"Peaks of Yemen I Summon"

"Peaks of Yemen I Summon"

Poetry as Cultural Practice in a North Yemeni Tribe

Steven C. Caton

Griot

London

This book is a print-on-demand volume. It is manufactured using toner in place of ink. Type and images may be less sharp than the same material seen in traditionally printed University of California Press editions.

University of California Press
Berkeley and Los Angeles, California
University of California Press, Ltd.
London, England

Printed in the United States of America

Library of Congress Cataloging-in-Publication Data
Caton, Steven Charles, 1950–
"Peaks of Yemen I summon" : poetry as cultural practice in a North Yemeni tribe / Steven C. Caton.
p. cm.
Includes bibliographical references.
ISBN 0-520-08261-3
1. Folk poetry, Arabic—Yemen—History and criticism. 2. Yemen—Social life and customs. I. Title.
PJ8007.2.C38 1990
398.2'095332—dc20 89-20524

The paper used in this publication
meets the minimum requirements of American
National Standard for Information Sciences—Permanence
of Paper for Printed Library Materials,
ANSI Z39.48-1984. ♾

For Hanni Schaaf Caton and William Charles Caton,
whose sense of adventure
has been an inspiration to me

Contents

APPENDIXES

Illustrations

Maps

Figures

Plates
(following page 126)

Acknowledgments

Above all, I want to thank Muḥammad bin Gāsim al-Hizām from Wadi Maswār, Khawlān aṭ-Ṭiyāl. Without his help I would never have finished this project or perhaps have even survived the field. He has an outstanding ear for his dialect, a deep sensitivity and love for tribal poetry, an uncommonly intelligent mind, and a fierce loyalty to our friendship that never wavered even in the most difficult of times. For his friendship, infinite patience, good humor, and steadfastness I will always be grateful.

I had the good fortune of striking up a friendship with two other tribesmen who took a keen and intelligent interest in my research. They escorted me to their villages, where I was an honored guest. There I had the opportunity of learning tribal customs related to social institutions like the wedding and religious festivals in which oral poetry plays a prominent role. Especially generous to me in this regard was the poet Ṣāliḥ bin Gāsim aṣ-Ṣūfī. Also extremely kind to me were Yaḥyā bin ʿAlī ash-Shanbalī and Ṣāliḥ bin Muḥammad al-Gīrī.

I wish to thank the Center for Yemeni Studies for having been instrumental in guiding and assisting me in the research, especially Dr. ʿAbdul-ʿAzīz al-Muqāliḥ, its director and now president of the University of Ṣanʿā, and Mr. Muḥammad ash-Shuʿaybī, who suggested Khawlān as a field site for me in the first place and continuously offered me sound advice and encouragement.

At the University of Ṣanʿā I benefited from the invaluable help of Professor Muḥammad ʿAbduh Ghanem, who gave generously of his time to help me analyze the meter of tribal poetry. I also wish to single out my friends Ṭāha Shamsān, for his assistance in translating the poetry, and Aḥmad ʿAlī al-Ḥājj, for preparing many of the Arabic transcriptions from tapes. The latter was also an excellent Arabic tutor.

Dr. ʿAbduh ʿAlī ʿUthmān and Christina ʿUthmān were a constant comfort: their advice was much appreciated, their company was always stimulating, and their knowledge of the country was invaluable to my research. Finally, Muḥammad Sharefaddīn and Ṣalāḥ Nahdī were also very helpful in offering encouragement along the way. Muḥsin al-Jabrī was kind enough to share his considerable knowledge of Yemeni poetry with me, and to him I am also extremely grateful.

Many other people in Yemen, too numerous to mention here, either directly or indirectly helped me in my research; I hope they will forgive me for omitting their names. In particular, every adult male or child of the Kibsies, who were my companions for one year, must have at one time or another given me a poem, a proverb, a new word, a Qurʾānic saying, or the like. But I wish especially to thank Muḥammad bin Muḥammad and his two sons ʿAlī and Yaḥya, Muḥammad Ismaʿīl and his son Muḥammad and nephew ʿAbdillāh, and finally Muḥammad bin Muḥammad al-Amīr and his relatives, who gave me many an excellent *zāmil* poem to appreciate and ponder.

Also instrumental in my fieldwork were the directors of the American Institute for Yemeni Research, Dr. Jon Mandaville and the late Dr. Leigh Douglas, as well as all the members of the institute, who taught me so much about coping with adversity. Mr. James Callahan of the United States Information Service and Mr. Tom Scotes, former United States ambassador to North Yemen, were also extremely helpful in expediting the bureaucratic process.

The research was done with the generous assistance of the Fulbright-Hays Program and the Predoctoral Research Program of the Social Science Research Council (1979–80). The writing of the book was partially supported by a 1988 Summer Stipend from the National Endowment for the Humanities, a 1988–89 postdoctoral Mellon Fellowship in the Anthropology Department at Washington University, Saint Louis, and a 1989 fellowship from the American Council of Learned Societies.

Among the many people who have read drafts of this book or its predecessor, my doctoral dissertation, I am extremely grateful to Lila Abu-Lughod, Roger Allen, David Edwards, Paul Friedrich, Dell Hymes, Peter Molan, Richard Randolph, the late Paul Riesman, Jerrold Sadock, J. David Sapir, Martin Schoenhals, Miriam Silverberg, Michael Silverstein, and Bonnie Urciuoli. In addition, I have presented parts of it in the form of lectures to students and faculty at Vassar, Carleton, and Hamilton colleges as well as the University of Chicago, Columbia University, New York University, the University of Virginia, and the University of California, Santa Cruz. Questions and critical comments from audiences at all these institutions were invaluable to me in writing (and rewriting) the book. Special thanks are due to Mary Kennedy for the line drawings in this book as well as to the University of California Press's referees for their painstaking reading of the manuscript. For their heroic efforts on this complex work I am extremely grateful to the editors Rose Vekony, Richard Miller, and Orin Gensler. But I would like to express my deepest appreciation to Dale Eickelman and Michael Meeker, who read the book in its entirety and whose astute and detailed critical comments vastly improved its coherence and overall readability. I took their excellent suggestions to heart and, I hope, successfully followed through on them.

A Note on Transcription

The transcription system of the *International Journal of Middle East Studies* is used here. However, because this is a study of an Arabic dialect and not the literary language, I have had to introduce certain changes.

Usually, though not always, diphthongs such as /ay/ and /aw/ are pronounced as long middle vowels (front and back), as in *bēn* (between) and *gōm* (people, nation). The classical Arabic phoneme *qāf,* pronounced in most standard varieties as an unvoiced uvular stop, is usually heard in Yemen as /g/. Thus, literary *qawl* (saying) is rendered as *gōl* in the dialect. I depart from this rule of thumb in words such as *qaṣīdah* (ode) that are well known as technical terms in Arabic literature and might confuse readers if they were to appear in their colloquial equivalents, but these exceptions do not occur often. Classical /ḍ/, pronounced as a velarized (or "emphatic") dental voiced stop, merges phonemically with /ẓ/, a velarized dental fricative. Thus, *ḍall* (go astray) and *ẓall* (be, become), which would be distinct in the literary language, are both pronounced with initial /ḍ/, here phonetically a fricative. A detailed description of Yemeni Arabic (specifically tribal) phonology is provided in Appendix A, along with information on syllable structures crucial for analyzing meter.

When Arabic words have become standardized in English (e.g. wadi, Mecca, Beirut), I use the accepted forms rather than a more accurate transcription. The two important exceptions are Muḥammad and Qurʾān. In addition, when persons specifically requested that their names be spelled in English in a certain way, I have respected their wishes in spite of orthographic conventions.

Finally, when the definite article *al* assimilates with the following consonant, I have noted the assimilation.

PART I

Background

1

Doing an Ethnography of Poetry

One of the lasting memories of my childhood is an incident that occurred at the inauguration of John F. Kennedy. Robert Frost was supposed to deliver a poem. He stepped to the microphone and began to read, or was about to read, when disaster struck. I believe that a strong gust of wind blew the piece of paper on which the poem had been written out of Frost's hands and carried it high over the heads of the assembly and out of the reach of the security officers who were scrambling vainly after it. The poem was not heard by those at the inaugural or by the millions of people listening on television. Since the poet had not memorized the poem and had no copy of it in hand, he could not proceed. This accident struck me at the time as of course unfortunate, but with the passing of the years I have come to see it also as supremely ironic.

When I was watching the inauguration, I was just about to leave childhood. Perhaps I identified with the scene more and more deeply as time went on because I saw what happened as symbolic of something that was taking place in myself. As with many school children who learn to love literature, I was first enthralled by the beauty of language in reading verse out loud. Then, as is perhaps also true of many of us, I learned to shift my appreciation from verse to the silent reading of prose, particularly short stories, novels, and drama. But rather than supplement my love of verse, the shift to other forms of literature seemed to supplant it. Some of us continue to read and write poetry, but not the majority. It becomes yet another school exercise, more and more remote from our everyday imaginings, which, like childhood, we outgrow. Perhaps what bothered me about the inaugural ceremony was a sense of incongruity at finding a poet—a craggy, white-haired old man at that—sharing center stage with the most powerful individual in the world, who happened to be youthful and handsome. The physical contrast embodied the discrepancy these two world-famous figures represented for me. Poetry was child's play, not the business of men, and certainly not the business of presidents.

There is always the suspicion in American culture, and to a lesser extent also European (though not Russian) culture, that political poetry, even in the hands of a master like Frost, can rarely rise above doggerel. A relatively famous American philosopher was once asked by a television interviewer why no great political poems had been composed in English literature. The philosopher did not contradict the assumption of the interviewer. His answer was that literature and politics had two different paymasters and could not mix.

About fifteen years after Kennedy's inauguration I found myself in Saudi Arabia. Again I am watching television, this time in an air-conditioned, prefabricated office in the middle of the capital. The scene: the king (who was Khālid at the time) has disembarked from his plane and is being greeted by a small crowd of well-wishers. In his entourage is his court poet. He holds his highness's attention for at least five minutes with a recitation of a poem. His highness does not seem impatient, and the poet is certainly not bashful or hesitant. The entourage listens respectfully, though I suspect that their interest (if not feigned) is more in the ceremony than in the meaning of the words. What interests me is that poetry should be tolerated, indeed embraced, by these dignitaries as though it were essential to the trappings of power.

I am next in a taxi, which is hopelessly stalled in traffic. To help pass the time, the Bedouin driver begins to recite a poem to himself. I have a hard time making out its meaning, but I think it is on the subject of love. I ask him to stop at a corner kiosk so that I can buy a newspaper, thinking it will provide more accessible entertainment than a poetic recitation, only to find displayed on the front page a text of a new poem about the Israeli-Arab conflict. My destination is the library of the University of Riyadh. As I walk down its corridors, I see public announcements about upcoming poetry recitations and contests.

After many such experiences I began asking myself: to what extent is poetry a key cultural event in this society, a part of its central political, social, and religious institutions? To what extent is this poetry entirely different from the poetry I grew up with and learned to ignore?

I spent nearly five years trying to answer that question—in North Yemen, however, not Saudi Arabia. The reasons for transferring to North Yemen (officially the Yemen Arab Republic, or Y.A.R.) were various and complex. Suffice it to say that the two years I spent in Saudi Arabia made me aware of the significance of poetry in the lives of Arabs and provided me with the competence in spoken Arabic needed to study it in depth. After arriving in North Yemen in January 1979, I spent roughly the next three years trying to complete the project I had first envisioned in Saudi Arabia. Twelve months of those three years (from November 1979 through October 1980) I spent doing fieldwork in an eastern region of the country known as Khawlān aṭ-Ṭiyāl, which I had been told was "rich" in oral, and specifically tribal, poetic traditions. The prediction turned out to be truer than I had believed possible.

Khawlān aṭ-Ṭiyāl is a *manṭigah* (region) belonging to the Bakīl Confederation [see Map 2]. In their poetry Khawlānis call their region the "seven tribes," though there is disagreement over which tribes to include in the illustrious roll. The seven most commonly named are Banī Bahlūl, Banī Shadād, Suhmān, al-Yamāniyatēn, Banī Ḍubyān, Banī Jabr, and Banī Sahām. It is not obvious where the territory of one tribe ends and the next begins. Subsections of different tribes usually mix in the same geographic region, and tribal affiliation is not of much consequence anyway except in critical situations such as warfare.

As one might expect in this part of the world, tribal social organization is patrilineal and patrilocal. Preferred marriage is with the patrilineal parallel cousin, though it is difficult to say how often the norm is carried out in practice. Except in the far eastern reaches of the country, tribesmen are sedentary agriculturalists who cultivate the many wadis of highland Yemen with a variety of crops including sorghum, barley, millet, vegetables, grapes, and the lucrative cash crop *gāt* (Catha edulis). Terracing is common, though not as dramatic as in other regions of Yemen. Irrigation is by rain water and well pumps.

Throughout Khawlān are to be found the religious elite known as *sādah* (sg. *sayyid*), who are reputed to be descendants of the Prophet

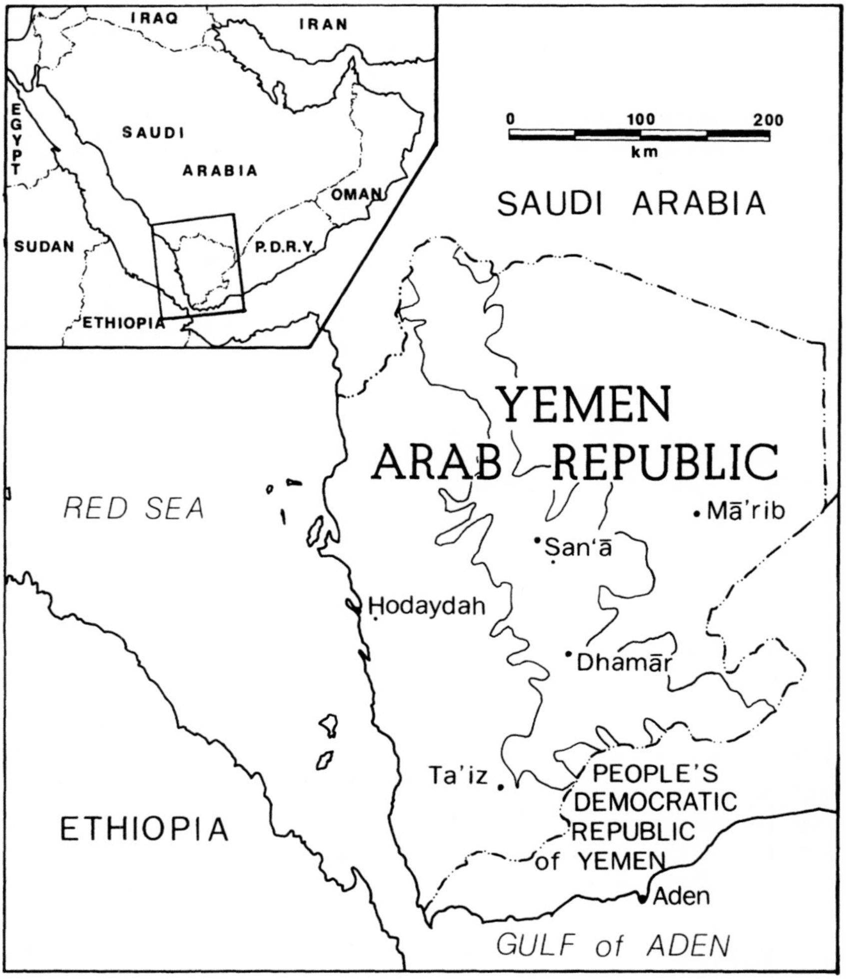

Map 1. Yemen Arab Republic.

Muḥammad. Though descent is important to their high social status, piety as well as religious and legal training are also essential, for the tribes look to them to solve some of their disputes (such as inheritance) according to the Sharīʿah. Most *sādah* live in one of the *hijrah* villages, a sanctuary set aside for them by the tribes, where they instruct the tribes on the credo and ritual of Islam, maintain a market where tribesmen may congregate without fear of blood feud because

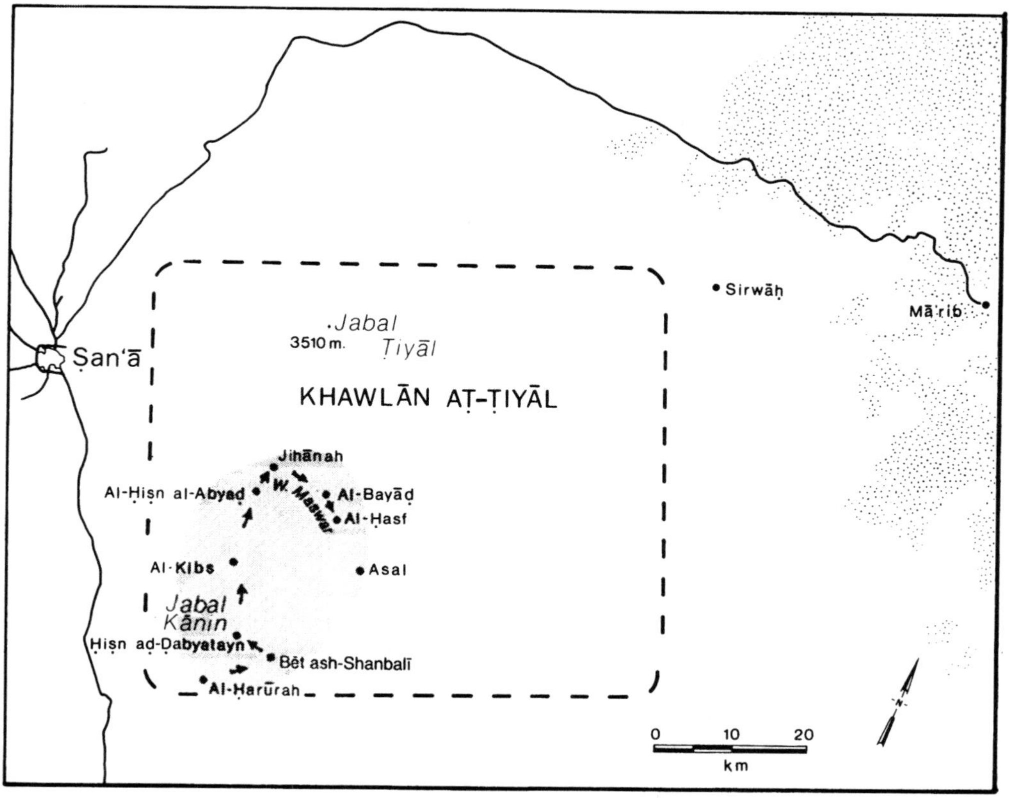

Map 2. Khawlān aṭ-Ṭiyāl. The boundary is only approximate and is represented by a broken line. The shaded region is al-Yamāniyatēn, one of the "seven" tribes. The route of my poetry-collecting trips is marked by arrows.

fighting is off limits there, and preach to the tribes in the Friday sermons. In pre-Republican Yemen (before 1962) the religious elite acted as the administrative arm of the theocratic state and were often in competition with the sheikhs over the governance of the region. Though their political power has been greatly eroded, they still retain enormous spiritual authority and hence indirect political influence.

The other important social group in the area is the servants, who usually live in tribal villages and are known as the *khaddām* (not to be confused with the *ʾakhdām*).[1] Their origins are less certain, though I will consider some myths about their descent in the next chapter on ideology. They are of low status because they perform various menial tasks considered too demeaning for tribesmen: butchering meat, circumcising the young boys, cutting hair, acting as masters of ceremonies at weddings, entertaining large gatherings with their drumming and other music-making, delivering messages to other villages, cooking and serving large ceremonial dinners, and so forth. In return for their services, the village households give them a small fraction of their agricultural products or else pay them a lump sum of money. Like the religious elite, they are under the protection of the tribes (each servant family becomes a client of a particular sheikh), but they do not carry weapons. They are not allowed to own tribal land, nor do their sons marry tribal women.

I will have more to say about one kind of servant, the *dōshān* (town crier), later in the book. He figures importantly in the production of tribal poetry, not as the composer of verse—for indeed he is excluded by his low status from taking part—but as a skilled musician who sings the verses of the highly prized *qaṣīdah* before a tribal audience.

The sanctuary in which I settled was located in a richly cultivated wadi. Nevertheless, aside from the grape arbors and fields of the ubiquitous and slightly narcotic *gāt* plant that checkered the flood plain and mountain terraces, there was little other vegetation. Except for a dusty clump of acacia nestled in the corner of some plot of land, nearly all the trees had been cut down for fuel long ago. Rainfall was not plentiful while I was in Yemen, and consequently the earth was desiccated. I was told that in wet years the wadi floor would be flooded in some places over a person's head; wild flowers would shoot up overnight from mountain crevices. At the sun's zenith, however, the hues that met my eyes were pallid and monotonous—mostly beiges, streaks of tan and gray. Only in the early morning and late afternoon light did the colors of the earth return to their deep chocolate browns and vibrant oranges and yellows. As if to offset the drabness of the earth, the sky was a dramatic canopy—alive with brilliant light, only occasionally blotted by dark clouds that massed behind the steep, volcanic mountains. At night the moon and stars were as intense as I suppose them to be anywhere on earth.

It was through this silent, nearly deserted landscape that I wandered alone from the sanctuary to neighboring villages where I hoped to meet poets or attend a wedding at which verse might be composed (see Map 2). The ground was hard and flinty. If one did not watch one's step, one could cut open a toe on a jagged edge; plastic sandals provided little protection. Had I been able to afford it, I would have hired a car, but I often managed to hitch a ride anyway. Besides, I traveled light, carrying only a small backpack containing a canteen of water, a little food, some small spiral notebooks, my tape recorder, and my camera. If I could find the shepherds' paths that crisscrossed the mountainsides, I could often save time and distance.

When I arrived at my destination, I was greeted hospitably by all except the stray dogs barking madly on the village periphery. I would be led through a cool, dark, and dry interior into the men's sitting room, offered a modest but delicious lunch, some scented and refreshingly cold water, and eventually a cup of tea. Polite inquiries after my health and the health of various of our common acquaintances in the sanctuary having been concluded, the session would begin with a brief interview, some attempt at gathering biographical information, and then a taping of the poet's own selection of verse. Sometimes I would spend the night, if one afternoon session was not sufficient or a big wedding celebration was to be held in the same village the next day.

On Fridays, the Muslim holy day, I did not have to leave the sanctuary in order to meet poets, for they came to it as members of various tribal groups. It was there that I tried to make the acquaintance of the poets. A friend of mine owned a store, and he would invite me to stand by the counter or else sit with him in its dark, musty, and cramped interior, where we loudly sipped our tea and chatted. Whenever a man reputed to be a poet came up to the store front, my friend would introduce me to him, and I would try to carry the ball from there. Sometimes they knew me by reputation or else recognized me from a television interview I did in Ṣanʿā.

That was how I met my closest friend and best consultant for my research project, Muḥammad. It was he who introduced himself, expressing interest in the project and offering to help. We agreed to meet in my house that afternoon, and he showed up at my doorstep with some of his friends—poets all. From that moment Muḥammad was to be indispensable to my project.

To learn the poetic tradition as well as become better acquainted with the devices of poetic composition, I made an effort to memorize individual poems recognized to be masterpieces. When I recited these by heart to poets, they took the project seriously. I also made an effort, even though it proved more than once to be embarrassing, to join in the chanting and composition of verse in public performances. I began by performing with the chorus in the wedding *bālah.* Linking arms with the young men of the village, I would join them in the circle in the middle of a large hall where the wedding festivities were held and chant with them the refrain line. This task is relatively easy and does not take much skill, though it is strenuous. While thus preoccupied, I could not, of course, tape the performances effectively or for that matter take photographs of the participants. The former duty was carried out by my friend Muḥammad, who soon became more adept than I at controlling the sound level and holding the microphone out of reach of the mischievous little boys who sought to sabotage the recording. Either I had become more confident, owing to a better understanding of poetic composition and delivery, or else I had become inured to my own embarrassment; in any case I threw caution to the winds and attempted one or two of my own lines. I learned more from making mistakes this way—because my friends were only too willing to gently correct me—than I did from listening to hours of tape recordings, and it always won the affection of my audience no matter how bad the verse sounded to their ears.

Had the opportunity presented itself, I would have apprenticed myself to a poet; unfortunately, all the poets with whom I was friendly were either too busy or else lived at too great a distance from my main field site to make such an arrangement practical.

I also initially regretted not being able to settle in a tribal village, for it would have given me a more intimate glimpse of everyday tribal life. But the sanctuary had its advantages. I was able to travel more freely because I was not tied down by specific tribal loyalties, and this freedom afforded me a better comparative perspective on the poetic system than I suspect I would otherwise have had. Then there was the tragedy that occurred to the sanctuary, a tragedy in which I was to be swept up. Ironically, it taught me more about the poetic system than years in a tribal village ever could have. But to understand that event, we have to backtrack a bit and fill in more information concerning Khawlān aṭ-Ṭiyāl.

The leading members of some "sheikhly" houses in Khawlān become chiefs of several villages in a given area. For example, in the territory belonging to al-Yamāniyatēn (see Map 2) there are approximately five major houses vying for this distinction. Not all tribal villages are under the authority of one of these sheikhly houses, for some maintain their own counsel; nor can it be said that one of these houses is significantly more powerful than the others and acts as a superordinate regional authority. This decentralization of power is characteristic of Khawlān and indeed of the whole Bakīl Confederation (in contrast with its Ḥāshid counterpart). Ever since the death of Sheikh Nājī bin ʿAlī al-Ghādir (1972?) there has not been a *shēkh mashshāyikh* (sheikh of sheikhs) to lead Khawlān and the Bakīl.

Actually, the sheikh is no more than a first among equals (for another view, see Dresch 1984). His responsibilities are to collect taxes for the government, act on behalf of his tribe in matters concerning the state and the confederation, mobilize men of the tribe and lead them into war, and of course solve disputes he is asked to mediate. He gets paid for his services but spends a great deal of his income on the entertainment of guests, an important ceremonial function. Some cynics claim that sheikhs deliberately stir up trouble in the hope of being able to line their pockets with additional revenues earned in the arbitration of disputes, which, if they resolve them, also enhances their reputation; but this would be a shaky strategy at best for acquiring power and maintaining it. Nor is the central state at present in a position to impose its authority over the rebellious tribes, either by threatening a show of force or by buying their loyalties through oil revenues as the Saudi regime has successfully done (though the discovery of oil in North Yemen in 1984 might alter the situation somewhat).

By presenting these facts baldly, I do not want to give the mistaken impression that Khawlānis feel a weak state or a decentralized system of internal sheikhly authority to be disadvantageous. On the contrary: even in tribal disturbances that seemed to threaten the stability and security of the region, the people involved rarely deplored (to me at least) the lack of a strong arm to impose a peace on warring factions. Only in the case of a massive *external* threat might such a step be seriously contemplated (and was actually taken in the Yemeni civil war when Khawlān was invaded by Egyptian forces); otherwise, I was told, "Every tribe in Khawlān wants to depend on itself." In other words, even though the tribes realized that a hierarchy of sheikhs could facilitate their dispute mediation, they preferred their autonomy to the intervention of a potential autocrat and the threat to their freedoms he would surely portend. The relevance of this point to the study of poetry will become clear in a moment.

It so happened that a young *sayyid* man who was visiting his natal village, the sanctuary in which I was living, stood accused by the tribes of absconding with two young tribal women. A war erupted between the religious elite and the surrounding tribe to which the girls belonged. This event was unprecedented because the religious elite are technically under tribal protection. I was in the sanctuary at the time of the abductions, busily collecting poetry that I began to notice was on the subject of the dispute. I saw outside my window the arrival of mediators, who were chanting verse exhorting the tribe to negotiate with the religious elite. The tribe responded with its own poems explaining why it felt it to be necessary to cleanse the stain on its honor by fighting it out with the sanctuary. This was the first time that I realized how important poetry is as a form of political rhetoric in dispute mediations.

But this use of poetry was not the only surprise. I began to understand too that warfare was far more complicated and subtle than the ethnographic literature on tribal societies in the Middle East had led me to expect.[2] More often than not, Khawlānī tribes tried to avoid exercising a kind of deadly brute force in which blood was spilled and men were killed; rather, they applied symbolic force, or a representation of the "real thing," whose aim was to achieve honor and not necessarily the liquidation of the opponent.

During the sanctuary's "war" with the tribe, *sayyid* marksmen kept watch on the roof of the house in which I was staying. I discovered, to my chagrin, that the house was directly in the line of enemy fire. At one point in the shooting I was summoned to the battlements to fulfill an unusual request: the marksmen wanted me to fix them some tea. One should never underestimate the Yemenis' wry sense of humor, especially their appreciation of the ludicrous, but I thought I had better show my solidarity anyway by brewing a fresh pot. Having heard what wonderful shots the tribesmen were, I crouched below the wall of the roof and inched my way forward apprehensively. Suddenly I noticed the look of nonchalance on my friends' faces and realized that the enemy bullets were missing their targets by a respectful distance of at least two feet. This shooting was no more than a game of violence, and it was explained to me as being necessary in order for the enemy to feel that it had reinstated the honor my village had besmirched. I hasten to add that the Yemenis were fully cognizant of the danger that symbolic force could evolve into a nasty war, but this occurred only when the financial and political stakes were high enough to goad certain troublemakers into fanning the flames of the feud.[3]

Since there is no strongman or central government to impose a peaceful settlement on them, it is imperative that contending parties be brought together to arrive at such a settlement (temporary in many cases) through argument and persuasion. In the absence of coercion and monetary influence, it stands to reason that the exercise of power entails persuasion, and persuasion in turn must be linked to oratory or political rhetoric (Caton 1987b). Burckhardt, the great Swiss traveller in Arabia, articulated this insight most succinctly: "A shaikh, however renowned he may be for bravery, or skill in war, can never expect to possess great influence over his Arabs without the talent for oratory. A Bedouin will not submit to any command, but readily yields to persuasion" (1831, 250). What is at stake is the ability of the sheikh to persuade the opponents to accept mediation; then, once the arguments of the two sides have been heard, he formulates a legal opinion on the case according to the dictates of *ʿurf* (tribal customary law); finally, he must persuade the sides to accept the final judgment (in which usually both are found somewhat at fault). Throughout this process the sheikh cannot appear to be dictating terms to the parties involved, nor may one or both of these appear to be coercing its opponent or the intermediaries into accepting its position, for such tactics would be tantamount to bullying and hence dishonorable. Each side, including the mediating sheikh (or sheikhs) and other dignitaries, may hope to influence public opinion only by voicing its point of view in the most appealing manner possible.

In such a communicative event it is clear that all kinds of verbal suasion will be exploited by the participants to achieve their ends, a study of which has not yet been attempted but would more than recompense its obvious difficulties with deep insights into political rhetoric. I will be concerned solely with the use of poetry in mediation, laying aside for the moment the crucial questions, Why should poetry be used in this process? and, How is it used? which cannot be satisfactorily answered until we know a lot more about the cultural concepts of poetry. The point I wish to get across here is that the composition of poetry is embedded in an extremely important political process—the dispute mediation—in which power, such as it exists in this system, must be achieved through persuasion. As I have already admitted, this interpretation has been complicated since the 1960s by the massive arming of the tribes and by economic development; but I believe that it still is basically true of the tribal system, though for how much longer is hard to say.

The significance of this point for the overall study cannot be overemphasized. What I wish consistently to demonstrate is poetry's centrality to the entire sociopolitical and cultural system, but this can only be done if the facts of tribal politics are examined within a theoretical frame that brings into relief this centrality. That is to say, I have argued for a concept of power to be understood essentially in symbolic terms, as persuasion (Caton 1987b); and insofar as this argument is convincing I must try to show that poetry is being used for persuasive purposes in the dispute mediation, a demonstration I will reserve for the chapter on the *zāmil.* But first I will set up an equation between power and a *culturally conceived* means by which to attain it, namely poetry.

A few months after the dispute broke out between the tribe and the religious elite, I had a distressing encounter with national security police, who quite naturally wondered what I, a lone American speaking Arabic, was doing in this politically turbulent region. To their credit, the police investigated my case with considerable kindness and dispatch, permitting me in fact to return to my field site to complete the study. When Muḥammad heard that I had been taken into custody by security police, he waited in the capital until I was released so that we could work together transcribing numerous poetry tapes.

Being held for questioning, though it should not have come as much of a surprise, was traumatic. I was depressed by the thought that my Khawlānī acquaintances must have complained about me or at least set me up to be taken. Perhaps I was naive to think that I could have ever won their trust, but the fact was that it bothered me terribly to realize that I had not. I also had to cope with the anxiety and sense of personal violation I felt when my notes, tapes, and photographs were confiscated, perhaps never to be returned—though in fact they were returned, every last item, and undamaged. Now I was haunted by a different question. Should I return to the same region or not? National Security asked me the same question, hinting that Khawlān was not the best place in which to conduct field research at that time. I could only answer them, and myself, by saying that I had already invested an inordinate amount of time there on this project and that it would take too much time and energy to relocate. Very much wanting and needing a vacation, preferably outside the country, I nevertheless decided against taking one for fear that my time in Yemen was running out or that I might not be readmitted into the country later. These were irrational fears, perhaps, given the way I had been treated by the authorities; but then who was to say that the treatment would be consistent?

I naturally was apprehensive on my first night back in the sanctuary (the meaning of which had by now become deeply ironic). My trust had turned to wariness, my affection to animosity. But I knew that I would have to conceal these feelings if I were to get my neighbors and friends to help me conclude the project. The need for concealment made me remember all the times I had made up things about myself, petty and harmless lies or half-truths every field-worker manufactures in order to make life bearable (for instance, I could not tell them that I am an agnostic or they would have shunned me completely); somehow the present context magnified those falsehoods, and with them my guilt and dislike of myself. I had even lost my enthusiasm for the project, wondering whether it wouldn't be better to return to the United States and do a library dissertation. Then I would be overcome by a certain sadness about the way things had turned out and no doubt also by more self-pity.

The next morning I went into the market as usual. There were no children playing in the street because of the ongoing hostilities with their tribal neighbors. People who knew me well greeted me joyously, though in my present mood I was not able to reciprocate. I was polite but reserved. Eventually the conversation turned to my brush with the law and how sorry people were to hear about it. Embarrassment on their part registered in the inflection of every remark and gesture, embarrassment coupled perhaps with relief that National Security had found me innocent of wrongdoing. One of my closest friends in the sanctuary, a man whose intelligence, charm, and sense of humor I greatly appreciated, invited me to join him and his family for lunch that day. The conviviality and relaxation of that meal put me at ease again—a classic case of breaking bread together reestablishing harmonious relations. I gradually began to feel that my return to the village might be tolerable after all. Ironically, the incident with National Security worked in the project's favor, for people now joyously proclaimed, "But you're innocent, you're innocent." Then, as if to make up for their embarrassment at having ever doubted me, they chewed my ear off about poetry, proverbs, and stories until the information was coming in faster than I could record it.

After about eight months in Khawlān I had collected more than enough material to see the general outlines of the poetic system. I spent the remaining four months refining that model before returning to the capital, where I remained for another year. Throughout that period friends from Khawlān, especially Muḥammad, visited me and helped work on the materials we had collected together. In addition, I hired another good friend, Ṭāhā Shamsān, who was more sensitive than most city slickers to the nuances of tribal speech, to help me with the translations. It was a wonderful period in which to review what had been accomplished and what still had to be done: transcribing and translating poetry, compiling and writing up my ethnographic notes on tribal social and political organization, and preparing preliminary drafts of dissertation chapters. In October 1981, after nearly three years in North Yemen and two years in Saudi Arabia, I returned to the United States.

When I was in the field collecting poems, I felt there to be two distinct but interdependent processes of appropriation at work. Taking down a poem is only one moment in a long chain of *reported* speech—from the poet to the reciter, from the reciter to the ethnographer, and from the ethnographer to the reader—and in each instance of reporting the speech is remolded and appropriated by the quoter.

For the ethnographer, the first process of appropriation is *understanding*. It is essentially a problem of linguistic reconstruction, that is, of recording the poem phonemically; glossing hitherto unknown words or grammatical constructions; obtaining background notes on persons, events, or places mentioned in the text that are usually of public knowledge and can be gleaned from nearly anyone; and gathering information on cultural references to belief and ritual systems. Each one of these operations of understanding is complex. The recording of the poem is not simply a matter of listening to the words and transcribing them onto paper; it is far more interactive a process between ethnographer and reciter (and in some instances between reciter and overhearers who are also familiar with the oral tradition and add their own two cents worth). Another major difficulty involves the difference in the appearance of the poem when it is chanted as opposed to when it is spoken. In the former mode the verse is more difficult to comprehend but at the same time its meter is more transparent (see Appendix B). Since music is an essential element of the aesthetic performance and since I was not yet certain whether the meter was essentially musical, verse-metrical, or some combination of music and verse rhythms, I was keen on transcribing the melody. But I was naive in thinking that this would be an easy task, for I discovered as many variants of a melody as there are, say, realizations of a phoneme, so that the musical transcription turned out to be an arduous task well beyond my meager musical training.[4]

How did I obtain a grasp of poetic form? In large part I culled it from the descriptions of informants who could tell me, for instance, that a poem called a *zāmil* has two lines, each of which is divided roughly into two parts and usually ends in a rhyming word. But on such matters of sound structure as metrical patterning informants could not articulate their knowledge. That the poem had a meter, and that the meter was regular, was almost invariably the extent of their comments.[5] Additional clues regarding the structure of verse were obtained by my "tampering" with lines and then asking informants whether one alternative was preferable to another (on analogy, it now seems to me, with the way linguists work on grammaticality judgments with native speakers). But the wonderful discovery was that the tradition has built into itself its own "response laboratory." In a dialogical routine two poets respond to each other's verse; the second poet must replicate as much of the form of the original poem as he can notice, and the audience criticizes the imitation if it finds it wanting. These reactions taught me how the native poet responded to the verse.

Given the impracticality of displaying all the collected variants of every poem discussed in this book, I have had to choose one text among several possibilities as representative of a particular poem. The question naturally arises as to the basis of this choice. In many cases I never came across significant discrepancies between variants of a poem; but if I did, I chose the variant that seemed to be the most generally known (if that could be ascertained) and provided notes on variant vocabulary and grammatical usage. Cases remain where the discrepancy is so great that several versions of the same poem must be represented.

What I have so far described is the laborious process of understanding a poem, an understanding that every participant in this oral tradition can more or less take for granted but which the ethnographer obviously cannot. I have maintained that this process is distinct from, though clearly related to, what I call the poem's *interpretation.* Whereas understanding may come automatically to the native speaker, interpretation may be problematical even for him.

In tribal society interpretation is sometimes, though rarely, a public act; it is more usual for each listener to form his own opinion silently on what the text means. I was obviously left in a quandary as to how to interpret poems when the interpretation was not openly worked out or discussed in a public forum (as it is, for example, in Western classrooms or literary journals). What I did was to interpret the poems in the same way that I would interpret, say, a Shakespeare sonnet—a process that is not yet, and probably can never be, "rule-governed" or subject to a methodology. I then presented the interpretation to one or more of my best informants and asked them if they agreed with it. Rarely did this question start a heated debate; more often the informant demurred. The trouble here is that tribesmen do not make their interpretation explicit. Instead they *react* to a poem's meaning (by laughing, composing another poem in response, keeping silent, and so forth), and that reaction betokens an interpretation the listener must *infer.*

It is important to remember that my interpretations were accepted by some people and rejected by others, the determining factor often being the listener's self-avowed political leanings. The interpretation of the poem (as in the case of most poems) is thus *politicized,* a condition that is of course characteristic of our tradition as well (W. Mitchell 1982; Rabinowitz 1987).

The major problem of translation is rendering the poeticality of these poems when this quality rests fundamentally on Arabic linguistic structure, vastly different from that of English. First, the metrical pattern depends on an alternation of syllabic weights between a light (Cv) syllable and a heavy one. (Other possible syllabic structures are elucidated in Appendix B.) By contrast, the predominant metrical pattern in English poetry has historically depended on syllabic stress rather than syllabic weight. Moreover, we might culturally apprehend a precise regularity in the metrical pattern as dull and monotonous, whereas in the Yemeni tradition it is positively valued. Even if one translates the Yemeni meter into a stress pattern, one is left with a difficult aesthetic choice: should one adopt strict classical meters, such as iambic pentameter, and thereby mirror the spirit of the original Arabic; or should one be more casual about the pattern by leaving, say, four heavy stresses irregularly distributed in the line and thereby gratify modern sensibilities?

Second, these constraining technical problems are only the tip of the iceberg. Much of the poeticality rests on allusion, elliptical reference to cultural beliefs and actual historical circumstances that require extensive commentary for the nontribal and non-Muslim reader. But such explanations of course mar the aesthetic impact of allusion as elliptical reference.

Finally, I have been speaking about the poem as though it were commensurate with the verbal text, much in the way we understand the notion of a poem in the West. But most tribal verse genres include compositions created in a dancelike performance which comprise an aesthetic-semiotic ensemble along with words and music. It is an aesthetic experience we have largely lost (except in opera).

The intractableness of this poetry to translation was beyond my talent to overcome in such a way as to present a satisfying aesthetic piece that remained wholly intelligible. In the end I opted for literalness, which would permit the Arabist to check the accuracy of the translation against the original text. I then supplemented the translation with however many notes were necessary to make both the content and the poeticality of the verse comprehensible. I do not pretend to have made a literary translation, only a literal one.

I prefer that this book be perceived as an ethnography, even though I am fully aware of how problematical that term has become in anthropology. Insofar as various theorists in "reflexive anthropology" understand the ethnographic enterprise to be vexed, this work is no less so, and for some of the same reasons (Marcus and Fischer 1986; Clifford 1988; Geertz 1988). But in fact I find the term *ethnography* far less problematical than *poetics,* which is in vogue these days among anthropologists who seem to have taken it over unreflexively. To suggest that one is doing an ethnography of poetry is to challenge one of the most serious shortcomings of Western poetics, namely, its failure to ground the theory of the poem and the literary institution in a theory of sociopolitical reality, no matter how it is represented ethnographically. Therefore, what I wish to emphasize is not the fact that poetics may illuminate our representations of ethnographic phenomena (Clifford 1988; Geertz 1988) but rather the reverse. I want to anthropologize poetics.

A full-fledged ethnography of poetry does not, to my knowledge, exist—certainly not for the Middle East and probably not for other geographic areas. Only Musil's pioneering *Manners and Customs of the Rwala Bedouins* (1928) comes close to being one. There have been, to be sure, several outstanding books written on the relationship of a particular poetic genre or of the poetic function in nonpoetic genres to various aspects of cultural life. I need only single out here Meeker's (1979) brilliant reworking of Musil's data on the Bedouin *qaṣīdah* and his arguments concerning the dilemmas of tribal politics in nineteenth-century Arabia; or Abu-Lughod's (1984, 1985, 1986) fascinating and evocative account of how Egyptian Bedouin women express their sentiments of longing and desire in *ghannawa* verse. Obviously, I owe a debt to these anthropologists as well as to other students of Arabic colloquial poetry, and I shall refer to them repeatedly in this work. But I think it is fair to assert that neither of the two works mentioned, nor any other, has made its focus the entire system of poetic discourse per se and analyzed the way in which that system reticulates with the social practices and cultural beliefs of a particular group of people. My aim, in other words, has not been to use the poetry to explore some aspect of sociocultural reality that is fundamentally of concern to myself, to anthropological research, or to linguistics. Rather, I came to Yemen to understand what tribesmen meant by poetry and analyze what they produced as poetry—in brief, to explore the aesthetic system of their verse—and at the same time anchor this production in their language and society. Not only do we have ethnographies on Tiv and Kaluli song (Keil 1979; Feld 1982), dance and the plastic arts (Thompson 1974), Australian sand paintings (Munn 1973), as well as Indonesian proletarian drama (Peacock 1968) and puppet theater (Keeler 1987)—to mention only some of the excellent work on art done by anthropologists—there has also been considerable attention paid of late to verbal art (Gossen 1974; Hymes 1981; E. Basso 1981; Tedlock 1983). I see this book as an extension of these traditions of research.

The fact, however, that no ethnography of poetry exists has made the task of writing this book more problematic than ethnographies ordinarily are. I have felt as though I were inventing a genre, if that is not too grandiose a description of the task at hand; but perhaps all anthropologists feel that way, or should. Here I was able to draw on the burgeoning ethnography of communication (Hymes 1974; K. Basso 1979; Heath 1983; Sherzer 1983; Bauman 1978; Beeman 1986; and others) for guidance and inspiration.

In brief, I came to study poetry in North Yemen because it seemed as though the culture was fascinated by it. To impart this fascination to the Western reader, I suppose it would have sufficed to represent the rich and complex use of verse in a variety of different social and political contexts and let the ethnography speak for itself. But my quarrel is not really with Western cultural assumptions of verse so much as it is with the literary critics and poets who harbor them and unreflexively construct theories of poetry based on them.

In an effort to challenge these views on a theoretical level, I have tried to develop a model of poetry as cultural practice in the conclusion. Whereas we do have plenty of examples of sociological analyses of the novel and other kinds of prose works such as drama, almost nothing exists in this line of research on poetry. Why? One reason may have to do with the historical development of poetry in America and Europe. It has a smaller readership than prose, its reception smacking almost of an elite preoccupation, and we tend to value "private" and "confessional" over "public" and "political" verse. Our poetry, as a consequence, seems much harder to ground in social and political reality. Another difficulty in developing a notion of poetry as practice is that poetic form is probably more deeply enmeshed in the structures of language than any other art form; but to appreciate this fact, an orthodox or more doctrinaire Marxist line would be of little avail, since Marxist theory has largely ignored the study of language (for reasons that need not be spelled out here).

Why, then, proceed in this direction? More obviously than in the West, poetry in tribal Yemen is both the creation of art and the production of social and political reality in the same act of composition. To compose a poem is to construct oneself as a peacemaker, as a warrior, as a Muslim. It seems to me that this fact is a critical insight into art as a *constitutive* social practice. It is one reason why I have chosen the term *practice* to describe Yemeni tribal poetry.

The other reason has to do with the sense of practice as *techne,* or the craft of fashioning verse. Poems in Yemeni society, or any other society for that matter, are not idly or haphazardly put together. The Yemeni poet must master a complicated set of interlocking practices, including rhyme, meter, alliteration, metaphor, formulas, speech acts, strophes, poetic exchanges, chants, and a host of performance routines. The sheer technical virtuosity required of a master poet in this tradition is staggering. This practice, which seems alien to most of us, is everyday cultural reality for Yemeni tribesmen. If this book awakens the reader to another kind of world, one very different from his or her own, a world in which poetry is centralized, not marginalized, in the arena of social and political conflict, and if that reader can learn, as I did, to be in awe of the craft needed to make that spectacle possible, then I will count it a success.

To reiterate, the basic point of the book is that the two kinds of practices—artistic and social—are indissociable. To fashion a poem is to engage in social practice. Each of the genre chapters in Part 2 elaborates this same basic point in different ways. In the two chapters devoted to the *bālah* I argue that this genre is to be understood largely in terms of the production of tribal ideology (*gabyilah*) or what it means to be a tribesman. But to grasp this point, we have to understand how the practice of composing a poem is simultaneously a practice that signifies "tribalness." We shall see how this problem relates to contemporary interest in the social construction of self, particularly in the Middle East. The paired chapters on the *zāmil* begin a shift in the analysis of techne from performance to the perfection or finalization of the text-utterance, a shift not completed until the third genre. I argue that the practice of composing the *zāmil* produces a certain ideology meant to be persuasive in the arena of political conflict. To understand the significance of this art of persuasion, we must reexamine some assumptions about the nature of power in tribal society as it has been described in the literature on the Middle East. The final two chapters on the *qaṣīdah* show how the practice of composing poetry has shifted onto the shoulders of the individual master poet, who is problematically self-conscious about the historical poetic tradition and changing social conditions. This person also gives voice to a political ideology relevant to the creation of the modern nation-state. The tribe becomes involved in state politics through the spread of its poetry on tapes sold throughout the market system. Of course, the state also tries to control this means of poetic communication to disseminate its own ideology among the tribes. In short, I will look at a problem rarely considered in the literature on the state: the way in which discourse, ideology, communicative practices, and state formation are interdependent. To us, this problem may seem all the more remarkable because that discourse is poetry; but to Yemenis, there is nothing remarkable about it. By the end of this book I hope the reader will understand why.

Yemeni tribal poetry is not atypical of verse found in other societies studied by folklorists and anthropological linguists. It is not "high" literature as recognized by the educated elite in Western countries or Arab society. For example, it is almost always spoken or chanted, not written; and it is cast in an idiom and linguistic register, generally known as colloquial, toward which the educated Arab elite has an ambivalent attitude, denigrating it for its supposed ungrammaticality while at the same time admiring it for its spontaneity and wit. To explore these unwritten forms of aesthetic expression, I have borrowed heavily from the tradition of folkloric research (Parry 1930, 1932; Lord 1960; Dundes 1980; Bauman 1978; Ben-Amos 1972). In particular, I am concerned with the need to study oral formulaic composition of verse in performance as well as the need to analyze folkloric works in light of their linguistic, aesthetic, and anthropological dimensions. Besides extending and enriching these descriptive goals in the genre chapters, I hope also to make a more theoretical point. The kind of data usually gathered by folklorists could be more usefully employed by sociological aestheticians who focus almost exclusively on written and "high" literary texts.

Finally, a few remarks on what this book is not about. I have little new to add about women's lives (Myntti 1978; Dorsky 1986) or women's poetry in North Yemen. Throughout my three years there I elicited information on both topics, but I was only allowed to speak to men in the tribal villages, and they usually stiff-armed the questions about women. My glimpse into this hidden world made me believe that women's verse paralleled to some extent the male genres, particularly the *bālah* and the *qaṣīdah,* and that among the eastern Bedouin the women competed with men for recognition of their artistic talents in public performances. I never heard a tribal woman deliver a poem, however, nor a man recite a composition by a female poet. The evidence was anecdotal, at best, and more often was simply not there for observation or recording by a male ethnographer. But I suspect that a female ethnographer would be amply rewarded for her time and patience.

I hope Arabists will find the data in this book interesting; but mine is a synchronic ethnographic analysis, not an attempt to reconstruct a pan-Arabic language, ostensibly frozen in Yemeni tribal poetry, or to relate the ethnographic findings to a historical reconstruction of a pre-Islamic poetry. I leave these tasks to Arabists better qualified than myself.

2

Gabyilah: Ideologies of Tribalism, Language, and Poetry

The term *gabyilah* (sometimes also *gabyalah*), derived from the same root as *gabīlī* (tribesman) and *gabīlah* (tribe), is used to refer to a general code of ethical behavior to which tribesmen say they adhere. Therefore, I will translate it as "tribalism."

Most studies of tribal societies, to the extent that they consider the cultural system at all, are content to equate the honor code with tribal culture as a whole. To be sure, the importance of the honor code should not be underestimated; but one wonders to what degree it is only a single piece of a more complex ensemble of values in tribal society. I begin with a discussion of the concept of piety precisely because it—not honor—heads the tribe's list of values. I mean to suggest not that piety is more important than honor but that it is crucial to a tribal definition of personhood and indeed may be in conflict with honor in a person's ego-identity. Furthermore, I (like the tribe) incorporate the notion of speaking Arabic—or, more exactly, a self-conceived "pure" and oral language with roots extending deep into a mythical past of the "original" Arabs—as part of tribalism. It too is not reducible to the honor code, though honor accrues to a person who speaks such a language. In Yemeni studies I would credit Adra (1982) with the first attempt to privilege *gabyilah* over the honor code, for reasons different from my own but still related to them. In this chapter I follow her lead.

Cultural notions of poetry are included in this discussion of tribalism rather than in a separate chapter, although the latter strategy would perhaps have been more appropriate, given their obvious importance to an understanding of local practices of verse composition. A separate chapter on folk theories of art would have drawn attention to this important topic, but it would also, I fear, have misrepresented their connection with the rest of social reality in tribal Yemen. In other words, I did not want to convey the impression that local terms and models of verse are self-contained and autonomous vis-à-vis other cultural spheres. As this chapter will make abundantly clear, to be a tribesman is to be a poet, and to be a poet is to be a tribesman. That is, the ability to compose verse is not something acquired or overlaid as some sort of cultivated veneer; it is thought to be inalienable from the person. Furthermore, by composing verse a tribesman demonstrates all the values that constitute tribalism: piety, self-possession, courage, honor, and so forth.

A brief comment is in order on why I have chosen to call tribalism an ideology. Though I would agree that ideology is a cultural system (Geertz 1973), my sense is that tribalism is connected with political action (or, more broadly, with power). It is utilized by cultural actors to try to persuade others to do one thing rather than another in a process of consensus formation. Thus, much of what is discussed in this chapter will seem to be part of a rhetoric of appeal used in various political contexts described in the rest of the book.

Values of Tribalism

"How would I have to raise my son for him to become a *gabīlī?*" I sometimes asked my tribal friends. One sheikh responded: "You must teach him four things: the dictates of Islam, how to shoot a gun, how to dance, and how to compose poetry." His prescription, though hardly complete, is as good a place as any at which to start the discussion of what it means to be a tribesman.

Piety

Islam is first on the list. The ancient Yemeni spice kingdoms predated Muḥammad, flourishing in what is commonly referred to as the age of ignorance, and the tribes know that they absorbed Islam into an established way of life. Their sense of their pre-Islamic past will be broached later in this chapter. Piety is a major criterion of character.

Tribesmen in the Zaidi (Shīʿā) sect pray three times a day and adhere closely to the tenets of Islam. But their attitude toward the *political* authority of Islam, which in prerevolutionary Yemen was the thousand-year-old Imamate as represented by the *sādah* religious elite, is more ambivalent. In the tribal view, at least, this ambivalence does not render their piety suspect but only their political allegiance, for they would fundamentally oppose any state compromising their autonomy. Otherwise religion is an inextricable part of tribalism. To label a man tribal is to expect him to be *dīnī* (religious), though of course it does not work the other way around.

The comment that I ought to teach my son how to use a gun has to be understood in terms of religion, but it particularly involves the cultural notion of honor. That is, one may be called on to defend Islam in a holy *jihād*, or more likely one may be required to defend one's honor (*sharaf*).

Sharaf

Though always on the lips of tribesmen, the word *sharaf* is not easy for them or the ethnographer to define. In general terms honor refers to a man's or woman's reputation for possessing virtues such as courage, wisdom, self-possession, honesty, and generosity—in short, all the ideals understood to represent *gabyilah*. Some people, however, embody these virtues better than others, and they have a reputation for possessing more honor. In part this reputation is ascribed to a person by virtue of ancestry. Thus, a born tribesman has more honor than a servant (*khaddām*) and, at least in the eyes of other tribesmen, also more honor than a descendant of the Prophet. But perhaps more significantly, honor is achieved; here Meeker's concept of the glorious deed (Meeker 1976) is helpful in understanding how honor is won or lost. In gift-giving, for example, honor is gained by generosity and lost by stinginess. Honor is accorded the courageous fighter but withdrawn from the coward. To wax poetic is honorable, to blather inconsequentially is not. But honor is as much an attitude as it is an act. To be self-possessed is more honorable than to be dumbfounded. And to respect the honor of others is in itself honorable.

As Bourdieu (1966), Jamous (1981) and Meeker (1976, 1979) make clear, one of the ways in which honor is achieved is to challenge another person successfully in a duel or contest of honor. The formulaic expression in Yemen for this challenge and counterchallenge is *daʿwā w-ijābah*. Poetry, as we shall see, is intimately bound with this routine and therefore, like a gun, is a weapon by which a man wins and defends his honor. A man may be challenged in verse concerning anything in his life: his family, his business affairs, a social slight, a lie, a broken promise, a stolen woman, a theft of land. A man who is challenged and cannot reply with his gun or his poetry loses face; hence the sheikh's counsel to teach my son the art of poetry. There is more to the explanation of that art than simply honor, however, as we shall see when we examine tribesmen's concepts of themselves as speakers of Arabic.

Karāmah

Another important act of *gabyilah* is hospitality, in which one's *karāmah* (generosity) is displayed. This value is so well known to be sacrosanct among Arabs as not to require comment. Honor redounds to the giver as well as the receiver of hospitality. The guest knows that he is being honored by the assiduousness of the host's attention to his needs and comforts; at the same time, by virtue of having performed this glorious deed of hospitality, the host becomes the object of the guest's praise. For example, it is customary when leaving the house of the host to proclaim loudly *akrimtū w-aslimtū* (you have been generous and have given), and the host replies with a barely audible *karāmah sahīlah* (generosity is simple). The host signals by his humility the fact that he would do anything for his guest, thereby ironically making himself out to appear grand. I have even heard the *dōshān* (town crier) climb onto the host's roof and acclaim his hospitality in rhymed prose to the rest of the village.

A great deal of wedding poetry is produced in reciprocity for the generous hospitality of the groom's family. Thus, after the guests have been fed dinner, they may be exhorted by the groom's father to rise and perform the *bālah*. On the one hand, failure to repay the host by honoring his son with verse would be a social slight. On the other, the guest also loses esteem, for he appears as less than noble in not being able to perform the glorious deed of composing. But having been hailed and praised in verse, the hosts must return the gift with poetry of equal or greater value, or else they too lose face. A potentially unending production of poetry is thus generated through reciprocity.

Shajāʿah

During my sojourn in Khawlān, I overheard a story of one man's daring exploits, which had captured the imagination of tribesmen. He was a young sheikh of the ʾAʿrūsh tribe, who had been attacked in his home at night by more than one assailant. He managed to drive the attackers away, but he was not content to let them escape and dashed off in hot pursuit. He managed somehow to pin them down with gunfire until reinforcements arrived, who helped him capture the culprits and bring them to justice. Of this young man everyone was saying *w-aḷḷāh, hū baṭal* (by God, he is a hero) and of his tribe *hum rijjālīn* (they are real men).

For the poet, as well, *shajāʿah* (courage) is an asset. In this society where poetry can be an intensely agonistic act, the poet puts on the line not only himself as artist but his whole person. In the wedding *bālah,* for instance, poetic composition becomes a poetic competition in which honor is the prize, and at one point in this earnest entertainment the poet must rely on the agility of his wit, the lightning flash of his imagination, to fashion adequate responses to other poets' challenges. Should the performance falter because of his clumsiness, he loses face. *Zāmil* exchanges entangle him in a tug-of-war between rival factions in which he may lose not only face, as in the wedding exchanges, but also power, as we shall see when we examine dispute mediations more closely. And the truly great poet, the *qaṣṣād* (composer of the *qaṣīdah*), may have to speak up against a leader, at considerable risk to his personal safety, in order to defend his tribe's honor. The poet then is as much a hero, and demonstrates as much courage, as the fighter sheikh.

Marūwah

In addition to courage, a man is judged for his *marūwah,* which I translate as self-control.[1] That trait was possessed by the legendary young sheikh, for in the stories about him he never lost his cool, even under fire. One is expected to maintain the same self-possession in other equally trying, if less dangerous, circumstances, as in replying to insults or suffering inflammatory accusations. On plenty of occasions ill-wishers might like to provoke someone, tweak his pride, or try his patience, but no matter how maddening these situations might be, the tribesman ought never to let them get the better of his emotional equilibrium. Yet this style, which reveals so much about the tribesman's dignity, should not be confused with turning the other cheek or, worse yet, emotional repression, which is just as alien to the tribal self. If the situation warrants it, then the white-hot fire of anger can flare up in the eyes, outrage stretch the mouth into a furious grimace, and the whole body tense up as if ready to spring at the object of its fury. But the actors should still be *self-conscious* of the response's stylization.

It is difficult for Americans to interpret the tone of such encounters, which appear to us to be potentially explosive. We arrive here at a vital distinction between real violence—brute force expended in an effort to coerce—and symbolic violence, whose aim is to make a statement about the actors, their relationship to each other, and the contest in which they are opposed. It seems to me that my white middle-class male culture possesses plenty of brute force but little of symbolic violence, and as a result perhaps we fear violence much more than the Khawlānīs because we expect the worst consequences from it. In Yemen I had learned to decipher scenes as stylized or symbolic violence and therefore feared the expression of it less, even in myself. How much of an insider I had become was brought home to me when I made a scene one day in the capital before some Peace Corps volunteers. They had treated me and some Yemeni instructors to a fancy dinner at a local restaurant and had carefully bargained with the owner ahead of time over the bill. The final check, however, amounted to much more than the volunteers had originally agreed on, or were even capable of paying, so a disagreement flared up with the owner. I tried to stay out of the ruckus at first, but when it was clear that the owner had not been altogether fair and yet refused to compromise, I had no choice but to put my oar in—not, as I recall, very happily. The argument proceeded like a dance. I would anticipate my opponent's move, as he would mine. Having to escalate the dispute because our restaurateur would not capitulate, I slapped the table with the flat of my hand, and he in turn grabbed the hilt of his dagger. I threatened to lunge toward him, fervently praying that the Yemeni instructors would restrain me, which they did, just as my assailant's assistants were holding him back, and thus we were pulled apart, publicly protesting this intervention but secretly relieved that it had happened. My Yemeni friends were all the time relishing this comedy, gleefully whispering into my ear, "That's right . . . you challenge him . . . the tribal way." Meanwhile the American volunteers were dumbfounded, no doubt convinced that their eccentric teacher had finally gone around the bend. By their standards perhaps I had, yet I distinctly recollect how controlled, and certainly contrived, the whole performance had been. Neither I nor the rascally restaurateur had lost his *marūwah*.

This mode of stringently controlling, though publicly venting, one's passions is perfectly suited to poetry. When we see later how massively the poet is restricted by conventions of meter, rhyme, alliteration, and line structure, we can appreciate the control, the self-possession, that this art form requires. Yet the poet is not suppressing or muffling his emotions. In the poems he speaks of the great passions that events have stirred in his breast and that have moved him to compose verse. Thus, the good poet may vent his passions but always in perfectly controlled techne. This may be why art is so closely connected with Aristotle's theory of catharsis. That is, emotions in drama or ritual are made governable by their transmutation into aesthetic form or the stylized release of passion.

Autonomy

If self-control is an ideal, then autonomy of the actor is one of the things it achieves. Unlike the other topoi discussed so far, there is no convenient term in the local discourse for the concept of autonomy. People used a circumlocution with me, *kull(a) ḥad yishtī yiᶜtamid ᶜala nafs-ah* (everyone wants to rely on himself). Of course, emotional independence is only a small part of autonomy; more important, it extends to economics and politics. It is the ideal of every young tribesman, for instance, to establish an independent household by building on land adjacent to his father's. When this ideal is unrealizable, and the young man has to live in the same house with his other relatives, his dignity suffers. I saw this happen to my closest Khawlānī friend, Muḥammad, who was unable to earn enough money in Yemen to establish his own home and wanted to emigrate to Saudi Arabia. Out of desperation he ended up joining the army when his search for employment abroad failed. His self-esteem turned into self-deprecation, which was transformed into resentment against his father.

Political autonomy can be threatened by the ambitions of a self-aggrandizing sheikh or the hegemonic drive of the central state. Rule over those who cherish their autonomy demands the art of persuasion, not coercion (Caton 1987b), for each person must be made to believe that he is a free agent. When conflict arises, therefore, one antagonist cannot bully the other, for such action would clearly violate his autonomy. Nor does one dare ask a powerful man or the state to intercede, out of fear that one would thereby become subject to his rule. The only way out of the dilemma is to seek restitution through a process of mediation with other equals. The mediators in turn cannot impose their decision on the contending parties without violating their autonomy. They must seek a consensus of opinion, freely given by the opponents and other observers at the dispute council, and then persuade the defendant to accept it; if he is honorable, he will. Just as feuding is a symbolic statement about honor, not actual coercion, so capitulation is a symbolic statement about mediation.

But suppose the parties in the dispute refuse to accept the consensus and attempt instead to coerce one another? In such a case they are no longer acting like true tribesmen and are no longer considered to be part of the honorable community. At this point the mediators may legitimately use coercion against the recalcitrant parties, if expulsion or shaming fails, because they are then judged to be flouting the consensus. Autonomy does not mean total independence from the collective will.

Land

No less important than these virtues in defining a tribesman is the right to own land. The story of my friend Muḥammad drives home the point. A landowner is considered to be autonomous or self-sufficient because he can live off the land (though the reality may be different), whereas a tradesman or a servant must exchange his labor for the products of the land and is thus considered to be inherently dependent. But the *sādah* (religious elite) too own land. What then distinguishes the tribesman from the *sādah?* The difference is the fact that the tribesman works his own land, whereas the *sādah* prefer to hire laborers for that purpose. As a producer, the tribesman is a *zirāʿī* (cultivator) and is proud of the fact. In owning land and, moreover, working it, a man constitutes himself as a tribesman.

The importance of land ownership to the self-definition of the tribesman is illustrated by the story of Ḥusēn. He had amassed a fortune through the industriousness and parsimony of his able sons working in Saudi Arabia and his own shrewd investment of their hard-earned wages in various enterprises in North Yemen. He was easily one of the wealthiest, if not the wealthiest, man of my village. At one point he petitioned the elders to allow him to buy land and build a permanent home on it for himself and his family, but they refused his request. He had offered them an extremely good price, far more than the land was actually worth. They told me, however, that he was not *muḥtarim* (respectful), and therefore they could not accede to his request. It turned out that Ḥusēn was of *khaddām* descent and therefore lacking in honor. Land is as important to the tribesman for its symbolic aura as it is for its economic value. Ḥusēn was not to be admitted into the charmed circle of honor by becoming a property owner.

Ideologies of Descent

Sūrah 34 of the Qurʾān mentions Yemen as the land of Sabaʾ which God had made "fair and happy." It had grown rich because God had appointed the stops of the incense caravan through the territories of the Sabaeans. Cities rose in the mountains, and a great dam was built, irrigating millions of acres and turning a desert into the breadbasket of Arabia. Monuments testified to the glory of the rulers, including the fabled queen of Sheba, who sent emissaries to all the empires of the ancient world. But the tale, as one would expect, is cautionary. The Sabaeans were greedy and called on God to "place longer distances between our journey stages" so as to increase their wealth. Incensed by their ingratitude, God caused the great dam to burst. A mighty flood was unleashed, destroying the cities. The fields shriveled up, and the gardens reverted to deserts, "producing bitter-fruit, tamarisks, and some few stunted Lote-trees." The Sabaeans' power was shattered, for God had "made of them as a tale (that is told)."

This story is almost archetypal of tribal ideals. Once again control over land, land that through labor can be made to bear fruit and produce other riches, is the source of honor and power. But control over land must be exercised with self-possession (restraint of greed) and piety (gratitude for what God has wrought), or divine retribution will soon follow.

As the holiest of Muslim books validates, the ancestry of the South Arabian tribes is the noblest. Their founder is Qaḥṭān (the Biblical

Yoqtan), who is said to be the descendant of Sām (the Biblical Shem); both names are very much alive in the Yemeni popular imagination. The capital Ṣanʿā is often called *madīnat sām* (city of Sām), the belief being that Sām founded it; hence it is the oldest city in the world according to popular reckoning.

A famous revolutionary poem begins, "Qaḥṭān is your ancestor and mine || the people of Yemen are your possession and mine." The rhetoric of the poem subtly reminds us that the *sādah* who ruled the theocratic state of Yemen until their overthrow in 1962 are descended from the Prophet, an ʿAdnānī Arab, and that all North Arabian tribes, which include the royal Hashemites, trace their descent from ʿAdnān, Qaḥṭān's collateral agnate. Hence they are all foreigners or outsiders, with no inherent legitimacy as rulers. The descendants of this same Qaḥṭān are believed to be the Sabaean and Hamdān kings, the masters of the fabled spice and incense kingdoms of South Arabia.

Or consider how the ideology has been absorbed in this line of poetry: "For *an-nigā* is like the columns of Sabaʾ || or Mārib Dam on its seven arches." The translation of the term *an-nigā* is problematic. In classical Arabic it has the general meaning "purity," but in the context of tribal society it can also mean a spotless reputation, and Landberg (1920–42, 3:2817) records that in tribal law it means to ḍeclare war on an enemy. (For a fuller discussion, see Dresch 1989, 49.) The metaphor is nevertheless clear: just as columns support a vault, or arches a dam, so *an-nigā* is a principle supporting order in tribal society. The ideology of history is a fertile source of rhetorical appeal.

Myths of descent are also important for legitimating the political subservience of the *khaddām* (servants). Note in this regard the alternative label for this servant category, *ahl al-khums* (people of the fifth), which is explained by different versions of the same origin myth. According to one version, they are descendants of ancient kings of South Arabia but proved themselves to be cowards in battle and disgraced their tribes, for a lapse in bravery is unforgivable. The sons' penalty was to forfeit their tribal (that is, honorable) status and serve the tribe in various ignominious tasks (enumerated in the next chapter). In return for these services they were to be paid one-fifth the booty captured in battle, though nowadays their fee is a fraction (less than one-tenth) of every tribal village household's income. This fall from grace is inherited by blood; hence their descendants are irredeemably of lower status. Recall that the old servant Ḥusēn could not buy his way into the kingdom of honor.

We may readily accept as common sense the idea that history can legitimate honor, but it requires a different shift in our way of thinking to realize that honor can redeem history (Meeker 1976). Various refrains are employed to explain the present: It's not surprising that ʿAlī turned out that way, given his father; or, Given the way ʿAlī has turned out, it's not surprising his father was that way. The latter more subtly suggests that the present validates and even re-visions the past (Given the way ʿAlī has turned out, maybe his father wasn't so bad after all). Present deeds can redeem the past as the past can validate present deeds.

This dialectic of history will be particularly apparent in the final chapter on the *qaṣīdah* when two old poets, both traditionalists, allude to the glories of Yemen's past in an effort to save its future. They re-vision the past in the present. We can also appreciate the great risk that the traditionalist stance takes, for if it fails to perfect the past in the present, if *gabyilah* falters, the past will be reviled. What is at stake is not merely the present moment but an entire history, which could become "a tale (that is told)." Tribesmen might wonder, How great could the ancients have been if their traditions have failed us now? For this very reason the traditionalist stance cannot be dismissed as simplistic, much less cowardly.

A Folk Theory of Language and Poetry

Tribal Arabic

Since the South Arabian kingdoms were located in the eastern part of the country, many Yemenis believe that it is in these regions, collectively known as *al-mashrig* (the east), that one can hear the purest spoken Arabic and the most brilliant tribal poetry. Sometimes this idea was propounded to me in terms of a gradient of language and poetry, starting from Mārib and Wadi Jōf (both located in the far eastern parts of the country), whose inhabitants are *badū* (Bedouin), where the lamp of tribal traditions is thought to burn brightest, and stretching westward to the highlands of central Yemen and then down to the coast. The farther one travels from the historical center of the Sabaean and Himyaritic kingdoms, the less intense is the flame. The highland *gabāyil* (tribes) that have always settled in remote mountain villages were so inaccessible to outside influences, or so the myth goes, that *gabyilah* still gives off there an incandescent glow; but among the coastal peoples, who have been overrun by the Ethiopians, the Turks, and other invaders over centuries of conquest, it has been all but snuffed out.

Those tribesmen who have been unaffected in their attitudes toward their spoken language by a standardized, literary education always have been extremely proud of their Arabic. They say it is not only ancient but also genuinely *ʿarab,* a belief linking notions of language with ideologies of descent. Purity of Arabic is associated with the ancient tribal kingdoms, and to maintain that purity is to maintain one's *gabyilah.*

Tribesman as Speaker

The true *gabīlī* is a man of his word. There is nothing worse than for him to be called *kadhdhāb* (liar). The insult flies like an arrow straight to the heart and requires an immediate, unretractable, and uncompromising reply: *anā daʿī l-ak* (I challenge you), with daggers resolutely drawn.

When someone responds to a request by saying, Yes, I promise to do that, *inshaḷḷāh* (if God wills), it may not be a real promise. The illocutionary intention of the speaker must be ascertained from a shrewd assessment of his past history, present circumstances, and future possibilities—in short, nothing less than the powers of a seer will do. But if one wants a true promise, then one must somehow wring out of the respondent *imānah* ([in] God's faith). That is final. That is as firm a commitment as one is likely to get. As an ethnographer I often needed firm commitments from my informants, so I vigorously wheedled promises out of them and would not be fobbed off with a halfhearted *inshaḷḷāh.* Deciding that I really did need a certain person to help me with some aspect of fieldwork, I would try, not very cleverly, to extort from him a muttered *imānah.* The tactic often backfired, for the interlocutor would feel pressed, perhaps even bullied. No tribesman lets himself be browbeaten, least of all by the likes of me, so I was often dismissed with the wonderfully deflective *aḷḷāh mustaʿān* (God is being asked for assistance).

Although it is important to be truthful and reliable, it is not necessarily a virtue to be frank and outspoken. In fact, a premium is put on the ability to allude to the truth rather than state it baldly. At the same time, the auditor has to be able to read between the lines, as it were, or infer the speaker's intentions and references, for these are rarely spelled out. The predicament resembles the problem of language for Hamlet: how to find direction through indirection and trap the conscience of a king. Note, however, the difference between indirection and misdirection: the latter, if carried out with malice, is lying, and that cannot be tolerated, neither in the tribesman's moral universe nor in Hamlet's.

The Poet

Tribal poetry is thought to be as ancient as the spoken language. I heard the opinion expressed more than once that Adam spoke in verse all the time and that the ancestors, the kings of Saba' and Ḥimyār, did likewise, for the gift of *hājis* (poetic genius) was as much part of their constitution as walking or breathing. Now, alas, they regret the foreign ways that have entered their world—the strange babble of tongues that can be heard on any street in the capital—and are eroding tribal traditions. Poetry has also been affected, they say, declining in use to a few occasions and mastered by only a handful of men. Significantly, some of the youths who emigrate to the cities or abroad return without knowing the old, customary greeting routines (Caton 1986), let alone the traditional poetic genres, for which they say they have no time and not much use. The old men of the tribe deeply lament this trend, fearing that no good can come to sons who abandon the ways of their forefathers. And of course they tremble to think what such a trend portends for the composition of poetry.

There are two general terms for "poet." One, the more marked form, is *hājis,* which is only used in reference to a genius—that is, a poet who can create verse *min rās-ah* (off the top of his head) and whose talent is as inexhaustible as a bottomless well. The other term is the relatively unmarked *shāʿir,* which may be applied to any poet, regardless of talent or productivity.

Hājis is also used to refer to poetical talent or inspiration, the Muse. An important set of terms, referring to various body parts and functions, contrasts with it. *Kabd* (liver) and sometimes also *galb* (heart) are the seat of *shaʿūr* (emotions), which is obviously related to the cycle of terms *shāʿir* (poet) and *shiʿr* (poetry) as one who emotes and the product of those emotions. These contrast with *rās* (head), which rules the faculties of *ʿagl* (judgment), *mukh* (intelligence), and *ḥalīlah* (imagination). A third, less localized agency corresponds to our notion of the soul and may be translated variously as *nafs* or *rūḥ*, the former having more the idea of individualness (ego) or personality, the latter representing a more spiritual essence. Usually *hājis* is classified among the mental faculties, since it is through these that man controls his emotions and imagination.

To a limited degree, the local theory has worked out the interaction of these faculties and their importance to poetic creation. Reason should control the emotions flowing from the liver and heart, disciplining them so that man does not fall prey to his passions (but not repressing them either). Whereas woman is conceived of as possessing as much intelligence as man (sometimes more), her ability to discipline her emotions and use her intelligence for constructive rather than destructive purposes, an ability controlled by reason, is, however, underdeveloped. (This idea is one of the ideological underpinnings for the various controls put on women, such as segregation, veiling, seclusion, and acts of modesty.) The emotions are easily agitated by outer events and in turn inspire the *hājis* to create poetry.

> O, O, my aching heart, || were I to say that I will hold my
> tongue, my reason [ʿ*agl*] would fly away.
> It is better that I utter my words to my audience || to launch
> my small poems on the waves of the air.
> (Muḥammad al-Gharsī)

> Son of Qāsim bin ʿAli said: "At night I sighed, || the spirit
> [*nafs*] is wasted and [so] the imagination [*ḥalīlah*] dredged
> up ideas.
> Father of Muḥammad sighed from the bottom of his heart
> while mankind was sleeping, || defeated [he was] in the
> world and sorry for its poets.
> O inspiration [*hājis*], as good as the wheat in the clay
> pots || on the waves of a pure sea [a pun on *baḥr* (meter)],
> scooped from its tidal rivers." (Muḥammad aṣ-Ṣūfī)

These two passages give us some insight into the cultural notions of creativity. It is dangerous to stir up the *hājis*, for once excited, it cannot be stopped without imperiling the poet's reason (as al-Gharsī fears). But the mad poet rolling his eye from heaven to earth will not do, for he should be in control of his passion. The poet suffers more than the rest of mankind by having to forgo sleep and peace of mind. Then we are told that the *hājis* dives deep into the imagination, pictured as a vast sea, and scoops from it the meter and the rhyme of the poem, its culturally most significant structures.

Some poets believe that chewing *gāt* will help focus their concentration on the act of composition while their *hājis* is hammering out the meter, rhyme, and images of the poem. For the longer odes they profess to require a certain amount of uninterrupted quiet; evenings are usually a good time to compose, after the guests have departed and the children have gone to bed. Even to the wedding *samrah*, which continues through the night, the poet may come chewing *gāt* to give himself energy and courage while participating in the highly competitive wedding *bālah*. (I have been told that *gāt* is chewed before going into battle to embolden men to commit valorous deeds.)

Themes versus Occasions

In the written dialect poetry of the towns and cities, known in Yemen as *ḥumēnī*, it is possible to speak of different themes in the verse, or at least the poets and critics of this tradition categorize poetry into genres on the basis of subject matter (al-Muqāliḥ 1978; Ghanem n.d.; ash-Shāmī 1965, 1974; al-Baradūnī 1977, 1981?): love poetry (*ghazl*), nature poetry (*aṭ-ṭabīᶜah*), social verse (*ijtimāᶜī*) (which can be further subdivided), and political poetry (*as-siyāsī*), attacking or defending the government. One can also type verse as being essentially religious (*dīnī*) or historical (*tarīkhī*) in subject matter. The tradition evinces a preference for certain kinds of verse over others, with *ghazl* enjoying great esteem and certainly the widest appeal, followed in order of appreciation by *aṭ-ṭabīᶜah*, then probably religious verse, social satire, and poetry with a political punch (cf. al-Muqāliḥ 1978 for this typical evaluation).[2]

Poems treating purely fantastic or imaginary themes are not taken seriously. In fact, I doubt whether they are possible in this tradition. The thoughts expressed in them are dismissed as hallucinations (*khadᶜ*) or, even worse, lying (*kadhb*). A poem is only composed in response to an *actual* situation, a momentous occasion (*munāsibah*) or a sociohistorical issue (*gaḍīyah*). I recall a tribal sheikh who, when asked by an Egyptian schoolteacher in my village to compose a poem spontaneously, wanted to know what issue he was to address. "Make up anything you like," was the response, to which the sheikh demurred, explaining that whereas he could compose a poem with rhyme and meter, there would not be much point to it if it did not treat some significant and actual social problem. Since he happened to be in the village market, he chose this scene as an "occasion" and facetiously began his ode in the solemn invocatory style, *yā jālisīn ʿala d-dukākīn* (O you who sit at the store fronts), which by the way is in perfect meter and has a neat internal rhyme (*-īn*). Laughing at this story, another poet friend of mine explained, "Exactly, for every poem there is a *munāsibah*. You see how ridiculous it sounds when it doesn't have a significant theme."

By *significant* we are to understand two types of social context: tribal ceremonies like weddings, religious festivals, and dispute mediations; specific historical events like wars, natural disasters, the occupation of the Ḥaram Mosque in Mecca by Muslim extremists, and the visit to North Yemen of Qaddafi; or more personal situations connected with the life of the poet. We shall see that the performance-composed genres like the *bālah* and *zāmil* are closely tied to tribal ceremonies, whereas the *qaṣīdah* is inspired by some *gaḍīyah* (issue) of burning interest to the poet and his tribal audience and is ordinarily not composed in a ceremony.

Unless they are already well known, the special circumstances under which a famous poem was composed are recited, for without such knowledge the poem would not be understood. Contrast this view of the poem as text-utterance with our own, wherein we believe the text, at least ideally, is self-contained so that it can be understood in its own terms.[3]

The Poem as a Political Act

Above all, a tribesman does not compose poetry purely for the sake of art. His sensibility does not separate aesthetic expression from the practical realm of life, for every poem is at heart a political and social act. The composition is in response to some actual, concrete event that always has practical or spiritual import for the community. Tribesmen hold a fundamental belief in what we might for now call the efficacy of poetry. The poet has power over men, and poetry is a deeply political act. By eloquence he can stir or, better yet, captivate an audience; if his poetic talents are truly outstanding, the chances are greater that the audience will do his bidding. Many anecdotes confirm this susceptibility to, fascination with, and awe of the poetic word. My favorite story is reported by the great Danish explorer Carsten Niebuhr, who traveled in Yemen in the eighteenth century with a party of scientists and scholars, of which he was the only survivor:

> The best poets are among the Bedouins of Dsjof. The Schiech of that country was, a few years since, imprisoned in Sana'a. The Schiech, observing a bird upon the roof of a house, recollected the opinion of those pious Musulmans, who think it a meritorious action to deliver a bird from a cage. He thought that he himself had as good a right to liberty as any bird, and expressed this idea in a poem; which his guards got by heart, at length reached the Monarch's ears, who was so pleased with it, that he set the Schiech at liberty, although he had been guilty of various acts of robbery. (Niebuhr 1972, 2:263)

Although I have no inkling who the poet was, the "Monarch" was probably the Imam, who was no fool when it came to handling tribal personalities and affairs. The story nicely illustrates how even the most implacable foe can be moved to clemency by an appeal to his sense of humor and, most important, his love of poetry. Sworn enemies engaged in mortal combat may at the same time harbor the greatest respect for each other, founded on no more than mutual admiration of each other's talents. A friend returned one day from battling one of the Khawlānī tribes in a bitter regional dispute. Disgruntled though he was with the sheikh, who adamantly refused to capitulate to the region's demands of mediation, he nevertheless admired his *qaṣīdah,* exclaiming to me, "By God, that son of a whore is indeed a poet!"[4]

The American poet Robert Bly has ruefully confessed, "Political concerns and inward concerns have always been regarded in our tradition as opposites, even incompatibles" ([1970] 1985, 131).[5] Yemeni tribesmen, however, think that poetry is too precious *not* to use for pressing public issues and that it can have a transformative effect on them as well; hence it possesses considerable power. They believe that it is poetic *form* which gives it this power. Let us now explore their "conscious" knowledge of this poetic form—that is, what they can actually say about it—while continuing to investigate the transformative power of poetry.

Poetic Chanting and Verse Forms

If one asks tribesmen to define poetry, one receives a fairly standard reply. First, it reveals a close connection in their minds between poetry and vocal music (and, more remotely, dance). They carefully distinguish between two kinds of vocalizing in the musical performance of poetry, *ghinā* (singing) and *ṣayḥah* (chanting; literally "yelling" or "shouting"). Only tribal males chant. Moreover, the term *ṣayḥah* has warlike connotations, for it also refers to battle cries. We will come across this sense of the word again in *bālah* verse, which can be seen as a metaphorical battle between poets.

Singing and chanting are marked by distinct modes of voice production. In *ghinā* the voice is low and soft, whereas in *ṣayḥah* it is a high tenor, creaky, almost a falsetto, bellowed out as loudly as possible. One explanation of the loudness is that this verse is intended to be heard by the public, but it is also, like its high pitch, hard on the vocal cords—deliberately so, for chanting is supposed to be a test of the warrior's strength and stamina. This fact is evident in *bālah* poetry performances in which the poets teasingly insinuate that their opponents' voices are growing hoarse and breaking, a sure sign that they are not up to the rigorous physical demands of this art combat. A creaky voice (a phonetic term for a crackling sound made when the vocal cords are in a certain position) can be commonly heard in everyday conversation, especially by tribal elders engaged in public encounters where "face" is involved, such as greeting exchanges (Caton 1986). It has the connotation of virility or manliness.

Each of the performance genres, the *bālah* and *zāmil,* is composed on traditional tunes (*laḥn,* pl. *ʾalḥān;* an alternative term is *nīyah,* pl. *nawāhī*), which more or less everyone knows how to chant. As my studies into the musical dimension have revealed, some of these tunes are identified with particular tribes. So strong, apparently, is this feeling of identification that a poet in one performance found it distasteful to compose poetry on a chosen tune because he asserted that it was "the Bani X's," with whom his group was at war. The *qaṣīdah* is yet again different from these performance genres because it is not composed by the poet with a standard tune in mind; indeed, it is ordinarily not composed to music at all. Only after its verbal text has been completed by the poet is the *qaṣīdah* given to a *mulaḥḥin* (someone who fabricates tunes). He is not a tribesman but a member of the *khaddām* who sings the verses to tunes he supposedly has created himself; he is accompanied, or accompanies himself, on the drum or tambourine. These performances can be beautiful, depending on the voice and musical skill of the singer. The greatest singer of Khawlān, al-Baddaʿ, was a favorite with taxi drivers and their passengers, who would cease their conversation long enough to listen to his clear, powerful, and sometimes haunting tenor on the radio. In such moments one would marvel at the way the voice and the words perfectly matched the physical setting as the car raced over the monotonous, hot, stark, and noiseless plains.

Besides music, the other ideas connected with poetic form are meter (sometimes referred to as *baḥr* but more commonly known as *wazn*) and rhyme (*gāfiyah*). The poet says he retrieves these from deep inside the "sea" of his imagination. In addition to meter and rhyme poets talk about alliteration, *takrīr al-aṣwāt f-il-bēt* (sound repetition in the line), as another important aspect of poetic form.

It is interesting that these same poets are unable to articulate the many different patterns of meter that are in traditional use. The most they are able to say about meter is that it is the essential component of verse, that it is based on the weight (*wazn*) of sounds and that it should be regular in its patterning. About the patterns themselves they are silent, and linguists must construct them on their own. How one might proceed in this work is discussed in Appendix B, but the aforementioned finding is not unusual. As Jakobson reminds us, "The poet's metalanguage may lag far behind his poetic language" ([1970] 1981, 139).

This metalanguage includes terms for other poetic structures as well. *Bēt* (pl. *ʾabyāt*) refers to the line of the poem, whereas *ḥarf* (pl. *ḥarūf*) is its hemistich. Take, for example, the opening of this famous *qaṣīdah:*

> – ∪ – | – ∪ –| – ∪ –| – –
> ʾibn[a] saḥlūl[a] b-iḷḷāha yitwakkal ||
> – ∪ – | – ∪ – | – ∪ – | – –
> rabb-ana l-gādir al-gāhir al-mitʿāl
>
> The son of Saḥlūl in God relies || Our Lord, the All-Powerful, the Vanquisher, the Supreme Being

This is one complete *bēt,* which is composed of two hemistichs or *ḥarūf.* The tribesman will analyze the verse into these constituents as well as point out that a rhyme (*gāfiyah*) occurs at the ends of the two hemistichs, namely /-al/ (repeated in the first hemistich of the following line) and /-āl/ (repeated in the second hemistich of the following line). The fact that the rhymes contrast in terms of vowel length (long vs. short) is not something he can explicitly articulate, though his audience certainly expects it, for it will chant in unison the final rhyme /-āl/ after each line, and if he were suddenly to insert a short instead of a long vowel, it will call him on the "mistake" (that is, if he did not do it deliberately). The audience response is proof, if one needs it, that structures of line and rhyme are psychologically real entities.

The audience may also exclaim *aḷḷāhu akbar* (God is great) after hearing this first line of the poem, not because it is the first line, nor because it invokes God's name (which the beginning of every poem is supposed to do), but because it has concealed within it poetic devices that win their admiration. It is the second hemistich that garners particular praise, but when asked what precisely is so wonderful about it, listeners usually respond, Can't you hear the repetition of sounds? The exasperated ethnographer then queries, Do you mean the repetition of the /a/ sound? To which the equally hapless reply comes: Yes, but there's much more. Can't you hear it? Then the informant usually repeats the line over and over again for the ethnographer to catch the patterning. Besides the alliteration of the long /a/ vowel, one can also point to the repetition of /g-r/ as in *al-GādiR* and *al-GāhiR* and a dense network of grammatical parallelisms (Jakobson [1966] 1981). "The poet is more accustomed to abstract those verbal patterns and, especially, those rules of versification which he assumes to be compulsory, whereas a facultative, variational device does not lend itself so easily to a separate interpretation and definition" (Jakobson [1970] 1981, 136). Rhyme and meter are thought to be obligatory structures of the line; alliteration (by which I mean here both the conventional consonance and assonance) is optional.

What about the meter, then? "Oh, it's there all right. Can't you hear it?" (this said in an exasperated tone that implies I must be deaf if I can't). "Sure, sure, I can. Uh, what can you tell me about it?" Again, there is a long silence. The poet then punches out the meter for me by clapping his hands four times in each hemistich. Each clap occurs where every foot (indicated here as |–⏑–|) begins, the clap thus dividing the hemistich into smaller, highly regular rhythmic units I call a *juzʾ* (a general term meaning "portion" or "section," which is not, as far as I know, part of *their* metalanguage). The beat is particularly discernible in the first line, and no doubt for this reason the first line is usually repeated several times by the singer or by the person reciting the work, so that the audience can firmly grasp it in their "inner ear" and listen for it in the subsequent lines.

The terms for meter, *baḥr* and *wazn,* have interesting connotations. The former is the word for "sea" or "ocean," and in the context of the poem it suggests not only that the poet's imagination is deep but also that the meter sounds like waves incessantly washing ashore. The latter has the literal meaning "weight," and it is not implausible that the weight of the syllable, which forms the basis of the meter, is being subliminally experienced here as an alternation of "light" and "heavy" syllables, an important clue to the structure of syllables on which the meter rides.

Other terms that are part of the poetic metalanguage refer to categories of verse. The *bālah* (pl. *bālāt*) is used for the poem (actually called the *qaṣīdah* of the *bālah*) composed in a chant during the groom's *samrah,* the session spent every evening in dance, poetry, and general merrymaking. I was never able to ascertain the exact derivation of the word, but probably it is related to the root *B-L-W* with its general meaning "to put to the test" or "a heroic performance." The term *bālah* thus suggests a heroic contest. When we examine in depth the performance of this genre—the fact that it is a competition between poets in which the prize is honor—this interpretation will seem even more plausible. It must be borne in mind that this genre is defined (by tribesmen) as that of poems composed in the wedding *samrah;* in other words, the genre is not defined in terms of what it is about (our Western obsession with subject matter) but in terms of what it *does* in social context. The analysis of genres must proceed according to the categories of performance.

Two closely related genres are the *zāmil* (pl. *zawāmil;* there is also a verb *zammal* meaning to compose a *zāmil*) and the *razfah* (pl. *razafāt*). (In Khawlān the alternative term *ḥaṣaʿah* is also, though less frequently, used for *zāmil.*) When I first began collecting texts in oral recitations (not yet during in situ performances), I kept confusing the two because on paper, and even in recitation, the *zāmil* and the *razfah* appeared to be indistinguishable. Not until I actually observed them being performed did I grasp the central differences between them. They have different melodies on which the texts are chanted; the *zāmil* is performed only outdoors, the *razfah* only indoors; the *zāmil* may be danced to the *bara*ᶜ but more often is not, whereas the *razfah* is always danced, and then to its own peculiar steps (the men turn while holding on to each other's arms as if they were doing the fox-trot); and the *zāmil* has a much greater range of use in social context, being performed not only at the wedding *samrah* (the only occasion for *razfah* composition) but also at the wedding *zaffah* (procession), the religious festivals, the dispute mediations, and the ceremonies of atonement. Once again the importance of these features of performance practices to a cultural classification of genres is clear.

The derivation of the term *zāmil* is even more obscure than that of *bālah*. One knowledgeable informant told me that *zāmil* is related to words like *zamīl* (crony, companion) and *zamālah* (comradeship, companionship), from which he not unreasonably concluded that this poem is intended to be performed among pals or friends. Note that *zamīl-ī* (my pal) is a commonly used possessive form of the word, carrying with it pleasant connotations of conviviality, loyalty, and solidarity. Whether or not my informant's derivation is linguistically correct, his speculation is interesting for what it reveals about the cultural conception of this genre (he was not alone in putting forward these claims about the term's meanings). In other words, the *zāmil* performance presupposes tribal bonds of solidarity among its participants, though the precise meaning of this solidarity shifts from one social context to the next. Thus, when the performance occurs at, say, a wedding, its meaning presupposes the solidarity and merriment of in-laws who are about to become members of the same moral community; in the course of a religious festival its meaning shifts slightly, presupposing the in-groupness of the *ʾummah* (community of faithful); and in the context of the dispute mediations the meaning becomes one of steadfastness, solidarity, and resolve of the litigants and mediator in the face of conflict. An important dialectic occurs between poetry and social action, for the *zāmil* both transforms the social context, through its association with the idea of solidarity, and is in turn transformed by it, through that context's specific meaning. (I cannot venture a derivation of the term *razfah,* as my questions about it drew a blank from virtually all my informants.)

Let us now turn to the most famous of all genres, the *qaṣīdah* (pl. *qaṣāʾid*). (The term *qaṣṣād* is often used for the poet of the *qaṣīdah,* and the verb *ʾaqṣad* means "to compose a *qaṣīdah.*") I say "famous" for a number of reasons. The *qaṣīdah* is well known throughout tribal

Yemen, whereas the *bālah, zāmil,* and *razfah* genres are not always found in other regions or else are known by alternative terms. Outside the tribal areas, among the literate urban populations, the term *qaṣīdah* is also recognized as referring to a long, lyric ode composed in the highest standard Arabic and cast in an aesthetic mold formed more than a millennium ago in the pre-Islamic era; it has survived to the present day virtually intact. Because most tribesmen are not aware of the written tradition of literature, they cannot understand their *qaṣīdah* to be an outgrowth of this same tradition. They see their poem as stemming from an ancient *oral* system. The literate, urban elements of the population, however, would conceive of the tribal *qaṣīdah* as a debased form of their own *written* genre. Despite these differences in the ways that the urban literate and tribal nonliterate groups understand the origin of their own and each other's *qaṣīdah*s, the contemporary forms of this poetry are considered by both groups to be enough alike as to constitute one genre. The idea of a genre shared by urban and tribal groups has significant implications for its survival as a viable art form in a changing society, as shall be explained in the concluding chapter.

Note that the poem of the *bālah* genre is also called a *qaṣīdah,* and we shall see that at least as *texts* they are astonishingly alike in basic content. What principally distinguishes them is once again a criterion of performance, in this case that the poem of the *bālah* is the most markedly performative of all the genre compositions, whereas the *qaṣīdah* is diametrically opposed to it (and to the other genres as well) in not being composed in a performance at all.

Because the tribal *qaṣīdah* is not composed in an oral performance embedded in some social ceremony, its subject matter (topical allusions) somehow becomes more noticeable (again only in contrast with the other genres in the poetic system). Here we can apply to some extent the idea of classification by topic—that is to say, a religious poem (such as a devotional to the Prophet or a poem about the *ḥajj*), a love poem (*ghazl*), or a political poem (*siyāsī*)—but it still has only a limited validity. More important to the local conception of the poem is that it have some kind of gist or central point at which one arrives after a series of preliminary speech acts have been ritually performed (invocation of God, praise of the Prophet, greeting of the addressee in the poem, if there is one, and so forth). Hence the term *qaṣīdah* is related to the dialectal word *gaṣd,* which can mean "goal" or "aim," "meaning" or "significance." In ordinary, day-to-day interaction people are constantly asking of themselves and each other *mā gaṣd-uh?* (what's his point? what's his intention?). This question does not indicate that communication is inherently inscrutable; quite the contrary, it shows that it is inherently to be construed. Thus, in a crucial sense the *qaṣīdah* is understood on the part of the poet to be the art of conveying his *gaṣd* to his audience and on the part of the audience to be the art of interpreting it. If the poem is felt to lack a particular *gaṣd,* it is ridiculed.

The poet's intention must relate to a specific and actual historical situation, so that in interpreting the poem the audience will instinctively relate what he says to what has happened or is happening. In addition, the intention must include an analysis (*taḥlīl*) of the problem as well as some sort of solution to it (*ḥall al-mishkilah*). It is therefore thought to take more than poetic talent to compose the *qaṣīdah;* it requires a deep intellect and a wisdom gained through wide experience in the world. At work is not merely the abstract talent but also the mind and heart behind the creative vision.

What also makes the *qaṣīdah* stand out is that it is the most valued of all poetic genres. The *bālah* performance on the groom's wedding night may have a special place in people's hearts, and *zāmil* poems of great wit and pithiness delight all connoisseurs of poetry, but for the tribesmen the *qaṣīdah* commands awe; only those poets dare compose it who are not afraid to be compared with the best of their generation and of their ancestors. Any poet who aspires to reach the pinnacle of his art and become famous has to prove his mettle in this genre.

Evaluation

The cultural criteria for evaluating a poem have been mentioned in passing; let us summarize them here. A good poem reveals the author's intention (*gaṣd*), which is related to some actual social ceremony or historical event and is not imaginary or fanciful. Though the intention should be implied through allusion or veiled reference, it must still be forcefully expressed. Of all subjects, politics or social criticism is preferred over erotic or humorous verse. A high premium is put on technical mastery of the verse forms, especially the meter, which should be regular, though rhyme and alliteration are also important. In the musical genres, particularly the *bālah,* the poet should have the stamina to carry his lines on the musical chant through many long evening performances. In addition, he should show his ability to analyze a particular issue current in the political community. And if he is challenged in verse, he has to be able to respond with a poem of the same genre, replicating or actually surpassing in intensity the verse forms of the original.

In this chapter I have constructed certain patterns of cultural interpretation having to do with tribal concepts of personhood, language, and poetry, all of which have been subsumed under the general term *tribalism.* In later chapters I will show that this ideology is critical for understanding how producers and receivers of poetry interpret not simply texts but also the acts of composition that result in texts. From now on, however, this ideology will remain in the background. What we need to grasp is the system of poetic practices that not merely is shaped by the ideology but directly and concretely helps to constitute that ideology.

3

The Social Production of Poetry

In the previous chapter we learned of the ideal that everyone in tribal society ought to compose poetry; it is part of what it means to be a tribesman. Poets, therefore, are not specialists. They only do especially well what everyone in the population ought to do as a matter of course. But the practice of the ideal raises the question of how composition of poetry is learned in the absence of formal instruction such as that provided by a school of poetry or a master-apprentice relationship. By the time males reach adulthood, they are able to compose verse according to the rules of poetic genres (meter, rhyme, line structure, symbolism, speech acts, and so forth), yet it is not at all clear how they master this ability. The question is not only one of production but also one of reception. How do they learn to interpret verse in ways that are deemed culturally appropriate?

I argue that common patterns of speaking in everyday discourse, which all children are socialized into producing, build a competence in basic structures related to poetic composition. As Friedrich (1979a) reminds us, drawing his insight from Sapir (1921a, 1921b) and the Prague School, poetry is ubiquitous in ordinary conversation: the poet has only to intensify (Friedrich's formulation) or foreground (Prague School terminology) the aesthetics of communication in the production of verse.

In other words, cultural conventions of art are grounded in real-world, everyday, practical activities of the society in which that art is produced and received. This shift in thinking about the production of art, as Geertz ([1976] 1983) was perhaps the first to realize in anthropology, originated in Michael Baxandall's *Painting and Experience in Fifteenth-Century Italy* (1972). A later, and for my purposes clearer, example of this new direction of research is Svetlana Alpers's *Art of Describing* (1983), about seventeenth-century Dutch art. Whereas art history has traditionally understood the Dutch paintings of this period to be imitations of the Italian Renaissance style, she argues to the contrary that the Dutch were embarking on a different enterprise. Whereas the painters in the Italian tradition narrated stories or allegories on canvas or else depicted ideal forms of beauty, as in their representation of the nude body, the Dutch artists were more interested in providing an empirical, rather than an ideal, representation of the world; they were more interested in the seen, in its surfaces, than in idealized projections of the painter. Moreover, she argues that this representation of the world is in keeping with a host of practices in Dutch society of that time: a public fascination with the camera obscura, which projected a moving picture of the outside world onto a two-dimensional surface by way of a lens affixed to a wall; mapmaking as a hobby among ordinary citizens; the Baconian interest in experimentation; the manufacture of lenses that magnified a previously unseen world of life, which was then described by draftsmen; and so on. These practices prepared the viewer to look at a painting as a way of describing the world. The aim of Alpers's analysis is not simply to uncover the conventions by which paintings may be viewed in a culturally and historically valid way. It is also to explain these conventions as being rooted in certain practices basic to a society.

Following Baxandall and Alpers, I too stress the relationship between poetic and other social practices in the culture. What is at stake here is the fact that the diverse competences poets need to carry out their daily speaking activities are also the competences they use in constructing their poems. Later in the chapter I will show how children's verbal games, tongue twisters, juvenile and adult riddles, proverbs, work songs, various speech acts such as greetings, hymns, and other devotional practices, and daily formulaic sayings build a competence in structures such as rhyme, alliteration, metrical patterning, the interplay of speech and musical structures, and allusion or veiled reference, all of which are the stuff of poetical practices.

How Poetry Is Learned

No formal instruction in verse composition exists among the tribes as it did, for example, in medieval Ireland (J. Williams 1971). From infancy boys and girls hear their parents and older siblings recite poetry. They also are exposed to poetry performances during wedding festivities, though I cannot say how much of them they actually understand when they have only just learned to talk.

By the time they are teenagers, boys and girls are usually segregated at public events; therefore, I was unable to observe the progress women were making as poets at this age. When they reach puberty, males are already considered old enough to know how to shoot a gun, dance, and compose poetry, so they are encouraged not only to observe the wedding celebrations but also to participate actively in them. In the poetry performances they usually perform in the chorus, a minimal participation requiring only that they keep the rhythm and the melody distinct while repeating a standard refrain like *lēlah wa bālah wa yā lēlah bāl* (night and *bālah* and O night of the *bāl*) or some other combination of words. I use the adjective *minimal* to describe their participation advisedly, for it takes quite a bit of stamina to chant in a high-pitched tenor for minutes and sometimes hours on end while keeping in unison with the rest of the group. Judging by the number of times the more experienced performers reproached us for cutting up the rhythm or failing to enunciate clearly the refrain, these skills did not come especially easily to my young cohorts either. Our task was nevertheless simple in comparison with what the others had to do in the performance (of which more later). If a young man begins to show a poetic talent by composing the shorter *zāmil* pieces or a line in the *bālah* performance, he will be applauded in his efforts and encouraged, but he has to practice the art and nurture his talent out of sheer love of the craft. No one will push him to excel.

It is important to note that the *zāmil* (and to a lesser extent the *bālah*) contains most of the metrical patterns used in the *qaṣīdah* as well as many of the latter's complex structures of rhyme and alliteration, so that those young men who wish to test their talent on the longer, more difficult ode will have already encountered the rudiments of its structure in the verse genres they practiced at wedding ceremonies.[1] Creating an ode involves, to be sure, far more than simply joining together some of the smaller poems, for the parts of the *qaṣīdah* are specialized to fit neatly into a larger, unified architecture. My point is only that the foundation for this ode's verbal patterns is already laid in the wedding poetry the young men practice before greater poetical ambitions begin to stir in them.

A youth's first odes are usually on the theme of love (*ghazl*). He faces perhaps the toughest audience of his life, for the girl who is the object of his desire may repay him with scorn and ridicule, especially if his verses do not pass muster. An approving glance or smile, however, would probably be enough to spur him on to scale even greater poetical heights: was it not said of Ibn Sinbul's verses, which are still recited in Khawlān more than a century after his death, that they would incite women to proclamations of love even when they had never laid eyes on him before? Perhaps the youth's sweetheart will reward his efforts with similar favors.

Is this early interest in lyrical and romantic poetry an expression of the first awakening of sexual desire in the boy? Given that males and females are segregated and that there are virtually no public forums in which it is permissible to express erotic desire, there may be a cultural presupposition that so highly structured a symbolic medium as poetry tutors control over one's passions; hence the expression of desire in verse is deemed safe. But perhaps there is also a sociological explanation for this early interest in romantic poetry. Before a man marries and has children, he is considered to be too immature to speak out on topics relevant to the village, the tribe, and the nation. Indeed, until he has achieved these signs of adulthood, his views may not even be politely listened to. Older, established poets tend to dismiss their youthful efforts at romantic verse as unrepresentative of their best work, even when they concede that a particular poem is a fine composition. The problem is that the theme of early poems is not "serious" enough. Even when these poets do on occasion compose love poetry, the poem usually contains a lengthy and important segment on local or national politics, as if to redeem it in the estimation of the poet and his audience. In other words, the only theme a young man *can* talk about is love, for he lacks the experience or authority to comment on social and political matters. When the poet has established himself in a household and is ready to take on adult responsibilities, he is able to voice his opinions on moral issues of great (or small) public concern. By this time too he and his companions know whether he possesses enough talent to become a major poet or *hājis*.

If a young man does appear to have the potential to become a major poet, he may end up working closely with a talented, established poet, who will help him improve his craft. This is not a formal master-apprentice relationship as in a bardic guild. The student does not live with the master, no money is exchanged, and no special deference is paid to the more accomplished artist. The older poet is often a relative or a close family friend, has known the "pupil" since boyhood, and accedes to his request for advice and guidance as a favor to a kinsman or fellow tribesman. It is difficult to know how common such informal teaching is in Khawlān. Muḥammad al-Gharsī, considered by many to be the region's finest poet, briefly attached himself to aṣ-Ṣūfī, who is recognized in his own right to be a fine technician, and the latter told me in an interview that he learned his art from his father, but I was never able to get reliable information on informal teaching.

The Poet as Specialist

The ideal in tribal society is for every man and woman to be a poet—that is, to be able to compose at least the wedding and *ᶜīd* festival poems. To what extent, then, is a specialization in poetry possible?

Those men who have reputations as *qaṣṣād,* or composers of the *qaṣīdah,* are considered to be better than ordinary poets and are referred to as "true" *shuᶜarā* (sg. *shāᶜir* [poet]). By virtue of their talent they are called on to reply to the poetical challenges hurled at their tribe, or else they take it on themselves to speak out on moral issues that particularly perturb their consciences—often, as we shall see, at considerable risk to their own safety or well-being.

The reward for their efforts, besides the obvious pleasure that the practice of their art gives them, is an enhanced reputation for *sharaf* (honor). This reputation for honor precludes the poet from publicly accepting money for his work. In private some Yemeni poets have boasted to me that, for example, a Saudi prince was moved to give them a munificent present in appreciation for a dedicatory poem, and sometimes one hears insinuations that so-and-so was paid a handsome sum by the president of the Y.A.R. for a poem supporting one of his policies; but it was made perfectly clear by the tone of the conversation that accepting remuneration is considered shameful.

It may help to shed light on this attitude if we contrast the poet's position with that of another wordmaster in Khawlān (and Yemeni society in general), the *dōshān* (pl. *dawāshīn*), who is a true specialist. The term is difficult to translate, but it is probably derived from the root *D-W-SH* which has the general meaning "palaver" or "babble" and is related to the noun *dōshah,* meaning a clamor of voices. Thus, the *dōshān* is something of a professional town crier who depends on his booming voice for his living. He utters praises of the groom and his family at the wedding ceremony in rhythmic prose, acts as a master of ceremonies on public occasions, relays messages from village to village or enemy to enemy during times of war, and greets the returning pilgrim with pious epithets. Like the low-status *muzayyin,* he belongs to the servant category known as the *khaddām* and as such, unlike a real tribesman, he cannot possess honor. Like all servants, the *dōshān* accepts payment for his work, either in the form of money or else as a part of the harvest of each household he serves in the village.

As the soul of the poet is expected to be noble and virtuous, so the character of the *dōshān* is reputed to be base and not a little mad. He may flatter a benefactor with a well-turned phrase or publicly abuse him with outrageous insolence, and though such recklessness in the face of tribal authority may seem a sign of courage, one must remember that he is protected from reprisals by his *hijrah* status. I was told that only children, women, and the *dōshān* would curse a person in public; Khawlānīs have a proverb, *rāmī b-il-ḥijār wa lā shatam l-ir-rijāl* (throw stones, but don't curse a man). A tribesman who is attacked by the *dōshān* would more than likely ignore him on the grounds that it is beneath his dignity to challenge him; but because of his very immunity from challenge or assault, the *dōshān* is both scorned and feared. His silence may have to be bought. A particularly alliterative Yemeni proverb is *ʾigṭaʿ lisān ad-dōshān b-il-iʿṭā* (cut off the *dōshān*'s tongue with gifts). This last expression best conveys the attitude toward taking money for verses—it implies that the act is part of the market rather than a symbolic exchange in the "glorious deed" of honor.

Another specialist to be distinguished from the poet is the *mulaḥḥin* (singer). He is a *khaddām,* like the town crier. If he has musical talent and a good voice, he may learn to play the *ṭabal* (drum) and even the *mizmār* (flute) and perform at the groom's wedding *samrah,* for which service he may obtain as much as two thousand Yemeni riyals (approximately $444 in 1981). If he has a truly outstanding voice, then a poet may give him his compositions to sing, though he, not the poet, composes the melody (*laḥn*). In the days before the tape recorder, verses were sent from one tribal audience to the next via the *mulaḥḥin,* who may have memorized a hundred compositions or more; his performances were well attended and generously remunerated.

Such public performances are much less common today. Indeed, I never actually attended one or heard of one being held. We might, therefore, jump to the conclusion that the technologizing of poetry deliveries through the tape recorder has destroyed the *mulaḥḥin*'s living. But the opposite has occurred—at least for the most gifted singers—for nowadays the *mulaḥḥin* tapes his songs and sells them to the stereo stores for hundreds of dollars, which, since he does not have to give the poet a royalty, is clear profit. (The most famous singer of tribal Yemen is al-Baddāᶜ, who hails from Khawlān.)

There is a clear division between the poet and the *mulaḥḥin*. The former creates the word; the latter carries it like a messenger (and is often addressed as such in *qaṣīdah*s). Though the voice delivery of the *bālah* and *zāmil* superficially resembles the singing of the professional messenger, it is culturally distinguished as *ṣayḥah,* which literally means yell or shout and may be used to refer to the war cry, whereas the voice of the singer is called *ghinā,* which literally means singing. It is commonly said that only women, children, and the public singer would burst into song. And I have been told that a tribesman would be afraid to publicly sing poetry to the *ṭabal* because such an act would shame his kinsmen, who might actually cut his throat in retaliation.

But the sanction works the other way too. Neither the town crier nor the singer may publicly compose *shiᶜr* (poetry), which is the exclusive privilege of tribesmen. Not even in the wedding performances do they participate. From *dōshah* and *ghinā* money can be made; *shiᶜr* can bring honor, and honor is possessed only by tribesmen.

Discursive Practices and Poetic Composition

The picture I have drawn of poetic practices may lead to the mistaken impression that only a few gifted persons are poets. In fact, the ideal is that every tribesman should be a poet or at least that every tribesman compose some poetry some of the time. In the absence of specialists or training in poetry, how are tribesmen able to learn verse composition? As youths they gain practice in crafting meter, rhyme, poetical exchanges, and so forth by taking part in poetry performances during the wedding celebrations and ᶜ*īd* festivals. But they learn how to produce verse in other ways as well. More exactly, they pick up from everyday conversation those practices that reinforce the skills of verse composition.

Proverbs are favorite bon mots among Yemenis, particularly tribesmen. One reason is that they are miniature poems and thus appeal to their aesthetic sensibilities, as does this saying: *al-wāʿid k-ar-rāʿid w-al-īfā k-al-maṭarī* (a promise is like lightning and fulfillment [of the promise] is like rain). Another reason is that like most tribal poetry, they *allude* to reality rather than nakedly refer to it, thus allowing the speaker to avoid, as the philosophers would say, making ontological commitments. If a friend refuses to lend money, the tribesman does not criticize him directly—Say, what about the time you wanted to buy some *gāt* and I lent you a hundred riyals—instead, he makes his point with a proverb: "The son of Khawlān says, 'What is mine is my friend's, and when I have nothing, I have no friend.'" A whole moral code is brought crashing down on the other's head (friendship is sacred and not for sale); the proverb refers to a current social situation, and because it is in the form of reported speech, as all proverbs inherently are, it alludes to the ancestors' moral reproach, which ought to deeply shame the addressee. Allusion is also playful because it is at heart a game of interpretation, even a duel of wits, which is such an important aspect of poetry performances. Hence, the addressee is expected to respond, preferably with his own proverb, and thereby to start another round of provocation and retort.

By mastering these kinds of aphorisms the young man begins to acquire a grip on the art of poetry with which they share many forms—sound symbolism, reported speech, pithiness, and allusion—though they are not regular enough in meter or rhyme to pass for genuine poems. Still, many proverbs are incorporated into highly structured verse, with little hammering needed about their edges to make them fit. More interesting, many poems have lines that sound like proverbs, though they are the poet's own invention, and one suspects that in time they will enter into the cache of proverbial lore.

Children's word games are another training ground in composition. Boys told me that they invent a special vocabulary when they refer in public to subjects they do not want others to understand (reminiscent in function of pig latin). For example, a boy draws his companions' attention to a girl in the street by saying, "Muḥammad, look at the *ʿunaybah*" (grape; diminutive form, feminine gender). If he is overheard and reprimanded for the remark, he can always deny referring to the girl. Whether his denial will save him from a box on the ears by an elder is another question. The point is not whether he can get away with it but the pleasure of veiled reference in this wordplay. Elders often recognize it for what it is and make allowances.

The words to a variation of musical chairs teach children the rudiments of rhyme:

yā dīk yā ṣayyāḥ || yā dākhil al-gariyah || bi-ghēr ijnāḥ

O rooster, O crower, || O you who enter the
village || Without wings

Though the meter is not regular (it is based on a common one in Khawlānī poetry), the rhyme scheme, *aba,* is.

The following tongue twister reinforces principles of internal rhyme as well as alliteration.

bāb-akum al-bābēn yā ghurābēn
mā yiftaḥ al-bābēn yā ghurābēn
ilā bi-miftaḥēn

Your door, the two doors O you two crows
Two doors won't open O you two crows
Except with two keys

Because the meaning is virtually nonsensical, the listener pays attention to the utterance's message form.

Better yet, of course, if one can create an utterance in which allusion or veiled reference, as exemplified in the boys' speech, is combined with the intricate verbal patterns of the tongue twister or the musical ditty. It is often called *lughz* (riddle). Here is one in the form of a poem about sexual intercourse:

dagagt al-bāb ḥatā kalā matan-nī || fa-lamā kalā matan-nī
kallamat-nī
fa-gālat lī ʾayy ismaʿēl ṣabr-an || fa-gult la-hā ʾayy ismā ʿīl[a]
ṣabr-ī

I knocked on the door until my back grew weary, || and
when my back grew weary, she spoke to me.

She said to me: O Ismael, patience! || I said to her: Hey,
Isma, my patience is spent!

Note the puns *kalā matan-nī* (my back grew weary) and *kallamat-nī* (she spoke to me), or the play on *ismaʿēl* (the man's name) and *isma ʿīl* (Isma is spent).

Work songs can be heard echoing in the valleys during the planting and harvesting season. They are known as *hajl* or *hajīl*. They combine certain verse structures with a quick rhythm and descending melody:

ʿalī musammā ḥaydarah
yaḍrib b-is-sēf ʿasharah
min al-yahūd al-fajarah w-al-kafarah

Ali who is called *ḥaydarah*
Strikes with his sword
Ten of the shameless and nonbelieving Jews.

muḥammad, yā muḥammad
muḥammad, jīt azūra-k
lā dākhil gaṣūr-ak

Muḥammad, O Muḥammad,
Muḥammad, I have come to visit you,
[I have come] into the interior of your castles.

When pushing a rock out of the way, one might sing this song:

ḥajr wa sīrī sāyirah
wa lā takūnī ḥāḍirah
aw min ḥajr as-sāyilah

Stone, go away!
Don't be there!
A stone in the wadi plain

Dozens of these work songs are part of the average person's repertoire. Prayers and religious hymns, with their countless repetitions of refrains such as "God is forgiving, praise be to God, there is no God but God," or "father of religion, father of the Muslims, may God keep our master Muḥammad clear of confusion," also instill sensitivity toward rhyme and rhythm.

Even greetings have a patterning that might be described as poetic in the Khawlānī sense:

> ḥayya l-bēt w-ahl-ah → ḥayy aḷḷāh man dakhl-ah
>
> Long live the house and the people in it! → Long may God preserve the one who entered it.
>
> min al-ʿāyidīn as-sālimīn → ʾaʿāda-kum aḷḷāh b-is-sālimīn
>
> The celebrants of the *ʿīd* are in good health → May God keep you among the ones in good health.
>
> ḥajj-in zāyirīʾ aw ḥarīw-in mugambaʿī → inshaḷḷāh
>
> A *ḥājj* pilgrimage or a groom-to-be → if God wills.[2]

Notice how the greeting exchanges employ formulaic phrases—that is, relatively fixed linguistic expressions preserved for their own sake—similar to our *hello, good morning,* and so forth. As is the case in other Arabic dialects, there are hundreds of these formulaic expressions, and they ornament every conversation. It is extremely important to know how to link formulas together and use them in the appropriate social contexts. Thus, ordinary discourse already prepares the would-be poet for the use of formulas in the *bālah* performance, where, however, they serve a very different function.

Everyday discursive practices, then, teach children and reinforce in adults many aspects of poetry—rhyme, meter, alliteration, puns, line structure, reported speech, organization into strophes, allusion, and sound symbolism—which we shall see intensified in verse genres. But another aspect may be even more salient for an understanding of tribal poetry. Not only is the poetic form of these practices reflected in the verse, but *the speech acts of greeting, prayer, invocation of God's epithets, and so forth become the stuff of poetry.* A *bālah* poem, for example, will contain numerous greetings of various men in the wedding party, religious invocations of God, and prayers offered on behalf of the Prophet. Because many everyday speech acts comprise the content of the performance poetry, all tribesmen are able to participate in the composition of some verse some of the time.

For example, in the greetings we have just examined, we find paired expressions in which the second formula (or the response) is more intensive in "illocutionary force" (Searle 1969) than the first formula (or the initial utterance). Thus, "My greetings to you" may be the response to "Greetings"; similarly, "And peace be upon you as well as God's mercy and His blessings," the response to "Peace be upon you"; "May God grant you His blessing and protection this morning," the response to "Good morning." This pattern, in fact, reflects a religious model of speaking imposed on Muslims in the Qur'ān (Caton 1986). In composing poetry, more or less the same formulaic expressions are used, except that the intensification of illocutionary force is conveyed by a metaphorical phrase tacked on to the formula. "And peace be upon you as well as God's mercy and His blessings" may become in poetry "And peace be upon you as many as there are stars in the summer sky," where the metaphor conveys the sense of the greeting being offered up innumerable times to the addressee and thereby honoring him. Of course, to make the formula fit a precise metrical verse pattern, certain syllabic alterations have to be made in the everyday greeting, but the changes are usually slight (the technicalities are discussed in chapter 4). The point to bear in mind is that much of the content of the poems, consisting as it does of a series of speech acts, is rehearsed in everyday speaking practices and therefore at the command of the competent tribal speaker. What I have illustrated for speech acts of greeting could be repeated for religious acts and challenge-and-retort routines.

Another kind of speech act that finds its way into poetry stems from an insult. Angered, a tribesman grasps his *jambiyyah* (dagger), removes it from its scabbard, and challenges his opponent—not to duel but to answer the charge that he is dishonorable. The insulted party has just performed an act of *daʿwā* (challenge), accompanying these grand gestures with some performative phrase such as *anā daʿī l-ak* (I challenge you) while at the same time handing over the dagger to a third party (any responsible adult who happens to be on the scene is morally obligated to intercede as judge if no official elder is present). Meanwhile, the opponent, if he is also an honorable man, takes out his dagger, hands it over to the mediator, and wipes his brow with his thumb, saying *w-anā muʿayyib* (and I am the offender). He has just performed an act of *ʾijābah* (retort) to the challenge.

This practice is at the heart of much social interaction (many times even as a parody of the game of honor). It does not always lead to a confrontation, as in the above scenario, nor is it often expressed in a ritually elaborate form; the challenger may simply grasp the handle of his dagger without removing it and challenge the other with a look of displeasure. But the meaning of the act is the same: the challenger feels that his honor has been impugned by the man he addresses and demands satisfaction.

Poetic composition is deeply implicated in this social exchange, as we shall see when examining various genres more closely. A poet often will challenge another person to respond to his verse with a composition of comparable, if not better, artistic merit (the poem is culturally conceived to be a weapon much like a dagger or a gun), thus initiating the challenge-and-retort routine. If the person who has been challenged fails to respond with a poem of at least equal value, he loses face, having failed in the glorious deed. This type of poetic challenge and retort is particularly evident in dispute mediations.

The Technologizing and Marketing of Poetic Production

The tape recorder and the market system are important means through which poems are recorded and disseminated in modern tribal North Yemen. Contrary to what some students of folk traditions have found to be the case elsewhere in the world, technology and modern economics have not inhibited the oral tradition. As I have already pointed out, the text is no longer memorized by the *mulaḥḥin* (singer) and then disseminated in live performances before an audience; rather, his performance is commissioned by a stereo store, and the tape is then sold in stores around the country or exchanged privately among friends. Often the poet recites his poems directly into a tape recorder (in a plain speaking voice), and the copies are then sold throughout the country, though it is still the case that he does not openly accept money for his recitations. Ostensibly his goal is to achieve greater fame by reaching a national, as opposed to a local, audience.

The tape recorder can be an important stimulus to poetic production apart from the (secret) economic gain it may bring to the poet. A man may hear a tape and become inspired to respond to its poetry by composing a verse of his own, which he then tapes and sends to the original poet, who in turn may reply to the reply with another tape. Thus, it is possible for poets who might not otherwise hear each other's work or get in touch with each other about it to exchange verses fairly easily. (An example of such an exchange originating through tape recordings can be found in chapter 8.) The tape recorder has also significantly altered the way in which the poem is assimilated by the audience. In the past, when the poem was disseminated by the singer, the audience had to catch the poem on the wing, as it were, but now the tape recorder allows them to intervene, altering the whole process of understanding and interpretation. The tape recording can be stopped, replayed, and advanced so as to allow its audience a more active role in the poem's appropriation. I have sat in on several afternoon *gāt* chews where the assembly would listen to poetry tapes and utilize the recorder in the manner described to enhance the listening and interpretive experience.

Though the tape recorder acts as an aid and stimulus to poetic production in one sense, one would suspect that it would alter that production radically. One might predict, for instance, that poetry tapes played at wedding ceremonies or religious festivals would gradually supplant the composition of verse in performance—which, as we shall see, is the hallmark of these celebrations—thereby extinguishing an important mode of its production. It remains to be seen whether this will happen, but when I was in Khawlān this orally composed verse tradition seemed to coexist alongside the taped *qaṣīdah.* The explanation has to do, in my opinion, with the different cultural conceptions of these two kinds of verse, which make one amenable to taping and the other not. The whole point of the *bālah,* as tribesmen describe it, is to be a game in which poets compete by spontaneously composing lines of verse to see who can outwit whom. To listen to the tape of such a performance would be to participate as a receiver, not as a producer, and thus to alter fundamentally the experience of this work of art. The *qaṣīdah,* by contrast, is not improvised in a performance but is composed independently, as a finalized utterance, and hence lends itself more readily to tape recording and reproduction without distorting its original aesthetic purpose. For the time being, at least, these two modes of reproduction flourish in parallel.

As far as I know, no poet uses the tape recorder in composing the *qaṣīdah,* recording and playing back successive versions of lines. But most of the *qaṣṣād* I knew were literate, and some wrote down the texts of their poems as they composed them. The degree to which writing intruded in the process differed from poet to poet, however:

for some it was merely a way of recording the lines they had already finished and ordered in their head; other poets would write as many as four drafts before they would be satisfied with the final result. But writing was by no means an essential aspect of poetic composition, for many poets of the *qaṣīdah* (among them the finest in the tradition, like Muḥsin al-Bowraʿī) were completely illiterate. Writing, of course, never entered into the composition of verse in performance, such as the *bālah* and the *zāmil.*

Though the market has been an important economic force in Yemen for centuries, it is doubtful that poetic production has ever been an economic good entering into its system of exchange. In the future the market may fundamentally transform the tribal poet's relation to poetic production from one in which honor is created to one in which money is earned. For the present, what is apparent is the *political* importance of the marketplace to poetry production: it is a relatively easy means by which the government can try to persuade the public to support its policies by hiring poets to compose verse touting its programs. Radio and television, on which much tribal poetry can be heard, are also important channels of government propaganda. But the marketplace is harder for the government to control than these other media, so it can become a source of antigovernment rhetoric secretly used by the public. When in the late 1970s, for example, the poet al-Gaʿshamī of the al-Ḥadā tribal confederation openly deplored in verse the assassination of his much-beloved president al-Ḥamdi and, moreover, strongly implied that his successor al-Ghashmī was responsible, he was imprisoned for several months. His *qaṣīdah* was then, and still is today, available in the market despite the fact that it is blacklisted by the government.

The Tribal Poetic System and the State

Just as tribal society spills over into the urban realm, so does its poetry, and this is not necessarily a modern phenomenon. Even more important, the state tries to use these poets for its own rhetorical purposes. In this regard a tribal poet, Ṣāliḥ Saḥlūl, is reputed to have been the first person to have declared to startled Yemenis over the radio the outbreak of the 1962 Yemeni revolution—in tribal verse. In the past some of the Imams were known to compose poetry in tribal genres such as the *zāmil;* that is, rather than persuading tribal poets to compose this verse for them, they did it themselves, especially when they (like imams Yaḥyā and Aḥmad) were already accomplished poets in the classical style. For example, a tribal delegation might importune the Imam with a poem (or series of poems) and he would reply, as the cultural system requires, with a poem of his own, replicating the verse he received. As these rules are quite specific with regard to rhyme, meter, alliteration, and various speech acts, his reply would require an intimate knowledge of the tribal poetic system.

It is thus clear that the state attempts to appropriate the tribal poetic system for its own political purposes, excluding the *bālah,* which is composed in a performance and is not ordinarily taped. And clearly when still most of the country's people consider themselves to belong to some tribe, it is wise for the state to do so as well. This is especially true when one bears in mind the fact that the state does not control the tribes by a monopoly over wealth or by coercive force, if it controls them at all, but rather by persuading them to back the regime. In other words, state power is fundamentally based on rhetorical appeals meant to influence the opinions of the religious elite, the urban bourgeoisie, and the tribes.

The Social Contexts of Poetic Production

The social contexts of poetic usage may be divided into two broad categories: tribal *ceremonial occasions* and key *historical situations* tied to the personal life of the poet or to the affairs of the community (village, region, nation, or world). These two kinds of contexts differ in their use of poetry. Poetic production is a norm of social action in the former but is voluntary in the latter; it is found in specific rituals in the former but is open-ended in the latter; it must be public and collective in the former but may be personal and private in the latter. All genres with the exception of the *qaṣīdah* are composed in the context of tribal ritual, of which we may distinguish at least four types: wedding celebrations (*zawāj*), *ᶜīd* festivities, tribal dispute mediations, and *hajr* (ceremony of atonement).

In the course of a wedding ceremony there are two crucial events in which *zāmil* performances are the norm: the *samrah* and the groom's *zaffah.* The noun *samrah* is derived from the Arabic Form I verb *samar,*

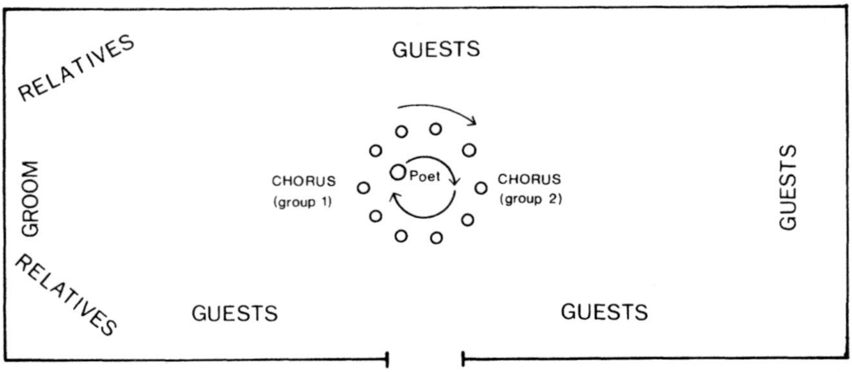

Figure 1. Bālah performance.

meaning to spend the evening with friends in restful, idle conversation. Tribesmen gather after dinner to sit and pass the time in someone's *mafrāj* (sitting room), sometimes nearly until dawn, chatting, playing games, and perhaps even dancing. The groom's *samrah* is supposed to have the same elements of relaxed amusement, but it naturally differs in that the caliber of entertainment is much higher. Professional musicians, a drummer-singer and a flute player, are usually hired to perform the music to which the assembly can dance the *mizmār* (named after the flute), and all the adult guests are obligated to contribute some lines of verse in the competitive *bālah* poetry or the *razfah*.[3]

The excitement builds as the guests arrive in groups of about five to ten during the early evening hours. They are the ones referred to in the poetry as *ʾajānib* (foreigners). Their *zāmil* poem echoes in the wadi basin in which they are walking and carries through the stillness of the night on high-pitched voices. Upon hearing their chant, the host of the *samrah* dispatches some young men to greet them at the village entrance with gun salutes and rounds of exploding firecrackers. The thoroughfare to the groom's house beckons in soft white light emanating from the garlands of bulbs strung across the house walls and is astir with children scurrying about and adults doing their rounds of visiting. There is no mistaking the groom's house, which is ablaze with lanterns, strings of bulbs, and torches. Its colored, stained-glass windows glow invitingly like embers in a hearth.

The arrivals are conducted to the *dīwān* (hall) in which the celebrants, including the groom, are waiting to receive them. They have to make their way up the narrow, low stairway past the first floor, which smells of fresh hay and animal dung, past the second floor, where the kitchens are only just closing down, though the odors of cooked food linger in the corridor, and up to the top—the men's section—where dozens of pairs of identical sandals are strewn outside the door. The wise concoct some excuse for taking their sandals with them into the room or else secrete them in the folds of their clothing, for otherwise they are likely to lose theirs or grab shoes of different sizes in the mass exodus at evening's end.

When the delegation has stepped into the room, the assembly rises to its feet to perform the moving ritual greeting known as *ḥāl.* Room is then made in the already packed hall for the new arrivals. The most prestigious personages, such as sheikhs, are seated nearest the groom; the rest may sit anywhere in the circle according to their preference. Usually a soft, thick oriental carpet is spread under the celebrants for their comfort during the long hours of the groom's *samrah;* the water pipe is also available, the tobacco laced with the finest incense and the water delicately scented. Each male wears the Yemeni dagger (*jambiyyah*)—a curved silver blade with a gazelle-horn handle inlaid with old coins—and brings a rifle, which he hangs by its leather strap on the wall pegs. These weapons are symbolic of male fighting prowess and hence honor, and the poetry is full of allusions to them.

The groom has already changed into his brand-new set of clothes during the afternoon *zaffah* (procession). He is distinguishable from the rest of the company by the *mushgarī* stuck into the right side of his headdress, a sprig of the green, sweet-smelling basil known as *shadhāb,* thought to be a prophylactic against bad luck or disease. Alternatively, he may don a wreath (*ʾiʿkāwah*) of the same plant. His hands are hennaed for the same reason. Throughout the wedding ceremony the groom has to maintain a rigid pose and does not participate in the events, such as the afternoon *gāt* chews, the dancing, the poetry, or the shooting matches. He is a passive onlooker.

Approximately one hour after the evening prayer, when the guests have been fed dinner, the professional musicians play a stirring drum salute called the *tamsīḥ,* which incorporates in its music the rhythms of the famous *baraʿ* dance (see Adra 1982). This salute is a signal that the poetic events and dances of the evening are to begin. Once I attended a *samrah* at which the host jokingly reprimanded his guests when the evening wore on without a poetic performance forthcoming. "Here I have fed you," he chided, "and now you must honor me with poetry."

Wedding celebrations may last several days, if not weeks, depending on the social prominence of the groom's family, and it is expected that a *samrah* be held on each evening of the celebration. On the *lēlat ad-dakhlah* (night of consummation) the festivities reach their greatest intensity. Guests who cannot attend every night of the celebration try to attend at least that evening. Two genres of poetry are commonly performed at the *samrah,* the most important being a competitive verse composition known as the *bālah* (the other being the dance-verse genre called the *razfah*). A wedding celebration is thought to be lacking if one or both of these genres is not performed; therefore, a special onus is placed on the guest to contribute in this way to the evening's entertainment.

As for the *zāmil* performance, I have already remarked that it occurs en route to the groom's village, but that is not the most crucial ceremony in which it is heard. Far more important is the groom's *zaffah,* the procession which begins at his house, slowly and majestically winds its way to the mosque, and then retraces its course. At the head of this procession are the village servants, who drum loudly the beat of the *baraᶜ* dance. Immediately behind them are the guests of the wedding, all of them adult males, marching in columns with their rifles slung over their shoulders. They are wearing multicolored turbans, jackets, and skirts. They form what might be called the chorus of the *zāmil* performance, one half chanting the first line of the poem and the other half chanting the second and final line; the poet usually comes from their ranks. If they feel so inclined, they might begin a dance to accompany the poetic chant and drum or shoot their rifles at an improvised target. All around them are the adolescent boys, too young to shoot off rifles or compose verse publicly, who gleefully light firecrackers and hurl them in the air to land usually underfoot or on the shoulders of the unsuspecting marchers, who cannot sidestep fast enough the flashing, hopping strings of fire. In the rear of the procession is the groom along with some friends or relatives bearing on their shoulders his *mazharah* or bouquet, which is composed of branches of acacia and sprigs of basil decked with strings of different-colored berries, hollow eggs, and various other charms believed to ward off evil and bring good health, fertility, and prosperity. Sometimes a picture of the Ḥarām Mosque in Mecca is stuck inside the bunch of plants, a reminder of the fundamentally sacred significance of the entire ceremony. As in the *dīwān,* the groom is expected to maintain a solemn, dignified, and basically passive mien throughout the procession. Although the women are not publicly present, they can be heard performing the peculiarly shrill ululation of joy (*taghrīd*) from the house rooftops. Their black, veiled figures lean over the parapets four or more stories above the street, from where they throw candy to the children, who chase after these prizes through a haze of blue smoke rising from the exploding firecrackers. The whole affair is a cacophony of noise, a swirling mass of movement and color.

The ideal of the poetic performance is that the guests compose a *zāmil* to which the hosts respond; this exchange is then repeated as often as inspiration allows. The tone of the exchange may be one of friendly teasing, of mutual recognition of honor expressed through praise and lofty compliments, of greeting, or of pious sentiments. The following is an example of such an exchange. First the host's poem:

> From us, good evening, [as many times as] the star revolves in the sky, || [As many times as] the rifle hits with its accurate bullets.
> O greeting to the guest, greetings from us all, || Which London announces and is broadcast in Iraq.

The illocutionary force of the greeting is intensified by the metaphors of revolving heavenly bodies and the deadly accuracy of tribal marksmanship. Now the guest's poem:

> Greetings from us. May thousands fill your mountains. || O defenders of the tribal border with the barrel of the rifle,
> We came from the same origins. || No one abandons his kinsmen until he dies.

The guest poet returns the greeting with equal force and addresses the hosts as "defenders of the tribal border," meaning that they are therefore honorable men. Because the guest is a relative by marriage, he feels obligated to attend the wedding and affirms this obligation by declaring, "No one abandons his kinsmen until he dies." The ideal of sociality understood as balanced exchange is upheld.

Enough has been said for the time being about the wedding ceremony as a context for poetic production. Now let us turn our attention to the two major religious festivals in the Muslim calendar: the *ʿīd al-kabīr* after the holy month of fast, Ramadan, and the *ʿīd aṣ-ṣaghīr* that marks the end of the annual pilgrimage to Mecca. Unfortunately, I had the opportunity to observe only one of these festivals (at the end of Ramadan) while I was in Khawlān, though I was assured by tribesmen that the same rituals are enacted in both.

On the first morning after the fast had been officially declared at an end, the old and young adult males of the village in which I was staying convened in the *sēlah* (flood plain) to greet each other with salutations peculiar to the *ʿīd.* The flood plain has special significance. In the Yemeni highlands most villages are built on rock outcrops that jut upwards from the wadi floor, the fertile fields surrounding them irrigated by canals that drain the wadi's plain when it is in flood, during the rainy season twice a year. The rest of the time the wadi floor is dry and used for a variety of purposes, including the transport of animals, the passage of people between villages located along the plain, as the meeting ground for tribal delegations who have been sent to a village to mediate one of its disputes, and for open-air markets that convene once a week. A mosque is usually situated at the rim of the flood plain and the village, casting its sacred canopy over these people and their activities. In short, the flood plain is a general thoroughfare bringing fertility, religious blessing, and hopefully also security. It is not surprising that the religious festival marking the transition of the fast and the beginning of a new year is held in a place saturated with the symbolism of passage, for, as Van Gennep ([1908] 1960) understood, ritual time is often symbolized by movement in space.

In the cool hours of early morning on the first day after the fast, the hamlet of Bēt al-Bahlūlī sends a delegation of adult males to march in the wadi toward the hamlet of Dhu l-Mukh, which in turn dispatches a group of adult males toward the former, the two groups meeting halfway. At the head of the delegations are the servants of their respective hamlets, drumming the rhythms of the *baraʿ* dance. The men behind them chant a *zāmil* poem appropriate to the religious occasion:

> The month of Shawāl for Arabs is proclaimed || As the time to break the fast for those who have fasted.
> Happy is the faster who has been loyal to [God's] demand, || And to those who have not—may they be damned!

We have put our trust in God. || Our lot can only increase
through His generosity.
O Lord, let rains give us (water) to drink || And irrigate the
crops and fields.

Again, the unmarried boys watch from the sidelines, the women from their houses. As soon as the two delegations stand facing each other a few yards apart, the elder of the first arrivals begins the greeting. "Peace, O tribesmen [lit. faces]," he shouts in a high, creaky voice that rises above the din of the drumming and chanting as a signal for the crowd to be silent. The elder continues as before: "May God restore us and you to the saved and the healthy." The presupposition of this formula, of course, is that those addressed are true believers who have remained steadfast in Ramadan. As soon as the elder has finished, the men of the opposing delegation intone in unison the response: "May God restore us and you to the saved and the healthy. May He protect them [the rest of the tribe] from harm." A reception line is formed by the initial group, which now welcomes the new arrivals individually. Each man shakes the other's hand and quickly kisses the back of it, muttering *min as-sālimīn* (among the saved), a shibboleth among the community of the faithful.

Smiling and laughing, the group now either prays in the mosque at the rim of the flood plain or else retires to an open-air site to hear a sermon about the significance of the *ʿīd* and then join in communal prayer. This activity may last a half hour, after which time they retire to their villages behind the drummers, once again chanting *zāmil* poems. The next morning the villagers visit each other and perhaps exchange gifts, the children often skipping from door to door to receive candy; at noon relatives assemble for large communal feasts. Everyone is very much relieved that the hardship of the fast is finally over, though perhaps their joyous mood is also tinged with a slight anticlimactic feeling because the drama of self-discipline that marks the fast has ended.

By far the most important social context in which *zāmil* poetry is composed is the dispute mediation. When a serious conflict breaks out between two or more villages or tribes or two different tribal sections—a conflict that might involve a dispute over land (private property or tribal boundaries), women (abductions, runaways, adulteries), or water rights—warfare among the contending parties often results. It should be repeated that the fighting at first is often a kind of symbolic violence in which the offended party tries to restore its honor by a show of force, and almost immediately after the first shots have rung out, intermediaries arrive to try to persuade the parties to agree to a truce and settle their differences peacefully. Only when the stakes become high, as in cases where considerable sums of money change hands, is there a real danger of physical violence and bloodshed.

Let us take a hypothetical example of a dispute mediation. Suppose that Bēt al-Bahlūlī has accused Bēt al-Mukh of having committed some offense (as determined by the code of customary tribal law), such as laying claim to land that it regards as its own property; if Bēt al-Mukh refuses to acknowledge the former's claim, a conflict will inevitably ensue. No violence or symbolic show of force need break out unless Bēt al-Bahlūlī feels that its honor has been challenged by the usurpation of its land, the killing of one of its villagers, or similar action. Should the village go to war, however, the countryside is alerted by the reports of rifle fire. Soon after the outbreak of hostilities the prominent tribal leaders along with other influential personages in the region, such as the leading religious elite, convene and march on the village to persuade its inhabitants to agree to a truce (*ṣulḥ*). This group of intermediaries is commonly known as the *wāsiṭah*.

The intermediaries may arrive chanting a *zāmil* poem (the chanting is not obligatory), announcing its intention of mediating the dispute and offering up cows or sheep for sacrifice as tokens of their sincerity and good faith. If Bēt al-Bahlūlī, the plaintiff in the case, agrees to a truce, it sets the conditions in numbers of cows, sheep, guns, and, in the most serious conflicts, even hostages, which Bēt al-Mukh, as the defendant, must hand over as a pledge of its willingness to discuss and resolve their differences honorably.

These demands are put forward by the intermediaries in the form of *zāmil* poetry. Since there are usually several intermediaries working to resolve any one dispute, they each march separately in the flood plain with their delegation and stop outside the defendant's village, while chanting all this time the two lines of verse in which they have couched their persuasive rhetoric. As in the wedding procession, the performers march in columns, though without a drummer at their head, and are received with the characteristic *ḥāl* greeting by a line of elders from the village. They then disband to await on the sidelines the arrival of other intermediaries or enter the village to discuss the problem with the defendants.

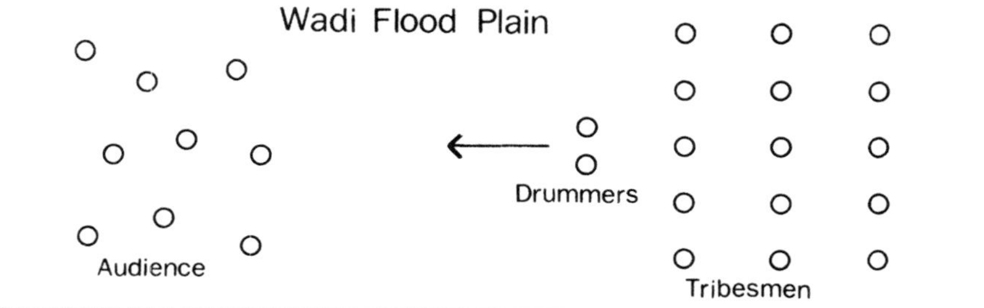

Figure 2. *Zāmil* performance.

In this society, steeped in the courtly ideal of hospitality, there must be a luncheon and *gāt* chew for these distinguished visitors before all parties can sit down to discuss the conflict. If they arrive at some sort of resolution, they depart from the village and deliver it to the plaintiff, again couching the terms of the proposed settlement in poetic form. Now another round of talks, this time with the opposing side, begins, and the plaintiff's response is carried back by the *wāsiṭah* in the form of another *zāmil* poem.

If a resolution is arrived at quickly, the offending party or accused accepts the judgment of the intermediaries as to their guilt and the punishment prescribed by tribal law. If, however, the conflict is not resolved quickly, the fighting escalates, and yet more mediating groups intervene to try to negotiate a settlement; in the most tragic cases a whole region may be embroiled in an unending cycle of truce, negotiations, and war. When events reach this boiling point, the tribes of the entire region may send their delegations (usually including one or more poets if these are not already present among the sheikhs) to the main assembly place, known as the *masrākh,* to discuss the emergency. These delegations arrive chanting a *zāmil* poem that expresses their moral attitude toward the conflict. And so the negotiations continue until a "final" resolution is reached (though in actuality the dispute may languish without ever being permanently settled by tribal law).

Whenever a judgment in a dispute has been rendered (and accepted) according to tribal law, it is customary for the defendant to perform a ceremony known as *hajr.* It is a public ritual of atonement and acquiescence to the sentence, which he carries out by marching with some sheep, cows, or camels to the door of the plaintiff's house (or the entrance to his village) and chanting a *zāmil* in which he expresses his contrition. Upon arriving at the house or gates of the village, he sacrifices the animals he has in tow.

All the above cases—the *bālah* performed in the groom's wedding *samrah,* the *zāmil* poetry composed for the wedding *zaffah,* the *ʿīd* festivals, and the dispute mediations—involve institutional contexts for the production of poetry. But a great deal of verse is composed in everyday, personal, but still intensely public, contexts, and it is to these situations that I now turn.

It is practically impossible to delimit a class of occasions on which someone might use *zāmil* poetry for his own personal ends. Specific examples must suffice to illustrate the point. For instance, in a local market I came across a wandering beggar poet who assailed his customers with recriminatory poetry if they proved ungenerous or unkind—verse variously intended to embarrass or amuse his audience depending on how charitable it had been. Once I was riding a bus on which more boarding tickets had been sold than there were seats available for passengers, with the result that a luckless rider who happened to be an old tribesman had to sit on the floor of the vehicle. Resenting the injustice of not having been given a seat like everyone else when he had paid for one, he composed a *zāmil* on the spot voicing his complaint. It had its intended effect: everyone on the bus started to laugh when they heard his poem and taunted the ticket taker, who in turn relinquished his seat to the now greatly mollified old man.

These are humorous and somewhat trivial examples (except to the persons involved), but the public and strategic use of poetry may occur on other, more serious, though still nonceremonial, occasions. A poet from Khawlān by the name of ʿUbād ʿAlī had once served in the special guard of the *ʿāmil* (administrator) of Maḥwīt district in North Yemen, who happened to be a prominent Khawlānī sheikh. At one time during ʿUbād's service the payment of the guards' wages fell into arrears, so they called on him, as poet spokesman of their group, to appeal to the administrator for the back pay. He delivered the following *zāmil:*

> Greetings to the *ʿāmil* from a soul [lit. heart] among us, || [Greetings] as great as His lightning flashes and [as many as] the raindrops.

The men are in a bad way, O youth, our courageous leader, || Still no expenses are forthcoming, nor have you given us [our] salary.

The sheikh paid his men and then responded to ʿUbād's poem with one of his own:

Greetings to the poet al-ʿUwal, our affection || [Greetings as great as] their floodwater irrigates in every wadi the parched earth.
O God who art one, with regard to the point you mentioned, our sentence is: || No one wants his group to work for nothing.

The response replicates the meter and rhyme of the original, thus framing it as a retort to a challenge. In other words, the verse form indexes the social encounter between the poet and the sheikh as one that crucially entails honor (a response to a challenge); thus social acts may spur not only the composition of poetry but also the way that composition may frame these acts or provide them with a context in which they may be culturally meaningful.

One of the folk heroes of Khawlān, Nājī bin ʿAli al-Ghādir, led the royalist forces during the Yemeni civil war (roughly 1962–1969). Having exhausted his stock of grain, he importuned the people of ʾAsal to sell some to his tribe, but they refused. He thereupon composed the following fiercely scornful *zāmil:*

Al-Ghādir says, "you have been generous, O people of ʾAsal, || May God increase your flock of sheep.
We asked you to give us grain and you said, 'Not a cupful.' || Ask about us, whether we live or die."

The opening line is deeply sarcastic, and the second is all the more dramatic because the people of ʾAsal condemn themselves in their own words.

I have said nothing about the *qaṣīdah* because, in contrast to the other poetic genres considered in this work, it is not usually produced in the context of an institutionalized activity like a wedding. Thus its pragmatic use is confined to actually occurring, sociohistorical events such as natural disasters, political assassinations, disease in the community, or a regional war. The performance genres, by contrast, figure crucially in institutionalized settings. Within this category the characteristic that marks the *zāmil* as a genre distinct from the *bālah* is its use in a greater variety of social situations—the groom's wedding procession, the march to the groom's *samrah,* the religious festivals, the dispute mediations, and the ceremony of atonement—whereas the performance of the *bālah* is restricted to only one of these. Thus, the relationship of these genres to each other can be summarized as follows:

Historical Time, Nonperformative	Ritual Time, Performative	
	Restricted	Unrestricted
qaṣīdah	*bālah*	*zāmil*

The distinction between historical and ritual time is one I use for analytical purposes and is not necessarily recognized in the cultural system.

This chapter concludes the overview of background information needed to understand the practices of producing and receiving poetry that are examined in detail in the rest of the book. One problem still remains, but it is so technical that I have decided to address it in an appendix rather than in the main body of the text. This problem concerns the analysis of verse meter. I noted difficulties with it in the previous chapter when I stated that poets are unable to articulate explicitly the metrical pattern even though they insist that there is one and that it is regular. I contend that at this point a comparative theory of verse meter must be gleaned from linguistics, and I construct such a theory in Appendix B.

PART II

The System of Poetic Genres

4

The *Bālah*: Poem as Play

> The rhythmical or asymmetrical arrangement of language, the hitting of the mark by rhyme or assonance, the deliberate disguising of the sense, the artificial and artful construction of phrases—all might be so many utterances of the play spirit. To call poetry, as Paul Valéry has done, a plaything with words and language is no metaphor: it is the precise and literal truth.
>
> Johan Huizinga, *Homo Ludens*

Of all the genres in the tribal tradition, the *bālah* is perhaps the most fascinating to study and thrilling to watch. It is, to a greater extent than any other Yemeni verse, composed *in* a performance (Parry 1930, 1932; Lord 1960). It is poetry created spontaneously before an audience, not prepared in advance and then delivered by a reciter. The audience witnesses an *act of creation,* which in and of itself is of aesthetic interest.

The *bālah* is also the most inherently collective and dramatic of all the poetic genres. Always more than one poet composes the verse, and they enter into a *competition,* which is referred to in the poetry as a *laʿbah* (game). This cultural notion reinforces the aesthetic experience of composition as an act, for in a game what is suspenseful is carrying out an act to an undetermined outcome according to specific, collectively shared rules. Poets are carefully monitored by the chorus, the audience, and each other to make certain they follow the rules of the game. A secondary, though still important, element of this game is musical—the chanting of the verse, whose complexity is unparalleled in the poetic system and deserves close scrutiny. In one sense, the social import of the performance is, as far as the explicit cultural system is concerned, a game intended for the amusement of the groom. But I shall argue in the next chapter that there is a deeper purpose to this game, namely, the ideal self of the *gabīlī* (see chapter 2) is constructed in the course of the performance.

In describing the structure of the *bālah* I distinguish between the turn, the speech act, and the hemistich. The first is a technical term from the literature on discourse analysis (Goffman 1981) that refers to the opportunity to speak accorded in simple succession or alternation to individuals, as, for example, the turns taken by different news announcers or panelists. *Bālah* poets take turns showing off their talent; the halves of the chorus take turns with each other, repeating parts of the performance; and members of the audience take turns expressing their evaluation of poets' verse. What a poet does in his turn is to execute a conventional speech act (for example, a religious speech act such as an invocation of God, a prayer for the Prophet, or a challenge and retort exchanged with another poet). It is important to bear in mind that this speech act is similar in content to ones examined in the previous chapter: there is little if any difference here between poetic and social practice except in the degree to which poetic form has been foregrounded (Mukařovský 1964) or intensified (Friedrich 1979a). A speech act is generally completed in two consecutive hemistichs, with each hemistich being stitched together from formulas expressing the content of the speech act (including the ideals of tribalism) by the thread of a regular meter and rhyme.

Nonverbal Aspects of the Performance

The Performers

There are three types of performers in the *bālah:* poet, chorus, and audience. The roles alone are fixed, the persons who assume them varying greatly in the course of the evening, even in the course of a single performance. No one decides in advance who is to be a chorus member, who is to be a poet, and who is to be in the audience.

In keeping with the ideal of *gabyilah,* every tribesman may have a turn at composing verse. After dinner has been served, the assembled guests are exhorted *gūmū!* (rise!) and asked to perform. If a guest is not confident in his ability to compose verse, it may be better for him not to attend the evening's festivities, but the sin of omission dishonors the groom. If someone is, like a sheikh, a person of renown, then he may not be able to avoid attending the celebration. Because of these strong obligations to compose poetry at the wedding celebration, the art is cultivated by all, if, alas, mastered by only a few.

Dance Movements

As described in chapter 3, the *samrah* involves a huge gathering (in the grandest wedding upward of a hundred people may be squeezed into one room). The groom, his immediate relatives, and his closest friends occupy the seats of honor at one end of the hall. The other guests, crouching with their backs to the wall, may sit near the groom, if they are particularly important; otherwise, they sit wherever they want (see Fig. 1).

A small group of men—approximately six to ten in the average performance—form a circle (*ḥalgah*) in the middle of the room. They face inward, their arms clasped around each other's shoulders or waists and their feet slowly moving in a simple side step (clockwise or counterclockwise; the direction of movement does not seem to matter). This circle of men is what I call a chorus, though in Arabic they are referred to as *ṣaffēn,* literally two ranks (lines or groups). One rank or *ṣaff* chants a refrain, and the other chants a certain part of the verse, the two groups thus alternating their chanting throughout the performance of a single poem. The choristers are often the younger men of the wedding party, sometimes even adolescents, who may not yet possess the requisite skill to compose verse but are learning it by performing in the chorus.

The poets, whoever they turn out to be, shut their eyes as they listen to the chanting, their faces tense with the effort of composition, their lips silently forming the lines that spring from their imagination. Confident that they have composed a well-formed verse, their faces brighten, and one among their number (which varies from two to five or even more) moves decisively toward the circle and breaks through the linked arms of the choristers, who close ranks behind him.

The poet is now in the center of the performance, in the middle of the *samrah,* and at the heart of the wedding festivities. The collective attends the individual's chant to see how well he plays the game. Cupping one or both hands to the sides of his head, sometimes even plugging his ears with his thumbs (see Plate 8)—a gesture that simultaneously projects the verse off a natural sounding board so that the whole noisy assembly can hear it and blocks out any palaver that might disturb his concentration (coincidentally this attitude is reminiscent of the *muʾadhdhin,* who calls the people to prayer)—he walks half of the circle's circumference and at the same time chants the first hemistich (*ḥarf*) of his turn. Depending on the particular chant, the chorus might intrude at this juncture with a choral refrain, but in any case the poet finishes his turn by chanting the second hemistich and continuing around to close the circle. (In the case of a third hemistich, which rarely occurs, he describes another half-circle.) He then immediately exits from the middle of the circle, and the chorus meanwhile picks up the chanting of the last hemistich of the poet's turn, alternating it with the refrain line. Now it is up to his rivals to continue building the poem. The performance ought not to depend heavily on the contributions of one person, for then it is no longer felt to be an evenly matched competition.

Throughout the performance the audience is hardly ever still, except when a poet enters the circle, at which time most people want to hear what he has to say and evaluate it. They are quick to laugh at a witty line or exclaim *aḷḷāhu akbar* (God is great) in reaction to a particularly good metaphor or adroit turn of phrase. If the poet's gift to the groom is unsound because it breaks the rules of composition, they will start shouting boisterously *ḥarf magṣūṣ* (a broken hemistich). Occasionally such rowdy criticism incites a quarrel between the poet and his audience, but he is more likely to amend the fault by quickly fashioning another hemistich. If he cannot make a speedy recovery, he will inevitably give way to another poet and thereby lose face. As soon as the poet has exited the circle and the chorus has begun chanting again, the audience usually attends to its own matters—resuming a conversation, smoking the water pipe, joking, or just dozing to the hypnotic drone of the chant.

To summarize, the performance is made up of three concentric circles: the inner one is described by the poet's turn, the middle one comprises the chorus, and the outer one is formed by the seated audience. The penetration of the inner circle by the poet emerging from the outer two and then the exiting back into them is perfectly iconic of the ideal that everyone—whether a member of the audience or the chorus—may be a poet; no one is privileged. In addition, and much more significant, is the fact that the closer someone is to the center, the more intimately he becomes involved in the compositional process: the audience reacts to the poem, the chorus "carries" it (the Arabic word is *shall,* which means lift or carry), and the poet composes it. And whereas the audience and chorus look inward, the poet faces them in the middle by looking outward: the individual is alone and being judged by the collectivity. It is certainly the ultimate moment of truth, when honor is being tested and is either recognized or repudiated.

Music

Each genre of performance-composed poetry (*bālah, zāmil, razfah,* and *rōshān*)[1] has its own set of melodies on which the poetry is chanted. I taped eleven melodies for the performance of the *bālah* in Khawlān, though I suspect that more exist (and was told as much by informants). The melody is chosen by the chorus at the beginning of the performance. Its members huddle together, trying out various tunes in a low but barely audible voice until one is found that all like. Then the two ranks burst into full voice (or *ṣayḥah,* the cultural apperception of which was described in chapter 2), delivering in a high register the standard refrain line, which varies only slightly from melody to melody. The chorus has to keep singing in unison and in key through endless rounds of repetition, which drum the music of the chant into everyone's "inner ear."

The following example shows a *bālah* tune with the refrain "And O night of the *bālah* and O *bāl,* night of the *bālah* and O *bālah.*"

The syllabification of the line is noteworthy for several reasons. Not every syllable is assigned to a single note; rather, often a syllable has to be stretched across several notes depending on the length of the melody (in other words, there are more notes than syllables). However, usually a long vowel is stretched, as in the above example, over two notes (*ya-a*), whereas a shorter vowel is held for only one (*wa*), so that there is a rough equivalence between musical time and syllabic quantity (or weight). Alternatively, the heavy syllable may be divided into two short ones (*ya-wa* for *yā; ba-wa* for *bā; le-ya* for *lē*).

I [Poet] refrain → filler → 1st hemistich (beginning)
II [Poet] 1st hem. (end) → filler → 2d hem. (beg.)
III [Poet] 2d hem. (end) →
[Rank 1] filler → 2d hem. (beg.)
IV [Rank 2] 2d hem. (end) → refrain (beg.)
V [Rank 1] refrain (end) → 2d hem. (beg.)
etc.

Figure 3. A schema of one type of *bālah* performance. Roman numerals represent complete musical lines.

A poet is now ready to take the first turn at composing verse in the performance. He has two tasks before him: to compose a turn of poetry with the correct meter and rhyme and to chant this verse to the melody.[2] His problem is to intercalate these two systems.[3] To illustrate, let us consider in detail the chant to which the above refrain belongs. The poet begins his turn by chanting part of the refrain *wa ya-a le-e-lah ba-a-lah* to the first third of the melody (see Figure 3). Then he inserts a filler, *ʾa-la-a,* on the following three notes and, after pausing briefly at the rest, begins the first hemistich. His problem, though, is that he cannot complete the hemistich on the melodic line. Therefore, he starts the melody over again (chant II) and completes the first hemistich. He still has about two-thirds of chant II left, which he resumes on the filler and the start of the second hemistich. He comes to the end of chant II before completing the second hemistich and hence must take up the melody a third time (chant III).

At this juncture the chorus joins in, taking up the chant from the poet without losing a note. The chorus divides into two ranks. The first rank repeats the filler and then the second hemistich to the end of chant III. The second rank immediately completes the hemistich on the first part of chant IV and begins the refrain on the last part of the chant. The first rank then has to complete the refrain on the beginning of chant V and start the second hemistich on the end of it. In this manner the two ranks of the chorus alternate until the next poet takes his turn, after which they pick up on the second hemistich of the new verse. Various other possibilities exist for the interaction of poet and chorus, but this one presented the most complex antiphonal structure I heard.

The role of chorister requires considerable skill. The first rank has to hear the poetic line and chant it exactly as the poet delivered it, and it only gets one hearing to do so. Once the poem is in full swing, this rank will sometimes anticipate the poet's end rhyme. It joins him as he is completing the turn, having second-guessed what he will say. It is only able to do so, however, in the beginning of the poem, when the highly formulaic language makes verse composition relatively predictable. In any case, chanting in the chorus requires stamina, good memory, and steady concentration.

Verbal Aspects of the Performance

The Hemistich

I have been stressing the aesthetic apperception of the poem as a process of composition rather than as a finished product. Because the *bālah* is poetry of the immediate present, the poet cannot polish the lines or elaborate the structure of the rhyme or images in the body of the poem. The poet is not nostalgic for the text, which has been forgotten, because he can always quickly create another; besides, it was never meant to outlive the moment of its composition. To paraphrase D. H. Lawrence, all is flying and lightness of touch, a quivering of surfaces, an open-endedness of a wind forever in passage.

What is foregrounded in the poet's and audience's attention is the system of rules—the poetic code—by which the utterance can be produced in a performance. True, spectacular verbal maneuvers such as skilled punning or alliteration are greatly admired, but what everyone is listening for is the poet's adhering to the rules of the performance while at the same time making such brilliant plays on words. This is one of the reasons that the poem is called a game.

METER

When a poet steps into the circle to take his turn in the poetic composition, one of the notions of correct form in verse that he has to obey is meter. The performance of the *bālah* rests on a limited number of meters—usually two—compared to the total of eight or more that exist in the tradition. The most common pattern (known in classical Arabic as *al-basīṭ,* though this term has no currency among the tribes) is an alternation of a four-syllable foot |– – ⏑ –| or its variant

|⌣–⌣–| with a three-syllable foot |–⌣–| and its (infrequent) variant |⌣⌣–|. Thus, the first turn in the above example of a *bālah* poem scans metrically as follows:

> – – ⌣ –| – ⌣ – |– – ⌣ –| – ⌣ –
> w-abdaʿ bi-dhī lāmiʿ al-bārig wa dhī lāḥ[a] bih ||
> – – ⌣ –|– ⌣– |– – ⌣ –| – ⌣ –
> yā man daʿ aḷḷāh karīm al-kaff[a] mā khayyab-ah
>
> I begin with Him who flashes the lightning and causes it to appear. || O he who calls on God, the Generous One, He does not disappoint him.

A much less frequently encountered meter in the *bālah* (similar to classical Arabic's *al-mumtadd,* though again it should be stressed that this term has no currency in Khawlān) is based on an alternation of a three-syllable foot |–⌣–| with a four-syllable foot |–⌣––| (and its variant |–⌣–⌣|, but this pattern occurs in only two performances I recorded in the region, and thus it is safe to conclude that it is relatively rare.[4] (For a justification of the scansion and the details of the analysis of the metrical pattern, see Appendix B.)

RHYME

The rhyming rule of the *bālah* is fairly simple in comparison with that of other genres. The first poet establishes the pattern, but there are only two possibilities. The hemistichs of the same line either rhyme or contrast with each other. Once the specific pattern has been established, the rule is that subsequent poets may not repeat the rhyming words used in previous turns (though they may use homonyms). If they do, the audience will catch the mistake and cry *ḥarf magṣūṣ* (a broken hemistich), and unless the poet can quickly rectify his mistake, he will forfeit his turn.[5]

FORMULAS

As in the case of other oral poetry, the *bālah* is constructed out of relatively fixed linguistic expressions known as formulas.[6] The formula is used as a building block to construct a regular meter in a rapid-fire performance. One widely heard *bālah* formula used in addressing tribesmen at the *samrah* gathering is:

– –[⏑]–| – ⏑–|–
y-abtāl ʿūj al-kirāsī[7]
O holders of the curved rifle butts

This formula occurs nine times in my collection, always at the beginning of the hemistich. It thus has a precise position in the meter. The following are the nine hemistichs in which the formula is used:

– –[⏑]–| – ⏑ –|– –⏑–|– ⏑ –
1. y-abtāl ʿūj al-kirāsī *ḥāliyāt an-numar*
O holders of the curved rifle butts, *beauties of the number*

– –[⏑]–| – ⏑ –|– – ⏑ –| – ⏑ –
2. y-abtāl ʿūj al-kirāsī *takrimū man dafar*
O holders of the curved rifle butts, *you welcome the arrival*

– –[⏑]–|– ⏑ –|– – ⏑ –| – ⏑ –
3. y-abtāl ʿūj al-kirāsī *taṭʿanū f-in-nahūr*
O holders of the curved rifle butts, *you stab in the neck*

– –[⏑]–|– ⏑ –|– – ⏑–| – ⏑ –
4. y-abtāl ʿūj al-kirāsī *shalliyīn aṣ-ṣamīl*
O holders of the curved rifle butts, *wielders of the club*

– –[⏑]–| – ⏑ –|– – ⏑–| – ⏑ –
5. y-abtāl ʿūj al-kirāsī *maddiyīn aṣ-ṣawāb*
O holders of the curved rifle butts, *adherers to the right path*

– –[⏑]–|– ⏑ –|– –⏑ –|– ⏑ –
6. y-abtāl ʿūj al-kirāsī *ḥāliyāt al-ʾimān*
O holders of the curved rifle butts, *the beauties of the safety catch*

– –[⏑]–|– ⏑ –|– – ⏑ – | –
7. y-abtāl ʿūj al-kirāsī *kulla fannān*
O holders of the curved rifle butts, *everyone is an artist*

– –[⏑]–| – ⏑ –|– –[⏑] –| –
8. y-abtāl ʿūj al-kirāsī *gōm shibbān*
O holders of the curved rifle butts, *a tribe of youths*

– –[◡] –| – ◡–|– – ◡ –| – ◡ –
9. y-abtāl ʿūj al-kirāsī *fī nahār al-fiyūd*
O holders of the curved rifle butts, *in the days of pillage*

The poet's challenge is to finish the hemistich by linking the fixed formula with other traditional formulas or original phrases, both of which have to fill out the remaining metrical pattern (–◡–|–◡– or its truncated form found in examples 7 and 8, which are chanted on a shorter melody).

It is useful to think of the traditional stock of formulas and epithets available to poets as a system. As Parry explains, "We may say that any group of two or more such like formulas make up a system, and the system may be defined in turn as a group of phrases which have the same metrical value and which are enough alike in thought and words to leave no doubt that the poet who used them knew them not only as single formulas but also as formulas of a certain type" (Parry 1930, 85). Compare examples 1 and 6. Though the idea or principle behind the use of the concluding formulas is the same (describing some beautiful part of the rifle such as the registration number or the safety catch), the phrases are not verbatim repetitions. By analogy the poet knows that (1) *ḥāliyāt an-numar* and (6) *ḥāliyāt al-ʾimān* are the same formula but altered at the end to meet the requirements of the rhyme. He might in another performance end the hemistich with *ḥāliyāt al-giṣāb* (the beauties of the gun barrel) if the rhyming syllable were *-āb*.

What has just been said about construction by analogy of the end-of-hemistich formula could just as well apply to the initial one. The expression

– –[◡]–| – ◡ –| –
y-abtāl ṣafr al-jarāmil
O holders of the yellow rifles

also occurs at the beginning of the second hemistich, is metrically identical to the other formula, and is similar to it in idea. A variant of this formula, *y-abtāl ṣafr al-majārī* (O holders of the yellow barrels [of the rifle]) is frequently heard as well. Another analogous formula with a slightly more varied wording is

– – ∪ –| – ∪ –| –

yā kāsibīn al-jarāmil

O ones who grip [clutch] the rifles

Undoubtedly other formulas similar to these exist.

Parry might have schematized the above formulaic systems as follows:

1a. y-abtāl *ʿūj al-kirāsī*
y-abtāl *ṣafr al-jarāmil*
yā kāsibīn ṣafr al-jarāmil
yā kāsibīn *al-majārī*

1b. ḥāliyāt aḍ-ḍarāb (beauties of the trigger)
ḥāliyāt *al-ʾimān* (beauties of the safety catch)
ḥāliyāt *al-giṣāb* (beauties of the barrel)

Selection from the system of formulas is only half the problem, for the poet has to know how to combine them into the syntagmatic or sequential unit of the hemistich so it will scan according to the desired meter. Combining 1a, the initial formula, with 1b, the end-of-hemistich formula, could generate the following metrically correct and semantically coherent *bālah* verse equivalents, all of which could be used in various performances:

y-abtāl ʿūj al-kirāsī *ḥāliyāt aḍ-ḍarāb*
y-abtāl ʿūj al-kirāsī ḥāliyāt *al-ʾimān*
y-abtāl ʿūj al-kirāsī ḥāliyāt *al-giṣāb*
y-abtāl *ṣafr al-jarāmil ḥāliyāt aḍ-ḍarāb*
y-abtāl ṣafr al-jarāmil ḥāliyāt *al-ʾimān*
y-abtāl ṣafr al-jarāmil ḥāliyāt *al-giṣāb*
y-abtāl ṣafr *al-majārī* ḥāliyāt *aḍ-ḍarāb*
y-abtāl ṣafr al-majārī ḥāliyāt *al-ʾimān*
y-abtāl ṣafr al-majārī ḥāliyāt *al-giṣāb*
yā kāsibīn al-jarāmil ḥāliyāt *aḍ-ḍarāb*
yā kāsibīn al-jarāmil ḥāliyāt *al-ʾimān*
yā kāsibīn al-jarāmil ḥāliyāt *al-giṣāb*
yā kāsibīn *al-majārī* ḥāliyāt *aḍ-ḍarāb*

yā kāsibīn al-majārī ḥāliyāt *al-ʾimān*
yā kāsibīn al-majārī ḥāliyāt *al-giṣāb*

The above formulaic types are of medium complexity in *bālah* poetry.[8] My intention was not to demonstrate the system in its full "productive" power but to illustrate how such verse is constructed from many systems of formulas.[9] A competent poet of this genre will have learned a large number of these formulas and have become adept at combining them so as to form a regular metrical hemistich, tinkering perhaps only with the end of the last formula to make it fit the rhyme.

To what extent a whole *bālah* poem is constructed of formulaic expressions may be gauged from the sample text provided in Appendix C; the formulas there are italicized, and every line contains at least one formula. Bear in mind, however, that the sample poem does not contain a lengthy development section, in which the use of formulas tends to decrease and the ingenuity of the poets is tested to compose "fresh" verse suitable to conditions of a specific performance or sociohistorical context. Here is the translation of the sample text. The refrain is "O night of the *bālah,* and O *bālah* of the evening, and O *bāl*":

1. And O night of the *bālah:*
Poet 1 Verily, I begin with Him who causes the lightning to flash and Him who makes it appear.
Verily, O he who prays to God, O Generous One, [he] will not be disappointed [by Him].
2. And O night of the *bālah:*
Poet 1 Verily, I praise God [as many times as] the east wind blows.
Verily, [as many times as] [God] causes rain to fall from the sky.
3. And O night of the *bālah:*
Poet 2 Verily, I invoke God who was at the beginning [of Creation] and the end.
Verily, I praise God millions of times that we count.
4. And O night of the *bālah:*
Poet 1 Verily, we will be saved from the Fire, whose flame is frightening.
Verily, on the day the Accountant reckons [the good and the evil] of all who approach Him.

5. And O night of the *bālah:*

Poet 1 Verily, He who is Leader of the bees which harvest and manufacture it [i.e. honey].
Verily, O God, we beseech You who are far and near.

6. And O night of the *bālah:*

Poet 1 Verily, Preserver of the ships on whose waves one is brought to safety.
Verily, I mention Muḥammad, God's blessing on *aṭ-Ṭayyibah.*

7. And O night of the *bālah:*

Poet 2 Verily, I mention Muḥammad since his mention is a duty.
Verily, He intercedes on our behalf [with God, to keep us out of] Hell, whose heat is blazing.

8. And O night of the *bālah:*

Poet 1 Verily, O God, we implore You to spare us from calamities.
Verily, I say good evening, I am of men who love war.

9. And O night of the *bālah:*

Poet 2 Verily, good evening to you, verily, you are the fanged lions.
Verily, O men of the *ḥaḍramī* [i.e. from Hadhramawt] blades, sharpen the fine cutting edge.

10. And O night of the *bālah:*

Poet 3 Verily, long life [i.e. greetings] to all of you, and may you not see any calamities [in life].
Verily, O thousands of welcomes innumerable.

11. And O night of the *bālah:*

Poet 3 Verily, I serve the two groups [i.e. of the chorus] who are wearing the *jambiyyah* and scabbard.
Verily, they who meet in the bulwarks of every fortified mountaintop.

12. And O night of the *bālah:*

Poet 2 Verily, long life and health to you [i.e. greetings] [as many times as] they press the grain on the grinding stone.
Verily, generosity to the guest, even in lean years.

13. And O night of the *bālah:*

Poet 4 Verily, O blessed evening when a friend meets his friend.
Verily, O welcome to the guest far and wide.

14. And O night of the *bālah:*

Poet 1 Verily, I serve the happy groom fine perfume.
Verily, and [I serve] the foreign [i.e. outside the village] guest melon and grapes.

15. And O night of the *bālah:*

Poet 2 Verily, may God preserve you all [i.e. greetings], O you who know the correct customs.
Verily, you meet in the bulwarks when trouble has started.

16. And O night of the *bālah:*

Poet 1 Verily, O welcome to al-Ḥukaymah [one of the poets in the *bālah*], who says what pleases him.
Verily, [welcome to him] [as many times as] His lightning flashes and has watered the parched land.

17. And O night of the *bālah:*

Poet 2 Verily, May God preserve you all, O you who butcher sheep (for the feast).
Verily, O men of generosity, long has this been our custom [i.e. to honor the guest by slaughtering sheep for him at lunchtime].

18. And O night of the *bālah:*

Poet 3 [Unintelligible line.]

19. And O night of the *bālah:*

Poet 1 Verily, in that house there will be neither sheikh nor army captain.
Verily, the wild lion is in the mountain, and the fox is in its lair.

20. And O night of the *bālah:*

Poet 3 Verily, O welcome to the guests as a group whose honor is precious.
Verily, and the groom—we will even add to all he wants.

21. And O night of the *bālah:*

Poet 1 Verily, O Ṣāliḥ [the groom's father], may God give you long life, do not remain a fugitive from us [i.e. do not flee your obligations as a host].
Verily, He [the host] is a solid, well-built fortress and not dilapidated villages.

22. And O night of the *bālah:*

Poet 3 [Unintelligible line.]

23. And O night of the *bālah:*

Poet 1 Verily, O Ṣāliḥ, long life to you, do not tear your *magṭab* [the male tribal skirt].
Verily, two thousand prayers for the Chosen One who is at aṭ-Ṭayyibah [i.e. buried in Medina].

Table 1. *Poetic Turns Composed by Each Poet in the Performance*

Poet 1	*Poet 2*	*Poet 3*	*Poet 4*
1			
2			
	3		
4			
5			
6			
	7		
8			
	9		
		10	
		11	
	12		
			13
14			
	15		
16			
	17		
		18	
19			
		20	
21			
		22	
23			

Four poets in all participated, and their contributions are listed in Table 1. The first poet clearly dominated the performance, probably because he had the advantage of choosing a rhyme with which he was comfortable, and it took time for the second poet to get used to it. The general pattern of such performances is for one or two poets to dominate, and the poet who establishes the rhyme has a "lead" over his competitors. (Note that the chorus did not call out *ḥarf magṣūṣ* [a broken hemistich] on the second hemistich of turn 9, whose rhyming word repeats that of the second hemistich of turn 6, because *ṭayyibah* is used to indicate Medina in the one and the dagger blade in the other. The same principle applies to the rhyming word of the first line of verse 14, where *ṭayyibah* has the meaning "fine" or "exquisite.")

FORMULAS, ICONIC INDICES, AND IDEALS OF SELF

We should take careful note of what sort of meanings are being conveyed in this typical *bālah* poem. For example, the assembly at the performance is described by formulaic expressions emphasizing war and prowess in combat. The poet of turn 8 says, "I am of men who love war," in other words, he is always eager to go into combat in defense of his tribe. The assembly is greeted as "fanged lions" (turn 9), which is another formula like *stabbers in the neck* or *wolves of the darkest night,* suggesting the fierceness of the tribal warrior. And when the poet addresses the assembly as "men of the *ḥaḍramī* blades," he is elevating the status of the group, for the blades in question are the finest of their kind in Yemen. In the context of this formula's use the poet improvises an end of the line with the imperative "sharpen the fine cutting edge." Then in turn 11 he exhorts his group to unite in the formula "who meet in the bulwarks" (i.e. one is solidary because one fights together with, not against, these men). In short, an image of the tribesman is constructed by the use of formulas expressing piety, courage, prowess, and other qualities of the ideal tribesman. Far more than just the composition of a poem takes place in this performance; a construction of self is achieved in the act of address.

This construction is achieved through what Peirce (1932) would have called an iconic index. According to his theory of signs, a symbol is a general category of sign that has a conventional relationship with the object it stands for, whereas an index is existentially related to its object in space and time. The last element in this tripartite schema is the icon, which stands for its object by virtue of some natural or cultural resemblance to it. In the *bālah* performance a formula like *wolves of the darkest night* is an icon (i.e. a conventional metaphor) and is at the same time an index because the formula is used in addressing the chorus or audience. The usage points to *these* men as the embodiment of the ideal traits of fierceness and valor.

In what sense is a self emerging or being constructed in this indexical act? Isn't the poet merely referring to a self the addressee is supposed to already possess (i.e. have internalized)? In other words, how do we know that the indexical act is creative in the constructivist sense? The first interpretation is more conservative, the second more radical.

George H. Mead, among others, expounded the notion of the self as being reflexive and emergent (Mead 1934, 1964). It is the latter assertion that may be, if at all, controversial; namely, that we are not born with a self but acquire it in a process of socialization. Mead's thinking was original precisely to the extent that he emphasized communication as necessary, indeed crucial, to this emergence of self. A child acquires a sense of who he is as a social being (Mead's *me*) by virtue of the reactions (Mead's *significant gestures*) that his actions provoke (such as in games). From these reactions (mostly verbal) he constructs an image of himself that people hold up to him and he internalizes. As an adult, however, a person faces periodic crises or otherwise highly problematical situations in which conventional role behavior (the *me*) will not carry him over his difficulties. Now the person (Mead's *I*) attempts spontaneously and creatively to overcome dilemmas. To solve them, he has to be able to represent to himself his actions in the problematical situation; in other words, he still relies on a reflexive capacity exercised in a communicative act. If he succeeds, his new *I* will be incorporated as part of his conventional behavior (his *me*). The self emerges, then, in two different time frames, according to Mead: during childhood, when adult roles are being internalized, and during adulthood, when problematical situations require new inventions of the self.

In the wedding *bālah* both the young and the mature participate; but the adolescent or young adult males are in the chorus, and for the most part they are addressed by older poets. In other words, the wedding is one of those public occasions in which the young are made aware of, and reminded of, who they ought to be by the elder males of the community. This reminder is perhaps most urgently necessary for the groom, who is about to assume adult responsibilities in life. A mirror is held up to him of who he must become, whereas the other adult men may recognize in that same mirror the *me* they already are (or should be). But the condition for this internalization of the *me* is a semiotic (Mead's *communicative*) process in which a value-charged icon (such as a formula) is used as an index in conjunction with adolescents. By thus conjoining a Peircean notion of sign use in concrete acts of communication with Mead's arguments concerning the emergence of self, I argue for the more radical or constructivist interpretation of what is happening in the *bālah* performance.

Other tribal values besides warfare and defense of the group's honor are being communicated, however. Take, for instance, the value connected with welcoming the guest. This value of generosity (*karāmah*) is stressed in turn 12 when the poet says, "They press the grain on the grinding stone. || Verily, generosity [is prescribed] to the guest, even in lean years," or in 14, "[I serve] the foreign guest melon and grapes" (nonpareil fruits offered as refreshment). In turn 17 the poet addresses the assembly as "you who butcher sheep," meaning that they serve meat at their meals whenever a guest visits; he adds, "O men of generosity, long has this been our custom." The wedding celebration is one of the focal occasions in which *karāmah* must be practiced by the host village or tribe in exchange for poetry, and again we see how the poetry constructs the assembly's ideal self.

The playful aspect of the *bālah* allows its practitioners gently to poke fun at some of these same values. Note, for example, the last portion of the poem in which the father of the groom by the name of Ṣāliḥ is teased by his poet friends. "Don't flee the assembly," they say because of his consternation at how much this wedding will cost. And the admonition to him, "don't tear your *magṭab*" in rage over the expenses, drew a hearty laugh from the audience. This humor presents us with the more human side of the situation in which the father has done his duty to his son and honored guests, but the duty can also be expensive and discomforting, as every father of a groom there knew. Other, more fascinating dimensions of this routine will be described below.

NONFORMULAIC LINES

It would be a mistake to assume that a poet's skill is judged solely by his handling of stock formulas. Quite the contrary: in addition to these stereotypical expressions a poet is expected to show some spark of originality. Take, for example, the following hemistich, which evoked laughter from the audience:

> massā-k b-il-khēr m-al-jabbān mittammarah [10]
>
> Good evening to you, [as great as] the station wagon bumps
> [on the road]

The formula is the stock greeting *massā-k b-il-khēr.* What follows is a nonformulaic expression intensifying the force of the greeting, an expression introduced by the relative pronoun *mā* (that which), the idea being that the poet wants to wish the person hello as many times as a car traveling over the unpaved, wheel-rutted roads of Yemen bounces and jostles. The poet has combined his competence in skillfully using formulaic expressions with imaginative invention to produce a metrically regular line. He is playing the game to the hilt.

The guest list, which varies from wedding to wedding, is a factor of the context that can inspire originality in the poet's forms of address. In welcoming me to the groom's celebration, one of my friends composed the following turn:

> wa sēf gad jā min amrīkah wa huh miktahal
> yisajjil al-bāl f-id-dīwān yā bāl bāl
>
> And Sēf has come from America, and he's got *kohl* on his eyelids.
> He records the *bālah* poetry in the reception room, O *bāl bāl.*

While I was among the tribes in Yemen, I assumed the name Sēf. Though it is a custom among males, especially on occasions like weddings, to color their eyes with black, blue, and brown antimony—partly for decoration and partly because of its presumed medicinal properties—the poet was, I believe, trying to convey the idea that I was living and acting in their midst like a tribesman. (The rhyme of the second hemistich is faulty, but the audience did not object.)

In a different performance the following turn was composed, again in recognition of my presence at the celebration:

> yā marḥabā sēf dhī jā l-iz-zawāmil yishill
> min kāb dēfid wa wāshinṭon wa lā gad zaʿil
>
> O welcome to Sēf, who has come to collect *zāmil*s,
> from Camp David and Washington, nor has he tired yet.

This is quintessential Yemeni allusion. The turn is certainly humorous, but it could not have been entirely innocent, for at the time of its utterance the Carter administration's attempts to mediate between Israel and Egypt were in full swing; the poet is suggesting the possibility of my being a political agent of the United States. The last part, which I translate as "nor has he tired yet," may have the meaning that I am indefatigable in my efforts to collect poetry or that I am a tireless spy. In a sense it represented a challenge to my honor. Had I been skillful enough to retort, I certainly would have won considerable respect from my audience. Instead, a friend came to my rescue by composing a verse in reply.

The Turn and the Speech Act

When one listens to a turn, one is struck by its internal coherence.[11] Its two (rarely three) parts are interrelated. The first turn in the sample poem illustrates the point:

> Verily, I begin with Him who causes the lightning to flash
> and Him who makes it appear.
> Verily, O he who prays to God, O Generous One, will not be
> disappointed [by Him].

The coherence or unity of the turn has to be understood in relation to a speech act—in this case an invocation and praise of God to which both hemistichs contribute. The first hemistich invokes God as the wielder of awesome powers. The second hemistich continues this description and exhorts the assembly to pray.

What are these speech acts? And once we have delineated them, can we discern a whole into which they are organized? Most important, what social meaning, if any, do these speech acts convey in the context of the wedding *samrah?*

Most performance-composed, formulaic poetries reported in the literature have been of the epic genre—that is, heroic-dramatic narrations of presumed historical or mythological events (cf. Bowra 1966). In the oral literature from the Middle East outstanding research has been done in particular on the Banī Hilāl cycle of Arabian legends by Connelly (1986) and Slyomovics (1988). In the context of these epic poetic traditions the formula has been analyzed as a building block in the rapid construction of a rigidly metrical line that advances the movement of a *story*. The poet uses formulas to describe the hero's mount and its trappings, his ride into battle, and the action sequences of the war. How the poet actually links these formulas in a metrically regular sequence more or less resembles the process for the *bālah.*

There is an important difference in the *content* of the formula for the *bālah* as compared with that of these other genres. It does not function to describe or name characters, advance a plot, or depict a scene, for there is no narrative in the poem. Besides its poetic function of building a regular meter, it performs various *speech acts* (Austin 1962; Searle 1969) whose primary relevance is for the wedding celebration. These are quintessentially *social* speech acts, among them the greeting of members of the audience; thus, social interaction becomes poeticized, a point that I will return to again in the conclusion of this work.

RELIGIOUS SPEECH ACTS AND THE BEGINNING OF THE *BĀLAH* POEM

The first turn usually opens with one of two formulas, either *I begin with You* or *In the beginning.* The former also begins a special religious speech act, the *invocation of God.* In Islam this act is known as *duʿā* (from *daʿā* [to mention, to call]) and is a kind of pious good work. The Qurʾān reminds the devout Muslim that "the most beautiful names belong to Him" and then admonishes the believer to "call on Him by them" (sūrah 7, verse 180). The Qurʾān thus specifies how the speech act is to be performed. One calls on God by using epithets describing His essence or being. In the orthodox "high" tradition of Islam these epithets are handed down as *al-asmā al-ḥusnā* (the beautiful names), but the local religious tradition goes beyond these by supplying its own descriptive phrases. A *bālah* poem could thus open with an orthodox performance of the speech act:

> w-abdaʿ b-ik adʿī-k y-ar-raḥmān y-al-mugtadir
>
> I begin with You, I invoke You, O Merciful One, All-Prevailing One

where *ar-raḥmān* (Merciful One) and *al-mugtadir* (All-Prevailing One) are part of the Qurʾānic tradition. But the following hemistich may just as well open the poem:

> w-abdaʿ bi-dhī lāmiʿ al-bārig wa dhī lāḥ b-ih
>
> I begin with Him who makes the lightning flash

in which God's all-powerful nature is rendered in imagery more tribal in origin.[12] In daily life God's epithets in the *duʿā* are invoked repeatedly; the more times His names are mentioned, the more pious the act appears to be. This *intensity* with which the act is performed finds its correlate in the poetic context of the *bālah* in the *mā* phrase, which metaphorically conveys the number of times the act is performed. For example:

> w-abdaᶜ b-ik adᶜī-k mā yitlō jamīᶜ ad-darūs
>
> I begin with You, I invoke You [as many times as] they recite all the *darūs*.[13]

The image embedded in the phrase signifies a great amount of something (in this case the many times that the Qur'ān is read over the sick) and intensifies a speech act of invocation.

After God has been invoked by the poet, performance turns are devoted to the act of *praising God,* which is sometimes known as *ḥamd aḷḷāh* or *tasbīḥ*. Like the act of invocation, this act too has its roots in Islamic ritual. The string of beads many pious Muslims finger during the day is called *masbaḥah* (that used for praise), which comes from the same root as *tasbīḥ* (glorification of God). Rapidly clicking the beads between thumb and index finger, Muslims mumble under their breath formulaic expressions of praise such as *Aḷḷāh is great, Aḷḷāh is sublime, There is no God but Aḷḷāh, Praise be to Aḷḷāh,* sometimes hundreds of times at a stretch. The intention behind this utterance is by sheer repetition to manifest one's love of God. This intensification of piety is communicated in *bālah* poetry either through enumeration or through the use of the relative *mā* phrase and a metaphor.

> I have praised Him thousands of times, [as many times as] the bird has spread its feathers in flight. || O God, the praise is Yours, [as many as] the raindrops that fall.
>
> We praise God the number of times you, O moon, and the sun [have appeared in the sky]. || He who causes the raindrops to fall and irrigates every desiccated wadi.
>
> O God, the praise is Yours, [as great as the number of times] they read in the *dhāriyāt*.[14] || You have kept us out of Hell, its hot fire.

The speech act following the praise of God is the *mention of the Prophet Muḥammad and ᶜAlī*.[15] The turn devoted to this speech act is also constructed out of formulaic expressions:

– – ∪ – | – ∪ – | – – ∪ – | – ∪ – ||
w-adhkur muḥammad ṣalāt aḷḷāh ʿalā ṭayyibah
w-adhkur muḥammad *ka-mā gad dhikrat-ah wājibah*
w-adhkur muḥammad *shafīʿ an-nās sīd al-bashar*

I mention Muḥammad, prayers of God on his city (Medina)
I mention Muḥammad, *because his mention is a duty*
I mention Muḥammad, *Healer of the People, Lord of Mankind*

∪ – ∪ – | – ∪ – | – – [∪] – | – ∪ –
shafīʿ-anā min jahannam yōm bardan wa ḥarr
shafīʿ-anā min jahannam *y-ibna ʿadnān*
shafīʿ-anā min jahannam *ḥarr-aha l-muḍlimah*
shafīʿ-anā min jahannam *ḥarr-aha l-kalīl*[16]
shafīʿ-anā min jahannam *ḥarr-ahā w-al-lahāb*
shafīʿ-anā min jahannam *ḥarr-ahā dhī yikill*

Be our intercessor [to keep us] from Hell, on the Day of Cold and Heat
Be our intercessor [to keep us] from Hell, *O son of ʿAdnān*
Be our intercessor [to keep us] from Hell, *its shadow-casting heat*
Be our intercessor [to keep us] from Hell, *its exhausting heat*
Be our intercessor [to keep us] from Hell, *its heat and flames*
Be our intercessor [to keep us] from Hell, *its heat that torments*

When ʿAlī is mentioned, a special formula is used, followed by one of that caliph's epithets:

– – ∪ – | – ∪ – | – – [∪] – | – ∪ –
m-ansā ʿalī rāyiḍ al-mēmūn gāṭiʿ rugab
m-ansā ʿalī rāyiḍ al-mēmūn *damm al-kufar*
m-ansā ʿalī rāyiḍ al-mēmūn *dhī lā yigill*

I don't forget ʿAlī, protector of the faithful, cutter of necks [of unbelievers]
I don't forget ʿAlī, protector of the faithful, *blood of the infidels*
I don't forget ʿAlī, protector of the faithful, *who do not lessen [in number]*

These religious speech acts establish, especially by means of the first-person indexical, that the utterer is a pious Muslim, an ideal among tribesmen. In other words, they are performative in two ways: not only do they create a poem in their very utterance but they simultaneously identify the poet as a true believer.

In Islam faith is a matter of deeds. Needless to say, these become hollow if they are not inspired by a devout religious sentiment, but the latter in turn must be expressed in a correct and controlled outward form.[17] Hence faith is above all manifested in speech. For example, I was told that the most important part of prayer is the words, many of them exact recitations of Qurʾānic passages, which of course are believed to be divine revelations. Many kinds of good works in Muslim ritual are performed by *utterance,* several of them already discussed as speech acts in *bālah* poetry.[18]

The question still remains of why it is important for the poet to evince a pietistic attitude in the performance. Here one must recall the groom's *samrah* in which it is situated. I would argue that the poet is doing more than demonstrating his own piety, though undoubtedly that is at stake; he is also being an exemplar, an icon of piety, for the groom to model himself after in his adult life. We have already seen that belief in the Islamic credo and the practice of Islamic ritual constitute one of the core ideals of the tribal concept of self. It is not just in mosque prayer that the celebrant can embody his fervor but also in the act of speaking during the poetic performance, to which the groom is such an attentive witness. In other words, not only does the poet make himself (over and over) into a pious Muslim by his controlled, but passionate, acts of invocation, naming, praising, and prayer, but he also "invites" the groom—who is about to assume the mature responsibilities of a member of the Islamic community—to do the same. Needless to say, the young man has long ago been instructed in the correct performance of religious ritual. What is being impressed on him at the wedding, and at this particular juncture in the poetic performance, is the *ideal* of piety: it is exhortative, not didactic. And the invitation becomes all the more appealing or persuasive by being clothed in beautiful poetic form.

SPEECH ACT OF GREETING

The poets continue the compositional process by acting out greetings to each other and to various important guests or friends in the audience. Anyone addressed in such a turn of greeting has to have the social grace to reciprocate with his own verse. In this manner discourse exchanges are built into social interaction. This greeting routine raises many interesting points of social significance, but let us first determine how the turn is constructed by the poet.

The poet may begin the turn with a formulaic greeting taken from everyday conversation and adapted to fit the metrical pattern --⏑-|-⏑ (with an alternate first foot ⏑-⏑-). Here are some examples of beginnings of the first hemistich:

masā-k b-il-khēr (Good evening to you)
ḥayyā-kum al-kull (May God grant you all long life)
yā marḥab aḍ-ḍēf (O welcome to the guest)
w-abgā-kum aḷḷāh (May God make you live)
min-nā masa l-khēr (From us, good evening)
yā marḥab ahlēn (O welcome, welcome)

Through deft syntactic paraphrase the poet fits the formula into the requisite meter. Take, for example, the ordinary greeting *masa l-khēr* (good evening), a genitive construction that literally translates as "evening of goodness." The problem is that the poet needs a "light" third syllable. One solution is to change the beginning of the formula to *masāk*(*a*) (your evening) and then convey the idea of goodness by a prepositional phrase, *b-il-khēr* (with goodness), which conforms to the meter, yielding the first expression cited above; another is to preserve the greeting formula *masa l-khēr* but shift it in the hemistich so that its initial weak syllable is in the desired third position. The poet then simply fills in the first two heavy syllables with the prepositional phrase *min-nā* (from us), with the result *min-nā masa l-khēr.* Neither strategy violently distorts everyday speech, nor does the more poetic greeting seem stilted in comparison to its ordinary equivalent. On the contrary, to my ear it has a very natural ring, important because social act and poetic performance end up fitting each other perfectly. Indeed, the two have become so tightly synthesized that they are not readily distinguishable.

As in the case of the religious speech acts, the rest of the hemistich is built by means of an intensifier phrase conveying the general force of the utterance. An important and well-known norm of Arab social interaction is to perform a greeting with an effusive show of warmth. In everyday conversation this enthusiasm is conveyed by special linguistic phrases and a complex system of gestures and facial expressions. The norm of conveying intensity is carried over into the corresponding speech act of the *bālah.*

The poet has at least five formulaic ways of expressing the intensity of the illocutionary force of greeting:

1. *mā* phrase with metaphors expressed in formulas
2. Comparison of intensity with a huge expanse conveyed in the expression *min hānā lā* (from here to)
3. The image of a greeting filling (*malā*) an enormous space
4. The active participle *wāzin* (weighing), expressing the idea that the greeting weighs a great quantity
5. Enumeration in high figures

This list is far from complete; it contains only the most frequent formulaic patterns in the corpus. Let us consider the formulaic systems of each of these options in turn.

To create the metaphor of the intensifier *mā* phrase, the poet has available several fairly deep formulaic systems. Here are two:

—| — — ⏑ —| — ⏑ —
mā shaddū ʿalā bū ʿajīl
mā shaddū ʿalā *marjabah*
mā shaddū ʿal *as-sāfirah*
mā shaddū *wa fōg ad-dawāb*

[as heavy as] what they loaded on the car
[as heavy as] what they loaded on *the draft animal*
[as heavy as] what they loaded on *the vehicle*
[as heavy as] what they loaded *and is on the mount*

—| — —[⏑] — |(— ⏑ —) or (— —)
mā yigrōn f-il-ʿādiyāt
mā yigrōn f-idh-dhāriyāt
mā yitlō ʾayāt furgān
mā yitlō jamīʿ ad-darūs
mā yitlō jamīʿ as-suwar

[as many times as] they read the War Steeds [Sūrah 100 of the Qurʾān]
[as many times as] they read the Winds [Sūrah 51]
[as many times as] they read the Criterion [Sūrah 25]
[as many times as] they read all the *darūs* for the sick
[as many times as] they read all the sūrahs

The two verbs used in the second formulaic system, *yitlō* and *yigrōn,* are not identical in meaning; the former refers to spoken recitation (as opposed to chanting or *jawwād*), and the latter to silent reading. It is interesting that *yigrōn* is employed instead of the colloquial *yigrō.* The more classical-sounding equivalent better suits the meter.

> – | – – ∪ – |– ∪ –
> min hānā ʾila l-gāhirah
> min hānā *yishill lā gaṭar*
> min hānā *yishill lā wiṣāb*
>
> from here to Cairo
> from here *let it reach to Qaṭar*
> from here *let it reach to Wiṣāb* [a region in Yemen]

The last three formulaic options display virtually no depth and do not need illustration.

The second hemistich of the turn usually begins with an honorific form of address:

> – – ∪ – |–(∪–|–)
> y-ahl al-jarāmil (O people of the rifle)
> y-ahl an-niṣāl al-ḥiḍārim (O people of the *ḥiḍārim* blade)
> y-ahl an-niṣāl al-gadīmah (O people of the ancient blade)
> yā ghuddat al-khashm (O vanquisher of the nose [of the opponent])

The epithets imply that the addressees are warriors, defenders of their people, conquerors. The poet is honoring them by casting them in the image of the ideal tribesman. Having invoked the military image, the poet then tells us how intensely the addressees fulfill the ideal:

> – – ∪ –| – ∪ –| – – ∪ –| – ∪ –
> yā ghuddat al-khashma w-antū taṭʿanū f-ith-thughar
> yā ghuddat al-khashma *w-antū tantamū f-il-ḥarab*
> yā ghuddat al-khashma *w-antū tidhagū kulla bāb*
> yā ghuddat al-khashma *w-antū muʿlagīn an-nār*
> yā ghuddat al-khashma *yā dhī tinzaʿūn ar-riyāt*
> yā ghuddat al-khashma *yā dhī takwuh al-gargarah*
>
> O vanquisher of the opponent, and you stab in the neck
> O vanquisher of the opponent, *and you unite in war*

O vanquisher of the opponent, *and you force open every door*
O vanquisher of the opponent, *and you light the fires [as a war signal]*
O vanquisher of the opponent, *O you who rip out the enemy's lungs*
O vanquisher of the opponent, *O you who brand the neck*

To summarize, in a performance turn devoted to a greeting, the first hemistich contains the greeting formula and then some metaphorical phrase conveying the intensity of the poet's feeling in the speech act. The second hemistich comprises a laudatory address, usually a martial image, which is then filled out and intensified in a subsequent description.

I have already made the point that the greeting not only fulfills a social norm of speaking at the wedding but also alludes to the important ideal of honor connected with the tribal concept of self. Moreover, by virtue of the fact that this allusion is made in the vocative, the selves of the others are constituted in social interaction. That is, the poet holds up to the addressees an image, albeit an idealized one, of what they are like as tribesmen; the self becomes reflexive through the mediation of a linguistic act (Mead 1934, 1964). In view of the performance's social occasion, on another level the poet is offering this ideal image of the self not only to the addressee as generalized other (Mead 1934, 1964) but particularly to the groom.

The poet's skill entails the ability to situate the performance in its concrete setting by little details of reference and address. The speech act of greeting (though this is no less true of the religious acts previously discussed) anchors the poem in a concrete context, a specific social situation. In the Western tradition the relationship between poetic text and social context has become severed, largely owing to the conditions under which the printed word is produced; the writing of the text is not coterminous with an ongoing social or political event. Hence it is virtually impossible for us to imagine an aesthetic that is sensitive to the specific context of its production, and if we can nonetheless imagine it, we may still have trouble appreciating its value as art. At least three distinct reorientations are required: the poem must be understood as a work wrought in the course of a performance; the performance should be situated in some specific social context which it affects and even perhaps transforms; and insofar as the details of the poem are sensitive to that context, the poem is appreciated by its audience as a valued work of art. Can anyone doubt that a poet needs considerable skill, not to mention a cool head, to fashion lines that meet stringent compositional rules in a rapid public performance, while at the same time adapting the allusions in these lines to the concrete details of the social context? More important, can we appreciate the extent to which this art form is constitutive of social reality in many more immediate ways than Western literature?

CONCLUDING THE *BĀLAH* POEM

There is no way of knowing at what precise point in the performance a poet will decide to close the poem. Poets do not confer with each other, and there is no prescribed sequence of speech acts leading up to a conclusion, although many performances do end right after a poet's intervention in what appears to be an overheated exchange. By contrast, if the inspiration of the poets is flagging, then someone steps forward and utters the closing speech act, a religious one. The frame is thus complete, the performance ending on the religious note with which it began.

The act that closes the performance is a religious exhortation of the assembly to pray for the Prophet Muḥammad. As was the case particularly with the opening speech acts, the close is composed by linking together a number of different formulaic expressions. The first of these in the hemistich is the formula *w-al-khitm* (and in conclusion), which parallels such formulas as *f-il-bidᶜ* (in the beginning), which open the performance. Linked to it is the formula *ṣallū ᶜala l-mukhtār* (pray for the Chosen One [the Prophet Muḥammad]). The two formulas comprise the following portion of the hemistich:

– – ⏑ –| – ⏑ –| – –[⏑]
w-al-khitm(a) ṣallū ᶜala l-mukhtār

The sequence needs to be completed by a phrase scanning as –|–⏑– and containing the final rhyming word. The following are examples taken from my corpus:

bū fāṭimah (the father of Fāṭimah)
dhī hū fahīm (he who is wise)
sīd ar-rusal (lord of prophets)
sīd al-fiyāt (lord of societies)
sīd al-jadūd (lord of our ancestors)

The last three expressions are all alternates of the same formulaic type; only the object of the Prophet Muḥammad's lordship changes to fit the rhyme.

Thus, in the *bālah* poem collective and controlled composition, as represented by metrically regular formulas shared in the oral tradition, reasserts itself over the (potentially disruptive) play of individual pitted against individual in free-wheeling verse, which we shall encounter in the next chapter. In the name of Islam social conflict is brought under control.

In the *bālah* aesthetic form clearly becomes fused with social function, and poetic production creates social acts. To assert this point is not to deny that poetic form has its own immanent and irreducible reality: after all, the structure of the musical melody, the intricate interchange of poet and chorus, the pattern of syllables comprising the meter, the rhyme scheme, the use of formulas in a performance, the unity of performance turns, the speech acts and their precise ordering—all these are the "specific" of aesthetic phenomena in this genre of poetry. Nor does this analysis necessarily lead to the obverse case, where social reality becomes absorbed in aesthetic acts and loses its integrity. Rather, it suggests that the apperception of aesthetic form is never divorced from its social meaning: the different melodies are evocative of different tribal groups, and chanting in general has strong associations with warfare. It suggests that the antiphonal exchange between poet and chorus hints at the complex polyphony of the individual and the collective; that the rules of composing the meter and the rhyme are the rules by which a social game of honor is played; that the formulas are never merely devices that construct the aesthetic artifact in the course of a performance but refer to crucial aspects of sociocultural reality (military prowess, piety); that the speech acts are more than just material for verse because they constitute sociocultural reality (a religious invocation, a greeting, a challenge); that the exchange of poets' turns is not only a drama that heightens aesthetic interest in the performance and captivates the audience, but also is interpretable as a *daʿwā w-ijābah* (challenge and retort) with the attendant meanings of honor; and that the bringing of the *bālah* to an end, in addition to providing poetic closure, checks the potentially invidious consequences of social competition.

5

The Poetic Construction of Self

I will never forget the first time I observed a *bālah* performance. The technical description in the previous chapter reveals that it is a complex and beautiful art form, and it thoroughly enthralled me as it did its Yemeni audience. Yet it thoroughly mystified me too: it was completely different from anything I was accustomed to. I was also charmed by the playfulness of the interaction and the great humor that was displayed, all seemingly for the sake of entertaining the groom; yet at the same time there was something disquieting—or rather, downright chilling—about the aggressiveness of this interaction, which seemed to belie its appearance as a game. It was this tension or contradiction between what was manifest and what was hidden that I had somehow to interpret and explain.

In the previous chapter I outlined the intricate patterns that comprise the game of the *bālah*. Now we must peer behind the game to confront its seemingly more ominous and sinister reality. What I will argue in this chapter is that the game is a deeply serious one of self-confrontation over the problem of violence in an honor-driven society. The solution to this problem, I maintain, is presented in the *bālah* and entails the construction of a certain kind of self. That is, the poet, in the act of constructing the *bālah* poem, constitutes himself as a tribesman capable of containing violence in the symbolic game of honor. To support this argument, I will refer back to ideas of semiosis and the self broached in the previous chapter. But to begin, let us consider the treatment of the problem of the self in cultural studies of the Middle East.

Cultural Notions of Self and Poetics in the Middle East

Unbeknownst to either of us, Lila Abu-Lughod was working on Bedouin poetry in the western desert of Egypt at the same time as I was studying tribal verse in the eastern region of North Yemen. Her principal concern in her sensitive and compelling ethnography *Veiled Sentiments: Honor and Poetry in a Bedouin Society* (1986) (see also Abu-Lughod 1984, 1985) is the way in which poetry relates to concepts of self—particularly, though not exclusively, among women—in Bedouin society. Her work persuaded me that some of the poetry I had collected in male rituals could be reanalyzed with issues of personhood or self in mind. (Extensive and exhilarating discussions with the late Paul Riesman at Carleton College strengthened this conviction.) Let me reconstruct her arguments and then clarify how my views build on and diverge from them.

Ideologies of honor and gender have primacy over sociopolitical organization in explaining passions and poetry in Abu-Lughod's analysis. Bedouin women, like men, are considered honorable as long as they adhere to the code of modesty, which requires, among other things, that they not publicly reveal their love for certain kinds of men or display their sexuality. Being honorable also means that they strongly believe in their own dignity, autonomy, and independence, all prized values of self. If a woman sees these values threatened—for example, if a neighbor encroaches on her property, or if she is forced to leave a situation in which she has had a say over her affairs and enters another, in which she becomes a dependent—then she may feel rage and resist. The dilemma is that public expression of such sentiments would be tantamount to an admission of dependence, loss of emotional self-control, and hence loss of honor.

The question Abu-Lughod then poses is, What communicative strategy or style is adopted by Bedouin women to express rage or love without at the same time admitting to weakness and a loss of honor? Abu-Lughod discovered that poetry became a major vehicle in this society for the expression of such sentiments. She then asks a second question, connected of course to the first: Why should poetry be considered a culturally appropriate and valued vehicle for this purpose? In other words, why should one be able to vent one's passions in verse, not in everyday language, without losing face?

Abu-Lughod provides several answers to these questions. She writes, first of all, that the audiences for the *ghinnāwa* verse are usually intimate friends or close relatives with whom a woman need not be modest and hence with whom an expression of passion is "safe," that is, does not have terrible consequences for the woman's honor. The second answer has to do with the rigid form of the verse, its high degree of conventional structure, which gives "a certain amount of protection for the individual in expressing the 'deviant' sentiments of dishonor and immodesty" (Abu-Lughod 1986, 239). In particular the author argues that "formulaic language, or rather the communication of sentiment in poetry, allows individuals to frame their experiences as similar to those of others and perhaps to assert the universality of their experiences" (Abu-Lughod 1986, 239). In other words, the individual is speaking not just for herself but for the entire community, so that the expression of sentiment is made less risky by being depersonalized (or at least deflected from her own person). But in another passage Abu-Lughod gives a different explanation for the link between honor and poetic composition, an explanation I find more interesting: "By channeling such powerful sentiments into a rigid and conventional medium and delimited social contexts, individuals demonstrate a measure of self-mastery and control that contributes to honor" (Abu-Lughod 1986, 245). To put the same point differently, the discipline of poetic composition, because it involves control over self, is also an act of creating honor, which entails mastery over one's emotions. The third explanation has to do with the cultural conception of poetry as persuasive, presumably more persuasive than other kinds of discourse, a finding consonant with those of other researchers in the field (Meeker 1979; Caton 1984); from this fact Abu-Lughod concludes that poetry is uttered in an attempt to persuade the hearer (ultimately the beloved) to do as the lover beseeches. If the persuasion works (I presume some mechanism of reported speech to account for the transmission of the poem from its originator to the beloved, with nonthreatening intimates as intermediaries), then the poet, who appears weak in her admission of vulnerability, will actually be strong, for she will have gained honor through the other's capitulation to her demands. Poetry becomes a weapon in the war of love rather than in the love of war.

Stimulated by Abu-Lughod's analysis, I have worked out the relationship of poetry to self or personhood in the Yemeni tribal male world in a somewhat different way. For one thing, I have started out with the question, What is a *gabīlī* (tribesman)? which I have tried to answer in chapter 2, rather than with a dominant ideological system such as the honor code. Discovering a cluster of ideas and values for the tribe's own concept of the tribesman (which include, but do not necessarily privilege, the honor code), I then proceeded to explore what relationship, if any, exists between poetry and personhood. The major difference in our approaches, however, has to do with our aims. I intend to show how the act of composing a poem in the *bālah* is also an act of *constructing* the self, an aim consonant with a larger purpose: to demonstrate that in the form and content of artistic—specifically poetic—acts, the structures and meanings of a society are created.

The cultural system of honor places great stress on the glorious deed, and I contend that the spontaneous composition of verse is one such deed. The agon of this deed manifests itself, first of all, in the formal intricacies of the verse composition but also, more significantly, during the middle portion of the poem's construction, when the poets enter into an exciting routine of challenge and retort. Here the poets issue derogatory or otherwise politically provocative remarks, often in a jocular tone of voice, addressed to another poet or a member of the audience, who is required by the honor code to reply in kind. This routine not only heightens the excitement of the game; it also creates an important dramatic conflict, which adds to the aesthetic appeal of the poem, and represents to the groom—who is about to begin adult life, in which such things count—what the ideal of honor is all about.

This agonistic construction of self has an interesting correlate in the verse. As we have seen, the first portion of the *bālah* is highly formulaic. Many poets take part in constructing this half of the poem. Then, quite suddenly, one poet will challenge another poet, the two of them dueling in verse to demonstrate to themselves and the assembly that they are men of honor. The content of the challenge is entirely unpredictable—a slur on the other's talent, a mischievous allusion to some political trouble, or anything else that might spring to mind—but the onus is on the challenged to respond quickly with an original retort. The verse in this segment tends not to be formulaic because the challenges and comebacks are truly spontaneous, unlike the first half of the performance. This free-wheeling routine requires the utmost quick-wittedness, imagination, talent, and sheer poetic dexterity to create verse *de novo* that still obeys the rules of meter and rhyme—the rules of the game—and evinces the self-possession or control, the *marūwah,* of the ideal *gabīlī.* One does not enter into such a routine lightly, for if one is beaten at one's own challenge, the outcome is a disastrous loss of face. Ultimately, then, the best poet is the one who can construct the most honorable self.

The game of honor is not all there is to the *bālah* performance, however. In the first part of the poem various obligatory speech acts are performed, such as invoking the names of Aḷḷāh, praying on behalf of the Prophet, and greeting various fellow poets and guests in the assembly. I have shown elsewhere (Caton 1986) how a concept of person as an honorable and pious Muslim is constructed in speech acts of greeting. This piety is intensified by other religious speech acts incorporated into the poetic performance. Along with the routine of *daʿwā w-ijābah,* which is constructive specifically of honor, this segment helps to create a full, rich, and complex self of the *gabīlī.*

In explaining how the self of the *gabīlī* is constructed, I will refer to the rules of verse composition outlined in the previous chapter: the movements and music of the performance, the verse meter, the rhyme, and the various speech acts performed by means of a fairly elaborate system of formulas—all of which help to constitute the game. But this chapter concerns mainly the middle portion of the *bālah,* in which the self is constructed and revealed to the groom. I summarize at the end of the chapter the arguments concerning the construction of the self in the light of this verse analysis.

The Speech Act of *daʿwā w-ijābah* in the Development of the *Bālah*

I have been arguing that in the course of composition an icon of the ideal Yemeni tribal male self is being created. Through verbal ritual acts in the beginning of the performance the poet creates himself as a pious Muslim. In the section devoted to the routine of greeting he depicts the addressee as an honorable man and himself as a pious Muslim, a symbolic act reciprocated by the addressee in what Mead (1934) would have called a conversation of significant gestures. Piety is a state of grace that cannot be maintained once and for all without further effort. It must be constantly regained. Similarly, honor has to be achieved over and over in glorious deeds. Hence the significance of the *bālah* as a public, symbolic act in which these aspects of the tribal self are constructed. Note, however, that the groom does not participate in this act. He is an anxious, though passive, onlooker who is about to become an adult and will have to act as these men are now acting before him, these paragons of tribal virtue (as revealed in the poetic performance). It is for him, ultimately, that they are constructing this ideal self, so that as a man he will know how to strive to become pious and honorable too.

The performance has been relatively tame thus far, its fun consisting mainly in seeing whether the poet has the wherewithal to create metrically regular lines that accomplish various speech acts simultaneously. The players have done little more than establish themselves as competent poets. Now the question is whether they have the mettle to withstand the challenge and retort.

Several routines are possible. The first one I will consider involves the host and guest at the *samrah*. The poets participating in the performance are expected to compliment the host for his generous hospitality, an important and highly valued norm of social etiquette.[1] After complimenting the host, the guests can begin the extended routine of sparring with him, each razzing the other in the hope of getting a laugh out of the audience. Here is the text of one such routine (see Appendix D for the Arabic transcription):

1. *Host:* Welcome to whatever you demand, even if you say, "Irrigate the fields [*nisānī*]!"[2] || It [the food] will come in the dish or it will come in a gunny sack [i.e. as grain].

2. *Host:* It's the game of the *bālah*, all of it, see, it has pleased me [*ʿajā-nī*][3] || Whatever you have demanded [in the way of hospitality] you have received: why this mischief?

3. *Guest:* O Saʿd, I know the generosity of the Yemeni[4] || The Arabs are hungry, they no longer want the *samrah*.

4. *Guest:* O Ḥājj, welcome, as many as there are minutes and seconds || And if your father were still alive, O Nāṣir, he would give all his property [to feed his guests].

5. *Guest:* Muḥammad has committed a disgrace; he has given four cups of tea || Black minted tea from the Emirates.

6. *Guest:* Go away! Count the *zāmils*! May you have a pain in

the pupil of the eye! || I want food, even if he entertains me with a cigarette.

7. *Host:* You want us to give you what has been prepared [for the meal] and what is in our garments || And if you want a little army bread, [go and get it] in the Naḍārah market.

8. *Guest:* I ask you for the dough that [sticks] to the fingers || And you, if you are not content [with the request], there will be fighting with stones.

9. *Host:* We have ground the grain [in the mill] and the camel is in the irrigation ditch || There is no guest among us, and you get yourself off to Sharārah [a quarter in Ṣanʿā].

10. *Guest:* Is there any love for this home? If there isn't, then I am alone [in my love for it] || How come the groom is your kinsman and we forget his happiness?[5]

There are obviously two sides in this little altercation—the guests' and the host's—each of which has its spokesmen poets. At the very beginning of the performance guests had complained that the host had been remiss in his hospitality (a more or less ritual joke that starts the teasing routine), so one of the host poets composed turn 1 to reassure the guests of the host's generosity. They may have anything they want, he says, even if they demand that the host irrigate their (the guests') fields—a generous offer since water is a scarce commodity in this arid land.

The poet of turn 2 "keys" (Goffman 1974) the guests' complaining as being in the spirit of the poetic game. Such a metapragmatic comment is not at all unusual in the course of the *bālah*. In the opening verses poets sometimes refer to the joy they experience in playing the game with such "heroes" and "friends" in the chorus and audience, a remark intended to exalt or glorify the very act in which all are presently engaged. In the development section of the performance, however, such commentary by the poets on their own and each other's performances becomes far more frequent and significant. For example, the comment in turn 2 allows for interpreting the rather outrageous insinuations of host and guests as a *game* of challenge and retort, not the real thing, which would surely lead to fighting. The function, then, of metapragmatic reference in this context is important and self-evident (it will come up again in turn 10). But metapragmatic reference is significant in another sense: it can become the basis of the game of honor itself. That is, poets tease each other by criticizing the way they perform the game in which they are currently engaged. Thus, the ability to reflect and comment on the verbal acts one is performing is a key feature of this game (as it is of most games).

Having commented on the performance in terms which allow it to be interpreted as a friendly game, the poet of turn 2 jokingly challenges the guest poets to explain their "mischief" when they have received everything that tribalism requires in the way of hospitality. In other words, this poet presupposes that he and his group have been honorable men.

This challenge is taken up by a guest poet in turn 3. His strategy of attack is to declare that he, the guest, knows the norms of Yemeni hospitality and that the host (Saᶜd) cannot pull the wool over his eyes by insisting that he has acquitted himself in his hostly duties. He implies that the host is miserly, an extreme fault in a tribesman's character. In other words, the host has fallen far short of the ideal of the Yemeni self. The poet drives home this attack in the next hemistich. He asserts that the guests have not been given enough food and are still hungry and that hence the evening's *samrah* has been spoiled; by rights they should quit the game, for as a poet said in another performance, *mā yitlaᶜ al-hājis illā saᶜīdah malān* (the *hājis* [poetic genius] is only inspired when its happiness is full [in other words, on a full stomach]). The same sentiment is expressed by the poet of turn 6. He curses the host for his miserliness, wishing him a pain in the eye; after so many *zāmil*s have been composed that afternoon in the *zaffah* and that evening on the way to the *samrah,* the poets deserve to be fed for their efforts. This poet demands his due even if all he gets to eat is one cigarette (that is, the host is so cheap he will substitute smoke for food).

The poet of turn 4 adopts another tactic by which to shame the host. He calls on the honor of the host's father to bear witness to the disgrace suffered by the guests. He contends that the father would have spent all his wealth, if necessary, to satisfy his guests. According to the logic of honor, this attack implies that the host's present ignominious deed reflects not only on him but also on his ancestors.

Turn 5 is humorous but requires a lengthy explanation. The joke pivots on the word *ṣiyānī* (sg. *ṣīnī*), a small porcelain teacup made in China, found in virtually every Yemeni household. The guest asserts that his host is trying to serve upward of one hundred people at the gathering with only four *ṣiyānī*, a broadly farcical image. Then he further piques his opponent's ire by suggesting that he is serving black minted tea from the Emirates, a cheap and much inferior blend. The term *miniᶜniᶜ* is an invented passive of *naᶜnaᶜ* (mint), its guttural consonants adding to the tea's distasteful image. This hemistich garnered kudos from the audience.

This bellyaching is too much for the host poet, who launches his counterattack in turn 7. Again, the humor depends on the use of terms with highly specific referents. Tribesmen sometimes secrete pieces of bread or other food in the folds of their garments as an emergency provision for times when they get hungry on the road and there is nothing else to eat. The poet charges that because the sumptuous wedding feast was not enough to satisfy the rapacious appetite of the guests, they are now clamoring for even the miserable scraps hidden in the host's garments. The next salvo is just as adroitly delivered. *Siḥtēn*, more commonly known as *kidm*, is the army bread served to soldiers. Made from a mixture of various coarse grains and presumed to be nutritious (and I know it to be delicious), it is readily available at a low price in one of the capital's markets, but it is generally disdained by all locals except the poor. Most households bake their own bread, which is softer, more delicate in texture, and more subtly flavored. By referring to it in his verse, the poet means to imply that the guests could only be of low status if they stoop to eat *kidm*.

Turn 8 continues the joke on the host. "The dough that [sticks] to the fingers" is a reference to a food called *ᶜaṣīd*, which is like a huge dumpling set in a heavy chicken broth and eaten by scooping up a bit with the fingers, then dunking it in the boiling soup before bringing it to the mouth. The poet warns that if the host does not provide the assembly with this delicacy, he will hurl stones in retaliation for this slight to their honor.

The host has been falsely accused, cries the poet in turn 9, for nothing has been spared to ensure the guests' complete comfort and satisfaction. Then he seems to insinuate that the riffraff attending the wedding celebration does not deserve the effort wasted on it. Also siding with the host is the poet of turn 10. He expresses his love for the host and calls attention to the groom, whom the guests have neglected to mention in their verses. He admonishes them for this oversight as well as for their waging of this "dispute," which threatens to spoil the joyousness of the occasion.

A heavy element of self-mockery is at work here, but at times the act of challenge and retort can become rather prickly and provoke some heated exchanges, as we shall see in the next example. When players of the game go too far in berating their opponents, usually someone, like the poet in turn 10, intercedes to calm them down and nudge the performance into alignment with its original purpose, which is to flatter the groom and his family.

An important aesthetic lapse in this segment of the *bālah* has implications for our understanding of the relationship of poetry to social action. The meter is rather irregular in some turns. (No one shouted "a broken hemistich," though whether the audience failed to catch the mistake or was enjoying the interchange too much to interrupt it, I cannot say for certain.) The fact that the meter becomes irregular is not surprising when we realize a second important fact about the aesthetic structure of the development section: namely, the incidence of formulaic usage has significantly declined. In fact, none of the formulas I have traced in the beginning of the performance occurs in the above-cited text. Obviously, a shift in aesthetic focus has occurred from the "correct" composition of metrically regular lines of verse that also perform various speech acts to an *improvisational* skill in devising witty, imaginative, and original verses in a dramatic exchange.

In essence, this part of the performance is greeted the most enthusiastically by the audience because it is now witnessing the true glory of the poetic deed. The greatest test of the poet's art is to keep the verses coming in a fairly standard form while replying to the specific accusations of the opponent, accusations that might come from any quarter of daily life. In turn, he must keep the opponent off guard by challenging him in a novel way; the more original the verse, the harder it is to top.

There are other ways of enjoying the game of the *bālah* than teasing the host or the guests. As we have already seen, a poet can also refer to the performance itself, heckling the other poets participating in it, defending friends who have been criticized, expressing his delight or chagrin at the poetry, exhorting the audience on the sidelines to join the performers, and so forth. Here is an example of such a routine in ten lines out of a twenty-nine-line poem (see Appendix D for Arabic):

10. The *bāl* and the company of men fill me with delight, but I am not lazy || For indeed the *bālah* is of no use to someone who is dull [i.e. not quick in fashioning responses].
11. O time of the *bāl* in the *dīwān,* whoever comes [to the *samrah*] will carry [the lines of verse] || I love the *bālah* with such heroes for men.
16. *Poet A:* O time of the *bāl,* and how many ignorant poets there are || He who does not correct his lines has no place among us.
17. *Poet B* [taking up A's challenge]: May God grant you long life, O poet; as for me, I am not lazy || If you have a hemistich, produce it and the boys will carry it.
20. *Poet C* [defending A, attacking B]: Don't criticize my namesake's poetry if it's short or long || The rest of his [B's] poetry is the worst it can be.
21. *Poet C* [attacking B]: May God preserve you, O poet, I see that you are hoarse || I am one of the men who produces and carries [the verse].
23. *Poet A* [responding to B]: You [who call yourself] a horned ram, you are our lamb || We will not play the *bāl* all night long; see, don't shudder with fright [i.e. shudder at the butcher's knife that cuts the lamb's throat].
26. *Poet B:* From the abundance of poetry that is on you, you might stumble || O His pity, O my namesake, see that you don't give up [the performance].
27. *Poet A:* And to you greetings, as many as fit in our [tribe's] borders and the village || O Fakhri [ʿAbdullah], long life to you—you're a horse's ass.
28. *Poet C:* O *bāl,* don't wear out my people [i.e. the assembly] with a bombardment of sayings || Each person is fashioning a rebuke and is cutting an unreasonable cut.

Turns 10 and 11 contain within them various assumptions about the ideal nature of a *bālah* performance. The poets cannot be lazy, for otherwise no poetry will be produced; nor can they be dull-witted to come up with well-formed verse. Furthermore, they suggest that anyone who comes to the *samrah* is expected to join in the performance. For all these reasons—that poets are bright and assiduous, that the men in attendance form an illustrious company—participating in the *bālah* is a pleasure.

The first challenge is hurled by Poet A to the assembly at large, as if to say, All right, who's brave enough to take me on? Poet B takes up his challenge in the next turn (17); he says that he is not lazy because he has already contributed a number of turns to the performance, implying that Poet A has yet to prove his skill by composing more than one turn. Hence, he returns the challenge with the taunt, "If you have a hemistich, produce it and the boys will carry it." Poet C comes to the defense of the initial challenger, Poet A, with the admonition, "Don't criticize my namesake's poetry if it's short or long," and then attacks B's poetry as the least skillful of all. He follows up this attack with the rebuke, "I see that you are hoarse"; in other words, although B may have boasted that he is prolific, C reminds him that his strength is failing and he might not be able to continue much longer. Poet C boasts, by contrast, that he does possess the stamina to produce and carry the verse in the chant. This poet, then, has not only defended a friend, and thus shown himself to be honorable in one sense, but he has also demonstrated spirit in defying his opponent, thus enhancing his reputation for honor.

Now Poet A rejoins the fray. Having previously been challenged to compose more verse, he does so in turn 23: "You [who call yourself] a horned ram, you are our lamb || We will not play the *bāl* all night long; see, don't shudder with fright." This is indeed a witty line. The epithet *horned ram* is an honorific, referring to brave fighting men. Poet A is debunking his opponent for applying such a vainglorious attribute to himself, substituting in its stead the image of the meek lamb. It is a clever remetaphorizing of the opponent; it lowers him several notches on the scale of heroism, since lambs are both stupid creatures and ready victims of the sacrificial knife. In the next hemistich the poet extends the metaphor by implying that it is the *poetic* blade that will victimize the opponent, but given that the performance will not last all night, the opponent need not shudder with fright. This turn is superior for two reasons: first, because of the ludicrous image of the tribesman turned lamb, which amused the audience; second, because of its skillful ironic use of metaphor, which, moreover, is extended over the entire turn. The poet has more than vindicated himself in this performance; he has indeed topped his opponent.

Poet B now has his back to the wall. He has been attacked by two men in the performance, one of whom has delivered him a stunning retort. He must come up with a rejoinder of equal or greater wit and poetic imagination to save face and maintain his reputation for honor. His turn (26) is addressed to Poet A: "From the abundance of poetry that is on you, you might stumble || O His pity, O my namesake, see that you don't give up [the performance]." He portrays the task of composing verse as a great burden and warns the challenger not to take up more weight than he can carry. But in the next hemistich he goads him on, telling him not to be daunted and "give up." Though his rejoinder does have some force, it is not as strong as A's challenge, nor did the audience seem as moved to laughter by it.

Poet A answers back in abusive terms, calling him in the next turn a "horse's ass." This retort goes too far, and Poet C, who had been defending A in this performance, now reprimands him: "O *bāl,* don't wear out my people with a bombardment of sayings." He suggests that the game of challenge and retort has perhaps become too heated and threatens to boil over into a physical altercation, which would spoil the mood of the celebration. Therefore, he warns, the poets should temper their aggressive verses. There is nothing persnickety in this suggestion. As we know, it is the duty of a tribesman to intervene in disputes before they erupt into real violence. A mediator is considered to be honorable precisely for this reason. Hence, Poet C has constructed himself as an honorable person at this juncture of the performance.

The *Bālah* as Symbolic Violence

The metapragmatic frame of the poem reveals that the performance is a game; but like all games, it is deadly serious. Its performance at the height of the wedding ceremony in what is probably the most important moment in the groom's life helps both to allay his anxiety *and* to create it—allay it because the fun temporarily takes his mind off the impending consummation of the marriage; create it because the message at the heart of the performance is frightening enough to make any man pause at the threshold of adult life.

In the poem life is represented as an unremitting contest of wills. The contest, fortunately, is portrayed largely in the form of *symbolic* violence; that is, the search for honor should be understood essentially as a game, and the *bālah* goes a long way to bring home this comforting message. When the players lose sight of this all-important *gaṣd* (intention), a wise old man steps into the fray to remind them of it, thereby retrieving the altercation from the brink of disaster. The performers hold up a mirror to everyday life, for the contest of honor, as Burckhardt understood when he described the stylized or ritualized manner of Bedouin raiding, should similarly proceed like a game. When real violence erupts, a wise old man, a sheikhly mediator, must try to prevent bloodshed between the two contending parties by persuading them to resolve their differences peacefully. Violence must be contained in the metaphor of the game.

But what is frightening is that the metaphor, like any true dialectic, contains the seeds of its own contradiction, for if one plays the game according to its ultimate logic, passions build; the frail vessels that are the human selves may not be able to contain them, and they may overflow into homicidal acts. There is always the potential for the laughing, boisterous mask to be torn away to reveal a hideous face of murder. The tribesman is supposed to know how to channel passion into controlled or stylized violence and thereby diffuse its explosiveness, but the *bālah* warns that such *marūwah* cannot be taken for granted. One must train oneself to achieve it, just as one must steel oneself to face it, as for example in performing the *bālah*. Becoming and being a tribesman is a matter of self-discipline.

I will return to the lesson of the *bālah,* that the pursuit of honor is symbolic violence, when considering a dispute mediation in Chapter 7. Indeed, one suspects that the actors involved in the dispute are expected to recall that lesson as well in order to avoid the more drastic consequences of the feud. But for us, the outsiders, it helps to recall the *bālah* in order to put violence in tribal society into a proper cultural perspective. Mediation is condoned, not brute physical force. As soon as the contest does turn to physical force and hence can no longer be interpreted as a game of honor, every effort must be expended to stop it, or else all is lost. When the peacemaker in the *bālah* yells to the contestants, "Don't frighten the groom!" he is in fact saying, Don't scare us out of our wits by the evil that your heedlessness portends. In short, the creators of the *bālah* recognize the precariousness of the game of honor in everyday life.

The Emergence of Self in Play

Mead (1934) speaks of the self emerging or being constituted in concrete social interaction, and his master metaphor for this social interaction is the game. It is worthwhile to explore the nature of the game as it relates to the problem of self-consciousness, and for this purpose Gadamer's discussion in *Truth and Method* ([1960] 1986) will prove helpful.

The key insight has to do with Gadamer's realization that play's "mode of being is self-representation" ([1960] 1986, 97). To some extent performing any structured activity entails representing that activity to oneself, but Gadamer asserts that "one can say this all the more when it is a question of a game" ([1960] 1986, 97). The reason is that the primary goal of the game is to be found in the game itself, a partially self-enclosed activity played out according to its own rules. Of course, the game may also serve important psychological functions for the actors (e.g. an outlet for their aggressions) or have cultural symbolic significance (e.g. representing masculinity), but it is not the only activity that can fulfill these purposes. To explain why a player does what he does according to certain strict rules is to appeal to a logic inherent in the game itself. To be engaged in a game, then, is to represent to oneself what one is supposed to be doing in the very act of doing it. A player dribbles a basketball down the court because he is supposed to move the ball from one spot to another in precisely this fashion, and as he is engaged in this activity, he is representing himself to himself as a proper player, or even a skilled player, of the game. Once we shift to the consciousness of the players in the game, we are really talking about their *self-consciousness.* Gadamer maintains that "the self-representation of the game involves the player's achieving, as it were, his own self-representation by playing" ([1960] 1986, 97).

Gadamer is quick to add, however, "All representation is potentially representative for someone" ([1960] 1986, 97), and this statement is no less true of play. The player in the game always has to have some other player to compete against, though that other player might be himself or a machine. Hence, in play one is representing one's playful role not simply to oneself but also at least to one's opponent and perhaps even to an audience. I might take this point further than

Gadamer by adding that the player also represents his opponent *to* that opponent (and perhaps to the audience) in the course of play. In other words, one tries to show one's opponent to be a "bad" player of the game (or in some cases to be a "good" player of the game). Thus, playing is an act of reflexivity, primarily of representing one's own act to oneself and to the other while performing one's role as a player.

It is no wonder, then, that Mead seized on the game, with its phenomenological essence of self-representation, as the prototype for understanding the emergence of self in a social interaction. When I speak of the poetic construction of self, I have in mind this emergent process in the *bālah* performance. What is the problematic situation that the actors are representing to themselves and to others? As we now know, it is the profound problem of violence, which emerges in the middle section of the poem, the challenge-and-retort routine. An actor represents himself to himself, his opponent, and the audience as an honorable man by issuing a challenge to a status equal. He *must* issue a challenge, for honor is primarily achieved in glorious deeds. He also represents his opponent as an honorable man, though simultaneously and implicitly posing the question, Who is the *more* honorable? It is precisely the answer to this question that they try to negotiate.

But a more profound question also is being asked and answered: how can we keep this game of honor going without risking real violence? The solution is prefigured in the enactment of the game, the representation *of* the self *to* the self as controlled passion. One actor responds to another's challenge with a retort that is electrified by his provoked passion *because* it is transformed into artistic beauty. Herein lies the relevance of poetry for the construction of the self in this culture and, one might add, of art in Aristotle's cathartic theory of the emotions. The various ways in which an actor may respond to a challenge are represented and self-consciously evaluated. The audience applauds controlled passion with "God is great!" By contrast, calling someone a horse's ass—an attempt at verbal coercion—contravenes so many rules of social interaction that it is roundly censured, mainly by laughing the person out of the poetic arena. Should real violence erupt, the actions of both challenger and respondent are represented as heinous by the mediator. In brief, the poet in the *bālah* acquires self-consciousness by acting out *marūwah* and then reflecting on it. One reason all celebrants at the wedding are encouraged to participate in the performance might be that they may thereby heighten their own self-awareness in regard to the problem of controlled passion. And because self-awareness comes in an act of poetry, so highly valued an experience of reality in this society, it fills the actor with awe and wonder.

There is another reason, however, that the construction of self is poetic, a reason that transcends this particular event and culture. For someone to represent himself to himself, his ego must temporarily step back from the stream of events and bracket them in experience. He must, in other words, achieve aesthetic distance from life. Then, literally playing with the possible representations of this life, he must fashion them into some larger whole, a construction, which he presents to himself and then attempts to embody in life. Achieving a sense of self is as great an undertaking as creating a work of art.

Conclusion

The *bālah* performance embodies the totality of the ideal tribal, male self. What is at stake here is not simply a "reflection" of certain ideals but the construction of such a person in a poetic performance.

The chant is culturally interpreted as a battle cry, and the men in the chorus are described in the performance as heroes. The act of composition is referred to as a game and is meant to be a form of generous gift-giving to the groom in exchange for his bounteous hospitality in the wedding feast. Through such metaphors the *bālah* is construed by the tribe as a glorious deed.

The deed begins with the religious acts of invoking God's names, praying for the Prophet, and mentioning ʿAlī, acts that make of their speaker a pious Muslim. First-person speech indexicals, among other linguistic cues, critically link the pious act to the speaker and hence help to construct the person. Poetic form (meter, rhyme, and formula) and musical chanting are tightly organized. This artistic poise, maintained in the outpouring of religious zeal and, later, of agonistic passion, is a mark of *marūwah,* one of the central values of the *gabīlī.*

In the subsequent greeting routine the utterer recognizes the honor of the other while demanding from him recognition of his own. Though expectations of regular poetic form continue into the development section, what is now foregrounded is the relationship of verse to the specific context of the performance, which intensifies the experience of the poem's occasionality. For example, the poet must select certain persons who are present, mentioning them in such a way that they stand out as individuals (e.g. the verses dedicated to me, pp. 97–98). Moreover, the verse ought to show some original spark, usually in the metaphor conveying the intensity of feeling with which the other is greeted.

In a sense, the poets are warming up to the exchange of challenge and retort, when the poetic deed becomes truly glorious. Here the need of poetic form to meet the contingencies of context—in this case the specific allusions made in the other's attack on the self—becomes even more urgent. Individuals attempt to score points off each other, thereby enhancing their own reputations, by the imagination and wit of their verbal maneuverings. The collectively shared system of formulas by which the opening of the *bālah* is created seems conspicuously absent in the development section because novelty of composition is being foregrounded. The poet has to rely on his own spontaneous resources; he is alone facing the rest of the world. The poets who triumph in this strenuous test become the embodiment of the heroic self.

But as in real-life encounters of challenge and retort, things may go awry. One poet cannot go too far in provoking the other, for then a controlled game of honor may erupt into the chaos of brute force, which, as the mediating poets remind the contestants, will scare the groom and destroy the harmony of social relations. In a profound moral lesson the *bālah* prefigures to its audience what can happen to social order when individual striving continues unchecked. The beautiful poise of the adult male comes undone, exemplified in a meter that crookedly limps along and a wit that has descended to name-calling in a language no better than the *dōshān*'s. For this reason the mediating poets must intervene between the contestants to reassert collective control over the performance as embodied in the formulaic close, with its regular meter.

But it is for the groom, above all, that this performance is held. He who is about to enter into adult life must internalize the ideal self exemplified in the game of the *bālah*. He must make himself over into the tribesman the images of the *bālah* create. And this transformation is all for a good purpose, for we shall see in examining the next genre, the *zāmil,* that violence is at the heart of the problem of the political order in tribal society.

Plate 1. Muḥammad, my friend and consultant, with his nephew (*left*) and son (*right*).

Plate 2. A photograph reputed to be of the great sheikh and poet al-Gardaʿī, taken more than fifty years ago. Myth has it that he lost his nose in an attack by a mountain lion.

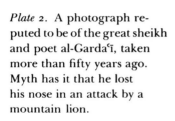

Plate 3. A wedding procession. Grooms' wedding bouquets are in the background. Servant drummers are in the foreground.

Plate 4. Three grooms (wearing sprigs of sweet basil) at their wedding.

Plate 5. A *bara*ᶜ dancer.

Plate 6. A *zāmil* chorister.

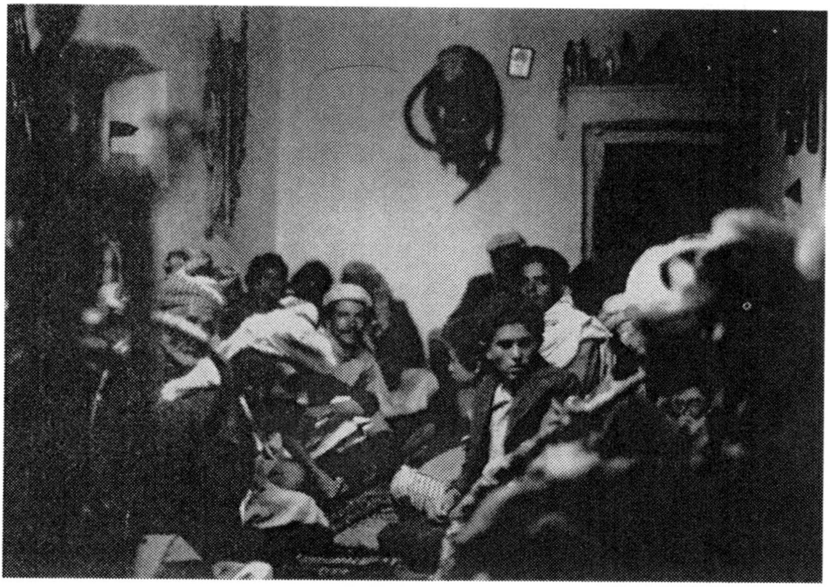

Plate 7. A typical wedding *samrah.* Water pipes in the foreground and hanging on the wall.

Plate 8. A *bālah* poet chanting his verse and surrounded by the chorus.

6

The *Zāmil*: Between Performance and Text-Utterance

In this chapter I analyze the *zāmil*, a genre that resembles the *bālah* in that it is composed in the course of a performance. But it is also close to the *qaṣīdah* in that the emphasis shifts from the act of composition to its final product or text-utterance. The rich, complex, and dramatic art of the *bālah* performance is present here only in an attenuated form. In the *zāmil* the chanting is still important, but its structure is simple. Only one poet composes the verse lines, not a group of poets in competition with each other. In addition, the roles of the chorus and the audience are greatly diminished. Since the utterance is brief—a complete *zāmil* poem comprises only two lines—there is no time pressure on the poets. The constraint rather becomes one of compression and terseness.

All Khawlānīs acknowledge the *zāmil* to be a great art form, so in what quality of aesthetic experience does its greatness inhere? Once aesthetic attention is deflected from the act of composition in a performance, it turns to its end product, the text-utterance. Greatness in the *zāmil* genre is determined by the intricacy of the message form, how effectively it conveys a meaning or feeling, and how well this meaning or feeling achieves a goal related to the social context. In detailing the conventions of this genre, I will expand the discussion of meter, rhyme, alliteration, and formula broached in the last two chapters and deal also with onomatopoeia, allusion, poetic dialogue, audience interpretation of utterances, and other topics. In the next chapter I will situate the aesthetics within their cultural context to show how closely art is related to political concerns.

Performance

One of the main characteristics distinguishing the composition of the *zāmil* poem from that of the *bālah* poem is the fact that only one poet is responsible for creating the text (a tendency observable also in the *qaṣīdah*). Recall that in the *bālah* more than one poet participates in the act of composition, since competition and conflict among these poets constitute an important aspect of the performance. In the case of the *zāmil,* however, there is no collective responsibility for the composition of the poem (whether in a spirit of competition or one of cooperation), and actors cannot switch roles during the performance. In other words, a member of the chorus cannot become a poet, or vice versa. A poet, though, may join with the chorus in chanting the utterance he has composed.

Besides the poet, the *zāmil* involves a chorus of men, as does the *bālah,* but its functions are far more limited. Whereas in the *bālah* the chorus alternates chanting a refrain line and the second or last hemistich of the turn, in the *zāmil* performance there is no refrain. Instead, one group of the chorus is given the first line of the *zāmil* poem and the second group the final line, and they take turns chanting. Furthermore, the metapragmatic function that the chorus and audience perform in evaluating a turn of poetry is eliminated, so that the other game-like element of the *bālah* disappears.

The audience of the *zāmil* too is passive. It does not openly judge the verse as in the performance of the *bālah* but silently takes in the spectacle. What it sees is ranks of men marching toward it like an army unit on parade in a dusty river bed (*sēlah*). What it hears is their high-pitched chanting of the poem. These men are decked out in full tribal regalia, rifles slung over the shoulder; they walk in a brisk step, sometimes hand in hand. At wedding ceremonies and the religious festivals the marchers might be preceded by a couple of servant drummers, in which case the poetic performance might be accompanied by a *baraᶜ* dance (see Plate 5) because the musical drumming is the same for the performance and the dance, each involving rows of men moving in coordinated steps (though the steps and body movements become more complicated in the dance). Consequently, a *zāmil* performance may include poetry and instrumental music as well as song and dance unified in a whole; the dance, however, is not an obligatory element of the performance, and I in fact rarely observed it.

After it has been given the words to chant, the chorus delivers them in a march. The specific starting point is less important than the destination, where the audience receives and greets the performers. For example, in the religious festivals the villages in a tribal region dispatch performers (poet and chorus) to march to a meeting place, where they celebrate the occasion with prayer, outdoor sermons, shooting matches, dancing, and other activities. At the rendezvous the performers are met by an audience that arrives only minutes before from other villages, chanting its own poem (thus the performers in one performance become the audience in a different one). Or, as in the case of a tribal dispute, the contestants and the intermediaries may agree to meet at some neutral point, where they can negotiate their differences peacefully, and it is to this meeting place that the various tribal delegations march, chanting poems expressing their own point of view in the controversy. In the wedding celebrations the performance of poetry can occur in the context of two important ceremonial events—the groom's *zaffah* (procession), which is conducted to the village mosque and back to the groom's house, or at night when the guests march to the village for the groom's *samrah* (beginning the performance just outside the village entrance). The action of the march, for all the ceremonies, spatially (and iconically) symbolizes the alignment of poet and chorus with audience: the audience is the goal toward which the performers are marching and the group to which in essence the poem is addressed.

The conditions under which the *zāmil* is performed are also different from those of the *bālah*. It is always performed outdoors, either in the day or at night (the *bālah* occurs only at night and indoors). The importance of *laḥn* (melody) to the delivery of the poem cannot be overemphasized, despite the fact that the overall musical performance is far less complex than it is in the *bālah*. I was once conversing with a man who claimed to be able to compose poetry, so I asked him for a sample of his work. On the spot he composed a *zāmil* on a specific issue I chose for him. I later showed it to one of my friends, who is renowned in Khawlān for his *zāmil* poetry, and his reaction to it was, "Well, it has a rhyme and a meaning—he does treat the issue in question—but it can't be chanted on any known *zāmil* tune, can it? He's all right when it comes to composing *qaṣīdah* poetry, but he's no good for the rest of it." The remark is revealing on several counts. It points out normative aspects of a *zāmil* poem expected by a tribal audience: rhyme, meaning (that is, an issue), and performable music. It also suggests that music is not as important for the composition of the *qaṣīdah*, though the latter is often set to music by a professional singer after he has been given the text by the poet.

The poem the man composed was chanted to the following melody:

This is only one of at least eleven distinct melodies I collected for the *zāmil* genre in Khawlān, and it remains for an ethnomusicologist to determine whether still more exist and to what extent they are unique to this region or are known throughout tribal Yemen. Many of them have a two-part structure where the second half is a natural cadence of the first.

The poem's text, however, need not be chanted for it to be passed on. I collected many *zāmil*s through plain-voice recitation. Thus, both the composition and the delivery of the *zāmil* poem are relatively more independent of music than is the case for *bālah* poetry.

Oral Tradition and Interpretation

The fact that the text of the *zāmil* poem may be recited independently of ritual occasions may explain why the oral tradition has preserved *zāmil* poems that are more than a hundred years old. Such poems are still recited in *gāt* chews and occasionally at wedding ceremonies. The reciter tells his audience who the poet was, if his identity is known (it generally is), and the *munāsibah* (occasion) for which it was composed and includes other historical information to clarify references in the utterance. The reciter can be anyone in the assembly who happens to know the poem, for Khawlānīs, unlike other Arab societies, do not have a professional or official *ḥāfiḍ* (memorizer) who assumes the main responsibility in the speech community for transmitting oral literature from one generation to the next.

The reciter in the following is Ḥusēn Ṣāliḥ from Khawlān. He spoke to me at a small gathering of friends:

> This is a *zāmil* that belongs to [*ḥagg*] al-Gardaᶜī [see Plate 2]. Do you know who he was? [I shake my head in the negative.] He was a great sheikh, of the Āl Murād, they live far, far from Ṣanᶜā in the east [*al-mushrig*], a little bit outside Mārib and north of Bēḥān. *Tamām?* ["OK?" I nod my head to indicate that I am following what he says.] *Tamām!*
>
> And he said [Ḥusēn recites in plain voice]:
>
> yā dhi l-maṣāniᶜ dhī badēt-ī || mā shī ᶜala sh-shārid malāmah
> qūlū li-yaḥyā bin muḥammad || bā naltagī yōm al-giyāmah
>
> O these fortress towers that have appeared before me || there is no blame on the fugitive.
> Tell Yaḥyā bin Muḥammad || we will meet on the Day of Resurrection.

One member of the audience repeated the rhyming syllable *-āmah* at the end of each line, and when the poem was completed the whole audience grunted *wa huh!*, which literally means "and it!" but loosely translates as "bravo!" Ḥusēn continued with his explanation:

> "O these *maṣāniᶜ*," that is to say [*yaᶜnī*], "O these big houses" . . . see [*shūf*], in the east the houses are built like a stronghold [*galᶜah*] because the tribes are constantly warring with each other and the people inside them have to defend themselves. As to the hemistich "There is no blame on the fugitive," well, see, the Imam—that was Imam Yaḥyā back in the forties—had imprisoned al-Gardaᶜī because this sheikh was taking money from the British to make trouble for the Imam on the borders. He was taken to the prison here in Ṣanᶜā, you know . . . [Someone interrupts: "You know the one they call Fortress Ghamdān?" I indicate I understand the reference, and Ḥusēn continues.] Well, al-Gardaᶜī escaped. He jumped from his prison window—and it's way up above the street by several stories—and was able to crawl to safety on a broken ankle to the house of some friends in the city, who then smug-

gled him out. He arrived at his home [*bilād*] and spoke this *zāmil*. [Ḥusēn repeats it one more time.] Thus, when he says, "There's no blame on the fugitive," he means that he was imprisoned without cause, unjustly, and that is why he escaped. After this he says that the Imam—Yaḥyā bin Muḥammad, he was the Imam—that he and al-Gardaᶜī will meet after they're dead, when all souls are called before God and the Prophet (may God bless him) to be judged.

S.C.: OK, I understand the *zāmil* now much better, thank you. But what did al-Gardaᶜī really mean? What was his intention [*gaṣd*] when he said, "We will meet on the Day of Resurrection"?

H.S.: What do you think?

S.C.: Well, I'm not sure . . . maybe, that the sheikh won't obey the Imam. Maybe, that he refuses his rule [*ḥukm*].

H.S.: That's it [*huwa huh,* said rapidly with rising-falling intonation]. See, he would later murder the Imam.

Bear in mind that Ḥusēn had to go into a more elaborate explanation of the historical context than would have been necessary had he been speaking to a native Khawlānī. The reciter feels it to be his responsibility to tell the listener as much information as is needed for him or her to understand the gist of the poem. As for an interpretation, it was rarely volunteered by the reciter unless he was specifically asked to give one by a questioner in the audience. Usually it was assumed that each listener understood the poem in his own way.

Variants in the Text-Utterance

Different versions of the same poem often exist in the oral tradition. Many changes come about through lexical substitutions, which clarify the meaning of the poem for speakers of a particular dialect. Thus, in one version of al-Gardaᶜī's poem *ḥuṣūn* (fortresses) was substituted for *maṣāniᶜ*, and in another *mā b-ish* (there is no) for *mā shī,* these alternates being more intelligible to a nontribal audience. The first substitution alters the meter somewhat, though it is still within the bounds of permissible variability.

More significant alterations of the text can occur, as in this variant:

yā dhi l-ḥuṣūn dhī badēt-ī || mā b-ish ʿala sh-shārid malāmah
law shī maʿī ʿishrīn rāmī || nidkhil li-yaḥyā lā magām-ah

O these fortresses that have appeared before me || there is no blame on the fugitive.
If I had with me twenty marksmen || we would enter Yaḥyā's palace.

The aesthetic structure of the original is considerably changed. The rhyme scheme is of the type *a* || *b*, whereas the original has only end-of-line rhymes. Note also the internal /ī/ rhyme in the first hemistich of the second line, *law shī maʿ-ī ʿishrīn rāmī.*

How does one explain, however, the radical alteration of the second line's meaning? Ḥusēn's version (which is the one I commonly heard in Khawlān) is far more radical in its defiance of Imamate authority. In that poem the sheikh is denying that the Imam has any legitimate right to rule over him (and, by extension, over the tribes) because he and the Imam are equal. The only authority he recognizes is Aḷḷāh's, not the representation of divine authority on earth by the Imam. Whereas the second version *appears* more drastic in its reaction to the Imam—the poet is, after all, alluding to his assassination—it does not imply even remotely that Imamate rule is in principle vulnerable. In other words, what is being called into question in the second version is the rule of only one man; what is being called into question in the first is the rule of a whole system of government. The first version would no doubt appeal to those Khawlānīs who actively sympathized with the revolutionary overthrow of the Imamate, whereas the second version would be preferred by those who did not oppose the Imamate as much as they did this particular Imam.

Yet a third variant of the same poem attributed to al-Gardaʿī exists. It is identical to the first version except for the fact that a third line has been added on:

yuḥrim ʿaley-ya gaṣra ghamdān || wa lā ḥufar l-ī gabra gāmah

Ghamdān prison is forbidden to me || even if a six-foot grave is dug for me.

I obtained this version in the capital from an amateur folklorist who originally hailed from Khawlān but was born into a famous *gāḍī* (judge), not tribal, family. I expressed surprise at hearing a third line, since I was told by tribesmen that the *zāmil* had only two. When I repeated this version to my Khawlānī friends they offered the opinion that it was from a *qaṣīdah,* not a *zāmil.* The ambiguity, however, is not surprising, since many poems that end up as *qaṣīdah* start out as *zāmil* (much as a short story may be expanded into a novel). The third line has some interesting aesthetic parallelisms, such as the passive-voice *yuḥrim ʿaley-ya* (is forbidden to me) and *ḥufar l-ī* (is dug for me), both of which occur at the beginning of their respective hemistichs; but it is the rhetorical meaning these parallelisms help to bring out that needs examining. The use of the passive voice is crucial in the context of the first hemistich, "Ghamdān prison is forbidden to me." Obviously, it is not the Imam who forbids the prison but Aḷḷāh, and it is He whom al-Gardaʿī obeys. Once again this stance undercuts Imamate authority and reinforces the meaning of the first version. The second hemistich suggests that the sheikh will defy the Imam's orders even if such a rebellion spells his death sentence. Superficially this hemistich could be interpreted as simple hyperbole, but in fact its meaning is deeply ironic when one bears in mind the historical facts, for it was the Imam who was to die at the hands of the sheikh, not the other way around. Interestingly, the Ṣanʿānī informant who gave me this variant was deeply involved in the Republican side of the Yemeni civil war and vehemently opposed the idea of Imamate rule.

It is virtually impossible to say which version of this *zāmil* is the original. I doubt that it matters to the tribesmen; even if one could prove to them which is "authentic" and which "spurious," they would not stop using the latter if it suited their own political purposes.

Formulas

The poetic form of the *zāmil* poem is more interesting than its musical structure. The constraint of composition in the *zāmil* is not one of time (as in the *bālah*) or of expansion (as in the *qaṣīdah*) but just the opposite: it is *compression.* Since the first line of the poem is usually set aside for recognizing the honor of the addressee (usually in a greeting containing laudatory epithets), there remains only one line in which the poet can address the issue in question. Terseness of expression is the rule, if not the tyranny, of this genre. At its best the *zāmil* is an aphorism (which can be plainly seen, for example, in al-Gardaʿī's poems).

One can reasonably argue from these facts that there is less need for formulas in the composition of the *zāmil.* Speed of composition, though indeed a factor, is less pressing than in the *bālah.* Where formulas are useful is in the first line, containing the speech act of greeting, and in more minor ways in the appeals to tribal values heard in political rhetoric. I was always struck by the fact that the first line, when devoted to the greeting and address of the assembly, was formulaic, whereas the second line contrasted with it in uniqueness of reference and composition. This effect heightens the feeling of compression, for if the first line is set aside for preliminaries, one expects the second to carry the poem's punch.

The expectation that formulas will be less useful to *zāmil* composition and performance is borne out by certain demonstrable facts about their occurrence in the poetry. First, my formula index for *zāmil* poetry is one-fourth the size of that index for *bālah* poetry. (A formula index is based on the number of separate items [i.e. types of formulas] and their recurrence.) Second, a major difference is the line length of formulas in the two genres. It is not uncommon to find in the *bālah* a formula taking up nearly half the hemistich or even, in a few cases, its entirety with the exception of the end rhyme. But in *zāmil* poetry formulas are short, never more than three words, and therefore encompass only a fraction of the entire line.[1] A final difference in the use of formulas in these two genres is the nature of the "systems" of formulas they rely on. The *zāmil* does not have the range of choices or the complexity of paradigmatic associations that one finds in the *bālah.* The most likely reason for this difference lies in the meters employed. Because of a greater number of diverse meters in the *zāmil* than in the *bālah,* we cannot expect to find formulas used throughout the corpus, if the previous definition of formula (a fixed expression used recurrently under identical metrical conditions) is correct. Perhaps formulas in the *zāmil* tend to be short so that they can be altered somewhat to fit a variety of meters.[2]

Meter and Rhyme

In *bālah* poetry I found only two metrical designs; the pattern --◡-|-◡- is predominant. This situation is exactly reversed in *zāmil* poetry. Several distinct metrical patterns are used (see Appendix B), but the most prevalent *bālah* pattern is the least popular *zāmil* pattern, and the design ‒‒∪‒|‒‒∪‒ is the most favored. The sheikh's poem clearly fits this latter pattern.

An obligatory caesura may occur in the middle of the line, as in the sheikh's poem, or more rarely in the last third of the line, but almost never in the first third.

The end-of-hemistich rhymes follow three schemes: (1) only the ends of the second hemistichs rhyme with each other (*x* || *a*, *y* || *a*, where *x* is a sound different from *y*); (2) all hemistichs rhyme with one another (*a* || *a*, *a* || *a*); (3) the first hemistichs rhyme with each other and the second hemistichs rhyme with each other, but the rhymes are different (*a* || *b*, *a* || *b*).

Line-Internal Rhyme

Another way in which the poem as a text-utterance is experienced in this genre is through line-internal rhyming. Take, for example, the opening hemistich of a famous poem:

> ḥayd aṭ-ṭiyāl aʿl*an* wa nādā kulla shāmikh f-il-yam*an*
>
> "Mount aṭ-Ṭiyal," he summoned and cried to every peak in Yemen

The end rhyme *-an* is anticipated in the word *aʿlan*. This internal rhyming is not accidental but is considered to be a feature of an aesthetically superior poem. Other, more obvious examples can be mentioned:

> yā salāmī ga*wī* mā yigraḥ al-lē*wī*
>
> Greetings as powerful as what the regiment fires [by rifle]

The repetition of *-wī* sets up an internal rhyme, which is continued in the next hemistich:

> f-il-hawā l-ah du*wī* lā ʿarḍa l-ah l-ayy-ah
>
> In the air it has a bang, nothing can stop it

Note that the line starts conventionally enough with a greeting expression accompanied by an intensifier—a typical pattern, except for the fact that the intensifier has been chosen because of its euphony: *salāmī gawī*. Following it comes the second intensifier, introduced by the common *mā* phrase, although no formulaic expressions occur within it; *yigraḥ al-lēwī* has been chosen for its fine euphonic possibilities and does not appear anywhere else in the corpus. Obviously, formulaic usage has given way to other sound potentials—alliterative patterns, internal rhymes, sound symbolism—which enhance the vividness of the imagery. We have entered an aesthetic world different from that of the *bālah*.

Several degrees of complexity are possible in the construction of an internal rhyme. For example, it is easy to see that scheme 2 is more complex than scheme 1:

1. a | a || a
2. a | a | a | a || a

Scheme 2 demonstrates that the hemistich can be made structurally more complex by repeating the internal rhyme more than once. But in certain patterns, repeated sectioning by rhyme occurs not just in one but in both hemistichs:

3. a | a || a | a
4. a | a | a | a || a | a | a | a

Thus, one can vary the pattern of internal rhyme according to whether one or both hemistichs are sectioned and according to the number of repetitions of an internal rhyme.

Next, the two hemistichs may not rhyme with each other:

5. a | a || a | b
6. a | b || a | a

And one can have an internal rhyme that is different from both end-of-hemistich rhymes:

7. c | a || c | b

Obviously, the possibilities are many. In actuality only some of them occur in my corpus with any frequency, but there is no reason to assume that a poet cannot produce the rarer schemes.

What seems to be important is the difference between a hemistich in which internal rhyming has occurred once and hemistichs in which it has occurred more than once. (Internal rhyme, as I use it, is the repetition of the rhyming sound [i.e. the sound that comes at the end of a unit of verse, such as the hemistich]. The repetition of any other sound in the line is, according to my analysis, alliteration.) To illustrate a *zāmil* composed on a pattern of first-order complexity (single repetition of the internal rhyme), consider this poem:

– – ⏑ –| – –[⏑] – | – –[⏑] –| – – ⏑ –
yā marḥabā milyōn min ʾaʿsh*ār* mā shāʿ al-mith*ār* ||
(a) (a)

– –[⏑] –|– –[⏑] –| ⏑ –[⏑] –| – – ⏑ –
b-iḍ-ḍēf wādi l-ḥ*ār* w-al-wiṣāl dhī jā min ḥar*ūb*
(a) (b)

– –[⏑] – | – – ⏑ – | – –[⏑] – | – – ⏑ –
tarḥīb min-nā l-ah yamidd ath-th*ār* garrarnā gar*ār* ||
(a) (a)

– – ⏑ –| – –[⏑]–|– – ⏑ – | – – ⏑ –
lā m-aktafā b-id-d*ār* wājib nirfaʿ-ah fōg al-jan*ūb*
(a) (b)

O welcome, ten million times, as many times as the lightning flashes || to the guest from Wadi al-Ḥār and the arrival who has come from Ḥarūb.

Welcome from us to him extends, we have decided to wreak revenge || If he is not content with the house, we will raise him on our shoulders.

The rhyming pattern is scheme 5. The object is to make the repetition regular from line to line in the poem. In the first hemistich of both lines the rhyme occurs in the third foot, in the second hemistich it occurs in the second foot.

It is much more difficult to construct a hemistich in which there is a double repetition of the end rhyme. In fact, I have only one such example in my corpus:

⏑ –[⏑] –| – – ⏑ – | – – ⏑ –| – – ⏑ –
salām yitfarr*az* ʿadad-mā h*azza* fī rās an-nuk*az* ||
(a) (a) (a)

– – ⏑ –| ⏑ – ⏑ –| – – ⏑ – | – – ⏑ –
mā dhī yibī wag*az* f-il-ēdāt al-mujamm*az* l-ah sak*ī*ʿ
(a) (a) (b)

– – ⏑ –| – – ⏑ –| – – – |– – ⏑ –
yā marḥabā yijh*iz* bi-ḍēfān al-ʿ*izz* ahl al-miy*az* ||
(a) (a) (a)
[third foot short]

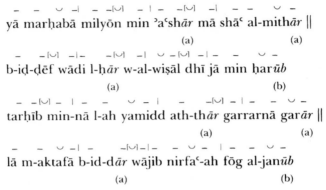

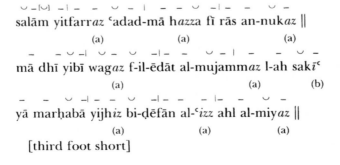

– – ∪ –| – – ∪ –| – – ∪ –| – – ∪ –
yā ḥayda mā yiht*iz* fiy al-ḥill al-ʿaw*az* rās-ah man*īʿ*
(a) (a) (b)

Greetings distinguishing [singling out] the company, as many times as they strike [with the hammer] on the top of the hill, || [as great as] he feels pain who wants to hold a live coal in his clenched fist.
O welcome provided to the mighty guests, people of distinction, || O mountain that does not tremble in difficult times, whose head is impregnable.

This poem was composed by an excellent poet of Khawlān. It is imperfect in its construction, for the meter goes awry (unless my transcription of it was faulty) in one place, and the occurrence of the internal rhymes is not quite regular. In spite of these deficiencies the poem was widely admired for its formal perfection by all who heard it. It is a rare example of internal rhyme having more than just a euphonic effect. The first hemistich has a greeting formula, *salām yitfarraz,* followed by an intensifier phrase similar to those found in the *bālah.* The sound repetition of *-az(z)* parallels the meaning of intensification.

The correlation of rhyme with meaning is rare but nevertheless exploited from time to time. Here is another example, the first line of a *zāmil* poem composed during the civil war by a Republican poet (al-Ḥadā):

∪ – ∪ –|∪ – ∪ –| – – ∪ –|– – ∪ –
ʾal-arḍ[a] ḥurriy*ah* wa ḍubbāṭ al-marākiz maṣriy*ah* ||
(a) (a)
– – ∪ –|– –[∪] – |– – ∪ –|∪ – ∪ –
gāyid la-hā sall*āl* w-al-mōhib la-hā raʾīs jam*āl*
(b) (b)

The land is free and the officers of the headquarters [of the republic] are Egyptian. || Its leader is Sallāl, and its inspiration is President Jamāl.

Sallāl is the name of Yemen's first president. He allied himself with Egypt in the hope of furthering the Republican cause in the civil war against the royalist forces of Imam Badr. Jamāl is the name of the former Egyptian president Gamal Abdel Nasser, who sent troops and military equipment to North Yemen under the command of the then colonel Anwar as-Sadat. What is interesting about the sound patterns in this poem is the way in which they reinforce the political rhetoric: the poetic figure of the internal rhyme *sallāl/jamāl* is a verbal icon of the political alliance linking the two countries. The same parallelism of sound and meaning is evident in the first hemistich: the internal rhyme *ḥurriyah* (free)/*maṣriyah* (Egyptian) links Egypt with the "free" revolution.

Alliteration and Onomatopoeia

There are two kinds of alliterative patterns. One is the repetition of individual phonemes (or a more "abstract" alliteration involving distinctive features). The other, which is more common, hinges on morphological patterns. Both phonological and morphological patterns are evident in the following *zāmil* from Khawlān:

> ⏑ – [⏑] –| – – ⏑ –|– – – ⏑ –| – – ⏑–|–
> salām yā ṣanᶜa ṣ-ṣanīᶜah[3] || w-ahl-ish[4] hum an-nās al-ᶜizāẓī
> ⏑ – ⏑ –| – – ⏑ –|– – – ⏑ –| – –[⏑] –|–
> jibāl-ạhā minḥah manīᶜah || mitḥaddiyah man kān ghāzī
>
> Greetings, O Ṣanᶜā, the blessed; || your people are noble.
> Its mountains are a fortress formidable, || threatening whoever attacks it.

These lines contain an obvious alliteration of the [+strident] feature and the [+nasal] feature. More interesting, however, are the consonantal patterns built from Arabic roots. For example, the root *Ṣ-N-ᶜ* is repeated in the words *ṣanᶜa ṣ-ṣanīᶜah* (Ṣanᶜa, the blessed), which is linked by rhyme to *manīᶜah* (formidable), creating a subliminal militaristic meaning of a city under siege but unbeatable. Note also the words *minḥah manīᶜah* (a fortress formidable): given that /ḥ/ and /ᶜ/ are both pharyngeal consonants (voiceless and voiced, respectively), one could argue on a more abstract level of representation that the same root is replicated in adjacent words. In the *bālah* alliteration occurs rarely, and almost never in its morphological variety, but it is highly prized in *zāmil* poems.

Onomatopoeia is also an admired feature of the *zāmil* genre. Here is an example that is particularly brilliant because it meshes internal rhyme with the speech act of greeting:

⏑ – [⏑] – | – – ⏑ – |– – ⏑ –
salām min-nā ṣarr[a] min ṣūd an-nukhar ||
– – ⏑ – | – – ⏑ –| – – ⏑ –
mathnī muʿashshar min lathīm akhshām-ihā

Greetings from us that whiz from the black [rifle] nose, ||
twelve [bullets] discharged from the opening of its nostrils.

The speech act of greeting is rendered metaphorically as the shooting of a gun (a tribal "salute"), and the gun is, in turn, metaphorized as a nose. On the semantic level the intensity of the greeting is conveyed in the image of bullets discharging in rapid fire from the rifle barrels. An icon of this image is in the internal rhyme. The sound symbolism inheres in the trilled /r/ of *ṣarr* (lit. issue, discharge), which suggests the sound of a whizzing bullet, and then is echoed in *nukhar* and *muʿashshar.* The iconicity gets still more subtle. Consider the words in which the trilled /r/ occurs and their order in the line. The sound is most intense in its first occurrence, doubled in the verb *ṣarr,* from the root *Ṣ-R-R;* next it is heard in the two-syllable word *nukhar;* and finally it occurs in the three-syllable word *muʿashshar.* In other words, as the sound of the bullet travels (and metaphorically also the greeting), its echo becomes fainter just as the word in which it occurs becomes correspondingly longer. Similar examples abound in the tradition: *salām ṭann[a] yitghaṭṭan* (greetings that peel like a bell). The verb *ṭann* (peel) begins with a strong initial plosive /ṭ/, which might resemble the sound of a hammer striking a bell, and ends with the doubled nasal /n/, a continuant that is dentally articulated and resonates with the initial sound. Here is another example: *bā ḥann*[*a*] *mā ḥannat lathīm al-kanad* (I moan like the opening of the *kanad* gun barrel). Like the verbs *ṣarr* and *ṭann, ḥann* (to moan, sigh, thunder) is also onomatopoetic. But I had difficulty hearing onomatopoeia, so I asked one of my friends to justify this impression. "You know," he said, "it's like . . ."—and then he heaved his shoulders and emitted a deep sigh on a beautifully articulated unvoiced pharyngeal (/ḥ/). The connection between sound and meaning was unmistakable. The repetition of /ḥ/ intensifies the pitying, lamentable feeling.

Sound symbolism reaches truly brilliant heights in this civil war *zāmil:*

– – ⏑ – |– – ⏑ – | – – ⏑ –| – – ⏑ –
lā tasmaḥō ʿaf*wan* gafā mā gad talaw*wan* w-alta*wan*

If you please, pardon someone who is wending a devious course.

Much is going on in this brief hemistich, but let us concentrate solely on the phrase *talawwan w-altawan.* Both words are derived from the same root (*L-W-Y*), but they are generated from different verb categories (Forms V and VIII). *Talaw-* and *w-alta-* form a sort of consonantal chiasmus (t-l-w/w-l-t), which dramatizes a turning back on oneself. Note too the effective use of the /l/ and /w/ to suggest a sinuous, gliding, or zigzag movement. Both sound patternings are perfectly congruent with the meaning. The poet is the Republican Sheikh Ṣāliḥ ar-Royshān from Khawlān, who is addressing the leader of the Royalist armed forces, Sheikh Nājī bin ʿAlī al-Ghādir. The gist of this snippet is that ar-Royshān is calling al-Ghādir a traitor because the latter had originally supported the republic and then switched his allegiances after the Egyptian occupation. It is his alleged betrayal of the republic that the poet wants to emphasize. He accomplishes his aim brilliantly by the selection of the glide and lateral consonants that suggest a slipperiness and sinuousness and by the chiasmus that iconicizes the shifting of al-Ghādir's commitments. If one remembers that this chiasmus is only one poetic figure in a densely textured line composed of meter, internal rhyme, and alliteration (like *gafā mā gad*), one can better appreciate the considerable art and craftsmanship that goes into the making of a *zāmil* poem.

Symbolism

A fairly common convention is to start a poem by addressing a messenger, represented by the image of a bird or the wind, whom the poet asks to carry his message. For example, a good friend composed a *zāmil* for me that begins:

– –[◡] –| – –[◡] – | – – ◡ – – – ◡ –| – – ◡
yā ṭēr yā siffāḥ min shaʿb al-yaman || balligh li-kartar dhī fiy
– | – – ◡ –
amrīkah mugīm

O bird, O winged one, from the people of Yemen || convey to Carter [this message] who in America is leader.

More than fifty years ago the armies of Imam Yaḥyā were advancing on the ʾAʿrūsh tribe of Khawlān, whose head sheikh was the father of the famous Nājī bin ʿAlī al-Ghādir. He is supposed to have said:

– –[◡] –| – – ◡ –|– – ◡ –|– – – ◡ –| – –
yā ṭēr yā ʿāzim wa gāṭiʿ l-il-marāḥil || ṭayyir wa khabbir bin
◡ –
jalāl
– – ◡ – | – – ◡ –|◡ – ◡ –| – ◡ –[◡] –| –
jīnā bi-ʾakhshām al-madalʿa w-al-jarāmil || silāḥ khawlān
– ◡ –
aṭ-ṭiyāl

O bird, O messenger, O crosser of the journey's stages, || fly and inform bin Jalāl: We have come with the nostrils of guns and rifles, || weapons of Khawlān aṭ-Ṭiyāl.

For an example using the wind, consider the first line of this civil war poem:

– – ◡ –| – – ◡ –| – – ◡ –| – – ◡ –
yā midhriyyah habbī wa nabbī majlis al-ʾamn al-ghabī ||
– – ◡ –|– –[◡] –| – – ◡ –| – – ◡ –
min baʿda thālith ʿām tamm aṣ-ṣulḥ[a] mā f-il-wajh[a] lōm

O wind, blow and blast the idiotic Security Council [of the United Nations] with the news || that for more than three years the truce has been at an end; on our faces there is no blame [for its violation].

We will encounter these conventions again in the *qaṣīdah,* where the messenger of the poem becomes incorporated into a lengthy speech act. This fact reinforces the intuition that the *zāmil* is an intermediate genre in the poetic system—halfway between the fully performance-oriented *bālah* and the text-oriented *qaṣīdah.*

Another and much more frequently employed convention of *zāmil* poetry is for the poet to address his "message" to a mountain, fortress, or other defensive bulwark, all of which are synecdochic images. Many *zāmil* poems, for instance, begin with an address to Mount Ṭiyāl, a feature of Khawlān that stands for the whole region. The celebrated poem by al-Gardaʿī that was the subject of analysis in the beginning of this chapter opens, "O these fortress towers that have appeared before me," where the village houses look like fortresses and stand synecdochically for the mighty people who inhabit them (and for whom the poem is intended). Following are two other examples of this convention. "Greetings, O impregnable fortresses" is nearly identical with the opening of al-Gardaʿī's poem. "O bulwark on the rim of Black Mountain" requires a bit of explanation. In Yemen, because of the rugged terrain, attackers take up positions on the mountaintops, building defensive bulwarks from the stones strewn about everywhere. As with all the synecdochic forms of address I have examined, their function crucially entails a rhetoric of address.

Not surprisingly, most symbolism in oral tribal poetry is of this conventional sort, and yet poets are constantly striving for fresh imagery, as, for example, in the modes of intensifying the speech act of greeting. It is precisely by casting a conventional sentiment in an original image or metaphor that a poet honors the addressee in the greeting, demonstrating his respect and affection for the other by polishing his speech.

My first example is a *zāmil* composed during the Yemeni civil war. Most Yemenis, especially tribesmen, had never seen an airplane before the Egyptians flew bombers over their villages and cities. This instrument of destruction impressed itself on the martial imagination of the tribesmen, and eventually a poet appropriated the image in this line of verse:

> – – ∪ –| – –∪– |– – ∪ –| – ∪
> ḥayyā bi-kum m-aṭ-ṭāyirah ḍallat taḥammal || min
> – ∪ – |– – ∪ –
> al-barinzāt ath-thigāl
>
> Long life to you, as great as what the airplane carries || of heavy bombs.

The poet is drawing an analogy between the intensity of his greeting and the powerful destructiveness of the bomb. But besides the original imagery, the line contains a heavy and no doubt intentional irony of wishing someone long life and intensifying the greeting by a destructive image. The poem is addressed to the enemy.

The appearance of the plane is almost as recent as the introduction of the automobile. In Yemen the car is no longer a luxury item, for with his new-found wealth acquired by labor in Saudi Arabia and the oil-rich states of the Arabian Gulf, the Yemeni citizen can afford many more Western products than his pocketbook previously allowed. The automobile is a particularly important feature of life in a society with virtually no system of public transport. Not surprisingly, the car has become a metaphorical image in tribal poetry, as can be seen in the following greeting:

> ∪ – [∪] –| – – ∪ –| – – – – ∪ –| – – ∪ –| – –
>
> salām l-ish yā ʿāṣimat ṣanʿā || mā ḥarrak al-mōtar masāmīr-ah
>
> Greetings to you, O capital Ṣanʿā || (as many times as) the engine moves its pistons.

The following poem, which I cannot resist quoting in full, dates from before the 1962 revolution. At that time a member of a distinguished *gāḍī* family from Khawlān was slain at the order of Imam Aḥmad. The Khawlānī tribes, obligated to protect the learned and religious elite within their territory, convened in the regional administrative capital to work out a settlement of their grievances with the Imam's personal representative.

The tribes of Khawlān chanted the following poem to the Imam's representative:

> – – [∪] –| – – ∪ –|– – ∪ – – – ∪ –|– –
>
> ʿirnūf ʿarnaf w-al-gabāyil sarrabat || w-al-jinna jābat min
>
> ∪ –| – – ∪ –
>
> gafā ḥayd aṭ-ṭiyāl
>
> – – ∪ – |– – ∪ –|– – ∪ – – – ∪ –|
>
> w-ash-shamsa faḍḍat w-ath-thirēyā gāranat || w-ad-dēwalah
>
> – – ∪ –| – – ∪ –
>
> khāfat ʿalā kashf al-jilāl.
>
> Mount ʿIrnūf is "ʿarnafing" and the tribes are mobilizing; || the jinn are roving in front of Mount aṭ-Ṭiyāl.
>
> The sun is rising and the Pleiades are conjoining; || the government fears exposure of its splendor.

The poem begins with the unusual and humorous neologism *ʿirnūf ʿarnaf*. *ʿIrnūf* is the name of the mountain at the base of which the tribes were meeting. The action predicated of this mountain is designated by the verb *ʿarnaf,* a verbal play obviously derived from the root *ʿ-R-N-F*. The semantic oddness of the neologism lies in the fact that an inanimate object, a mountain, is described as doing something. But notice the parallelism of this natural phenomenon and the social one, "the tribes are mobilizing," which is then extended hyperbolically throughout the poem. Nature is gathering its forces—first the *jinn* around the base of Mount aṭ-Ṭiyāl, then the sun rising, and finally the Pleiades in the sky—and by analogy the forces of society are also marshaling for the onslaught. The climax of the sequence delivers the punch of the poem, for faced with such universal opposition, the central government fears its overthrow.

Allusion

Closely connected with conventional symbolism is allusion. The key difference between the two is that allusion is a concealed reference, often occasioned by a concern for social, political, or religious censorship (though it need not be) and slightly mysterious because it requires interpretation on the part of the audience. A perfect example is in a *zāmil* that ends, "Say to Ḥasan and Badr, O Nājī, 'Silver has already turned to brass.'" This line was a subject of much speculation among my informants. One interpretation hinges on the immediately preceding linguistic context, in which the poet is enumerating the powerful weapons to be found in the Republican arsenal in contrast to the meager supplies (cartridge belts) available to the Royalists. Hence, on the one hand, the phrase may mean that the once-powerful army of the Imam (who had strong support from the northern and eastern tribes) had now become a ragtag outfit. On the other hand, it could be that silver is an allusion to the monarchy and that the phrase is supposed to mean that its political power has been debased (turned to brass). Either interpretation is legitimate, for the mystery created by the allusion is deliberate.

The Coherence of the Poem

How does one begin a *zāmil?* Recall that in the *bālah* it is obligatory to begin by mentioning God's name, which can be done by means of a number of different formulas. This option is common in the poetry composed on the occasion of the religious festivals (though not exclusive to it, for I have heard poems begun this way composed on the occasion of war disputes, for example). Another one of the most common ways to begin the *zāmil* poem is by the formula *So-and-so (the name of the poet) has said (or says)* . . . In many cases the verb of speaking is the most neutral one, *gāl* (he said), followed by the poet's name (where the author unequivocably takes responsibility for his composition) or his name with some epithet (e.g. *al-fatā aṣ-Ṣūfī* [the youth aṣ-Ṣufi]) or more simply a tribal designation (e.g. *ibna khawlānī* [lit. a son of Khawlān]). Yet another alternative is to refer metapragmatically to the poetic act with a formula like *yigūl al-baddāᶜ* (the poet says). What follows any of these options is some form of reported speech, the poem construed as "fixing" the actual words of the poet: these are the words that *he* said. Responsibility for speaking is being assumed.

After this beginning, a very common speech act is the greeting, as in these examples from various *zāmil*s:

> salām min-nā gāl al-ᶜawḍalī
>
> ("Greetings from us," said al-ᶜAwḍalī)
>
> yā ᶜutmah al-khaḍrā salām arbaᶜ miyyah
>
> (O ᶜUtmah [name of a village], the green [i.e. fertile] one, four hundred greetings)
>
> yā marḥabā yā dhī wafadtū ᶜand-anā
>
> (O welcome, O you who have come to us)

But the greeting may be implied and only the addressees mentioned. If a poem is composed in response to a previous *zāmil,* the line might begin with the metapragmatic reference "O you who composed the speech," which indexes the text as a response poem.

These preliminaries of address and greeting usually take up the first line of the poem. The second line introduces the subject, with a punch line at the end. Economy, not excess, is obviously called for; as I have noted, compression is the hallmark of this art form.

Zāmil Dialogues

When a poem has been addressed to someone or to a group such as a tribal delegation, the recipient is expected to reply with a poem of his or its own. Regardless of whether the challenge is friendly or hostile, a response is required. However, not all responses to poems are necessarily in answer to a direct challenge, for a poet may hear a poem by chance and decide to reply to it. I can recall several instances when I had presented my collection of poems to various poets and one of them said, "I want to reply to that," and he proceeded to compose a poem on the spot. The poem to which he was responding always had been composed recently and dealt with a contemporary issue.

A poet cannot respond to a poem in any way he wishes. He must recognize the genre and respond in kind. Furthermore, he must reproduce the rhyme scheme of the original, and if possible also the alliterative devices, and construct the line of the same length on the same metrical scheme. In the performance he must also know how to chant the poem to a given *laḥn* (melody) that is formally congruent with it. And he must make sure that his poem is in fact a response to the issues raised in the original—thereby demonstrating his grasp of its allusions or concealed references—effectively parry them, and answer the central criticism.

These dialogues are built into tribal ceremonies as exchanges between social groups. At a wedding party the celebrants are usually split into two groups: the hosts (the groom and his friends and relatives), and anyone who wishes to attend plus the relatives of the bride. At the wedding procession it is appropriate, indeed expected, that guests compose and chant poems in honor of the groom, to which the poet of the host party responds with an offering of its own. When the two religious festivals are celebrated at the ends of the Ḥajj and Ramadan, the month of fasting, various regional tribal delegations convene at a central meeting place, each party chanting one of its own *zāmil* poems; any tribal delegation may respond to one or more of these poetic offerings. Nowhere is the routine more important than in the dispute mediations held by the two conflicting parties and the intermediaries, which I will investigate in depth in the next chapter.

When I was in the field, the so-called hostage crisis in Iran was in the foreground of international news for several months. Since the Khawlānīs knew I was American, they often sought out my opinion on the matter, and I in turn solicited theirs. One man whom I knew to be a poet of some stature composed the following *zāmil:*

– – ∪ –| – –[∪] – | – – ∪ –| – – – ∪ –|∪? –
yā marḥabā yā sēf min nihjā fuwād-ī || yimlī suwāḥ-anā
– ∪ –
w-al-bilād [second foot long]

ʾamrīkiyah taʿlan ṣuḥuf-hā w-ar-rawādī || ʾash-shāh yiṭlub
  f-il-ḥidād

O welcome, O Sēf, from the bottom of my heart; || [let
  my greeting be bounteous enough] to fill our fields and
  countryside.
America broadcasts in its press and radio, || "The Shah
  wants asylum."

The poem is addressed to me. The second line appears to be not so much an opinion on the matter of the American hostages in Iran as it is simply a statement of fact—the Shah was at the time seeking asylum in a Western country. Yet since a poet acts as a spokesman for a group, this poem must be viewed as being sympathetic to America's position. In tribal law, after all, it is the custom for powerful sheikhs to protect fugitives who seek refuge from the wrath of their pursuers, with the understanding that they either help to negotiate a settlement between the two parties or expose themselves to the wrath of the opponent. America is like a powerful sheikh, and it was obligated to protect its protégé, the Shah, though it could expect reprisals from Iran—or so went the argument of many tribesmen. Thus, the poem is not simply a declaration of fact, a politically noncommittal statement.

One day I was chewing *gāt* with some tribesmen when another poet happened to hear me recite this *zāmil* and was inspired to respond:

ʾaḷḷāh bā yabgī-k yā dhīb al-miʿādī || min wasṭ[a] ṣanʿā lā
  murād
ʾīrān w-al-ʾāyāt fī shaʿb-ah yinādī || ʿalā yidī-nā bā yiʿād

May God preserve you, O wolf of the enemy; || [greetings]
  from the midst of Ṣanʿā to the Murād.
Iran and the ayatollahs among its people cry out || "[What] is
  owed us will surely be returned."

The aesthetic structure of the poem mimics that of the original. The meter and the relative length of the hemistichs are exactly the same. The rhyme scheme and surface segmental phonemes /-ādī/ and /-ād/ are reproduced. The only thing that the poet has not done is repeat the metrical error in the second hemistich of the first line—no doubt because he knew that the extra short syllable was an unintended irregularity in the metrical foot. The two poems are even parallel with regard to certain speech functions. The first line is devoted to a speech act of greeting, though the poet uses a laudatory formula of address, "O wolf of the enemy," by which he shows his respect for the other poet. The second line echoes an act of reported speech of the first poem.

As for its topic, the poem appears simply to be stating a fact: the poet is reporting what the religious leaders in Iran were demanding of the United States. But given the rhetorical nature of the routine—that one poem is composed in response to the challenging view of another—these "pure" declarative speech acts must be regarded as being other than what they seem. Just as the first poet was sympathizing with America, the second poet is acting as spokesman for Iran by demanding the return of the Shah and his wealth.

Thus, the two poems are linked as a couplet, a pair, and an exchange. This repartee, as we know, is called *daʿwā w-ijābah* (challenge and retort). Of course, the first poet did not issue his poem as a challenge to a specific person, though he knew it was likely that someone might take exception to his political statement and reply to it. Ideally, I should have shown the second poet's response to the first to see whether he would issue a second public statement, but the opportunity, unfortunately, never arose.[5]

The final series of poems I will examine here was composed in a very different mood and for a calamitous historical event, the Yemeni civil war. Khawlānī aficionados considered them to be among the finest of my collection, both from the point of view of aesthetics and from that of rhetoric. As they were composed by famous persons in a unique and historically significant period, they are of general interest to historians as well.

The first *zāmil* of the series is by the great Khawlānī sheikh Nājī bin ʿAlī al-Ghādir. He was sympathetic toward the republic at the beginning of the revolution; but when the Egyptians intervened militarily in the civil war and effectively occupied Yemen (much as the United States did in South Vietnam), he changed his mind about the justice of the cause and switched his allegiance to the Royalist forces, who were fighting to reinstate Imam Badr. He composed this poem, in which he defied the Republican sheikhs of Khawlān:

– – ∪ –| – – ∪ –| – – ∪ –| – – ∪ –
ḥayd aṭ-ṭiyāl aʿlan wa nādā kulla shāmikh f-il-yaman ||
– – ∪ –| – – ∪ –| – – ∪ –| – – ∪ –
mā bā[6] najamhur gat wa-lā nafnā min ad-dunyā khalāṣ
– – ∪ – | – –[∪] –|– – ∪ –| – – ∪ –
lā[7] yirjaʿ ams al-yōm w-illa sh-shams[a] tishrig min ʿadan ||
∪ –[∪] –| – –[∪] –| – – ∪ –| – – ∪ –
w-al-arḍ tishʿal nār w-imzān as-samā tamṭur raṣāṣ

"Mount aṭ-Ṭiyāl," he summoned, and he cried out to every peak in Yemen; || "We will never become a republic, even if we were to be snuffed out of this world forever;
Even if yesterday were to return today and the sun were to rise in the south; || Even if the earth were to burn up in fire and the clouds of the sky rain bullets."

The hemistich of the line is long—four feet. The meter is the same one we have seen in other *zāmil*s, and the rhyme scheme is *a* || *b* with an *a* | *a* internal rhyme in the first hemistich. One might argue that the verb *nafnā* (we are snuffed out) is onomatopoetic (especially the fricative consonant among the continuants, suggesting a heavy air-stream). But what is particularly striking about this poem is the logic of its rhetoric, a logic built entirely out of paradoxes—"if yesterday were to return today," "if the sun were to rise in the south," "if the earth were to burn up in fire and the clouds of the sky rain bullets." The poet is arguing hyperbolically that even if these impossible phenomena were to arise in nature, still the impossible—namely, Khawlān joining the republic—would not happen in society. Again an analogy is drawn between the immutable order of nature and the mutable order of society. This analogy will come up again in the next chapter when I discuss poetry as a form of political rhetoric in dispute mediations.

Let us now examine the response poem by the Republican Sheikh ar-Royshān:

– – ∪ –| – – ∪ –| – – ∪ – | – – ∪ –
lā tasmaḥō ʿafwan gafā mā gad talawwan w-altawan ||
– –[∪] –| – – ∪ – |– – ∪ –| – –[∪] –
al-mīj w-al-yūshin maʿā bū marwaḥah w-as-sūd khās
– – ∪ –| – –[∪] –| – – ∪ –| – – ∪ –
mā yigraḥ aṭ-ṭayyār ḍarb ash-shurfa w-ill al-mīmawan ||
– – ∪ –| – – ∪ –| –– ∪ –| – – ∪ –
gul l-il-ḥasan w-al-badra yā nājī gad al-fuḍḍah naḥās

If you please, pardon someone who has wended a devious course. || The Mig, the Yūshin with the helicopter and the fighter jet:
Neither cartridge belts nor M-1 rifles will stop the pilots. || Say to Ḥasan and Badr, O Nājī, "Silver has already turned to brass."

The aesthetic structure of the poem reproduces the rhyme and meter of the original, but it also *intensifies* some of these structures and hence surpasses the original. The first hemistich parallels the first hemistich of al-Ghādir's poem, but the internal *-an* rhyme has been topped by a two-fold, rather than just a single, repetition. This is only the tip of the iceberg, however, on which al-Ghādir's provocation founders, for the end of the first hemistich contains a clever use of sound symbolism I have discussed previously. The alternation of the glide and lateral consonants /w/ and /l/ suggests a sinuous motion perfectly in keeping with the meaning of someone wending a devious course. Earlier I pointed out the chiasmus in *talaw-* and *w-alta-*, which dramatizes in sound the Royalist sheikh's "turning back" on his cause. By contrast, the slightly onomatopoetic *nafnā* (we are snuffed out) in al-Ghādir's poem seems a feeble effort. Add to this comparison the intense vowel and consonant alliteration in *gafā mā gad* and it becomes apparent that this poet has gotten the advantage of his opponent.

Al-Ghādir made his point by a kind of hyperbole of logical paradoxes; the last ("even if the clouds of the sky [were to] rain bullets") is a synecdochic allusion to an imminent Egyptian invasion. The opposing sheikh picks up this allusion and makes it the thrust of his retort. He lists the kinds of weapons and military equipment the Republicans have received from the Egyptians and implies that the Royalists will be unable to defend themselves against them ("Neither cartridge belts nor M-1 rifles will stop the pilots"). Then, in a final brilliant stroke, he tops al-Ghādir's allusion in precisely the spot where it occurred in the original challenge—at the end of the poem, which carries the punch. Crown Prince Ḥasan and Imam Badr are to be told by al-Ghādir that "silver has already turned to brass"—a highly ambiguous phrase, as noted earlier. Whichever interpretation one chooses, the allusion has a strong aesthetic appeal; it certainly won high praise from its audience.

In the challenge al-Ghādir first spoke in the third person, then switched pronominal reference to the first-person plural, thereby pulling himself more immediately *into* the speech event. Ar-Royshān begins his poem by referring to the sheikh in the third person, then he brings him more immediately into the speech event by addressing him in the second person in the final hemistich ("say . . . , O Nājī"). Whereas the challenge is couched as a direct quotation, only the punch line of the retort is; but the effect of the latter is powerful, for it isolates and highlights the crucial allusion. The use of reported speech (the sheikh is supposed to relay his enemies' words) is also an effective taunt, for it reduces the opponent to serving as a mouthpiece or a carrier of other peoples' opinions, like a *dōshān.*

To this poem al-Ghādir later replied, once again in the same meter and rhyme:

– – ∪ –| – – ∪ –| – – ∪ –| – – ∪ –
mā yinfaᶜ-ak yūshin maᶜā-nā ḍidd-ahā l-antah majann ||
– –[∪] –| – – ∪ – | ∪ – ∪ –| – ∪ –
ʾal-gām titʾamman tilaggiy ad-dabābah shiṣāṣ [final foot short]
– – ∪ –| – –[∪] – | – – ∪ –| – – ∪ –
mā yinfaᶜ-ak sallāl l-al-ḥuḍᶜī wa la l-ᶜamrī haṣan ||
– –[∪] –| – – ∪ ∪? –| – – ∪ – |– – ∪ –
yiblīs w-anta l-laᶜna ᶜalē-k al-laᶜna f-il-gabr al-ḥiwāṣ [second foot long]

The Yūshin will not do you a bit of good. We have something to combat it. You are out of your mind. || The land mine is certain to leave the tank in pieces.
Of no use to you is Sallāl, the lunatic, nor al-ᶜAmrī Ḥasan. || O Satan, you are cursed, and the curse is in a narrow grave.

Whether because of a problem in the original or my own error, I cannot say, but the meter is faulty in two places. As-Sallāl was the first president of Yemen, who headed the republic during the stormy civil war years. Al-ᶜAmrī Ḥasan was the commander in chief of the Republican army (Stookey 1978, 258).

The poet has continued the internal rhyming begun in the original poem (repetition of word-final *-an*). He has also placed the word *majann* (crazy, foolish) in a position in the line where it echoes the insult *talawwan w-altawan,* thereby strengthening his argument that if ar-Royshān considers him to be a traitor, he considers ar-Royshān to be a fool. Furthermore, the parallelism of allusion at the end of the poem is continued in the reference to the curse of the narrow grave. But this poem does not match its provoker in poetic brilliance. Indeed, it deteriorates into name-calling and cursing, which, as we know from the *bālah* performance, is dishonorable, a harbinger of bloodshed.

To summarize, whereas in the *bālah* the routine of challenge and response is organized among the turns of a performance, in *zāmil* poetry this exchange is achieved among individual poems. This dialogue is subject to fairly precise conventions of meter and rhyme. More important, however, is the ability of the poet to pick up unconventional (nonobligatory) aspects of poetic form that are hidden, as it were, in an utterance—including internal rhyme, alliteration, sound symbolism, and the parallelism of reported speech and allusion—and use them to best his opponent.

Now that we have some idea of the aesthetic structure of the *zāmil* poem, let us probe the use of this genre in the war dispute mediation by considering an actual case study. I will be concerned, as in the chapter on the *bālah,* with developing a certain argument about the relationship of poetry to tribal culture, but I will also delve into the question of how power, not just the person, is constituted in poetic composition.

7

Power, Poetry, and Persuasion

What Western peoples might find strange, Khawlānī tribesmen take for granted, namely, that politics and poetics are inseparable. I have argued elsewhere for a reconceptualization of power in terms of persuasion rather than in terms of force, as it is usually conceived of in the literature on Middle Eastern tribal societies (Caton 1987b). In this chapter I will demonstrate the connection between the art of composing poetry and the rhetoric of persuasion. At the heart of this demonstration is the case of a dispute mediation involving two Khawlānī tribes during the course of which dozens of *zāmil* poems were composed. To analyze the poetry as a form of persuasive rhetoric requires some basic analytical concepts, which I cull from the writings of Kenneth Burke on the concept of identification, from Aristotle on rhetoric and discourse, and from James Fernandez on metaphor.

Persuasion and Rhetoric Defined

Burke's Concept of Persuasion as Identification

Burke's particular contribution to the study of rhetoric in his *Rhetoric of Motives* (1969b) is his idea of *identification*. Persuasion, according to Burke, logically entails conflict, for if actors are in perfect accord with each other, they do not have to be persuaded. To overcome conflict, actors have to see that they are in fact "consubstantial" with each other—that they share a common worldview and motivations or are otherwise part of the same moral community—by agreeing to *identify* with the images of themselves that they present to each other. If I present myself as an honorable person and my audience agrees to accept me as such, then we are consubstantial and have a basis for agreement. Note that identification is more than simple attribution of some quality (e.g. "He is an aggressive person"); it is the willing acceptance of that attribution by the actor, with the consequent sociopolitical implications (e.g. "He must curb his aggressiveness").

Burke's formulation of rhetoric in terms of identification is useful here for at least two reasons. First, it squarely situates the problem of rhetorical appeal within the problem of sociopolitical order (and not just economic advantage as in, say, advertising, which is only comprehensible within a larger system of capitalist competition and hence conflict in the sociopolitical order). It is from this vantage point that I want to examine the problem of the rhetorical use of poetry in Khawlān, that is, as a problem of political power. Second, according to Burke's analysis of identification, actors voluntarily *make themselves over* into the image of themselves expressed in the utterance. This way of looking at identification links persuasion with the construction of self, which was broached in the previous chapter. In other words, the creation of power now becomes integrated with the construction of self as an emergent phenomenon in social action.

Identification and Aristotle's Rhetoric

Immediately relevant is the discussion in Aristotle's *Rhetoric* on the means of persuasion. The first means is identification with the character or ethos of the speaker.[1] But the moral probity of the speaker is not sufficient for persuasion, which Aristotle insists is only effected by the speaker through his *discourse.*[2] When we examine the first stage of the dispute, we will see how the sheikhly mediator constructs himself and his addressees, the contestants, as honorable tribesmen by the way he speaks to them. Identifying with such an honorable image, the plaintiff may be persuaded to arbitrate rather than go to war.

In the second means "persuasion is effected through the audience, when they are brought by the speech into a state of emotion" (Aristotle 1932, 9). That is to say, the audience may be moved by feelings of shame, joy, anger, remorse, laughter, love, hatred, disdain, respect, and indignation, which will impel it to behave in the way the speaker desires. Aristotle remarks that this is probably the most common way writers on rhetoric have studied the tactics of persuasion, and the field has changed little since his time. In the first stage of the mediation we are about to examine, the sheikh is trying to instill in the listener an attitude of respect (*iḥtirām*) toward his person in order to then move that listener to acquiesce to his request.

Third, Aristotle writes that "persuasion is effected by the arguments, when we demonstrate the truth, real or apparent, by such means as inhere in particular cases" (Aristotle 1932, 9). It is clear that Aristotle viewed argument as the most significant means of persuasion, and his concept of enthymemes is useful in understanding how argumentation proceeds. Enthymemes are like syllogisms in philosophy except that their propositions are drawn not from exact science but from "common knowledge" and "accepted opinions" (Aristotle 1932, 6) or from "things contingent and uncertain such as human actions and their consequences" (Aristotle 1932, 5). Since they are founded on opinions or historical circumstance, enthymemes cannot yield an absolute demonstration of certainty or truth and are thereby different from true, dialectical syllogisms. Elsewhere in the same text Aristotle calls these opinions *topics* or *commonplaces,* which he presumes vary from culture to culture (the commonplaces in Sparta are not quite the same as those in Athens) and yet have a certain universal appeal, both in terms of content (e.g. everyone views death as undesirable) and in terms of logical form (e.g. in quantitative relations more of a good thing is better than less). These opinions are not in themselves persuasive, however, unless they are cast in the logical form of a proposition, such as, If we are honorable men [opinion] and honorable men do not bargain with terrorists [opinion], then we do not bargain with terrorists. The syllogism need not be expressed in such literal and explicit form. More often it is cast as a metaphor because metaphor is more appealing to the listener. I will expand on this point when I examine the nature of metaphor shortly.

Style is Aristotle's fourth means of persuasion. Any argumentation in rhetoric (as opposed to the ideal of dialectic) must be couched in a certain style "since it is not enough to know what to say—one must also know how to say it" (Aristotle 1932, 182). As Burke rightly emphasizes, it is at this juncture of the discussion in *Rhetoric* that Aristotle merges rhetoric with matters he had covered separately in his *Poetics* (as "pure" form or poetry for poetry's sake). Now he becomes engrossed in poetic form for use in political relations.

(There is yet another way in which poetic form works its spell; namely, certain meanings are always *covertly* created in poetic form and work subliminally to influence thought. Hence the covert ideological power of aesthetic form; it is no wonder that in so many cultures, Khawlān included, poetry is held in awe as a kind of wizardry.)

James Fernandez on Metaphor

Of poetic devices used in the fourth means of persuasion "it is metaphor above all else that gives clearness, charm, and distinction to the style" (Aristotle 1932, 187). James Fernandez's original and highly provocative notions of metaphor (Fernandez 1986) build on Aristotle's but go beyond them in a way that is useful for anthropologists.

Fernandez defines metaphor in general as "a strategic predication upon an inchoate pronoun (an I, a you, a we, a they) which makes a movement and leads to performance. . . . The metaphors in which we are interested make a movement. They take their subjects and move them along a dimension or a set of dimensions" (Fernandez 1986, 8, 12).[3] The strategic predication involves the placing of I and other pronouns on continua along which they can be moved. Fernandez explicitly invokes Aristotle here. Metaphor figures in rhetorical strategy as follows: "If you aim to adorn a thing, you must take your metaphor from something better in its class; if to disparage, then from something worse" (Aristotle 1932, 187). An example of Aristotle's proportional metaphor would be *Reagan : America :: leader : people :: parasite : host population,* from which one could say either that Reagan is a leader of his people or Reagan is a parasite of the people. Fernandez observes, "Each of these terms is a metaphor—the one abusive, the other ennobling" (Fernandez 1986, 18). And he paraphrases Aristotle when he explains that "we are generally inspired to metaphor for purposes of adornment or disparagement" (Fernandez 1986, 10). This praise or blame is obviously connected with feeling, Aristotle's second means of persuasion.

According to Fernandez, culture "is a quality space of 'n' dimensions or continua," and society "is a movement about of pronouns within this space" (Fernandez 1986, 13). The "quality space" is reminiscent of Aristotle's topoi with the exception that Fernandez would emphasize feelings or attitudes over ideas in culture, a marked departure from most symbolic anthropology (though that view is becoming more acceptable as a result of heightened interest in the anthropology of emotion). Metaphor is a crucial device in this movement of the self from one quality to another: "Language has devices of representation at its disposal, mainly metaphor, by which pronouns can be moved about—into better or worse position—in quality space. Social life from the perspective of this model is the set of those transactions by which pronouns, the foci of identity, change their feeling tone—the sense of potency, activity, and goodness attached to them" (Fernandez 1986, 13). Society becomes the arena of communication (what we might call pragmatics) in which this movement is accomplished.

The strength of this notion of metaphor lies not only in its remarkable subtlety and semiotic richness but also in its insistence on the importance of feeling tone and of the fact that metaphor entails not just intellection (or seeing) but also action. But the present study deals with the use of metaphor in the art of persuasion, an art ideally practiced in voluntary social action (for it makes no sense to persuade someone who can be compelled).[4] Burke is correct here, I believe, in invoking the concept of identification, for metaphoric images in rhetoric only *invite* actors to make themselves over into the (iconic) image. It is a question of voluntary action, where the actors allow themselves to be transformed by identifying with an image.

Summarizing, one can say, following Burke, that persuasion logically occurs in a situation of conflict, where those who are doing the persuading try to get the other to identify with them and thereby achieve commonality or agreement. This process can only succeed where the actors in the conflict are free to choose to identify or not to identify with others; one does not persuade in a situation of coercion. Various means can be employed to make the identification attractive, appealing, reasonable, or otherwise desirable. Following Aristotle fairly closely, I have delineated four such means: (1) the persuasive character (self) of the speaker, though it is *in* his speaking that his self is constructed (in ways already discussed having to do with poetic performance); (2) attempts by the speaker to arouse the emotion of his audience, which will impel it to act in a certain way; I take this means to be the traditional concept of oratory; (3) the argument, which is a kind of syllogism based on certain cultural presuppositions of reality (enthymemes) and which appeals because of its logic; and (4) poetic form (or what we have been calling parallelism), especially metaphor, because aesthetic form makes the underlying message appealing and signals covert meanings that work subliminally in the awareness of the auditor. With these basic analytical concepts, let us now attempt an analysis of *zāmil* poetry as persuasion in a Khawlān dispute mediation.

A Case Study

For the sake of clarity I have divided the dispute into three stages, though I hasten to add that these are my divisions as suggested by the data rather than ones Khawlānīs used in discussing the dispute. In the first stage actors attempt to construct themselves as honorable selves, an argument I have already made with respect to *bālah* poetry. They do so through a variety of means, including a show of physical force—what has come to be called *feuding* in the ethnographic literature—and the challenge-and-retort routines of poetry. In the second stage of the dispute the actors accept mediation of their differences; at this point they begin to use poetry to try to persuade the audience of the moral rightness of their position. This stage is really the heart of the mediation process. The third stage is the agreement of all parties to a general reconciliation or a collapse of the negotiation into violence.

In the dispute a fascinating dialectic is thus apparent between actual warfare or attempted coercion, on the one hand, and the symbolization of violence (in shows of force or verbal conflict), on the other. This dialectic has been anticipated in the *bālah* performance, but whereas there it was a game, here it is real life. As the dispute enters each new phase of mediation, more and more parties of the region become involved until the ceiling has been reached and there is nowhere else to turn except to the state. That option is undesirable, for intervention by the central government threatens the autonomy of Khawlān. Therefore, enormous pressure is brought to bear on the contestants to settle their differences (or at least shelve them) before their dispute threatens the political stability of the entire region.

Let us recall the ideal of self held up to the groom in the *bālah* performance. Honor must be constructed through a controlled (or stylized) act that *represents* violence but ought not to descend to it. When provocation goes too far, when name-calling threatens to disrupt the poetry of action, the culprit is reprimanded. So too in the case of the dispute mediation, where the stakes are much higher. The party that refuses to mediate threatens to destroy the game of violence and hence the whole social order.

As the discussion of the dispute proceeds, I will have occasion to bring up other points regarding the nature of mediation, the importance of persuasion, the crucial relationship of power to persuasion (rather than the threatened use of coercive force as it has often been understood in the ethnographic and theoretical literature on the Middle East), and, most significantly, the various ways in which poetry is used in this complex political context.

Stage One: The Reconstruction of Honor

At the end of 1981 a tribal dispute broke out between two of the seven tribes of Khawlān, the Banī Shadād and the Banī ʾAʿrūsh. In contention was a meadow both sides had claimed as pasture for their sheep. The Banī Shadād were accustomed to grazing their sheep on this meadow near the tribal border, referred to in the poetry as *ash-shaghāb,* generally ignoring their neighbors, who claimed the land as their own and wanted to have the matter settled through arbitration. One day the ʾAʿrūsh shot and killed their sheep, which were grazing in the meadow under contention. Rightly interpreting this aggression as an affront to their tribal honor and wealth, the Banī Shadād declared war. Almost immediately after the first shots rang out, messengers were sent to the surrounding districts to summon the intermediaries from among the leading sheikhs and religious dignitaries.

The first to arrive was Ḥusēn ʿAlī al-Gāḍī, sheikh of the Suhmān tribe. He marched with his delegation of fellow tribesmen to the meeting place (*masrākh*) of the plaintiff, the Banī Shadād. Though I did not witness this scene, I suspect it was like many others I observed (see chapter 3). The men must have tramped in rows along the course of the wadi, bearing rifles on their shoulders and delivering a poetic chant in a high-pitched tenor. No doubt their steady advance was being silently, if intently, watched by the Banī Shadād, some of whom ringed the defensive positions on the mountaintops and others of whom were forming a delegation to greet them at the assembly place. These are the words of al-Gāḍī's poem:

– – ∪ –| – –[∪] – |– – ∪ –| ∪ – – – ∪–|
1. bā nādiy al-masrākh yikhbir l-ī banī shadād || lā yihmilū
– – ∪ –|–
gadr an-nazāyil
– – ∪ – | – – ∪ –| – –[∪] –| ∪ – – – ∪ –|
w-at-tafrigah mā shī maʿā-nā khēr f-il-farād || w-al-ʿurfa l-ah
– – ∪ –|–
ʿaddat wasāyil

I call out to the *masrākh* to inform the Banī Shadād on my account, || do not slight the honor (*gadr*) of the guests.
Disunity—there is nothing good for us that comes from separation, || and tribal law (*ʿurf*) has numerous means.

To appreciate the grandness of the sheikh's opening gambit, I must explain that he brought to the assembly place some virgin women, who represent the honor of the Suhmān tribe. It is well known in the Middle East that one way in which a man's honor is measured is by the control he exercises over female relatives. Women are segregated from males and are required to avoid, if at all possible, even being seen in public. Hence, the sheikh must have been signaling that he trusts the Banī Shadād; he would not risk exposing his women to ignominy, and thereby jeopardize his honor, if he were not positive of their honorable intentions. He thus was not only making an explicit statement about his own honor; he was also presupposing an equally magnificent honor on the part of the plaintiff and thereby hoping to coax the latter into negotiations. The second line is a corollary to this argument. The sheikh reminds the Banī Shadād that their intransigence in the matter of war threatens to disunite the group, a needless consequence because tribal law provides alternative, peaceful solutions to conflict. The honor-bound tribesman is obligated to mediate.

The Banī Shadād were unwilling to sue for peace and rejected the sheikh's mediation. After repeated efforts to get the tribe to accept a truce (*ṣulḥ*), all of which failed, al-Gāḍī issued the following *zāmil:*

∪ – ∪ –| – –[∪] –| – – ∪ –|– – – ∪
2. ʿagāyir[5] as-suhmān jāt-ak w-al-makhālif[6] || lā[7] wasṭa
–| – – ∪ –
masrākh-ak nazīl

– – ⏑ –| – – ⏑ –| – – ⏑ –|– – –
ṭaff al-ḥarūbah w-ibdhal aṣ-ṣāyib[8] wa nāsif || mā ḥad[9]
⏑ –| – – ⏑ –
min al-madhhab yamil

The sacrificial cows of the Suhmān have come to you as have the women || to the midst of your *masrākh* descended.
Extinguish the wars, strive to follow good and be moderate; || no one will deviate from the principles [of tribal law].

The first line alludes to an event that took place on the sheikh's arrival at the meeting place. After having sacrificed some cows as a token of his solemn pledge to mediate the dispute impartially, he had broken his dagger (*jambiyyah*) over his knee and thrown it onto the carcasses, a dramatic gesture asserting his honor. The strategy of the rhetoric is transparent: remind the plaintiff of one's honor and hint that a refusal to negotiate risks an offense. The second line is an obvious admonition to follow the dictates of tribal law as well as a pledge to interpret that law impartially.

The Banī Shadād at first did not reply to al-Gāḍī's poems. Such a silence can either mean that the addressee is incapable of taking up the challenge because he is devoid of poetic talent (a condition impossible to imagine among Yemeni tribesmen who assiduously cultivate an ethos of poetry) and is thereby dishonored; or, more likely, it signifies a refusal to take up the challenge, which is a serious insult. In short, the Banī Shadād had no choice but to respond.

– – ⏑ –| – – ⏑ –| – –[⏑]–|– ⏑ – ⏑ –|
3. ḥayyā bi-man jā min gubal khawlān ʿārif[10] || wa muḥtarim
– – ⏑ –
sinnat bakīl
– – ⏑ –| – – ⏑ –| – – ⏑ –|– – – ⏑ –|
man jā wa ʿād-ah bā yiraddid kulla sārif[11] || w-illā fa-hū
– – ⏑ –
ʿābir sabīl

Greetings to those who have come from the tribes of Khawlān as experts in tribal law || and respect the traditions of the Bakīl.
He who comes intending to reproach every wrongdoer [is welcome]; || otherwise, he can continue on his way.

Refusing to believe that al-Gāḍī was impartial, the Banī Shadād's strategy is to show him to be unfair in singling them out for rebuke when their opponents had, after all, started the conflict by firing on the sheep. In their opinion he has disqualified himself as an effective and fair mediator. The end result ought to be that the two sides continue fighting so that the Banī Shadād can redeem their honor.

Note that this poem reproduces the meter and rhyme scheme of the sheikh's poem. By so doing, it frames the previous *zāmil* as a provocative challenge to which it is the retort. By challenging the Banī Shadād in the first place, the sheikh has honored them, for he has thereby made them his equal, and, as the logic of the dialectic would have it, the tribe has in turn honored the sheikh by taking up his challenge. By at least reciprocating, if not actually topping, his opening gambit, they have demonstrated themselves to be equals in honor.

The above interpretation strongly suggests that honor is at stake in this routine of challenge and retort; but what I wish to argue is that it would be a mistake of cultural interpretation to reduce it to honor alone. Honor is involved only as a means to an end, not as an end in itself. Both parties in the dispute, the combatants and the mediators, appeal to the value of honor to make their own positions more persuasive. Furthermore, it is by framing their encounter or rapprochement as honorable that they are able to enter into negotiations in the first place, for persuasion entails the equality of the parties involved (otherwise the threat of coercion would be imminent). The Banī Shadād felt dishonored by the treacherous act of the ʾAʿrūsh, but the sheikh has now bestowed honor on them by performing a glorious deed, so that they may enter the negotiations as equals. The honorable self is constituted in these acts, not for its own sake, but to make possible a negotiation.

Having been snubbed by the Banī Shadād, the sheikh's delegation chanted this poem:

⏑ – ⏑ –| – – ⏑ –| – – ⏑ – ⏑ –| – –[⏑]
4. barāya-kum w-iḥnā tawakkalnā || wa khāṭir[12] al-masrākh
–| – –
w-aṣḥāb-ah
– – ⏑ –| – –[⏑] –|– – – –⏑ –| – – ⏑ –| – –
yā kam ʿala l-masrākh nādēnā || jīnā li-ṣōt al-ʿizza ṭallāb-ah

Farewell, we are putting our trust in God; || goodbye to the meeting place and its proprietors.

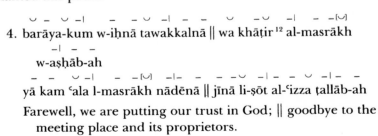

How many times have we called out to the meeting place ||
demanding an honorable reply.

The tone is clearly one of exasperation with the Banī Shadād, who in the estimation of the Suhmān have failed to act honorably by steadfastly refusing al-Gāḍī's offer of mediation. As soon as the sheikh departed, war broke out anew. The fighting lasted several days, but in spite of their superior numbers the Banī Shadād were once again unsuccessful in their bid to dislodge the ʾAʿrūsh from their defensive positions along the border.

Stage Two: Metaphorical Syllogisms

Khawlān was now sending other delegations to the assembly place in the wake of al-Gāḍī's failure. Among them were the Āl Shadēg, one of the important sheikhly houses of the region; delegations from Wadi Maswār, one of the agriculturally richest and politically most prominent areas of Khawlān; some of the *sādah* from the administrative center of Jihānah; and others. Given their eminence and influence, these personages could not easily be ignored by either of the contenders, who had to discontinue fighting long enough at least to listen to their exhortations.

In this second stage of the mediation process, characterized by the involvement of an ever-widening circle of negotiators, delegations arrived chanting poems in which they tried to persuade the Banī Shadād to mediate. Here is the poem chanted by the Shadēgī contingent as it marched onto the meeting place:

– ∪ –|– ∪ –| – ∪ –| – – – ∪ –|– ∪ –| – ∪

5. yā salāmī malā fajjat[13] al-wādī || yā gabāyil ʿal al-ʿizza

– | – –

mashbūḥah[14]

– ∪ –| –[∪]–| – ∪ –| – – – ∪ – | – ∪ –| –∪ –|

sharʿ al-aṣḥāb lā gad bada l-bādī || bā yigaddim ʿalā ṣāḥib-ah

– –

rūḥ-ah

O greetings [as great as] what fills the wadi's gap, || O tribes
clutching onto honor:
The custom of friends, if anything happens, || is for the one
friend to give the other his life.

Again the first line includes an appeal to tribal honor, which, it is hoped, will induce the two sides to settle their differences peacefully. But the second line adopts a new strategy. The poet, according to my informants, reminds the two sides that people sharing a common border are presupposed to be friends. In other words, the rhetorical appeal to the adversaries is now in the name of friendship; friends do not kill each other—they die for each other in a common cause—and therefore the two opponents should work toward peace. This meaning is nicely echoed in the alliterative phrase *ṣāḥib-ah rūḥ-ah,* which literally translates as "his friend his life"; the parallelism of sound (/ḥ/ and /ah/) and of syntax (possessive noun phrases) subtly suggests the interdependence of friends and one's own life. The effect of poetic form in such cases is covert and probably entirely unconscious, but not for that reason any less powerful an influence on the audience.

Metaphors seem to proliferate in the poetry of all parties at this stage. The Maswārī delegation chanted this poem:

– ⏑ –|– – ⏑ –| – ⏑ – – ⏑ –|– – ⏑ –|
6. yā gabāyil f-il-wasaṭ wāsiṭah || lā tadhillū f-il-baṭūn
– ⏑ –
ash-shaghāb
– ⏑ –| – – ⏑ –| – ⏑ – – ⏑ –| – – ⏑ –|
man yijāmil yiltaʿan shārib-ah || man taʿaywaj [15] nirdim-ah [16]
– ⏑ –
l-iṣ-ṣawāb

O tribes, in the middle [there are] intermediaries; || do not go astray inside the boundary of *shaghāb.*
Whoever is one-sided [or shows favor], his beard is cursed [i.e. his honor is impugned], || and he who deviates we will push him onto the correct path.

The beginning of the poem reminds the tribes that there are intermediaries present among them; therefore, they are honor-bound to listen to their exhortations. Then they are admonished not to go astray inside the boundary by, one presumes, ignoring the advice of the intermediaries. The phrase *go astray* hints at a metaphor. The intermediaries are to the warring tribes as shepherds are to their flocks—a political metaphor commonly used in the tribal rhetorical tradition to refer to governance. Certainly, the last half-line states that the opponents in the case have not acted according to tribal law and that if they continue to flout the law, they will be pushed onto the correct path—a clear allusion to the use of force, but this only under extraordinary circumstances.

When the religious elite of Jihānah arrived to help mediate the dispute, one of the Khawlānī sheikhs composed this poem:

– ∪ –| ∪ –[∪] –| –[∪] –| – – ∪– – ∪ –| – –[∪]
7. yā banī shadād y-aʿrūsh ḥill al-mishkilah || warridū mā kān
–| –[∪] –|– – ∪ –
burhān ḥākī f-ish-shaghāb
– ∪ –| – – ∪ –| –[∪] –| – – ∪– –[∪] –| – – ∪
kulla ḥad mutwassal inkār nukrī kāmilah || gāl milk-ah gabla
–|– ∪ –| – – ∪–
mā yinzil ar-rābiʿ kitāb

O Banī Shadād, O ʾAʿrūsh, solve the problem, || provide something as evidence that will speak about *ash-shaghāb* [the name of the tribal boundary].
Each person has prepared a complete and absolute denial; || he has said it was his property before [God] revealed the fourth sacred book.[17]

Here the rhetorical appeal is to the legal evidence that will establish the validity of the adversaries' claim to the land. This evidence is needed because, as the poet points out, both sides say their rights to the land are legitimate and ancient. Now legal deeds must back up claims.

Yet another poem composed during this second stage of the dispute warns of *tafrigah* (separatism, breaking away from the group):

– ∪– –| – ∪–| – ∪– – – ∪– –| – ∪ –|
8. yā salāmī y-al-wajīh al-malimmah || yā majiddah l-il-gubal
– ∪ – –
f-is-sadādī
– ∪ – –| – ∪ –| – ∪ – – – ∪ – –| – ∪ –|
khābirū-nā f-il-ʾamūr al-mihimmah || lā nugā shī mithla ṭēsh
– ∪ – –
al-jirādī

Greetings, O men of the assembly, || O you who are striving earnestly to stop the tribes from fighting.
Negotiate with us the important matters; || let us not be like the locust that wanders away from the swarm.

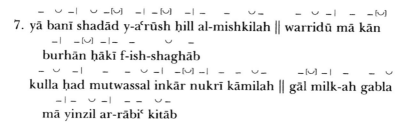

It is the last hemistich, containing the crucial metaphor of the locust, that warns against separatism. The allusion was intended for the Banī Shadād, since the general consensus of Khawlān was that this tribe was opposing the will of the entire region by persisting in a recalcitrant course of war against the ʾAʿrūsh. Note that *locust* is a laudatory epithet precisely because the insect is a feared predator (victorious armies on the move are sometimes described in the poetry as swarms of locusts). Once an individual locust wanders away from the swarm, however, it loses its way and perishes. The message to the Banī Shadād could not have been clearer.

Let us now consider the arguments of the opponents as expressed in their poetry. The ʾAʿrūsh had a stronger legal claim than the Banī Shadād to the boundary meadow because they could furnish documents such as deeds entitling them to the land as well as witnesses who swore that the border had belonged to the ʾAʿrūsh for as long as anyone could remember. For their part the Banī Shadād argued that the ʾAʿrūsh had no right to fire on their sheep, thereby provoking a war, and that to reinstate their honor, they would have to continue fighting. They too had witnesses to testify to their legal claims; and though they could not furnish written documents corroborating the oral testimony, they argued that the very presence of their sheep grazing on the land was proof that it belonged to them—an argument of possession by use.

The right of property is determined by sale or by ancient inheritance. This principle was well expressed in a poem composed by the ʾAʿrūsh and relayed to the intermediaries:

– ∪ – –| – ∪ –| – ∪ – –| – ∪ – – ∪ –
9. yā wisāṭah gayda-kum gāda-nī l-iṣ-ṣāyibī || w-al-ghawā
–| –[∪] –|– ∪ – –|– ∪ –
maddī-h dhillah w-il-akhḍā l-iṭ-ṭamūʿ
– ∪ – –|– ∪ –|– ∪ – –|– ∪ – – ∪ –
milka jadd-ī baʿda sīd-ī wa milk-ī baʿd ab-ī || w-al-jadūd
–| – ∪ –| – ∪ – –| – ∪ –
al-māḍiyah min gafā sām ibna nūḥ

O intermediaries, your order has guided me to the right path. || I will not give in to fear, no, nor submit to the greed [of the opponent].
[It was] my grandfather's property after my ancestor's, and

> my property after my father's; || [and so it goes] down the past generations all the way to Shem, the son of Noah.

In the first line of the poem the ʾAʿrūsh accept the exhortations of the intermediaries for both sides to do right (*ṣāyib,* as opposed to *ʿāwij* or *ʿawāj* [deviation from right]) according to the dictates of customary tribal law. In this manner they hope to show themselves to be compliant with the general consensus of the region. They also make clear that they will not be cowed by superior numbers among the Banī Shadād, who, they argue, would like to force them to withdraw their land claims. In other words, they imply that the Banī Shadād are acting like tyrants by trying to coerce the opposition into submission, thereby portraying their enemy as someone who threatens the egalitarian ideology. They especially will not give up when they believe greed to be motivating their opponents' desire to fight. Then, in the second line comes the claim of priority by ancient right of inheritance. The ʾAʿrūsh are a noble tribe and trace their descent all the way back to the "original" Arabs of Yemen—Shem, the son of Noah, and his progeny. Thus, the claim of inheritance is backed by prestige lineage. Or, to put the argument in other words, the ʾAʿrūsh are the descendants of the "original" and "noblest" of the Arabs, and if the latter determined the tribal boundaries and willed the partition to future generations, then their right to the land is unchallengeable.

Aesthetically this poem stands out in the corpus. In the first hemistich the /g-d/ alliteration and the internal /ī/ rhyme bind the line together and underscore the concept of "your order has guided me to the right path." A similar effect is achieved in the first hemistich of the next line through the syntactic parallelism that twice links "property" and "after." In this line too the repeated internal /ī/ rhyme draws the hemistich together as a unit and focuses the listener's attention on it. According to my informants, this poem was aesthetically and rhetorically the most effective I had collected in the dispute.

Of course, the ʾAʿrūsh were not alone in pressing their land claims on the basis of ancient inheritance. The Banī Shadād did so too. As one of the intermediaries quipped, "Each side has said it was his property before God revealed the fourth sacred book." The next rhetorical stance of the disputants had to be based on evidence substantiating each side's claim to the land. In response to the poem from the intermediaries enjoining the adversaries to come forward with such proof, the Banī Shadād composed this poem:

– – ∪ –| – – ∪ –| – – ∪ –| – – – –

10. yā ḥaḍrat al-ḥākim[18] wa yā ḥaḍrat gubal khawlān || mā ʿād

∪ –| – – ∪–| –

nubā daʿwā w-ijābah

– – ∪ –| – – ∪ –| – – ∪ –| – –

w-al-ḥadda mithl ash-shamsa w-an-naʿjah hiy al-burhān ||

– – ∪ –| – – ∪ –| –

dhī fattaḥat l-il-ḥarba bāb-ah

O honorable *ḥākim* [governor-judge] and honorable tribes of Khawlān, || we no longer want challenge and retort.
The border is like the sun, and the sheep are the evidence || which opened the door of war.

The expression *daʿwā w-ijābah* refers to the poetic dialogues of challenge and retort that the parties to the dispute were bandying about and which had clearly exhausted this poet's patience. The second line presents a rather unusual simile, "The border is like the sun," which I had to ask my informants to explain. They insisted that it meant the border is plainly visible to everyone—like the sun, a given, natural, and incontestable fact. The rhetorical sleight of hand here is to move the tribal border from the world of society, in which it is man-made and artificial (and therefore subject to negotiation), into the realm of intractable nature (and thereby place the issue beyond human politics and argumentation). The poet then follows up this rhetorical maneuver with the assertion that "the sheep are the evidence"—that is, because the sheep were grazing on the land, they had a right to be there, and their unjustified slaughter was the just cause of war.

This verse was not a convincing piece of sophistry to the ʾAʿrūsh, who responded thus:

– – ∪ –| – –[∪] –|– –[∪] –| – – – –

11. ḥayy aḷḷah al-baddāʿ mōla t-tēh w-aṭ-ṭughyān || man gad

∪ –| ∪ – ∪ –| –

fugid min-ah ṣawāb-ah

– – ∪ –| – – ∪ –| – – ∪ –| – – ∪

ʾabrazta burhānī mikattab w-ash-shahūd aʿyān || wa

– ∪ –| – – ∪ –| –

ʾajza-kum kull-an[19] darā bi-h

Greetings to the poet, the epitome [lit. the lord] of arrogance
and tyranny; || (greetings) to him who has lost his reason.
I have submitted written evidence and eyewitnesses; || of
your failure everyone knows.

Note that the response conforms to the aesthetic structure of the previous poem. The joke is that by imitating the original, the poet has framed the two responses as a challenge-and-retort routine, of which the Banī Shadād poet had claimed to have had his fill. However, this is only the first antagonistic thrust, for the poet next accuses his opponent of being arrogant and tyrannical because he persists in a course of action that flouts tribal consensus. Then the poet tries to clinch the argument with the observation that the ʾAʿrūsh have made good their legal claims to the land, presenting written documents and witnesses; the allusion to failure in the last hemistich probably refers to the lack of evidence on behalf of the Banī Shadād's claims to the land as well as their inability to usurp it in spite of their superior fighting power.

By topping their opponent with this deliberately provocative riposte, the ʾAʿrūsh in a sense precipitated another round of fighting with the Banī Shadād. But this latest conflagration did not appreciably change the situation, for the Banī Shadād failed to make the ʾAʿrūsh budge from their position.

Stage Three: "Resolution"

By now the ranks of the intermediaries had swelled to include all the major tribes of Khawlān. Once the entire region becomes involved in a dispute mediation, the pressure on both sides to compromise becomes very great, for there is essentially no other recourse for peaceful resolution of the conflict except the intervention of sheikhs from another confederation or the central government, which is not desirable if the region is to maintain its autonomy. Before such intervention the tribes acting as intermediaries will collectively lean on the recalcitrant parties to wring from them a mediated settlement. What we expect to see in this stage, then, is a consensus on the part of the intermediaries concerning the resolution of the case—that is, some judgment as to who is guilty, what the fines should be, and so forth.

At this stage the drama is at its height. The Banī Shadād, in our example, were defying the consensus of the region as a whole by refusing to accept an arbitrated settlement that would find them at fault. If they refused to compromise, the region would have no choice but to go to war against them, and because of the Banī Shadād's power, they might be able to withstand a general assault on their territories and avoid a rout. In other words, the punitive action might be protracted and not particularly productive. On the other hand, the Banī Shadād might only be bluffing; that is, they might only attempt to push the dispute to the edge of the abyss and then withdraw, hoping thereby to restore their wounded pride and also win the most advantageous settlement possible.

In the tribal councils the main weight of criticism had apparently fallen on the Banī Shadād for having steadfastly refused to accept a judgment from the intermediaries and opting in the last stage for war. This form of ʿ*awāj* (deviation [from the tribal law code]) came under attack in this poem from the intermediaries:

– – ∪ –|– – ∪ –|– – ∪ –| ∪ – – – ∪ –|– –
12. kāfī ʿawājah yā gabāyil-nā banī shadād || ʾal-ḥarba tālī-ha
∪ –
ṣ-ṣawāb
– – ∪ –| – – ∪ –| – – ∪ –| ∪ – – – ∪ –|
ʾin shī maʿa-k daʿwah ʿidī-h mā yinfaʿ al-ʿadād || shūf al-balā
– – ∪ –
rās ash-shaghāb

Enough recalcitrance, O Banī Shadād; || after war should come adherence to the tribal code.
If you have a challenge to make, give it—crying does not help; || see the distress on top of *shaghāb* [name of the tribal boundary].

The intermediaries are pointing out to the Banī Shadād that the war they waged in retaliation for the killing of their sheep should suffice to cleanse their honor. Now they are honor-bound to abide by the judgment of Khawlān in the dispute. If they persist in their aggressive tactics, their violence can only be interpreted as having an insidious intent. That is, everyone will believe that the Banī Shadād are trying to coerce the ʾAʿrūsh into giving up the boundary land by their use of force, and this action would make them out to be tyrants dictating their will to the rest of the region. No one can be tolerated who betrays such inclinations. In the second line the intermediaries urge the tribe to put forward its allegations against its opponents rather than whining about lost sheep, and they remind the Banī Shadād of the sorrowful consequences of war, which has left several of their men wounded.

But the appeal was to no avail. The intermediaries left the assembly place chanting this poem:

– – ∪ –| – – ∪ –|– – – ∪ –| – –[∪] –|–
13. w-iḥnā tawakkalnā ʿal aḷḷāh || nimshī ʿalā bābūr zājī
– – ∪ –| – – ∪ –| – – – ∪ –| – – ∪ –|–
lā budda-kum mā taʿwazū-nā || w-ad-damma rāyig f-il-miḥājī

We place our trust in God; || we ride in a powerful car.
No doubt you will beseech us || and blood will flow on the battlements.

By the expression "we ride in a powerful car" the intermediaries indicate that they are departing the assembly place by automobile; on a deeper level they allude to tribal government (a car being a symbol of the tribe or state). They are convinced that the Banī Shadād have made a mistake by going to war, for they surely will be beaten by the combined strength of the ʾAʿrūsh and the regional mediators.

The response of the Banī Shadād was haughty, contemptuously dismissing the intermediaries and their adversary, the ʾAʿrūsh:

– – ∪ –| – –[∪]–|– – – ∪ –| – – ∪ –|–
14. ʾaʿmāra-kum lā zād jītū || mā min miḥāḍir-kum birājī
– – ∪ –| – – ∪ –| – – – ∪ –| – – ∪ –|–
jā ʾal-ʿubēdī hū w-al-ajrab || dhī ṣaffa-hum min ṣaffa nājī

Do not ever come back again; || there is no end to your presence here [at the *masrākh*].
Al-ʿUbēdī has come, he and al-ʾAjrab, || whose group is the group of Nājī [bin ʿAlī al-Ghādir].

The two sheikhs, al-ʿUbēdī and al-ʾAjrab, had by this time joined the ranks of the ʾAʿrūsh as allies against the Banī Shadād, who were showing them utter contempt. Notice once again that the meter and rhyme scheme echo exactly the intermediaries' previous poem, thereby framing the exchange as another challenge and retort.

Having been provoked, these two sheikhs had to answer the Banī

Shadād with a *zāmil* of their own. It is a riposte to their riposte; all three poems thus form a chain of exchanges:

– – ⏑?⏑ –| – – ⏑ –|– – – ⏑ –| – – ⏑ –|–
15. lā milka ʿalā shōr al-ʿawājah || w-aḥwasta w-antah kunta zājī
– – ⏑ –| – – ⏑ –|– – – ⏑ –| – – ⏑–|–
ʾal-ḥarba mā hī shī zawājah || shūf ash-sharaf mithl az-zijājī

Do not persist [in heeding] the advice of deviation [from tribal law]; || you have become bowlegged when once you were strong.
War is not a wedding; || see [or beware]: honor is like glass.

The response is unquestionably more artful than its provocation. It is rich in metaphors. For example, when the poet observes, "You have become bowlegged when once you were strong," he is comparing the weakness of a man in the army whose legs are bent and can no longer endure the march with the moral decrepitude of the Banī Shadād. In admonishing that "war is not a wedding," the poet is reminding the Banī Shadād that they should not reenter the fray thinking it will be easy. Finally, he creates a complex metaphor between honor and glass: honor, my informants explained to me, is like a window through which one sees into the tribe's innermost character; honor, like glass, is fragile and easily broken; and once honor is shattered, it cannot be mended. The poet is alluding to the same rhetorical argument raised earlier in the dispute, namely, that it is dishonorable for a tribe to deviate (*taʿawwaj*) from the consensus of the group (in this instance the group being Khawlān). This is a powerful argument, and the Banī Shadād had to heed it carefully. The alliterations of /w/ in the phrase *w-aḥwasta w-antah* and of /sh/ and /f/ in *shūf ash-sharaf* underscore key rhetorical strategies in the poem—a rebuke in the case of the first phrase, an admonition in the case of the second. Note also that the rhyme scheme is more interesting than the one in the original. Together these poetic forms make this *zāmil* a more appealing piece of rhetoric.

Discussion of the Case Study

Each party in the dispute—including the opponents and the various mediators—constructs an ideal self, which it presents to the Other (in this example the whole of Khawlān). The ʾAʿrūsh say that they killed their opponents' sheep because the pasture is theirs; honor dictates that control over one's own domain be exercised, and the ʾAʿrūsh continue to exert control by occupying the meadow. Hence, they interpret their actions not as coercion but as a symbolic show of force connected with honor. The Banī Shadād try to wrest back the land by force, arguing that their actions are also honorable, first because they must avenge the killing of their sheep and second because they are honor-bound to regain control over what is rightfully theirs. Thus, both sides believe themselves to be honorable in resorting to force, and each presents itself to the other as ideal tribesmen.

The mediators, however, believe they are acting as honorable men by intervening, as in fact the tribal code dictates anyone in an impartial position must do. In this fashion they are representing themselves to the opponents as honorable men. At the same time they are holding up to the opponents the ideal of the tribesman who submits to mediation: after he has had a chance to reconstitute his wounded honor by a show of symbolic force, he accepts the verdict of qualified and fair judges regardless of whether he is found at fault.

It appears that the ʾAʿrūsh have land deeds to prove their ownership of the meadow under dispute. The Banī Shadād have used the same meadow for sheep grazing as long as anyone can remember and argue that possession is in this instance proved by use. The mediators clearly favor the arguments of the ʾAʿrūsh, although they will no doubt have to pay some damages to their opponents for the killing of their sheep.[20]

Let me summarize the points that I have tried to make in the case study:

1. Force is best understood as a symbolic statement of honor. As actual or attempted coercion it is criticized, except under very specific circumstances; for example, the intermediaries may try to coerce both sides into accepting a negotiated settlement to avoid the intervention of some party like the state, which would compromise regional autonomy. Such symbolic force does not preclude bloodshed, for in a glorious deed of raiding and warfare there is always the risk of loss of life or limb; but the aim of the bloodshed ought not to be coercion.

2. Symbolic force is a strategy not only by which honor can be regained (as in the first stage of the dispute) but also by which mediation is precipitated. The ʾAʿrūsh fired on the sheep to reconstitute their honor, but they also knew that once they had done so, the sheikhs would arrive to begin the mediation process. What they could not do is fire on the sheep, usurp the meadow, and refuse to mediate, for that would be coercion, and coercion is the first step toward tyranny, a threat to everyone's independence. The Banī Shadād would be allowed, indeed expected, initially to go to war against the ʾAʿrūsh to reconstitute their honor—bloodshed is a necessary risk in pursuit of the glorious deed—but next they would have to submit to arbitration and accept the regional consensus of opinion, even if it were against them. Sometimes parties are slow to accept a settlement because they feel their honor demands that they play hard to get, but everyone more or less knows that that is the reason for their recalcitrance, and it is tolerated for a while. However, the consensus in the above case was that the Banī Shadād's resistance was no longer defensible on the grounds of honor alone, and the interpretation was that they were harboring the darker motive of coercion. The ʾAʿrūsh accused them of that motive in the final verses, thereby making them out to appear as bullies and tyrants, an image that contravenes the ideal of the tribesman. By holding up this image to the Banī Shadād, they hoped to reverse the course on which their opponents were bent and persuade them to accept mediation at last.

3. Symbolic force and mediation are dialectically related in the course of the dispute; one cannot work in the absence of the other. I have already said that the initial show of force is meant to initiate the mediation process, for in the glorious deed both sides have the opportunity of showing themselves to be honorable and may thereby enter into the negotiations as equals. But the exchange of words, as represented in the challenge and retort of poetry, may lead to the shaming of one or the other actor (as indeed happened in the case study), which precipitates another round of symbolic violence out of which emerges a new verbal exchange, this time on a higher level because more mediators are involved.

4. The most important function of poetry in the second stage is to persuade the audience. Honor is created in the act of composing a poem, but it is not the only motive. Each side uses all the rhetorical

weapons at its disposal to present its position in the best possible light, and the intermediaries attempt by the same means to induce the two opponents to stop fighting and start negotiating. To accomplish persuasion, the challenge-and-retort routines can be used as a forensic device: one side presents its argument, the other side answers with a counterargument, and so forth. Issuing a poem as a challenge *invites* a response and thus begins a dialogue by which mediation has a chance of succeeding. The dialogue gives voice to each side and thus assures balance and fairness. The form of speaking here is congenial to the sense of freedom in action the tribal ethos requires.

5. Metaphor is a key element in the art of persuasion of the poetic dialogues. First, metaphor suits the taste for alluring depths of meaning. In using it, and using it well, one creates oneself as an ideal speaker. Second, because of its compactness of expression, metaphor becomes an ideal poetic device for the terse medium of the *zāmil.* Third, metaphor, as is commonly known, allows the perspective in which a particular reality is construed to shift, sometimes radically, so that the object appears wholly different when approached from different angles. Take, for example, the reality of the border between the tribes. In the literal sense a border (*ḥadd*) is what separates, thus creating social and political distinctions. But the sense of separateness can be muted by recasting the term, as one intermediary poet did, as meaning a line demarcating friends, an image that highlights unity, not separateness. The two opponents metaphorize the border in different ways. The ʾAʿrūsh identify the border with ancestral, even mythical, patrimony, as a partition sanctified by tradition, and thus "culturize" it. The Banī Shadād "naturalize" the border by identifying it with the sun, as something not man-made. The sun also has religious associations and therefore is not entirely devoid of the appeal to tradition either. The border becomes what each side metaphorically makes of it to suit its own rhetoric.

More than metaphor, however, is entailed in the persuasiveness of poetic discourse. Alliteration and internal rhyme were used to underline certain key ideas of the text, to channel the thoughts and emotions of the audience in certain directions (see, for example, the discussion of poems 5, 9, and 15). If the poet must know certain conventions in order to enter into this kind of discourse in the first place, he must also be able to manipulate for his own rhetorical purposes certain nonobligatory forms that may have a subliminal or unconscious effect on the listener and hence be all the more potent.

Conclusion

To compose a *zāmil* in accordance with the conventions of the poetic tradition is to have the power to enter into a certain kind of discourse in which honor is created or defended by the poet and persuasion is exercised. This aspect of power has to do with the construction of conventionally recognized verse. But one is a long way from actually controlling the discourse if one cannot exhibit skill in subtly channeling the thoughts and opinions of the audience in certain directions by the manipulation of such poetic forms as alliteration and metaphor. If by these devices one can top the opponent in the exchanges of challenge and retort, or conversely, if one has created a poem that is so artful in its form as not to be easily answered in the exchange, then one has shown oneself able to control the discourse and therefore be more persuasive. One has acquired power in discourse. Tribesmen say of certain poems that they are more persuasive because they are more artful, and the more artful they are, the more powerful their creators become.

This idea can be restated in the more technical language of semiotics. The poem becomes an icon of the discourse to be constructed by the respondents in the mediation and thus is "virtually" metapragmatic (Silverstein 1976, 1981). More exactly, it is an indexical icon in the sense that the poem is *addressed* to a particular other. The addressee has the option to cut off the discourse (to refuse to play the game), but this maneuver is fraught with potential compromises, for it may be construed either as incompetence or as coercion, both of which cause a loss of face. The other option is for the addressee to take up the challenge and obtain power over the opponent by either imitating the original icon or, even better, making the reproduction more vivid. Such a maneuver sends an implicit metapragmatic message to the original challenger, to the effect that he must now continue the process of modeling and intensifying the discourse in this manner or give up his presumption to power in discourse.

When a message is culturally construed as art and simultaneously is composed for communicative events such as mediations that are part of the core institutions of society, then art not only becomes intensely interesting to students of society but can be ignored by them only at their peril. But the case study should have served as a lesson to students of art as well. The poems appeared to be most artful when they were most engaged in political persuasion.

8

The *Qaṣīdah:* Individual Talent and the Cultural Tradition

October 15, 1979

Met Muḥammad Nāṣir al-Gharsī today.

I had gone to the President's house in the morning to rendezvous with the poet but was told that he had left in the President's party and I was advised by the guards to come back in the afternoon. In the afternoon I returned to the Presidential palace with my various letters of introduction in hand, hoping to meet the poet, but again I was told that he was unavailable. As I prepared disappointedly to head back to the city, a jeep pulled up alongside the road and the driver told me *he* was al-Gharsī. I wasn't sure whether to believe him, for I didn't recognize his voice as being the same one I heard on the many tapes the poet has recorded. In fact, the man to whom I was speaking turned out to be a close relative of al-Gharsī who had recognized me from the interview I gave on Ṣanʿā TV and knew all about my project. It would be an honor, he said, to help me with it. The best time to catch Muḥammad would be in the evening and he would drive me now to the poet's house so that I would find my way.

. . . When the time came to visit al-Gharsī, most of Ṣanʿā was without electricity. As luck would have it, though, I managed to find the street and passersby conducted me to the right door. I almost didn't knock. There had been so many disappointments. I knew that this individual was important to my project, but I didn't know whether I could calmly accept another setback, another delay, another foul-up. If I didn't go through with it now, however, I might not have another chance. I knocked. The door was opened and I was ushered into a room filled with people, though the candle light inside was too dim for me to discern the faces clearly. The man who got up to greet me said he was Muḥammad al-Gharsī. I must have stared at him momentarily, studying his voice to see whether indeed this was the man I had been waiting to meet all these weeks, for he sensed my skepticism and laughed, repeating, "Welcome, I am Muḥammad al-Gharsī." I too laughed in embarrassment. So this was the great poet at last!

The above passage is taken from my field diary. Muḥammad al-Gharsī is a Khawlānī who was widely regarded in Yemen as one of the finest tribal poets, if not the finest, which explains why I went to such lengths to meet him. One could go to practically any village to hear wedding *bālah*s, for poetry of that genre is composed universally. And though the *zāmil* is created by a single poet, no one person becomes famous for his *zāmil* compositions since, again, most individuals in the society are competent to compose *zāmil*s. But only some persons compose *qaṣīdah*s, and only a few of these poets are recognized as masters of the genre.

The relationship of the individual and his talent to the cultural tradition, an analysis of which has not been particularly pertinent until now, is the focus of this chapter. By *tradition* I do not mean a historical sequence of works canonized by a culture over a specified period of time, for it should be apparent by now that Yemeni tribesmen do not fetishize the works of their past as much as their literary, urban counterparts or Western societies do. Rather, I have in mind the cultural *practices* of composing a poem belonging to a particular genre; these practices constitute what it means to be a tribesman. In other words, what is transmitted in the tradition is not a body of texts but a repertoire of means—including the verse systems examined in the previous chapters as well as new ones employed in the *qaṣīdah*—by which distinctive poems, recognized as part of a particular genre, may be produced, and the mastery of which signifies that one is a tribesman.

The concept of the individual is perhaps more problematical than that of tradition. By *individual* or *individuality* I do not mean anything *necessarily* unique or distinctive about the creative artist, a Western and peculiarly bourgeois conception of the individual that cannot be assumed to apply to other cultures. Almost any artist, by the transformation of a uniquely personal pattern of experience into a communicable form of art, inevitably adds something novel to the art world.

Perhaps we should start with the Yemeni tribal poet's own conception of himself as an individual. In some important respects this cultural notion of the individual has great affinities with the nineteenth-century romantic idea of artistic genius. I noted in chapter 2 that there are many *shāʿirs* but only a few *hājis*es, that is, only a few poets endowed with enough talent and inspiration to create great works of art. This kind of person is somehow special. Emphasis is also placed in this culture on the emotions of the poet, which are stirred by the troubling events of his epoch, emotions so overpowering that they can lead to madness if they are not somehow disciplined in art. The nineteenth-century romantic artist did not disdain the crudities of politics or the sordidness of business and retreat into an empyrean realm of beauty. The greatest exemplars of the romantic artist—Wordsworth, Blake, Shelley, and Byron—were deeply immersed in the social and political turmoils of their day.

But the differences between the Yemeni tribal concept of the individual and that of the romantic poet are just as great and should not be minimized. The belief of the romantic artist—indeed that of all Western artists—is that the artist seizes on some essential or eternal truth about the world and expresses it in his or her work. Art is the touchstone of *universal* human experience. In Yemeni tribal culture, however, one rarely comes across this idea self-consciously expressed by either artist or public. If anyone has insight into eternal truths, it is the religious sheikh by his study of the Qurʾān, the *ḥadīth* (sayings of the Prophet), and the Sharīʿah (Islamic law), to which he applies himself with his own highly trained critical faculty and imaginative insight. The poet reveals only specific truths: he is concerned with providing solutions to particular and concrete problems of political action. Furthermore, whereas the romantic poet would talk about the particular, the concrete, and even the seemingly inconsequential as the exemplification of universal truth (the world-in-a-grain-of-sand outlook), the Yemeni poet works in just the opposite direction, using for his content not specific images of lived experience so much as allegories from proverbs, Qurʾānic maxims, or tribal lore as means of revealing the truth about the *particular* situation in which he and his community must live. For the Yemeni tribesman, universal truth is not problematical, for it has already been revealed; what *is* problematical is the specific, context-bound truth behind the concreteness of everyday life.

It follows from this differing relationship between the universal and the specific that the poem does not have the same value in the two cultural traditions. The poem of the romantic genius is naturally enough thought to be precious as a text revealing universal truth and therefore is to be preserved. In the Yemeni tribal tradition, however, the poem is not fetishized, because it is intended for use in solving a particular situation and then loses its import as new historical circumstances arise. The emphasis in the Yemeni case is not on the individual poem but on the *poetic system,* which the creative artist can exploit in order to generate a new response to an ever-changing social and political scene. A poem is not recycled from one generation of readers to the next if it no longer speaks to the contemporary social situation. If a poem is obsolete, a new one should be produced in response to new circumstances, crowding out the older poem in people's memories and affections. But God help poetry if tribesmen lose the abstract competence needed to produce new verse rather than imitate the old.

The industrial revolution, with its division of a totality or wholeness of life into discrete specializations or compartmentalizations, deeply affected the realm of art. Now the artist created art and became involved, say, in politics but as separate spheres of activity. True, some romantic poets, particularly Blake, wrote a lot of political poetry, but they were the exceptions. Byron fought in political wars *and* wrote poetry, but he only rarely saw his verse as a means of fighting the political order. In Yemen, however, the artist constitutes his self as a tribesman—and especially his political being—in poetry, primarily because the aesthetic has not yet been separated from other categories of experience. This relationship of art to the rest of life may now be changing, but as yet the Yemeni tribal poet is only on the threshold of modernity.

Though our analytical notion of the individual must draw on the cultural constructs of the individual in a given culture, it cannot be limited to them. The concept of the individual is partly reflexive; that is, a person is whatever that person *thinks* he or she is in a given society. This reflexivity is informed by two distinct symbolic patterns:

the cultural constructs of individuality, and the person's own understanding of his or her pattern of life experiences and how these have constituted him or her as a person in the world. If, for example, someone in our society says of herself that she is a poet, then on the one hand her understanding is informed by the cultural constructs of what it means to be a poet in society and on the other by her own life experiences as a woman of a particular race and class, a configuration of understandings that she shares with only a few other poets in her world.

But self-consciousness is only part of what constitutes individuality. There is also the question of how the person constitutes, or fails to constitute, this sense of self through creative or expressive acts in the world—in other words, freedom or will. Mastery over self-expression is achieved (when it *is* achieved) with, as well as against, the power of other individual wills—with, as well as against, a cultural tradition and material forces. It is never simply an automatic self-fulfillment but the *exertion* of will. In the process of exerting that will, of proclaiming one's freedom, one necessarily encounters the limitations to that freedom, and this discovery necessitates a remolding of one's understanding of self as well as a compromise with recalcitrant materials and personalities one is trying to bend to one's will. The individual, therefore, is someone who has balanced a sense of self with a will to power, on the one hand, and with his or her understanding of the forces that constrain it, on the other.

Having thus defined what I mean by the terms *individual* and *tradition,* I will begin to explore their relationship with a detailed description of the practices by which a *qaṣīdah* poem is created. In this way we will learn the poetic tradition for this genre, as we have for other genres in previous chapters. But we will also see how *individual* poets exploit different possibilities in the verse systems (meter, rhyme schemes, alliterations, sound symbolism, and so forth), thereby extending and transforming the tradition. To bring home this point, I will compare Muḥammad al-Gharsī's poetry with that of some of his closest competitors from Khawlān to see why he is so widely admired. Individual talent means the ability to realize novel patterns *inherent* in the verse system by exploiting that system superbly. In a broader sense, however, the individual talent of al-Gharsī represents a new model of what the *qaṣīdah* should be, a new genre, and hence a re-presentation of the tradition. The consequences of such redefinition go beyond aesthetics to the social construction of self. Al-Gharsī is representing himself as a different kind of tribesman from his closest competitors through the poetic practices he adopts.

But why should al-Gharsī's talent respond to the tradition in this fashion? There are many complex answers to this question—one of the most important surely has to do with his own personality—but I will focus on the one most consonant with sociocultural concerns. Al-Gharsī experienced in his job and his urban environment certain deep and widespread social changes, and in an unself-conscious way his transformation of the tradition is in response to these changes. I will argue that in effect what he is saying by this transformation—as evinced in the new form his *qaṣīdah* takes—is that a new kind of tribesman is needed to come to terms with a modernizing society. His voice, along with the ones to be heard in the next chapter, represents a part of an interesting and continuing ideological dialogue on the theme of tribalism.

The *Qaṣīdah* versus the *Bālah*

As a way of grasping the outlines of the *qaṣīdah* practices, let us consider in detail some of the differences between them and those of the *bālah:*

1. In the *qaṣīdah* the moment of inception is spatially and temporally separated from the moment of reception. Whereas the poet and the audience in the *bālah* are face-to-face, there is a distance between the poet and the receiver of the poem in the *qaṣīdah.* This distance is symbolized in the poem: the poet addresses a messenger, whose duty it is to deliver the poem to its receiver by traveling across a specified geographic space; the receiver may then answer the poem with one of his own and send it via another messenger to the first poet. We can assume that the *mulaḥḥin* (composer of song), given his role, is in most cases the messenger. In the *bālah,* on the contrary, the whole point is to respond directly and almost instantaneously to a challenge.

2. In the *bālah* the composition of the poem is a public spectacle to be enjoyed for its dramatic intensity. In the *qaṣīdah* the act of composition is under scrutiny by no one except the poet.

3. The poetic voice in the *qaṣīdah* is individual, not collective.

Since the poet is physically separated from the receiver of the poem and from an audience, and since it is rare for him to compose a poem jointly with another or to have his verse "edited" by another, the whole aesthetic experience becomes a solitary one. The poet in fact implies this individual voice when he starts the poem with "So-and-so says . . ."—referring to himself as the one who instigates the message and takes full responsibility for it. Later in the poem he declares that his mind and liver (the liver being the seat of the emotions) have become so disturbed by political events that he is moved to compose the poem. How different from the *bālah,* where no one person can take control over, and thus responsibility for, the composition.

4. The sociohistorical situation looms much larger in this genre than in the primarily oral one. This context has a very different relationship to the text-utterance than it has in the Western tradition, for it cannot always, or even often, be understood from what is said in the poem per se. Information on the context has either to be provided by the reciter or to be known in advance.

5. The words of a particular *qaṣīdah* poem are valued for their own sake, and if the poem is a good one, it is thought important to preserve them. In the *bālah,* by contrast, the words are forgotten as soon as the performance is over. Whereas in the past there were professional singers of verse whose task it was to preserve and musically deliver someone's poem (alternatively, a literate tribesman would be asked to write down the poem and then recite it), today the tape recorder has taken over the function of preserving the text-utterance.

6. It becomes possible to talk of an oeuvre in the *qaṣīdah* tradition because the text-utterance is preserved and originates from an individual. Such an attitude toward the verse genre is entirely alien in the *bālah,* where the rules of performance are kept in memory, and not the text-utterance.

The Question of Literacy

It is well known in Arabic studies that the high literary tradition has its own *qaṣīdah,* probably the most prized genre in all of written Arabic poetry. Its roots are in the beautiful pre-Islamic odes, also known as *qaṣīdah*s, which were composed by the ancient tribes of Yemen and the other tribes of Arabia. The tribal *qaṣīdah* is a juncture or point of convergence for the oral and purely tribal tradition and the literate and almost totally urban tradition. A highly literate *sayyid,* for example, once addressed the Khawlān tribes in a classical Arabic *qaṣīdah,* assuming that the tribes would be able to understand him because they also compose this ode. Indeed, one of the tribal poets took responsibility for responding to him. Though there are noticeable differences between the two poems, especially in the language, they were culturally classified under the same genre.

Is the tribal *qaṣīdah,* then, a genre in transition between the purely oral *bālah* and the literary genre of the high tradition? Furthermore, are the differences between the two genres produced by the medium of writing or at least by distancing media of "secondary orality" (such as the tape recorder) (Ong 1982)? Or are they to be attributed to the tribal, oral tradition itself, which simply conceptualizes the poetic experience as a gradient from the poem as a performance to the poem as a text-utterance, with writing or secondary orality being allowed to penetrate the latter end of the continuum, where it is compatible with the aesthetic structure and experience of a nonperformative, but still oral, poem? In other words, one way of formulating the question suggests that writing is crucial to the creation of the *qaṣīdah* and determines its potential forms. The other way suggests that the *qaṣīdah* had always been part of an ancient oral tradition and that writing fits into that process without disruption or distortion, an intervention obviously not possible in the *bālah.*

Support for the view that the *qaṣīdah* is not dependent on writing comes from the fact that many tribal *qaṣṣād*s (composers of the *qaṣīdah*) are illiterate. Al-Gharsī is highly literate; but Muḥsin al-Bowraᶜī, an old Khawlānī poet who is perhaps his closest competitor, never learned to read and write, and his *qaṣīdah*s are widely admired. A convincing argument that writing has significantly structured the aesthetic experience of the *qaṣīdah* simply cannot be made, though what *can* be argued is that tribal poets who are literate have used writing in the composition of their *qaṣīdah* poems primarily because the aesthetics of the genre permit it, not because they are literate. I would contend that the role writing has played in the structuring of the tribal *qaṣīdah* has only become important since the 1962 revolution, when education began to spread to the tribes.

One final point is in order before delving into the details of the genre description. I have noted that the tribal *qaṣīdah,* though not necessarily written, is still accessible to a literate and literary audience. This fact is important for political reasons. It means that the voice of the poet need not be confined to the tribal community but may be heard by the nation-state, and the poet may thereby try to influence its decision-making processes. Writing and media of secondary orality such as radio, television, and the tape recorder are important not only in the way they affect the structure of the poetic act but also in the way they make it accessible to a wider audience. We will see how Muḥammad al-Gharsī exploits these political possibilities in his composition of the *qaṣīdah*.

The Content of the Traditional *Qaṣīdah*

The *bālah* and the *qaṣīdah* are strikingly similar in the kind and sequence of routines the poets have to execute, and yet the discrepancies are significant.

1. Opening

Many *qaṣīdah* poems begin with the formula *So-and-so says,* in which the poet refers to himself as the speaker of the poem. By contrast, in the *bālah* no one person can assume control of the verse production, and in the *zāmil* the poet often (though by no means always) refers to himself as *lisna khawlān* (a tongue of Khawlān) and remains anonymous. But in the *qaṣīdah* it is the individual who takes charge of, and assumes responsibility for, the composition.

2. Invocation of God

The invocation of God in the *qaṣīdah* follows a standard pattern set in the *bālah* poem: first His name is mentioned, then He is beseeched for forgiveness and praised, and finally the Prophet Muḥammad and ʿAlī are mentioned with a call for prayers on their behalf, alluding often to their services to Islam and mankind. To perform these speech acts, the poet has available stock epithets and formulas from the Qurʾānic tradition.[1]

Here is an example of this routine from the Khawlānī poet Ṣāliḥ bin Gāsim aṣ-Ṣūfī:

O God, O He to whom your forehead you humbly bow in prayer || O leveller of the earth, O fixer in place of the seven seas,
In Your name and Your knowledge and the sūrahs of the Pen, Light, Prostration, Hūd, || the Throne, the Verse of the Throne [sūrah 2, verse 255], the Verse of the Sun and its blazing light,
Be swift with Your forgiveness and gentleness on the day we are in our graves, || O life everlasting, Your forgiveness in the darkness of the shadows,
Your forgiveness of us on the day of resurrection, on the day the angel Mālik drags || the criminals, the traitors, to Hell and its fire.
Praise be to You [as great as] the lightning's flash and the thunder's clap; || shower us with beneficent mercy and irrigate the country with rain.
Irrigate the gardens of Yemen, make green and bring forth every flowering branch; || the land lives and in it all the trees are in bloom.
Pray for Ṭāhā, man's intercessor on the day of judgment || the Chosen One, whose virtue was known in all regions of the world.
And al-Ḥaydarah [ʿAlī bin Ṭālib], who fought the infidels, the world can testify || [that] he revived the divine precepts and religious laws, and restored them to their former [exalted] position.
He who follows the Chosen One will reside in the midst of Paradise forever; || May God's prayer and blessing be upon you forever, O Chosen One.[2]

The more elaborate the content of these opening sections—and some of them have the exuberance and majesty of a Handel aria—the more intense the religious attitude in them and hence the more pious the persona of their creator. Some poets like aṣ-Ṣūfī, who always impressed me by his religious devotion, revel in these openings; others like al-Gharsī, who is more secular in his attitude, tend to keep them spare and sometimes even omit them altogether. These differences reveal the perspectives in which the poets wish their public to perceive them as persons.

3. Invoking the hājis

Next the poet alludes to his troubled mind and agitated emotions. Thus, aṣ-Ṣūfī complains, "The father of Muḥammad moaned from his heart while mankind was asleep," and another poet, al-Baddā, exclaims, "How the soul has been distressed and the heart is anxious." Al-Gharsī confides to his audience, "I moan in my aching heart," and al-Bowraʿī refers to himself as *al-muʿtani* (the one who is disturbed).

Note how the process of verse composition is metaphorized. The image is of someone extracting rhymes and meters from the sea (*baḥr* means "meter" and "sea"). The greater the poetic genius, the deeper the sea from which the poet "scoops" his verses. A rarer image is that of the planter, whose crop is his poem, which is harvested by the audience.

The discussion of the native theory of verse composition in chapter 2 revealed that the stimulus to the emotions and thoughts of the poet is something outside the person or body: a real historical social event (falling in love with a beautiful woman, a tribal war, a drought, a pilgrimage to Mecca or Karbala, imprisonment, a quarrel with a friend) is never imaginary. A poet is thought to be a particularly sensitive and intelligent person with a long-suffering soul. Al-Gharsī maintains a kind of cathartic idea of poetic expression: "I moan in my aching heart. || If I say I'll keep silent, then I'll lose my mind. It would be better for me to explain my words to the audience."

Here is a particularly fine passage from Muḥsin al-Bowraʿī on the same subject:

> The anxious one [i.e. the poet] said: || "Hand over [verses], O my genius || do not make excuses to me, || refrain from apologies.
> It is as if you relied on me || and then you left me in the lurch || in this ignominious time || helpless.
> It [his *hājis*] said, "Quickly I came to you; || I am not like one who vanishes [the moment he is needed]. || Seize hold [of me] to extract." || And he answered me in meters.[3]

There are a great many aesthetic details to admire in this poem, which I will refer back to later. In this entire introspective section, in which a dialogue is carried on between various facets of the poet's personality, it is the individual, not the collective, who is clearly seen to be the creative force behind the poem. Furthermore, the individual is often depicted as being solitary in his travails ("The father of Muḥammad moaned from his heart while mankind was asleep"). The act of creation, as in the case of writing, is a lonely, anxious one.

4. The Messenger

After the poet has revealed his troubled emotional state and invoked the *hājis,* another convention is introduced when he addresses a messenger, on whom he calls to deliver his poem to the intended audience. Usually addressed as *ṭārish,* this messenger may be a human being, such as a famous singer (*mulaḥḥin*), but he is just as likely to be a bird (*ṭēr*)—recall the analogy between the bird's song and poetry—or even the wind (*rīḥ, nōd*), for poetic speech is conceived of as something to be wafted on air. Al-Gharsī put it in one of his poems, "[It would be better] to dispatch my small *qaṣīdah* on the waves of the air."

Some poets develop this section into a full-blown dramatic scene extending for a dozen or more lines in which the messenger is given instructions pertaining to his itinerary and informed as to the places and people he will encounter en route. Compare the difference in dramatic qualities in the treatment of this scene by two Khawlānī poets, each outstanding in his way. The first passage is selected from a poem by al-Gharsī:

> O my messenger, I will dispatch you now, hurry || to where
> I specify, quickly, I beg of you.
> Now I will take you in a Cadillac taxi. || Go immediately to
> Taʿiz, the capital, your home.
> Submit my lines to the policeman in charge and make || the
> commander understand, inform him and tell him,
> "Remain where you are, may God preserve you."[4]

Al-Gharsī seems merely to observe the convention without doing anything aesthetically interesting with it. By contrast, al-Bowraʿī (who is from ash-Shanbalī) gives the messenger an elaborate set of instructions on how to get to Gaflān:

> O messenger, saddle yourself a horse, || bridle it and put on
> the fine spurs.

Fleet as the wind in some plains, || he is not bothered by distance or desert.
From the hamlet of ash-Shanbalī, sanctuary and community of Shiites, || vanquishers of the opponent with the shot that is on the mark.
To the people of exalted rank, || men of intellect, action, and gratitude.
Cross, O traveler, the two mountains ahead || and al-Ḥadā, the border of Bukhētī and Ziyādī.
And Asʿad, son of Saʿd, cross every wadi || and in the evening [arrive], for sure, in the plain of Dhamār.
On the second day, O my messenger, saddle early; || a level plain and roads [will be] on your right and left.
Wadi al-Ḥār, wend your way [through it] bend by bend || and at noon, [arrive] at Gaflān, Ṣayʿād ash-Sharafī.[5]

This itinerary is not something the poet has imagined for the sake of filling out a poetic routine. It is an actual route along which one would encounter the places and people he mentions. Nowadays the car often substitutes for the horse as the messenger's transport.

5. *Greetings*

Once the messenger has arrived at his destination, he is instructed to greet the recipients of the poem. There follows a section entirely devoted to this speech act, not unlike what we have already seen in the *bālah*. The greeting is a highly charged rhetorical act; far more is involved than merely a polite acknowledgment of the other person's presence. The degree of intensity in the greeting reveals the respect accorded the social status of the addressee. That intensity is created by the sheer repetition of greeting formulas, by the hyperbole in the metaphors designating the illocutionary force of the greeting formulas, and by various laudatory address terms accompanying the greeting. Following are three different examples of this routine, and as in the previous section, the more traditional the poet, the more time and care he takes in developing it:

Al-Gharsī: Welcome, welcome that ennobles || the people of the Kalashnikoff and the *jambiyyah,* || the people of the German and British rifles;

Welcome that fills the capital || and every tranquil place || and irrigates the green land;
Welcome, like the welcome of the rain || that fills its [Yemen's] villages and towns, || O tribe, you who stab in the vein.
O Uncle Ṣāliḥ, welcome || [as many times as] the morning breezes blow || and the cool wind stirs.[6]

Aṣ-Ṣūfī: Convey my greetings from Ṣāliḥ with the finest perfumes || mixed with rose water, ambergris, and saffron.
Sprinkle them on Wadi ʿAbīdah, who are generous to the guest, || people of noble souls and tender hearts.
Single out the sheikhs with rose water and *ʿūd* incense || as well as the individual members [of the tribe] with *kādhī* from Oman.
Greetings from Ṣāliḥ aṣ-Ṣūfī, ten times in full, || a gift for you, O men of glory abiding forever.
Greetings to you that fill the mighty fortresses and joyous houses, || an anchorage of courage, how many among them are defenders of the faith!
People of generosity and nobility, pickers of flowers, || who are from a glorious wadi and drink from fountains.
Wadi ʿAbīdah, whose people are crossers of bridges; || if their thunder claps, no safety from them [is found] on earth.[7]

Al-Bowraʿī: Convey [my greetings] from me, Ḥusēn, son of al-Jamālī || Bowraʿī, who possesses the fine safety catch [on a rifle].
O upper right and left arms [i.e. support of the tribe], || greetings to you that weigh as much as the *kafāfī* gun barrel.
And our nephews whose custom it is to be generous, || there is not a nephew [among them] who does not have the character of his uncle.
Whether in right, *ghawā* [?], or generosity, || our nephews are nothing less than lions and giraffes [i.e. distinguished among men].
Single them out with *nidd* incense and *ʿūd;* || they are wolves after blood in the fierce fighting.
They do not fear the enemy's advance || with German rifles whose handles are slim.

And all our brave friends, || Shambalī, including Khubēgānī
and al-ʾArwam.
With flowery greetings overwhelm || them who live in the
region of as-Sarīm and Jarāf.[8]

Al-Gharsī uses typical metaphors of greeting. Though he too embellishes his greetings in a conventional manner, aṣ-Ṣūfī develops an image—that of fine perfumes, which the messenger is supposed to sprinkle on the guests in their honor—through which he dramatizes the speech act. By contrast, al-Bowraʿī honors his addressee, his relatives in Bēt ash-Shambalī, by naming them with exalted epithets: they are generous to a fault—*jūd* or *karāmah* can be roughly translated as generosity or liberality and is one of the central values of tribal society—and they are fierce and fearless ("wolves after blood").

6. The Message

Once the messenger has greeted the assembly or audience, he must recite the poet's message (a message within the message, or reported speech). All the preceding sections have ceremonially led up to this one, the poem's heart. Imaging a journey helps create this effect, for one expects to be moving toward a goal, and when the messenger arrives, the goal is at hand. Because the *qaṣīdah* is expected to address a particular social or political issue, it does so here and affords the audience the opportunity to judge the poet's intelligence, courage, and ethical character. In other words, just as the middle portion of the *bālah* was the arena in which the true skill and courage of the performing poet was tested, so the message portion of the *qaṣīdah* is the touchstone of the great *qaṣṣād*. But the message portion is specific to a socio-historical situation, and one cannot make genrewide generalizations about its content. I will return to this problem after examining a couple of poems in detail.

7. The Conclusion

The poem usually concludes with a brief section in which two speech acts are performed. In the first one, man beseeches God to forgive him his sins on the judgment day, and the second calls for humankind to pray on behalf of the Prophet Muḥammad. A cursory examination of the concluding portions of three different poems shows that conventional epithets and formulaic expressions abound:

> *Al-Gharsī:* O Lord, I beg Your forgiveness, Your protection of me; || I have sought protection from You against idolatry.
>
> Remembrance of the Prophet [as many times as] the morning breeze stirs, || [as many times as] it rustles the trees, grape vines, and *rāk* tree.[9]

> *Aṣ-Ṣūfī:* O God, look favorably on my end, O rich and grateful being, || Your forgiveness and Your pardon and Your absolution and Your kindness are my security.
>
> And in conclusion, pray for the chosen one, moon of moons || Pray for him, all of creation, mankind and *jinn.*
>
> Ṭāhā, the beloved, the shining light—happy is he who visits him [i.e. makes a pilgrimage to his city, Medina], || he whose virtue God has announced in the sermons and calls to prayer.[10]

> *Al-Bowraᶜī:* And may prayer cover you [or, inundate you], O seal of the prophets, || [as many times as] the camel driver sings and the wind blows.
>
> [As many times as] the people cry out to you || for mercy, compassion, and protection.
>
> O bearer of glad tidings, O warner, O guiding light, || O intercessor for mankind [to keep him] from the scorching fire.
>
> He who hears the prayer for Ṭāhā many times || [as many times as] they read the fine pages [of the Qurʾān].[11]

Whereas aṣ-Ṣūfī and al-Bowraᶜī favor the format that has just been outlined, al-Gharsī does not employ it frequently. He often skips the preliminary invocation of God and the prayer for Muḥammad and ᶜAlī, though he may invoke the *hājis,* greet the addressee, and end the poem by asking God for forgiveness and calling for prayers on behalf of the Prophet Muḥammad. As a rule al-Gharsī gets to the point of his poem more quickly than the others and develops it with more care. The traditionalists among the listeners sometimes said his poems sounded abrupt, whereas the urban modernists were attracted to it for that very reason and because he seemed to deal with issues in a more direct, sincere, and comprehensive fashion. These reactions are important, for they suggest that the tribal *qaṣīdah* is being composed for two different kinds of audiences and, as a result, a new form of the same genre is beginning to emerge and thrive, particularly in the city. I do not want to suggest that al-Gharsī is the first poet to have adopted this urban tribal style, only that he is one of the greatest urban representatives of it.

The Poem as Consummate Form

The Line

The *qaṣīdah* line is structurally as taut and complex as any poetic verse can be. It accommodates a number of sound patterns including meter, rhyme, alliteration, sound symbolism, and pauses, which are artfully integrated to produce a massively rich, polyphonic texture. Here is the beginning of a poem addressed to the president of Yemen:

⏑ –[⏑] –| – – ⏑ – – – ⏑ –| – – ⏑ – – –
salām yā gāyid taʿiz || yā dhī maʿa-k manṣab wa ʿizz || ʾayḍ-an
⏑ –|– – ⏑ –
wa tārīkh-ak yazīd
– – ⏑ –|– – ⏑ – – – ⏑ –| – – ⏑ –
ʾant al-jamālī w-al-hamām || w-antah l-il-abṭāla s-sanām ||
– – ⏑ –|– – ⏑ –
mā yadhkur illā kulla jīd
– – ⏑ –| – – ⏑ – – –[⏑] –| – – ⏑ –
ʿabd aḷḷah al-jīd yinjab-ak || w-an-nās[a] kull-in yaṣḥab-ak ||
– – ⏑ –| – – ⏑ –
w-aḷḷah maʿa-k fī-mā tarīd

Greetings, O commander of Taʿiz, || O you of authority and nobility; || your history will increase [your fame].
You are handsome and generous; || you are the greatest of fighters; || only the best is mentioned.
ʿAbduḷḷah [father of the president], the excellent one, has conceived you; || Everyone wants to be your friend; || and God is with you in what you want.

Each line is composed of three hemistichs separated in recitation usually by a slight pause. No *zāmil* line could ever be that long or entail as many subdivisions. The rhyme scheme is relatively complex. The three lines share the end rhyme *-īd,* and each line has an internal rhyme: *-iz(z)* in the first line, *-ām* in the second, and *-ak* in the third. The two types of rhyme are fitted exactly into the meter and into the pauses to produce a precisely divided, linear structure. Where internal rhyme occurs in the *zāmil,* the rhyming sounds are found within the metrical foot, so that a sense of a periodic sectioning of the line is not as marked as in the *qaṣīdah.* Furthermore, in the *qaṣīdah* a tension arises between the identity of the end rhyme, which unifies the poem, and the diversity of the internal rhyme, which changes with each line—a tension that is musically effective.

Formulas

At this juncture it is appropriate to analyze the use of traditional formulas. Because they have to fit the metrical requirements of the line and be modified in accordance with complex rhyme schemes, they are not used frequently in the *qaṣīdah.* The following line is taken from the conclusion of the previous poem:

– – ⏑ –| – – ⏑ – ⏑ – ⏑ –| – – ⏑ –
w-al-khitma ṣallō yā ḥaḍūr || ʿala n-nabī badra l-badūr ||
⏑ –⏑ –| – – ⏑ –
shafīʿa min nār al-waʿīd

And in conclusion, pray, O assembly, || for the Prophet,
moon of moons, || intercessor [who keeps us out of Hell].

The poet has to bend the formulas to fit the ever-shifting contours of the meter, the rhyme scheme, and the placement of caesuras.[12]

Strophes and Refrains

Organization of lines into strophes becomes possible for the first time in the *qaṣīdah,* an effect achieved also by rhyme schemes and occasionally by refrain lines. Here is a dazzling example from al-Gharsī:

– –[⏑] –| – ⏑ – –| – ⏑ – ⏑ –| – ⏑ – –| –
kullēn[a] fī mārib-ah mārib || wa yishtow al-waḍʿa yitkharrib
– – ⏑ –| –[⏑]– –| – – – ⏑ –|–[⏑]– –| –
w-ibna sh-shaʿab ṭūl yitgharrib || w-ahl al-khudāʿāt titsarrib
– – ⏑ –|– ⏑ – –| –
l-ish-shaʿba yitʿaffarow shaml-ah

– – ∪ –| –∪ – –| – – – ∪ –|– ∪
b-il-kadhba w-ad-dijla w-at-tazyīf || bēn al-ʿawāṣim wa
– –| –
bēn ar-rīf
– – ∪–|– ∪– –| – ∪ – ∪ –| – ∪ – –| –
hādhā yiḥīlō ʾila t-tawḍīf || wa dhā yibō minn-ana t-tashrīf
∪? ∪ –[∪] –| – ∪ – –| –
wa yibīʿ min shaʿb-anā w-aṣl-ah

– –∪ –| – ∪ – –|– ∪ – ∪–| – ∪ – –|–
gad bāʿuw al-baʿḍa dhī bāʿū || wa kam ghalabnā wa lā ṭāʿū
– – ∪ –| – ∪ – –|– ∪ – ∪ –| –∪ – –|–
lākinna-hum f-il-ʾakhīr ḍāʿū || wa mithl-amā bāʿuw ibtāʿū
– –∪ –| – ∪ – –| –
yā bēʿat ar-rukhṣa b-il-jumlah

Everyone has a hidden aim in mind || and wants the situation to deteriorate.
The sons of the people are always migrating || and those who deceive are seeping in.
The unity of the people is divided.

Through lies, deception, and forgery || among the major cities and the rural areas,
This one is shifted into a position [of power] || and that one wants to be honored by us [i.e. be asked to take power],
While he sells a part of the people.

Some people have sold; || how often we have refused [to sell], even if they [i.e. the people who have sold] have obeyed.
But in the end they were lost, || and as they sold, so were they sold.
O what a cheap, wholesale deal that was!

The structure of the text is a series of couplets divided from each other by a half-line. Each couplet has the rhyme scheme *a* || *a* / *a* || *a*, though the rhyming sound is not the same from couplet to couplet. The unity of the couplet is reinforced by grammatical parallelism. The rhyming word in the first couplet tends to be a Form V verb, the rhyming word in the second couplet a Form II verbal noun, and the rhyming word in the third couplet a Form I weak verb. The half-line ends invariably in *-lah,* a unity in the rhyme scheme that is musically in tension with the variable couplet rhymes. Its semantic function is to complete (in some instances even to summarize) the ideas in the preceding couplet.

The refrain also exists in the *bālah,* but it is clear that its function in the *qaṣīdah,* besides structurally organizing the poem into strophes, is altogether different and more dramatic. Al-Gharsī composed several poems that illustrate the function of the *qaṣīdah* refrain to perfection. The one I will consider begins in standard fashion, invoking God's name and blessing, then glorifying the fierceness and bravery of the president's bodyguard, composed of men from all the great tribes of Yemen, whose names he mentions and praises. The sixth line of the poem becomes the refrain:

> O friend, be patient whenever things get bad. || No, no,
> O time, the law of the good is always envied.[13]

Its introduction at this point has the effect of suddenly breaking off the poem's conventional opening, of altering the tone, and of beginning the poet's subject. In other words, it has an aesthetic function of separating or delineating thematic material within the poem.

From now on, this refrain appears after every four or five lines. In lines 7–10 the poet complains of the way in which everyone in the guards seems to be picking on him and the terrible conditions of service. The refrain line reappears to counsel patience on the part of the poet. In the next five lines the complaint is developed further, but this time it focuses on the behavior of specific officers in the guard with whom al-Gharsī has a bone to pick. This section is again separated by the refrain line from the next five lines of the poem, which relate a particular incident in which al-Gharsī damaged an army vehicle, through no particular fault of his own, and had to pay for the repairs. Next, the poet muses over the possibility of forwarding his complaint to the president, to whom he alludes in the poem by the phrase "he of the star and eagle" (the two symbols of the republic), praising his nobility, generosity, and sense of justice. When the refrain line reappears, its advice to be patient seems to have paid off, for the poet now hopes that presidential intervention will clear up the confusion. But in the next section al-Gharsī continues to criticize some of the officers, especially their callousness toward the privates. His exasperation mounts, and again the refrain line comes in to soothe his temper as the concluding section of the poem begins. The poet mentions that the new commander of the guards is a decent fellow, but if nothing beneficial is to come from him, then the soldiers had better put their trust in God alone. The refrain line concludes the poem on a note of resignation. On the one hand, the refrain organizes the text by sectioning it off into higher-order units that have some sort of thematic coherence. On the other hand, it contributes a meaning that shifts subtly in mood and idea from one development section to the next.

It is interesting to contrast al-Gharsī's technique with that of the more traditional Muḥsin ʿAlī al-Bowraʿī. The latter also uses a refrain to separate couplets from each other: "God help and protect us from what we fear." The crucial difference in his use of a refrain is that it occurs after every couplet and is thus related to the rest of the poem more mechanically than organically. It does not have quite the dramatic, emotional impact of al-Gharsī's refrain.

Sound Symbolism

Onomatopoetic effects proliferate in *qaṣīdah* poetry, but I will limit my illustrations to two examples. The first is a strophe from one of al-Gharsī's poems we have already studied:

lākin wa lā budda min lākin || wa law tashūf al-hawā sākin
sākin wa lā tiḥsib-ah sākin || lā budda min hizzat al-mākin
yirjaʿ ʿala shaʿb-anā ʿagl-ah

But, and there is no end of but, || even if you see that the wind is calm.
Calm, do not suppose it is calm; || no doubt the powerful will shake [i.e. make heads roll]
And return the people to their senses.

The mood set by this verse is of the quiet before the storm. The first hemistich is an anticipation of something ominous to come, which is cued by the word *lākin* (but). The sound of this word has resonances in *sākin* (calm) and *mākin* (those who can make things happen) and invites consideration of the possible semantic relationships among the three words. Indeed, the meaning of the verse can be summarized as follows: there is calm (*sākin*), but (*lākin*) it is soon to be shaken by the powers-that-be (*mākin*). The second verse contains the onomatopoetic word *hawā* (air), whose meaning is reinforced by the succession of long vowels and sibilant and fricative consonants, which together give a breathy quality to the line. Though this quality is attenuated in the next line, it is still highly audible in the strongly fricative /ḥ/ phoneme of *tiḥsib-ah*. Then suddenly the tonal qualities shift radically: the long vowels in the middle give way to a series of double consonants in *budda* and especially *hizzat* that produce the aural image of something battering or buzzing with great force. The word *hizzat* (trembling, vibration, shaking) is, like *hawā,* onomatopoetic, the strongly pronounced voiced double sibilant /zz/ mimicking the sound of an electric current (the word is in fact used to refer to an electric shock). Each of the verse's hemistichs propels forward the meaning that is conveyed.[14]

I close this section with a few words about puns. Yemeni poets are generally fond of such word plays and try to use them as often as they can. Al-Gharsī uses a pun in the first line of one of his poems to great effect, encapsulating in it the meaning of the whole poem:

> Ibn Nāṣir said, "My feelings (*shaᶜūr*) have become confused || and, by God, barley (*shaᶜīr*) has thwarted poetry (*shiᶜr*)."[15]

The three key words of the poem—feelings, poetry, and barley—are all derived from the same root, *SH-ᶜ-R,* and thus are morphologically related. When the poet says "barley has thwarted poetry," he means that people today are more concerned with materialism (what they put in their stomachs) than with nobler feelings.

Metaphors

We have already seen the poetry of previous genres to be fertile fields of metaphorical imagery. In the *bālah* the images embedded in the *mā* phrase are metaphors for the intensity with which a certain speech act is performed—praising God, greeting a guest, and so forth. The *zāmil* contains a wealth of imagery including guns, hunting, monumental building, natural catastrophes, awesomely powerful natural agents such as lightning and thunder, marauding animals such as wolves, locusts, and hawks representing the fierceness of tribal warriors, mountains synecdochically referring to a tribe or tribal region and also used as figures of speech for impregnability, and glass symbolizing the fragility of honor. These metaphorical images are carried over into the *qaṣīdah,* with the crucial difference being that the poet is not bound by limitations of turn-taking in the performance or compression of the content and may thus take advantage of his freedom by developing his metaphor over several lines.

By way of illustration, consider this metaphorical passage from one of al-Gharsī's poems:

> What a pity, O people, O bridge crossers, || but the fact is that you are like a mirage.
> If anyone is thirsty and desperate for water, || he thinks it is a circular sea;
> If he approaches upon seeing it, || he finds nothing but barrenness.
> It is as if someone had said to you, "Turn to the rear!" || and the bugler sounded his salute in your ear.
> And all of you retreated, O cursed people; || may God rebuke your unconscionable souls.[16]

Al-Gharsī is rebuking his audience for being fickle in politics and spineless toward their enemies, who threaten the borders and infiltrate the country (the poem was composed in early 1979 during the war between North Yemen and South Yemen). He uses two different metaphors to convey this criticism, the first of which is that of the mirage. It seems to rise in the first line and then, like the thing it represents, hover and only gradually become distinct over the next several lines. The first line equates the people with the mirage. The next two lines are an exploration of that image: the first concretizes the illusion of the circular sea on the horizon of the desert toward which the thirsty traveler stumbles. The second reveals the image to be a lie, an illusion, but by then, one presumes, the traveler's fate has been sealed. One need not draw out the implication of al-Gharsī's rhetoric: the people's resolve to face the enemy is like a mirage. The fourth line contains a very different image, in which the people of the nation are likened to an army unit, which in the next line blindly obeys the bugle sounding ignominious retreat.

In another poem al-Gharsī predicts a grave social disaster that might destroy the foundations of the nation. The poet concretizes this apocalyptic vision in a series of natural cataclysms:

We have become riddled with problems, and advice has become useless, || and today [social] conditions as a result of these problems have become unmanageable.
O flood, flow from the crest of the mountain and [in] the flood plains; || O people of the thirsty fields, God has come with His flood.
Its beginning is erupting volcanoes and its end is earthquakes, || and I fear that catastrophes will take place from Ḥāshid to Bakīl.
The disasters will spread to all the people; || spreading to both its parts [Ḥāshid and Bakīl], until it [the country] punctures its tire.[17]

The first set of images has deep Qurʾānic associations—God's flood that cleansed the world and destroyed all except Noah's ark, and the divinely retributive earthquake to which sūrah 99 is devoted. The poet is tapping into the power of not-so-unconscious meanings in order to heighten the impact of his metaphor. The fourth line abruptly shifts to another image, seemingly prosaic and thus strangely dissonant, of puncturing an automobile tire (variants of this image include brakes malfunctioning, steering off course, a collision, engine failure), which conveys the sense of arrested momentum. This imagery too has powerful, though this time quite secular, associations with tribal or state governance. The driver steering his car, the shepherd overseeing his flock, the building standing on firm foundations—these are some of the symbols of governance: "You have been duped, O our people, and unwary; || the shepherd of the camels has lost his flock which have been neglected"; "We beg you to catch up with the confusion in the country; || build a building the right way—do not build on fragile walls"; "Among the foreign and domestic homes || we fear for the inhabitants that someone might wreck the ceilings" (al-Gharsī).[18] The metaphor thus becomes, in this context and with conventional symbolism in mind, slightly ambiguous. The poet, under the guise of talking about the ending of a flood, may be covertly introducing another idea—the ending of political order. There is no way to confirm this interpretation absolutely, especially when poets are reluctant to interpret their texts for their audience, but no one would absolutely *disconfirm* it either, and the interpretation is consonant with the notion of natural cataclysm being symptomatic of moral collapse. As in the previous examples, the metaphor is developed over several lines, a luxury of expansion denied the poet in other genres.

This technique allows metaphor to be transformed into allegory. An entire moral story can be filled out in the imagination of the listener. In one line from the previous poem "O flood, flow from the crest of the mountain and [in] the flood plains; || O people of the thirsty fields, God has come with His flood," the first hemistich invokes a natural agency that the listener expects brings destruction in its wake. But the second hemistich temporarily consoles: the fields are thirsty, and the flood is welcome. Moreover, the flood is God's—an agency of divine will. But the succeeding line is alarming and causes the listener to reassess his inferences: "Its beginning is erupting volcanoes and its end is earthquakes, || and I fear that catastrophes will take place from Ḥāshid to Bakīl." Obviously, this is a morally cleansing flood, an agency of divine retribution visited on the people of Yemen. Having apprehended a new kind of intention behind the use of the imagery, the listener now places it within an essentially Qurʾānic narrative whose rhetoric is replete with stories about natural disaster befalling cities and peoples who have betrayed their religions. In this way the imagery becomes allegorical because of the explicitly moral lessons to be drawn from the Qurʾānic allusions: something terribly wrong in the state has caused these disasters to happen. But there is still more if we consider the description of the flood flowing "from the crest of the mountain and [in] the flood plains" as bearing significantly on the interpretation. One does not at first notice its significance because of the fact that rainwater naturally flows from the mountains downward toward the plain; one therefore assumes that the poet is simply indulging in a bit of naturalistic description, not entirely gratuitous because this filling out of the image arguably enhances the poetic style. (Might not some American poet write, "The falling of the rain / beating down the petals, bloodying the drains"?) But this description is in the message portion of the poem, in which al-Gharsī is supposed to be making his point, and his point is political. Therefore, it is not farfetched to suppose that more is intended than a naturalistic description (or at least that other interpretations are possible): namely, the tribes that live in the mountains are specifically the objects of this retribution, which will spread to their two main confederacies, the Ḥāshid and the Bakīl.

Here is another example, this time from the poetry of aṣ-Ṣūfī:

> Ḥāshid summons Bakīl, the generous: "Let us break the shackles." || O people of the two wings, Yemen will not obliterate the traces [of its past glories].[19]

Aṣ-Ṣūfī is exhorting the Yemeni tribes to remember their heritage and act in the manner of the great spice kingdoms, which had been a power to be reckoned with in the ancient world. The reported speech, "Let us break the shackles," is a reference to the 1962 revolution, which overthrew the Imamate. At least some of the Bakīl joined the Ḥāshid in this fight against a regime that had kept Yemen backward and under its heel. It is thus an allusion to unified tribal action in the cause of the nation-state. The phrase "people of the two wings" is a metaphor referring to the Ḥāshid and Bakīl as the two wings of the state, which itself is like a bird with the Imam as its head—an image that, ironically, has been reabsorbed into the imagery of the Republican [anti-Imamate] eagle. The word *ʾathār* (lit. ruins, traces) is not devoid of powerful associations either. Though it occurs often in pre-Islamic verse as a reference to the traces left in the sand by the beloved's encampment, it is also used in contemporary Khawlān in describing the great ruins at Mārib left behind by the Sabaeans, the reputed ancestors of the Yemeni tribes. I assume that it is this latter association that the poet has in mind when he speaks of the *ʾathār* the Yemeni people ought not to forget. The poem contains mostly metaphorical allusions—an allusion to the civil war, an allusion to tribal unity symbolized in the wings of a bird, and an allusion to Yemen's venerable, awe-inspiring history—woven together to form a dense fabric whose weave is not altogether apparent. What holds them together, makes them unified and coherent? In a word, politics. But within that general semantic domain a host of other references link up with what we might call allegories of history.

The Individual Talent of Muḥammad al-Gharsī

Up to this point in the chapter I have been mainly concerned with genre analysis while at the same time suggesting that there are marked differences between poets in the way they exploit the genre conventions. I have not been keeping track of the three main Khawlānī poets to see how they differ, if at all, on every specific aesthetic detail; it is enough for my purposes in this section to have a general sense of the individuality of Muḥammad al-Gharsī as a poet. We have learned, for example, that he prefers to skip, or at least to pay only perfunctory attention to, the preliminary routines leading up to the message portion, in contrast to his peers aṣ-Ṣūfī and al-Bowraᶜī; that he excels in the use of rhyme schemes and refrain lines for the purpose of internally organizing the poem into strophes that are dramatically and organically connected; that he is a master of sound symbolism, particularly puns, which evince his sense of humor; and that he likes to create multilinear metaphorical allusions.

Important though it is to grasp this sense of al-Gharsī as an individual talent, it would be ludicrous to reduce his talent to these purely genre features. Probably more significant is the sense in which his career in the army and especially his friendship with the current president of Yemen have affected his poetry. That is, he has an individual public personality by virtue of the position he occupies in a vast tribal and national structure, which has helped to shape the kind of poetry for which he is celebrated and in particular the kinds of themes he talks about in his poetry. It is precisely this sense of his career and its relationship to his art that I want to examine in this final section.

Muḥammad was born in the mid-1940s in a small village (al-Ghars) near the southwestern border between Khawlān aṭ-Ṭiyāl and the Sinḥān tribe. Muḥammad said that he first showed interest in composing poetry as a love-struck teenager wooing a pretty girl. The story may be apocryphal; many poets, as we have seen, seem to think that that is how they began. More likely the boy's aptitude had already been apparent in the village wedding *bālah*s and, later, in the *zāmil* compositions, so that his father, himself a modest *qaṣṣād,* took the boy under his wing and encouraged him. Though he did compose love lyrics, he openly ridiculed these juvenile efforts as beneath his talent, a reaction that again fits the stereotype of the established poet who values only his mature political and religious output. After his father taught him all he knew, Muḥammad visited another Khawlānī poet, who will figure more prominently in the next chapter, Ṣāliḥ bin Gāsim aṣ-Ṣūfī, who is widely acclaimed for his artistic competence and particularly admired for his handling of metrical patterns. Under his tutelage Muḥammad mastered the techniques by which he became a major voice in the tribal tradition.

Although I was unable to get a detailed answer from him on this question, it appears that Muḥammad had gotten to know the current president of Yemen, ʿAlī ʿAbdullah Ṣāliḥ, when they played together as boys on the Sinḥān-Khawlān border. I assume that they went to the same regional elementary school to learn how to read and write. In any case, Muḥammad is highly literate, to the point where he can employ standard or classical Arabic grammar in his poems (for example, when he is addressing a Ṣanʿānī audience); hence, he is sometimes said to be the most eloquent (*faṣīḥ,* which also means classical or standard) of tribal poets.

Both Muḥammad and the young Ṣāliḥ joined the army and served on the Republican side in the civil war. It was during these years fighting alongside the Egyptians that Muḥammad was introduced to Nasserism. Perhaps it was because of this contact that he supported socialism (a characterization of his views he would publicly deny, though it is one I often enough heard expressed) and displayed sympathy with the Soviet bloc. Bear in mind that terms like socialism are always relative, for when one examines al-Gharsī's views closely, they are not much different from capitalism within a welfare state. He appears socialistic, however, in comparison with some other voices (heard in the next chapter). I am not certain of the exact reasons, but his friend ʿAlī ʿAbdullah rose relatively quickly through the ranks of the army and took his poet friend along with him. When Ṣāliḥ became president, Muḥammad was serving in the president's special guard and living in Ṣanʿā. Friendships do not always survive such rapid climbs to power; but a talented poet is useful to a man of power who is not particularly gifted as a poet. For example, I knew sheikhs in Khawlān who relied on the talents of one or more of their tribesmen to respond to poetic challenges they had received, simply because they were not themselves capable poets, and I suspect that al-Gharsī's relationship to the president is founded on the same dependence. One can surmise as much from the fact that al-Gharsī has taped at least one poem that he composed on behalf of his friend when the latter was commander of Taʿiz.

One might expect that al-Gharsī would have become merely the president's mouthpiece, a spokesman for government policy, but he is a more interesting character than that, as attested by the following story. While I was in Yemen, a tarmac road linking the capital with the eastern city of Mārib was being built. Lying between these two population centers, Khawlān was the most logical region through which to direct the road and therefore it was initially promised a section of it—

until Ṣāliḥ came to power and saw to it that the road would pass through territory friendlier to him than Khawlān, a classic case of pork-barrel politics intended to maintain the loyalty of grass-roots supporters. Such a road, among other things, becomes a major thoroughfare for the transport of smuggled goods from Saudi Arabia to the lucrative Ṣanʿānī markets, so that any middlemen stationed along it stand to make a handsome sum of money. If al-Gharsī had been merely a government stooge, he would have extolled the wisdom of the president's decision or at least have remained silent. Instead, he composed a poem that scathingly criticized it.

The poet faced a moral predicament. On the one hand, he owed loyalty to a friend, as prescribed by *gabyilah*. On the other, he owed loyalty to his tribe, which had been betrayed by that friend. In the end he chose loyalty to his tribe, a move that could have jeopardized not only his friendship with the president but also his army career. I suspect that al-Gharsī found himself increasingly at odds with the government and the army, for I heard a rumor shortly before I left Yemen that he had been kicked upstairs to a high-level post in which he was forbidden to compose any poetry. Working within the system has its price. Opposition did not cost him his life or his job; it cost him his voice. But he is part of a tradition in that respect too, for there are legends about poets who have been put in prison for their criticism of the central government. At some point in the career of every major poet a crisis of conscience leads to direct opposition with central authority, and for that reason the renowned poet must be possessed of courage as well as talent.

Al-Gharsī's Self-Proclaimed Masterpiece

As happened with so many other Yemenis, Ibrāhīm al-Ḥamdī's presidency sparked al-Gharsī's imagination and inspired him to compose what he considers to be his best poem. On the domestic front al-Ḥamdī acquired a reputation as a reformer and a developer. In international politics he was respected as a skillful diplomat who managed to keep Yemeni politics fairly free of outside control. Among other innovative policies, he encouraged the burgeoning of the local development associations (LDAs), which have taken the initiative in organizing most development projects, including the building of roads, clinics, and schools and the introduction of improved agricultural and irrigation techniques. In his foreign policy al-Ḥamdī avoided becoming subservient to Saudi Arabia and was beginning to establish cultural and military linkages with South Yemen before his assassination.

Al-Gharsī's masterpiece has to be understood in the context of al-Ḥamdī's presidency. Putting himself in the role of the spokesman of the people, al-Gharsī advises the president on a program that he thinks will serve the people's best interests, which he summarizes at the end of the poem. The twin themes of the poem are social and economic development, on the one hand, and political independence, on the other. (See Appendix E for Arabic transcription of the following poem.)

In my name and in the name of the army and in the name of the communities, || [in the name of] our heroes who defy the perils of death and destruction,
In the name of the army posts in the lofty mountains facing each other || I say, Long live the daring leader to whom no description can do justice.
Long live the free leader who leads Yemen and its convoys, || the army and the son of the people who in respect rose to their feet.
Nine million, and as God is my witness, the number is in decline || though perhaps its [Yemen's] number was eleven million or maybe more.
And all of them obey your orders, the forces are on the alert; || thousands follow your lead, O sir, thousands.
Do you not see those huge crowds and gatherings || awaiting your order to move on whatever you desire [lit. see]?
And all the hopes of thousands present and absent [from the country], || the aim of their intentions and serious wishes is to save the rural areas.
For the countryside needs able-bodied and willing hands; || like the capitals, take into consideration their situations and circumstances.
If you listen to the person guided by special interests, then every district remains isolated; || the fact of the matter is that we are a nation, not a collectivity of special-interest groups.

Yesterday we bolstered and unified disparate hearts; || ignorance is gone, the darkness of the nights and the eclipse of the sun have passed away.
Gone are the days of poverty, we have destroyed the walls [standing] || between [us] and progress as well as development—enough of life in the caves!
But we saw on the mosque ceiling the spider's web; || this is what has made Yemen carry weapons and swords.
O pioneer of progress, millions are hoping || that you will bring well-being and progressive views to the communities.
God has appointed you ruler of Yemen and has given you a capable hand; || but be gentle, O favorite of the people, be compassionate with us.
Take a good look at any underdeveloped province; || give it its fair share of education; bind together the separate groups.
We beg you to catch up with the confusion in the country; || build a building the right way—do not build on fragile walls.
For conditions are not the same—yesterday is the opposite of tomorrow, || and the waves of the Red Sea are roiled by the buffets of the storm.
Woven and spun threads are to be found at the spinner's; || wool needs to be carded before it is spun, for otherwise it remains only wool.
Among the foreign and domestic homes || we fear for the inhabitants that someone might wreck the ceilings.
Examine [the people] until you know whose hearts are evil; || know the results [of the examination] and how to deal with the [evil hearts] according to what they are used to.
One has knowledge—walk with him; and the other is his worker, || for mankind is various, his kinds are several.
You have a lot of experience in this matter; || do not flatter anyone—the person with right on his side fears no one.
Here I am, in the name of Yemen, demanding just demands; || I beg you [to give] your unequivocal decree without any meanderings or beating around the bush.

The first is to build the roads and repair what is broken || in the remote areas; please [go] and have a look.
Second, let our schools be built quickly || for the sake of educating the children: education and not clapping of hands.
Third, [see to it] that we obtain oil through the help of a mighty nation, || [that] we push our country forward after backwardness,
After the sediments [have settled], the standstills and ignorant minds || scooped from the depths of ignorance.
Fourth, open soon and not later the door of agriculture; || it is forbidden to allow our people to remain fasting from the previous night [i.e. not to eat during the night when they are fasting the next day].
These are four items whose advantages can be shared by all || among the government and the citizenry—you and I have their interests at heart.
Excuse me if the poet has gone on too long in his *zāmil,* || for poetry can spin on from the arrangement of rhymes and lines.

The poem does not begin or end by any of the conventional means I have described. It is pure message. Although unorthodox, this kind of poem is not unusual for al-Gharsī; it does, however, set him apart from many other tribal poets, for example, the two whose work I will examine in the next chapter.

Instead of the conventional opening, the poem begins immediately with an enthusiastic address to the president. The poet establishes himself, moreover, as the spokesman of the entire community, the vox populi. When he mentions that the population of nine million may be in decline, he is referring to the large number of Yemenis who have emigrated to other countries, implying that in addition to the many Yemenis inside the country supporting al-Ḥamdī, there are many outside who rally around him as well.

In line 7 the first and major theme of the poem is introduced: save the rural areas. Or, as the poet exhorts the president in line 13, "O pioneer of progress, millions are hoping || that you will bring well-being and progressive views to the communities." But he reminds the head of the government that this development policy has to be executed evenhandedly across the whole country and counsels him, in line 9, not to "listen to the person guided by special interests," for then every district benefits, and the president remains true to the idea of the republic. Otherwise, the nation risks being split asunder. These lines are an indirect and subtle allusion to the civil war, which had just been concluded (1971) after nearly ten bloody years ("Yesterday we bolstered and unified disparate hearts"). And when the poet says in line 10 that "ignorance is gone, the darkness of the nights and the eclipse of the sun have passed away," my interpretation is that he is alluding to the dark times of the previous Imamate, which for years had resisted instituting badly needed social, economic, and political reforms. As a result of malign neglect Yemen had become one of the poorest and most backward nations on earth. The attitude of the people is well summarized by the phrase "enough of life in the caves!" (line 11).

In line 12 the second and subsidiary theme is mentioned in a powerful allusion: "But we saw on the mosque ceiling the spider's web; || this is what has made Yemen carry weapons and swords." This line always produces much speculation among listeners. The spider is not necessarily a malign symbol in Muslim thought, for the religious tradition has it that Muḥammad took refuge from his enemies in a cave across whose entrance a spider wove a thread concealing his whereabouts. It is possible to interpret the spider as the protector of religion, represented synecdochically by a mosque ceiling, from the attacks of hostile forces against which Yemenis are exhorted to take up arms.

But the riddle is this: what precisely is the force that imperils the security of the country? Line 17 contains intimations of political threats confronting the country, cast in the allusion of a storm buffeting the Red Sea. It could be that the poet has in mind the turmoils in the Horn of Africa (the Marxist takeover of Ethiopia at the time and its bloody suppression of the Eritrean war of independence, or the feuds between Ethiopia and Somalia), which it was feared might spread to Yemen and Saudi Arabia on the other side of the Red Sea. In line 18 al-Gharsī presents us with another interpretive enigma: "Woven and spun threads are to be found at the spinner's; || wool needs to be carded before it is spun, for otherwise it remains only wool." On the one hand, this could be an allusion to the theme of social development in the country; in other words, the nation as it now operates does not benefit the people but must, like wool, be carded and spun before something can be made of it. On the other hand, al-Gharsī could be referring to the internal political situation, where the president is seen as a kind of spinner who has a controlling hand over the various political parties. Probably the poet has both meanings in mind, for it is not possible to preserve the gains of progress without securing internal political stability. So al-Gharsī advises the president to look carefully around him to determine who might be working against the interests of the country—those men representing the vaguely expressed threats in the previous lines—while at the same time expounding a platform for Yemen's development.

Of that program al-Gharsī mentions the building of roads first (line 24). The next recommendation is the construction of schools, which he puts forward in the form of a popular proverb: "education and not clapping of hands" (line 25). In other words, let us not just applaud the program of action; let us actually *do* something about it. Not surprisingly, the third plank in the poet's platform is the discovery of oil. For years the successive governments of Yemen have brought oil exploration companies into the country, with disappointing results. Since oil has been discovered in Kuwait, Saudi Arabia, the United Arab Emirates, and Oman, Yemen has assumed (rightly, it turns out) that it too must have underground reserves, which only some conspiracy has kept them from unearthing. Oil, the black gold of the Middle East, has made it possible for once desperately poor countries to suddenly blossom into powerful kingdoms. The fourth and final suggestion that al-Gharsī puts forward is the development of Yemen's agricultural potential. For centuries Yemen had been the breadbasket of the peninsula, growing rich on a diversified system of crops it used both for internal consumption and export. For instance, world-famous mocha coffee, grown in Yemen, once dominated the market. But more than changing world market conditions contributed to the demise of the agricultural system. For one thing, *gāt* became a lucrative cash crop, with most energies in the agricultural sector devoted to its growth and sale to the near-exclusion of every other crop. Another factor was the large-scale emigration of able-bodied Yemeni males to Saudi Arabia and the Persian Gulf, an agricultural force that was not being replenished or replaced. Given the large remittance payments from abroad, it was more economical for Yemeni households to import goods than to grow or husband them domestically. As a result of these developments the agricultural system has languished to the point of near-collapse. Al-Gharsī's suggestion, then, is both pertinent and urgent.

The penultimate line encapsulates al-Gharsī's rhetorical position in this poem, for in pointing out that this program of four recommendations is mutually beneficial to the government and the people, he transcends the arena of factional politics by saying that he supports the nation as a whole. Hence, the program will help unify the country after years of division and internal disarray. It is a formula, so to speak, by which Yemen can save itself.

Conclusion

In what sense, then, is Muḥammad al-Gharsī an individual, and what is his relationship to the cultural tradition? He is obviously not a traditional tribesman who has spent his life in the countryside tending his fields, attending the endless rounds of weddings and religious festivals, and contending in the equally endless political disputes of the tribes. Not that he does not from time to time do these things, or that his heart and mind are not with his relatives in the countryside when he is away from them in the city; but he surely has presented himself in his poetry as a tribesman of a different stripe. He is a man who talks about petty politics in the army, the scarcity of bread in urban markets, the housing shortage, or the governance of the country—experiences remote from the lives of his relatives back home—and these topics speak of a person engaged with the problems of an urban society and state government. Most important, one has the sense that al-Gharsī is self-consciously sounding the voice of a "new" tribesman. More and more, tribesmen emigrate to the cities or abroad, where they encounter an entirely different set of problems, to which al-Gharsī has responded.

To express his voice in the more traditional forms of *qaṣīdah* poetry is problematical, however. Al-Gharsī's life experience is no longer deeply involved in the rich ceremony of tribal life, and perhaps for this reason he feels alienated from the long greeting routine and the messenger scene found in the more traditional poems. What *is* shared in the urban context is Islamic ritual, and therefore it is not surprising to find al-Gharsī holding on to the religious invocation of the traditional *qaṣīdah* when he seems to let go of nearly everything else. What remains besides the religious invocation is the message portion, which in a typical al-Gharsī poem of the 1970s and 1980s is usually the major part of the text-utterance. As a result of these innovations—and it is difficult to say to what degree al-Gharsī alone is responsible for them—a new kind of *qaṣīdah* emerges, different in feeling tone from the traditional one. This *qaṣīdah* is rather unceremonious but elaborates on the problematic situation and its solution at great length, and then ends abruptly. The pace is more rapid, the tone more clipped, the analysis more direct and incisive. It self-consciously creates a rational persona—rational in the sense of problem-solving—saved from dryness by al-Gharsī's sense of humor.

Al-Gharsī has thus created a form in the *qaṣīdah* that expresses more closely the feeling tone of his experiences in the city, army, and bureaucracy. It is also a form that allows him and his audience to focus their attention on the problematical situations in their environments; that is, the sheer emphasis on the message portion draws attention to these problems and thereby gives the sense that the poet is someone ready to tackle them. He has transformed the traditional genre in a way that makes the poetic experience more vital to contemporary reality, or at least more vital to him and his fans. In the next chapter, however, we will see almost the reverse response to this reality.

9

Tribal Ideology, the State, and Communicative Practices

> The crucial phase of monopoly-capitalist development, including capitalist control of the advanced technologies of centralized amplification and recording, came also to include the intensive development of such machines as transistor radios and tape recorders, which were intended for the ordinary channels of capitalist consumption, but as machines involving only primary communicative skills gave limited facilities also for alternative speaking, listening and recording, and for some direct autonomous production. This is still only a marginal area, by comparison with the huge centralized systems of amplification and recording, based on varying but always substantial degrees of control and selection in the interests of the central social order. Yet though marginal it is not insignificant, in contemporary political life.
>
> Raymond Williams, *Problems in Materialism and Culture*

First Incident: When Syria withdrew from Nasser's United Arab Republic in 1961, Yemen's Imam Aḥmad was emboldened to oppose the Egyptian president's brand of socialism, which he felt was incompatible with the tenets of Islam. He expressed his views on the subject in a poem published in an Adeni newspaper on December 9, 1961.

Second Incident: It is said that one of the first things the Republicans did at the outbreak of the revolution on September 26, 1962, was to secure the Ṣanʿā radio station, and that one of the first things the citizens of Yemen heard on the radio the next morning was a poem composed by the tribal poet Ṣāliḥ Saḥlūl declaring the institution of the republic.

What both these incidents illustrate is the involvement of poetry in the declaration of state policy through the use of modern communications, especially the radio. These are the communicative means that Raymond Williams (1980, 56) argues are critical to the political order. In this chapter, however, we will see that the tape recorder is at least equal in importance to radio and television in disseminating and shaping state policy in tribal Yemen, a fact that requires some explanation.

Since the 1962 revolution Yemen, along with other states of the Arabian Peninsula, has undergone widespread and often rather disruptive social changes. Nevertheless, and as we saw in the last chapter, some tribesmen strongly believe that the changes have not occurred fast enough or equitably enough. In this chapter we will come across the opposite view, as expressed in a poetic exchange created by two of contemporary Yemen's finest tribal poets. They fear that modernization has led to Westernization and hence an abandonment on the part of Yemeni youth of ancient tribal traditions. This transformation of values, they believe, has weakened, and will continue to weaken, the country politically. In their opinion tribalism has been the nation's backbone from time immemorial; to threaten tribal traditions is to imperil the country's political independence, for Yemen will be gradually absorbed into the Western sociopolitical system. In the context of Islamic resurgence, which has vehemently rejected Westernization, this exchange of views in 1979 is highly significant. For this reason it also has great importance for the formation of government policies. The state, in effect, cannot ignore this vocal opinion without, as in the case of prerevolutionary Iran, endangering itself.

To interpret the poetic exchanges, let us first consider Yemeni tribal and state relations and the ways they may be affected by the communication practices involving the tape recorder and the market system. A look at the dilemmas facing a modernizing society like Yemen will also serve as a prelude to understanding the context of the poetic exchanges.

Tribe and State in Khawlān

Like Morocco, Iran, Saudi Arabia, Afghanistan, Libya, and Jordan, North Yemen has a sizable tribal population. However, the central government is still not strong enough to wield authority with the same heavy hand that, say, the government of Iran has in past decades. Politically the tribes therefore remain relatively autonomous. They are also quite well armed. In fact, to some extent the government depends on the armed tribes, especially in the east, to help defend its borders in case of external aggression, and it is always nervous about the possibility of tribal dissidence stirred up by its policies. In short, the tribes are a power to be reckoned with, and their actions and discourses are not taken lightly by the state.

As can be imagined, tribes and the state are at political cross-purposes much of the time. The Ṣanʿā regime would like to bring the tribes to heel; the tribes would like to remain autonomous while still influencing, if not controlling, the central state. Tribal sheikhs are obviously important for both the state (insofar as it can indirectly rule the tribes through them) and the tribes (insofar as their leaders can represent tribal interests in the workings of the central government). Besides the sheikhs, the other traditional arm of the state has been the religious elite.[1]

No research that I am aware of has been conducted on the way in which the tribes in the Middle East may attempt to influence state power through a communication system. In this chapter I suggest one such avenue of research by examining a poetic production that depends crucially on the tape recorder in the context of a market system. This demonstration is in keeping with earlier attempts in this book to argue that an understanding of tribal politics in the Middle East has been impeded by a neglect of the study of discourses critically related to power. Let us, therefore, turn next to a sketch of the communication system in question.

The Tape Recorder and the Market

The *qaṣīdah* lends itself to the intervention of tape recording without seriously distorting its aesthetic practice. Why? It is not the act of creation itself that is meant to be public but rather the text-utterance (or product); therefore, taping the poem does not seriously affect the artwork, for the tape recorder is designed precisely for this purpose. Its use is specifically tied to the vocalization (but not the performance) of the text-utterance, which is the focus of the *qaṣīdah* in illiterate tribal culture. The *qaṣīdah* is composed to be heard, and this hearing is what the tape recorder makes possible. This last fact is one of the reasons that tape recording is more suitable than writing to the reproduction of the text-utterance of the *qaṣīdah.*[2]

The other reason that the tape recorder is advantageous is that it not only makes possible the reproduction of the text-utterance but also actually sparks its *production.* The first poet whose work we will analyze in this chapter, aṣ-Ṣūfī, composed and then recited a poem that he taped and sent to his friend, a poet by the name of al-Maᶜlah, who hails from Dhamār. Al-Maᶜlah composed his reply, taped it, and sent the tape back to Khawlān, where aṣ-Ṣūfī listened to it. Poets can go to local markets or to the stereo stores in the major cities to buy tape recordings of the latest "hits," listen to them, and then decide whether they want to respond. If they do respond with a poem, they can tape it and send it by messenger directly to the poet or sell it to the stereo stores for distribution, on the assumption that the other poet will eventually hear the reply. The point is that the ease and economy with which a poet can make his work known to the public via the socioeconomic institutions connected with the tape recorder (as compared with the more traditional methods of face-to-face recitations or the *dōshān*'s singing) make it possible for poets to respond quickly to each other's work. Far from endangering the composition of *qaṣīdah* poetry, the new technology of the tape recorder has actually encouraged it, particularly in a social group many of whose members are illiterate.

As a result there are two social modes of poetic production. One is practiced in the older, traditional style of intimate, face-to-face gatherings around the illiterate poet or *dōshān.* The other is the modern, primarily urban style, which depends not only on new technology but also on a capitalist market system embedded within a far-flung social network (involving poet, technician-recorder, distributor, store owner, buyer, and audience) and is more likely to be, though not necessarily, tied to literacy.[3]

For the politics of the nation-state, the reproduction and dissemination of tribal poetry through the socioeconomic institutions connected with the tape recorder have enormous consequences. One might imagine that the effect is primarily one-way: that is, the central state tries to impose its control over tribal politics. There is no question that the national government does indeed try to co-opt the voice of various poets, as we have seen, in order to promote its own policies and agendas, but there is a major difference between communication media such as television, newspaper, and radio, on the one hand, and the tape recording industry, on the other, which makes the political effect a two-way street. The former media are almost invariably tied to large-scale capitalist enterprises and require relatively large amounts of money, whereas a tape recorder can be operated by anyone, and tapes can be readily and inexpensively produced, reproduced, and distributed to the population at large. Even more crucial is the fact that the former media, though not exactly easy for the central government to control, are certainly more controllable than the tape-recording industry. As happened, for instance, during the Iranian revolution, antigovernment tapes can be smuggled into the country because they are small, lightweight, and portable. In addition, almost anyone can afford a radio cassette player to listen to in the privacy of one's own home. North Yemen has a black market of officially banned tapes, which are available in the stereo stores or through private channels, and there is little that the government can do to suppress them. As a result of these factors the government can be challenged on tapes, which are then sold on the black market.

The Dilemma of Modernization

For our purposes it is not necessary to quote involved statistics for Yemen regarding the new hospitals, roads, schools, airports, power plants, factories, water treatment and sewage facilities, clinics, and other improvements that have been introduced since the beginning of the Republic in 1962 or to specify who has been the beneficiary of them. A great deal has been accomplished since then, and the hope is that a great deal more will be achieved, but fears also exist that this technological progress has to be paid for with a high, perhaps too high, political and moral cost. These fears will be discussed in our examination of the poetic dialogue. For now, it is important to understand the politics and economics of this modernization. Who funds it? Who directs it? What are its sociopolitical consequences?

Yemen is one of the poorest nations in the Middle East. The discovery of oil in 1984 in the eastern region of the country may in the long run make a difference in its per capita income, but it is too soon to tell. Oil prices, unfortunately for Yemen, became depressed when the discovery was announced. The country has no other major natural resources on which to base an ambitious development scheme. Although its labor supply is sizable—a large portion was exported to Saudi Arabia and the Gulf states during the height of the oil boom—its workers are basically unskilled and are mainly used only in low-paying, menial service and construction jobs (houseboy, gardener, street sweeper, car mechanic, and construction worker). Its only other major resource is the cash crops harvested from its extensive, but delicate, agricultural system; very few of these products are exported, however, and a disproportionately large amount of the cash crop is *gāt*. Vegetables are grown only for local consumption and often are more expensive than imported vegetables from Lebanon and Egypt, so that the price structure does not encourage agricultural production. In the late 1970s and early 1980s most of the able-bodied males who could have tended the fields had emigrated to work elsewhere in the peninsula; hence, it is not clear how well the agricultural labor force could have responded to increased demand for domestic products, especially since the income from migrant labor was higher than what could be earned from farming. This admittedly sketchy picture of the economic possibilities for development reveals that Yemen would have to finance that development from two major sources: foreign aid and remittance payments from migrant laborers. Indeed, both have figured prominently since the early 1970s.

These two sources of income are independent of each other and are controlled and administered through two different, though related, political agencies. Foreign aid, or that part of it that is nonmilitary, is channeled directly into the central government and managed by its Central Planning Organization (CPO). On more than one occasion I heard that a foreign government would give aid directly to a particular region, thereby circumventing the central government entirely, but I am not aware of any evidence to prove this assertion. Remittance payments go directly to the families and other relatives of the migrant laborers (money is sent back through the banking system) and are thus privately controlled. However, through local initiative and then government encouragement various regions of the country have started their own local development associations (LDAs), which have organized and paid for small-scale development projects with private and government funds. For example, if a wadi in Khawlān feels it needs a new clinic, it will ask its LDA to help finance the project, perhaps with the assistance of the CPO. There is another aspect of the private sector to consider, namely, the capitalist free-enterprise system, which takes the initiative to build certain kinds of facilities that will make its enterprises more profitable—hotels, for instance, for tourists; large housing complexes around the edges of the city to house foreign company employees; roads along which goods and equipment can be transported; and so forth.

Modernization in Yemen has proceeded, then, along a very different path than the one the Saudis or the Iranians have taken, simply because Yemen has not had the massive financial resources these nations have enjoyed and because the government has not directly controlled the process. Some developers have said that Yemen is blessed and, in a sense, unique among developing nations because of the local initiative demonstrated by the LDAs. Though the rulers of the state can only indirectly take credit for the beneficial results of economic and social development, they cannot, as in the case of Saudi Arabia and particularly Iran, be directly blamed for the consequences deemed harmful by some fundamentalist or conservative sectors of the population.

Even more than the economics of development, the politics of development are complex and to the nonexpert like myself remain something of a mystery. Donor nations such as Kuwait, Saudi Arabia, the Soviet Union, and the United States have an important influence on the central government as a consequence of their aid. But the pressure to institute sweeping educational, social, and political reforms does not come just from donor countries. It is also applied politically and militarily by the Marxist regime of South Yemen, which went to war with the Y.A.R. in 1979 and subsequently waged an internal guerilla campaign to pressure the Ṣanᶜā regime into continuing its political concessions. Saudi Arabia has been implicated in a number of coup attempts and, it is said, regularly infiltrates the northern borders to deal directly with the tribes. The increased power of foreign governments over the internal politics of Yemen is perceived by many, not just the two tribal poets heard in this chapter, to be a major threat to the political autonomy of Yemen. Indeed, like many other third-world countries, Yemen is caught in the unenviable position of having to play off one superpower against the other through clever dealings with their regional client states.

The expansion of the free-enterprise system has, to be sure, stimulated growth, but it has also had significant adverse effects on the social system. New companies have brought foreign workers into the country, who live by and large in the major cities and, whether rightly or wrongly, are sometimes perceived as having a malign influence on the Yemenis who come into contact with them. Not only urban populations are exposed to the potential ill effects, for many rural youths, not being able to find lucrative work locally, have had to migrate to the cities, where, it is feared, they will pick up all kinds of evil habits. The capitalist system has also encouraged a kind of materialism, which may be good for business, but some of the more religious and conservative elements deplore the neglect of spiritual values following an orgy of consumerism. Perhaps less obvious is the emergence of a new class structure, which divides the nation into groups that are arguably more opposed to each other than any others have been in Yemen's past.

Even in relatively remote Khawlān I could sense how modernization was having deleterious effects on tribal social and political institutions. Many of the young men who returned from Saudi Arabia or from schools in Ṣanᶜā had forgotten the customs that form an intense part of everyday life, much to the chagrin of their elders. Once I witnessed a scene in which a young man, dressed in all his newly purchased finery, was being greeted by an elder in the elaborate routine customary of tribal social interaction, but the young man was flustered because he did not remember the precise formulaic responses or their sequencing. His failure to perform them properly was in a real sense a failure to constitute himself as a member of the social group. Hence the young man's consternation; for though his new clothes might signal his incorporation into one sort of world, one that glimmers meretriciously and alluringly at a distance from the tribe, his speechlessness left him excluded from the world to which he had returned.

The Poetic Dialogue

In the context of the above remarks on modernization in Yemen, let us now consider a dialogue between two great tribal poets. The first is by the Khawlānī Ṣāliḥ bin Gāsim aṣ-Ṣūfī and was sent to his friend ᶜAlī Mugbil al-Maᶜlah, a poet and merchant from the Ḥadā tribe (a member of the Ḥāshid confederation). (See Appendix F for Arabic transcription.)

Said the youth, father of Muḥammad: "Everything comes to an end, || and every creature in the world will perish.
O bird, winged one, beat the air and depart; || convey an envelope containing a rhymed poem
From ʿAyn, Khawlān, which will not tolerate any good-for-nothing, || neither human devils nor jinn.
O bird, do not land except in Dhamār, the most beautiful || of all places which God has watered.
When you have arrived in the town, you must inquire || about the son of Mugbil Muḥammad, the best of men.
Of glorious majesty, very courageous, he would never be stingy, || the anchor of generosity and nobility of all time.
Lion cub of al-Ḥadā, whenever he sees the stranger, he receives him [in his house]; || he says: 'Welcome to you on the eyes.'
He goes out of his way to please the guest, || a lodging for the needy from far and wide.
Poet and merchant, there is none like him; || a liar is he who says he is like him, building his great deeds on high.
Maʿlah, the highborn, whose ancestry stretches back to the earliest times, || [is a descendant] of a group of Zaydi sons, offspring of snakes [an honorific].
The army of al-Ḥadā, which shakes the earth when it mobilizes; || in fear of it, the Russian army trembles as well as the American.
If he asks you: 'What is your news?' then tell him: 'I have come to you as a messenger || with a letter from the poet of the Khawlān army.
Your friend, who has stuck to his principles and never wavered, || keeps his friendship, secretly and openly.
Greetings to you [as many times as] His lightning flashes and rain falls; || From the mountain peaks all night long the thunder claps.
Irrigate the desiccated land, and with rain shower [the earth]; || revive its fruits and let the blossoms on the branches bloom.
May it inundate you, O judge of the people of reason and the people of solution [i.e. wisdom], || judge of virtuous and inspired people.

With musk, mastic, *nadd,* sandalwood, || ambergris perfume, rose water, and sweet basil
Especially for you [I give exquisite scents], O son of Mugbil, and hurriedly || from Ṣāliḥ aṣ-Ṣūfī, who gives them to you personally.
[As many times] [I give these greetings] as the Indian boat sailed and carried || goods from India to fill every store,
As many times as every believer spends the night praying || and obeys his God sincerely and thoroughly.'
O messenger, speak to al-Maʿlah, do not be timid, || [speak] truthful words from the best of friends.
Tell him: 'The son of Gāsim bin ʿAlī is weary || with a life in which the man of honor is degraded.
My heart no longer loves this life || If I am exhausted on the day of glory [?].
The hardships of time have left my heart numb. || Where can I get another heart in this lifetime?
I believe a heart cannot be exchanged || and the son of a Muslim does not become an infidel or a Christian.
Neither a pious man nor someone fasting attends a party || which every bum and drunkard goes to.
Honey from the stomach of bees does not turn into vinegar, || [the honey] that the bee manufactures at the beginning of ʿAllānī.
No yellow orange comes from the colocynth, || nor do the devil's figs appear in the pomegranate.
Likewise, the crab apple does not resemble the pure, dry dates || from the palm trees of Najrān.
Precious stones and pearls remain changeless for all time, || nor do sapphires change, nor coral.
And thus are people distinguished and set apart, || not being like people in other countries.
O nation of religion, none of you is ignorant; || the pharaoh and Hāmān have passed away from the world.
Nimrod, who was invincible, passed away, || and the prophet of God, Solomon, also.
The best and most beloved, the Chosen One, has also gone, || to whom God revealed the verses of the Qurʾān.
And al-Ḥaydarah, who with his sword threw to the ground

the enemies, || passed away after he cut off the heads of the horned ones [i.e. the most courageous, like rams].
What made you, O our free Yemen, become subservient || when you have so many young men who stab their opponent [i.e. are fierce warriors]?
I never would have thought that the towering peaks would be leveled || when its masters, who have protected them, are descendants of Qaḥṭān,
Who destroyed every attacker as soon as he arrived || with *shēsh khānah, hirtiyyah,* and *sulṭānī* [all old rifles],
And they took as booty the wealth of the Romans and that of Hitler, || the army of the Ethiopians, they, and the sons of the Turks.
O our people, every courageous person who meets us trembles; || it is our army which conquered Persians and Romans.
And today neither the Kalashnikoff nor the German rifle does us any good, || neither cannons nor machine guns.
O son of Yemen, your [only] aim is to relax in talk, || chewing *gāt,* whose leaves are picked from every garden.
Do you not know that the nations are infiltrating our people? || Communists, Baʿthists, allies of Qaddafi and Italians.
Nasser's party has taken root || as well as the Syrian party, the Baghdadi and Lebanese.
The pro-Western party from the north infiltrates || and the pro-Eastern party led by Mount Shamsān [the mountain overlooking the port of Aden].
And he who has entered the country does not say the *shahādah* [the Muslim declaration of faith] and does not believe in God; || this one is a Magi [adherent of Mazdaism, hence a heretic] and that one a pagan.
No one in all these parties says *bismillāh,* || in the name of God, the Creator of the universe.
O our people, wake up and get moving before you are lost; || do not be deceived by the atheists.
Enough of combing your locks, you fool; || be done with your hippiness, a thousand shames on your beards.

These pants are good and those pants are better, || green and red—you see, different designs and colors.
No such good news was ever received: || that our people are saved from the idolators.
O son of Yemen, if you keep your door locked, || neither idolators nor adulterers will enter.
O Maʿlah, advise the men of the people to remain tribal || before they walk zigzag paths and enter blind alleys.
O Mount Bēnān, tell the people what to do || while the leader of the nation strikes down every traitor,
Our distinguished leader, who leads the campaign || and seeks justice against every criminal after he has acquired proof.
The Almighty forgives the sins of anyone who sins; || he who repents and is faithful, God will forgive him.
O Lord, Ṣāliḥ calls to You and beseeches You || in Your name, Your knowledge and omniscience, O Generous One.
We have called on none but You in the past and [will continue to do so] in the future, || O You on whom we rely.
I ask Your forgiveness if my sins have overburdened me, || O You whom we beseech, O You of high degree.
Your forgiveness and Your pardon and Your mercy make easy for us; || in Your hands we are born naked on the Day of Resurrection.
On the day the scales tilt and balance, || O Everlasting Life, tilt the scale in my favor,
On the day when wise minds are baffled || and the angels Mālik and Raḍwān meet [to drag men into Hell].
My purest prayers for the Chosen One are recorded, || prayers and greetings from my heart and tongue.
O people, pray for the one whom our Lord favored, || Muḥammad, who lives in the Paradise of Eden.'"

An Arabic transcription of the first line will suffice to illustrate the fairly simple line structure in aṣ-Ṣūfī's poem:

– – ⏑ – |– ⏑ – |– – ⏑ –| – –
gāl al-fatā bū muḥammad kulla shī yukmal ||

⏑ – ⏑ – | – [⏑] – | – – ⏑ – | – –
wa kulla makhlūg[a] min dār al-ḥayāh fānī

One caesura divides the line into equal halves. The meter is a form frequently encountered in Yemeni poetry, with each hemistich ending in two long tones. The rhyme is perhaps the subtlest part of the poem's structure. On the surface it appears to alternate *-al* or *-il* at the end of the first hemistich with *-ānī* at the end of the second. But there is a "deeper" or linguistically more abstract relationship between the ends of the hemistichs, for almost without exception the first hemistich ends in two *closed* heavy syllables (CvCCvC), whereas the second ends in two *open* ones (Cv̄Cv̄):

First Hemistich	*Second Hemistich*
tawakkal	gayfānī
ʾajmal	ʾamzānī
tisʾal	insānī
yibkhil	azmānī
agbal	aʿyānī

In other words, there are two kinds of rhyme: one repeats the same phonological segments, and the other repeats the same syllabic structure. This rhyme scheme is an important element of the sound structure of the line, which al-Maʿlah would be expected to imitate in his response, according to the rules of poetic dialogue; hence, we must be on the lookout for it in his *qaṣīdah.*

The overall structure of the poem fits the conventional pattern outlined in the previous chapter.

1. Line 1 declares the poem to be a statement by the "father of Muḥammad," using the formulaic opening *gāl al-fatā.*
2. Lines 2–5 are a conventional address of the messenger (in the guise of a bird), who is instructed to deliver the poem to al-Maʿlah in Dhamār.
3. Lines 6–11 are devoted entirely to *mujāmilah* or the praising of aṣ-Ṣūfī's poet friend and of his tribe, the Ḥadā.
4. Lines 12–20 are the usual greeting routine found in all traditional poetry.
5. Lines 21–55 are set aside for the true substance or topic of the poem, its message.

6. Lines 56–64, which end the poem, are devoted to the glorification and praise of God, beseeching His forgiveness, and to prayers on behalf of the Prophet Muḥammad.

Section 5 interests us most, and I will shortly discuss it in detail, but for now let us observe how deeply, even startlingly, traditional this poem is in its format. I say deeply traditional because the poet does not omit a single routine expected to occur in the tribal *qaṣīdah*. He draws each one out, as if he were savoring its particular content and feeling tone. He takes his time where other poets who do not omit the routines might nevertheless rush headlong through them to get to the message portion as quickly as possible. Aṣ-Ṣūfī hoped by this poem to make his debut on the national stage as a major voice in Yemen, yet the particular form of the poem is archetypically tribal and sounds parochial to many ears, as if the poet were making no concession whatsoever to a wider, nontribal audience. This puzzle—the seeming contradiction between the tribal poetic form and the wider national appeal it is meant to achieve—I will try to solve later, after first examining the content of the poem more carefully.

Aṣ-Ṣūfī begins (line 21) by telling his friend how distressed he feels, though as yet he does not explain the reason. We have seen this move before as a conventional way of introducing the subject matter of the *qaṣīdah*. What is interesting is the way in which the poet states the dilemma of the contemporary social situation by which his *hājis* has been inspired to compose this poem: namely, he states it in a series of logical paradoxes (lines 25–31). Such a device was employed in the civil war poetry of al-Ghādir, who insisted that Khawlān would never join the republic even if a series of logical impossibilities were to become reality; and the audience probably makes an association between this poem and that other great one of the past, between aṣ-Ṣūfī and one of Khawlān's greatest tribal sheikhs, between this time and the period 1962–69 when Yemen was being fought over not simply by the Republicans and the Royalists but also by the Egyptians and the Saudis and by the Soviets and the Americans. These lines establish a parallelism between two kinds of discourses and in the process suggest an analogy between the two historical time frames in which the discourses are situated. Is this suggested homology between now and then, between one poem and another, between one poet and another, merely an accident? I don't think so. Aṣ-Ṣūfī talks about the present in much the same way al-Ghādir talked about his day, that is, as a time when Yemen seems to have become other than what it ought to be, twisted into an image of itself it no longer recognizes. The transformation is due to the changes the Egyptian occupation has wrought and the contemporary struggle for the soul of the nation.

Let us look more closely at the logical trope. Aṣ-Ṣūfī asks: does a Muslim become a Christian? does a pious man indulge in drink or associate with disreputable souls? does honey turn into vinegar or the orange develop from the seed of the colocynth? These paradoxes are intriguing but as yet abstract, without a concrete reference in the sociopolitical world, until the poet comes to the line "And thus are people distinguished and set apart, || not being like people in other countries" (line 31). The audience now realizes the issue to which the poet is alluding, namely, that the Yemeni people are a distinctive nation. Yet a paradoxical situation has arisen, in which they are becoming, by dint of personal choice or inevitable social pressures, like someone else. In a very important sense the whole issue of self, or identity, has come once again to the forefront of concern, only this time the issue is the identity of the nation-state.

The poet begins his appeal to the people (line 32) with the vocative *yā ʾummat ad-dīn* (O nation of religion, i.e. Islam), thereby encapsulating the essence of the people's identity in its commitment to Islam. He then proceeds to admonish that nation when he says, "None of you is ignorant," in other words, you have all been instructed in the credo and practices of Islam, so there is no excuse for backsliding. Next, he mentions certain great historical figures of the past (lines 32–35), which include the pharaoh who opposed Moses and his brother Aaron (who is called Hāmān in the poem),[4] Nimrod, the son of Cush, who was said in the Bible to have been a mighty hunter, King Solomon (considered by Muslims to have been a prophet), the Prophet Muḥammad, and al-Ḥaydarah or ʿAlī. The poet repeatedly says about all of these figures that they have departed (*sār*) the world. They all were great warriors in their own lands (ancient Egypt, Israel, and Arabia) who fought bravely to keep their countries free. One can find support for this interpretation in line 36, where the poet asks, "What made you, O our free Yemen, become subservient || when you have so many young men who stab their opponent?" I think it reasonable to assert that up to this point aṣ-Ṣūfī is warning his audience that although they were once a proud and mighty nation, they are now in danger of sharing the fate of other great nations in history, unless, like Moses or Muḥammad, they resist.

That Yemen was once a great nation he reminds his audience in lines 37–42. He alludes to the great tribes of Yemen through the synecdochic figure *al-jibāl ash-shāmikhah* (towering peaks) and, on the one hand, glorifies them by their pedigree descent from Qaḥṭān, the mythical head of the South Arabians in the genealogy of peninsular society, and, on the other hand, casts aspersions on them by suggesting that these peaks have been leveled—in other words, that the tribes have become powerless. He then proceeds to remind his audience of Yemen's past prowess in defeating its enemies. For instance, we are told that the tribes "destroyed every attacker as soon as he arrived" (line 38) and then in the next line these invaders are mentioned by name. The allusion in line 39 seems to be to Aelius Gallus, who was sent by Rome to crush the power of the South Arabian kingdoms because they had grown rich as middlemen, charging Rome an exorbitant price for transporting African, Hadhrami, and Indian incense used in funerary rituals. Mention of the army of Hitler is a confused reference to the German power backing the Turks in World War I, whose occupation of Yemen ended with their defeat by the Allies. The "army of the Ethiopians" is most probably the pre-Islamic Christian kingdom founded in Yemen by Ethiopian conquerors, who were subsequently defeated and driven out of the country by the Yemeni people. But aṣ-Ṣūfī reminds his audience that today the Yemeni people are unable to drive out invaders, for "neither the Kalashnikoff nor the German rifle does us any good." Yemenis are ridiculed in line 42 for caring about nothing except idly chewing *gāt* with their friends.

By setting up a parallel between present circumstances and past history, as-Ṣūfī is able to define a danger and a remedial course of action—if, that is, he can prod the country out of its lethargy. The past becomes an icon for the present, a redemptive way of being and acting in the present world. Tradition triumphs by returning the country to its genuine self, by reclaiming its destiny. We can now understand why the poem is self-consciously traditional in its form. Just as al-Gharsī's poem was stripped of nearly all ceremonial rhetoric, getting right down to the message because that mode was in keeping with the progressivism of the poetic voice, so in reverse aṣ-Ṣūfī's poem assumes the archetypical tribal mode, which is in harmony with his traditionalist and highly tribal stance. In other words, the traditionalism of the poetic form is harmonious with the traditionalism of the political point of view. But the connection between tribal poetry and the message of aṣ-Ṣūfī's poem will become clearer when we have completed the analysis of his appeal to the Yemeni people.

The enemies from without, who threaten the country's political independence, are named in lines 43–47. They are the communists and Baʿthists, the supporters of Qaddafi, the Nasserites, Syrian elements, the Iraqis, the Lebanese, and, for some reason explainable only by the rhyme, the Italians (or is this a reference to the Ethiopians?). The most important accusation comes in line 45: the pro-Western (i.e. pro-American) party that infiltrates from the north is clearly Saudi Arabia, though in keeping with the tendency to allude rather than specify, the name of the country is never mentioned; and the pro-Eastern party led by Mount Shamsān is clearly a reference to the Adeni government and its Russian allies. Aṣ-Ṣūfī proclaims all these elements in lines 46–47 to be godless and impious and for that reason subversive of the Yemeni political order. Then in line 48 comes his rallying cry to the people: wake up and do something before it is too late!

The ending seems disappointing, however, in that it does not give a positive, prescriptive program of action to redress the country's problems, much as, for example, al-Gharsī tries to do in his poem. What we get instead is a steady stream of denunciation of male youth. They are ridiculed for being vain and effeminate ("Enough of combing your locks, you fool" [line 49]), and their foppish dress, aped from the West, is satirized in the indirect speech of his sarcastic line "These pants are good and those pants are better, || green and red—you see, different designs and colors" (line 50). Pants, especially the tight-fitting ones worn by urban males, are not a manly attire among traditional tribesmen. Women in fact wear pants under their dresses, whereas men usually wear only a knee-length, heavily pleated wrap called a *magṭab* (a variant of which in the city is the *fūṭah*). In a tribesman's perspective, then, when the male youth adopt the Western fashion of wearing pants, they are acting like women, not men. The poet mocks the youth for being concerned more with the different fashions available in the market than with the significant moral and political predicaments facing the country.

Aṣ-Ṣūfī proposes two vague courses of action by which to avoid the erosion of Yemen's venerated traditions. First, in line 52 he exhorts the people to "keep your door locked," a phrase that has to be understood in terms of the conventional analogy between house and nation. Translated into concrete political terms, this closed-door policy would of course lead to tighter control over entry of foreigners into the country and perhaps even expulsion of many so-called undesirable elements. Second, and certainly more significant, aṣ-Ṣūfī beseeches people like his friend al-Maᶜlah to preserve the old tribal ways of life, for he is convinced that strong *gabyilah* (tribalism) will keep Yemen politically independent: "O Maᶜlah, advise the men of the people to remain tribal || before they walk zigzag paths and enter blind alleys" (line 53). The poet's appeal strikes a deeply sympathetic chord with a large segment of the tribal audience, who sense that political, economic, and technological changes since the revolution have altered the identity of Yemen beyond recognition.

How, then, does the poet intend to achieve his objective of retribalizing and retraditionalizing the country? He does not explicitly say. Are we therefore to account the poem a failure? After all, in the message section the poet is expected to provide an analysis of an issue and then a solution. But it is precisely at this juncture, I would argue, that the reason for the deep traditionalism of aṣ-Ṣūfī's poetic practice becomes evident, for this practice is, as I have hinted, a resplendent icon of the tribalism he espouses and encourages. By listening to this poem, by being moved by its beauty and persuaded by its message, the audience is admiring a part—a very important part—of tribalism itself; the listener not only admires it from a distance, as a viewer in a museum would a canvas, but actually participates in tribal practice, for the listening is part of the practice, part of being in the world the practice creates. In other words, aṣ-Ṣūfī's program of reform began in the very first line and continues to build to the end. The reform is a consummate text-utterance created in the traditional, tribal style. He puts forward a model of being-in-the-world, which through its beauty he hopes will be compelling enough to be emulated by further poetic production in the same vein. And if the composition of poetry is not just the creation of an artwork but, as I argued in the previous chapters, also social production, then it stands to reason that aṣ-Ṣūfī is creating the social tradition he is convinced will save the country, for being a tribal poet is inseparable from the other values and practices of *gabyilah*. Furthermore, he has directed his *qaṣīdah* at another poet, who, as we know, is expected to reply with a poem as good or better, so that the tradition not only is kept alive but is improved upon in the response poem. The hope is that the reaction will not stop there, that a wider listening audience made possible by the tape recorder will hear the poetic exchange and be moved to compose their own tribal poems, which in turn will inspire others to reply in kind, and so on ad infinitum—another reason that the tape recorder is considered to be an ally, not a foe, of tradition.

Let us now see whether indeed al-Maʿlah rises to the challenge offered by his friend. (See Appendix G for Arabic transcription.)

The brother of ʿAlī said: "Times are changing. || Some
places are desirable and other places are not.
Only You remain, O God, defending us from ignominy, || O
You who raised the sky without a column.
You level and raise [the earth]. You oversee and
contemplate. || Your judgment is sound. You are the one
and only God.
The Almighty who created the rain cloud [or flood?] and
dew, || He who created me, formed and made me,
He who created lightning in the midst of the sky and
showered || from the sky water which irrigates every
thirsty thing
And revived the earth, so that it could bear fruit. || And
mankind lives comfortably, Arab and non-Arab.
And the sun travels in its house for mankind, || providing
for man's livelihood with a generous hand.
[God is] sufficient for all creatures, lofty and secure, ||
creator of everything without forgetting a thing.
In praise of Him the thunder extols and the ground shows
obedience. || All the creatures of creation echo His praise.
And every creature praises and beseeches Him, || the master
of all things. He is a Just Giver.
I praise Him as many times as it rains in the evening. ||
My praise and thanks to my Lord as long as He may let
me live.
In every condition I praise Him. It is my duty. And I act || in
obedience to Him [in the power of] my best efforts and
abilities.
From now on, the sweetness of youth has vanished. || My
heart, O my friend, has exhausted me with despair.
What is wrong with you? The real man is the one who says

'I' (i.e. boasts of his own deeds), you idiot. || He does not say 'my father' [i.e. boast of his ancestry] even if he were a Lugmān [a famous tribal name].

If you do not betray the proverb, then you are a man after my own heart. || If the guest comes to you, say: 'Long life to the arrival.'

Welcome [him] and make him feel at home; greet him and be thrilled by his arrival at your door. || Cherish him; do not take him to a neighbor's house.

Slaughter [animals for dinner] in his honor. I am your father, do not disquiet or fail me. || Spend what you will from my house and storerooms.

Give presents, as I would, to your guest, O youth, and more. || You know the customs regarding my guests.

O my son, make sure that no effort has been spared for the sake of hospitality. || He who honors his guests is never a loser.

The consequences [of hospitality toward] the guest are an unmitigated blessing. || The guest is always right. You must not deny him anything.

From now on, welcome him and make him feel at home. || [Show him] a welcome [so great] it would fill Wādī Silᶜah and Harrān.

The land of al-Ḥadā is from the border of Kōmān to Mōkal, || from Gazan to Manāhil, the [tribal] border of Bēḥān.

Welcome to Gōsī, Ṣayādī, and the son of Ḥarmal, || who honor the guest, young and old.

[And welcome] to aṣ-Ṣūfī, the excellent one, whose heart opens to me, || Ṣāliḥ, son of Gāsim, the noblest person to have come to me

From the people of Khawlān. If the crisis worsens, || they are men of reliance on the day the roars of battle are heard.

Noble people, proud, enduring, and able to solve problems, || the sons of Ṣūfī are the noblest young people.

The district of Hanshal testifies to their greatness || as well as [the greatness of] Suhmi, Shadād, and Suḥmān.

Mount Lōz and the people of al-Bukērī, every man of them is a brave warrior, || [and every man] from the Banī Jabr and the people of Royshān.

And to Sheikh Ṣāliḥ for the amazing poem which has guided [us], || the youth, father of Muḥammad, has lived as the greatest of men.
I received a present which was like the most excellent date from Ḥalḥal ||or a date from ʿAlān and Bēʿān.
By it our courageous friend has made a statement. || I do not know for which [of my] deeds he is rewarding me.
Son of Gāsim, the noble one, who has copiously composed verse, || who scooped from the depths of the sea and gave me to drink,
As a gift, I gave him two thousand bottles of mixed perfumes: || rose water, *nadd, ḥāfūrī,* and sweet basil.
Greetings to him [as many times as] has flashed || the lightning and [as many times as] the thunder claps.
[My] greetings conveyed to the sheikh and his entourage || and to the farmers [as great in number] as a million *faddān,*
One hundred thousand multiplied by one hundred thousand multiplied by two hundred thousand [greetings] to be collected, || and [add] two million total to the account.
Do not fail to greet the youthful sheikh, O messenger, || and if there is any left in the total, give him sixty thousand baskets in greetings.
Greet the sons of Muḥammad when you have arrived || in the region of Nagādhī, which has shepherd and sheep [i.e. is well governed].
His sons and the sons of his brothers, let them take what they want || of the gift, the old and young [of them].
My friend Ṣāliḥ is a noble and a giant among men, || noble in character, who calls to me out of kindness.
Everyone in al-ʿAyn is to be given || a gift of twenty bottles of fine perfume.
He who honors the guest with sheep and sweets: || When the guest comes to him, he fills the stomach of every hungry person.
As for the dear, excellent friend who is brave, || with such verses he perfumes and intoxicates me.

I testify that he deserves renown for his honor. || I endorse [him] with my signature and acknowledgments.
On behalf of my friend Ṣāliḥ, I will declare in the roster || we have not seen the likes of his words before.
I sighed the way the courageous sigh who are defeated. || I sighed from a sorrowful and defeated heart
because of the evils of the times, which have left me speechless. || I composed and put into rhyme in order to bring up what nauseated me.
He who spends the whole night sleepless says || it is as if he dissolves on the fire of his tears,
because of the incident in the Ḥaram Mosque in Mecca, which is linked || to a party of germs, villainous people.
My heart is folded like a fold of yarn or thread. || Fire has burned my flesh and bones.
Iniquitous parties are fighting Islam, || and disturbances are destroying you, banner of Islam.
There remain the deceivers, every dim-witted ass || who wrongly fought the Prophet out of enmity.
Today, inside the Ḥaram Mosque of Mecca, are being brandished || guns of war, among them howitzers and mortars.
They rebelled against the Meccans, lighting torches, || regardless of the fact that the king and his assistants [were in the city].
They have menaced it with warfare [waged with] the M-1 rifle and machine gun. || Not even in such a manner did the pagans behave [before Islam].
In the *giblah* [the direction of prayer, toward Mecca] of the Arabs neither Ethiopians nor Makhwal || nor Khaybar nor Jāhiliyīn [the people before Islam] [behaved in such a manner].
When I heard the broadcast in the hills of Jarwal || transmitting the news of the sin, my tears flowed.
When I heard the news, my soul became hot as pepper. || Sorrow increased my anxiety and left my mind wandering.
The earth shook and trembled; the ground withered. || Every country cried in shock and grief.

Baghdad called Aden, the Levant, and Ṣaffi at-Tall, || and Syria warned Libya and Darmānī [Sudan].
Egypt cried out, and Beirut contacted Nōfal, || and the land of Yemen conveyed the message to London and Iran.
The Najd [Saudi Arabia] shouted and cried for the states to hurry, || and the Gulf warned Tunis and Bahrain.
Sharjah repeated [the news] to Kuwait, so that it would be on the alert, || and India passed on the news as well as Russia and Japan.
[All these states] despised all that the despicable party had done || in the Muslims' *giblah* by way of shameful deeds.
How much have we been angered by causes of distress! || How many problems, how many ignorant people!
What is the use of talking to our unarmed generations? || It would be like shouting to deaf people.
Our youth have strayed from the path of our past generations || in such a way that it leaves the bighearted hopeless.
How many tragedies do we suffer! The youth are stupid, || wedded to pride, rebellious, and good for nothing.
This one is a bum, and that one, if he dons a *fūtah,* wears it long, || and those who wear their hair long have adopted the style of the Christians.
So many people have we exhorted, hoping they would mend their ways. || As God is my witness, my heart bleeds over their loose morals.
We warn, admonish, and advise all who wear long hair || by means of messages [delivered in] sincerity and good faith.
Nothing among them is forbidden [*ḥarram*] or permitted [*ḥallal*], || but each goes about doing things willy-nilly.
What is your honest opinion about Banī Shaᶜfal? || What if I were to go and tell him to answer me the day we meet?
As God is my witness, they deserve to be beaten with clubs || and jailed in the Ghamdān fortress [in Ṣanᶜā].
Among our people, O son of Gāsim, is a generation that stumbles. || It distressed me before it bothered you, O Ṣāliḥ.
The time is out of joint, sweeping men's affairs along with it [lit. dragging along whoever is rolling a stone] || [sweeping

away] the customs of Tubʿ and Ibn Kanʿān [two ancient South Arabian kings].

He who recorded for Yemen a history in inscription || full of glory, majesty, honor, and certainty.

How valiantly did Sēf bin dhī Yazin fight, how fiercely did he wage combat! || He cleansed religion in Egypt and the Sudan.

And Shem, son of Noah, so many men did he defeat, || elevating the just religion above all others.

We have advised the bums to give up the sideburns, || the mutton-chops [lit. beetle] that they let grow under their ears.

We are following their example [i.e. that of the ancestors], O son of Yemen. || We are walking on the side of right, on the straight, high path.

O zealot, do not be lazy about performing your duties. || I beg you, do not reverse your nature and betray yourself.

Do not put your trust in time and the deceptive world. You are wise. || Caesar, the kaiser, and bin Marwānī have all departed."

The son of Mugbil says: "My heart was restless last night. || It dwells on subjects that mortify it.

The deeds of the daring cannot be compared with those of the weak, || nor gold bow down to *ḥumaygānī.*

The arrow of the bow is not equal to the mustard branch, || nor dirt comparable to April wheat.

Nor are almonds equivalent in price to horseradish, || and prickly pear does not have *murgān* in it.

I have never heard of pearls rusting, || nor is an ivory-handled dagger given [as a present] [when the gazelle handle is prized].

Rise, O messenger of the son of Mugbil, tighten the straps on the saddle of the female donkey, || [proceed] from ʿAns and pass behind Sufyānī,

Go into the heart of al-Ḥadā, the place of nobility and source of tribal traditions. || People on whom we can rely to defend our honor [lit. a people of reliance when anything happens to skin and cloth].

Son of al-Mughaddī and Kōmān of Lower ʿAnā, || al-Gaʿshamī, al-Jarādī, and the people of Ḥayyānī.

The men of al-Farāṣī, who are from the frightening ʿAbīdah tribe, || and the ʿAmās, who have many brave young men.
Al-Bukhētī, whose army is famous: when it mobilizes, || the earth shakes. It has youthful warriors.
Like Bukhētī is Muḥammad bin ʿAlī: when he pounces, || he deals the enemy a hundred blows.
And there is still the son of Gōs: in raids he is a deadly scourge || of deep-rooted glory, a sultan, son of a sultan.
The glory of al-Ḥadā, the marrow of Nājī, [is like] a branch that when it sways || frightens the towering mountain peaks.
If sounds of gunfire break out, al-Ḥadā is on the move. || Behind it so many Thubānīs and Ḍubyānīs do I find.
They attack the opponent with arrows from the long bow. || Ṣaʿdah and Hamdān are witness in Yemen [to their prowess].
[I honor] Ānis and Sāgīn from ʿAbdān to Nōfal || and Arḥab, sons of the people of Yaḥyā behind Sinwān.
O messenger, at Zirājah climb up the mountain || behind al-Ḥarūrah and to the left of the Qahlān borders.
Your path is al-ʿAyn, whose lightning has appeared || and has irrigated al-Ḥadā with the exquisite scent of musk and has inundated me.
At Sāriy al-Barg is pure water to drink, || but it caused sorrows in my heart.
Ask after the one who prolonged his stay in al-Ḥadā, || son of Gāsim, the excellent one, Ṣāliḥ who inquired about me.
[He is] from a Khawlānī group, the glorious army; when it is mobilized, || when it is determined [to march], they fire on it like rain.
Out of excessive fear our people deserted tribalism || after they had rallied their forces and equipment.
In the quickest way possible it [Khawlān] drove out the enemy from Yemen's land and eliminated || those forces advancing from the land of Egypt.
Greetings as many times as the lightning in the middle of the sky flashes || and his flood irrigates the quarter of Ghōshah and Haylānī.

[Greetings] everlasting to the Khawlān army, as many times as recited || ʿUthmān bin ʿAffān [the Qurʾān] and glorified God.
Greetings from the tongue of a poet who has not abdicated || his duty to rejoice when someone gives me [a poem].
He [the poet] accepts the response, no matter how much it might distress. || I repay him and please him in gratitude for what he has given me.
It would not be fair for the son of Gāsim to be neglected by us. || Rather, he should be paid double without charge.
I esteem whoever presents favors, || and he is still owed something additional [to be carried] on the shoulders.
And in conclusion, pray for one whom our Lord blessed. || [Pray] for Muḥammad and his people for all eternity."

From the first line al-Maʿlah's poem conforms to the metrical and rhyme structures of the original, including the subtle rhyme of the CvCCvC and Cv̄Cv̄ syllables:

◡ – ◡ – | – [◡] – | – – ◡ – | – –
ʾakhū ʿalī gāl[a] gad ʾal-wagta yiddāwal ||
– –[◡]– | – ◡ – |– – ◡ –| – –
w-aṭmāʿ bugʿah wa bugʿah mā la-hā mānī

The brother of ʿAlī said: "Times are changing. || Some places are desirable and other places are not."

Now let us analyze the organizational scheme of the poem for purposes of comparison with aṣ-Ṣūfī's *qasīdah.*

1. Line 1 begins with the initial formula *gāl* (he said), as did the first line of aṣ-Ṣūfī's poem. The rest of the line, like its counterpart, is a reflexive statement encapsulating the poem: "Times are changing."

2. Lines 2–12 are an invocation of God and praise of Him, paralleling the original.

3. Lines 13–23 form a block in which the poet addresses his son and tells him to live up to the great tribal traditions of hospitality toward guests. This section is clearly motivated by the general subject of the poem, the tribal traditions that are in danger of being

forsaken by the younger generation. On the one hand it points out what one of these great traditions is, and on the other it serves the younger generation as a lesson in tribalism.

4. In lines 24–29 al-Maʿlah greets Khawlān, aṣ-Ṣūfī's tribal affiliation, and praises its prowess and other attributes.

5. In lines 30–45 al-Maʿlah acknowledges the receipt of aṣ-Ṣūfī's poem, which he praises and for which he expresses his gratitude. Then he conveys his greetings to the poet and his family in al-ʿAyn by the conventional means of offering fine perfumes, incense, and other precious things.

6. The message portion is contained within lines 46–88, which I will discuss in greater detail below. It parallels section 5 in aṣ-Ṣūfī's poem.

7. The conventional theme of addressing a messenger and telling him to deliver the poem to the first poet is handled toward the end of the poem, roughly in lines 89–109.

8. Aṣ-Ṣūfī is greeted once again in lines 107–112; al-Maʿlah makes a special comment concerning the duty of answering a poem received from a friend. It is also a veiled rebuke of various Khawlānī poets who had failed to respond to a poem he had sent around to the eastern tribes.

9. The poem concludes in one line, the conventional invocation of the Prophet Muḥammad and call for prayers on his behalf.

A comparison of the two poems reveals that they contain the same kinds of elements, except that al-Maʿlah's poem tends to elaborate them more (especially the greeting routine and the invocation of God) and to switch their order (for example, the messenger scene is toward the beginning in aṣ-Ṣūfī's poem but toward the end in al-Maʿlah's). The real test, however, comes in al-Maʿlah's treatment of the basic theme. Like his predecessor, he begins by expressing his deeply troubled emotional state, "[I sighed] because of the evils of the times, which have left me speechless" (line 47), and we learn in line 49 the cause of his distress, "the incident in the Ḥaram Mosque." At the risk of slowing down the narrative a bit, let me make clear at this point the chronology and significance of the historical events surrounding this incident.

November 20, 1979, was the beginning of the Islamic year 1400, which because of its centennial symbolism was being celebrated with special fervor by worshipers inside the Grand Mosque of Mecca. The peacefulness of the early morning hours was unexpectedly shattered by volleys of gunfire and shouts of *al-mahdī* (the right-guided one) coming from a band of young men brandishing rifles. Hundreds of worshipers leaped up from their prayers and ran to shut the gates of the mosque, which was now declared occupied in the name of a new messiah; innocent bystanders were kept hostage. Of course, in the eyes of pious Muslims all over the world a sacrilegious act of enormous magnitude had just been committed against the most revered and holy of Islamic shrines. However, the long and drawn-out assault on the mosque by special forces of the Saudi Arabian army left them even more horrified because of the scores of dead it inflicted on both sides.

Lines 49–59 deal with al-Maᶜlah's emotional and moral turmoil over the event and also give a synopsis of what happened. When he heard the news, he tells us, his "heart is folded like a fold of yarn or thread. || Fire has burned my flesh and bones . . . my soul became hot as pepper." His outrage toward the men who so violently occupied the mosque in contravention of all the religious principles of Islam is expressed in the invectives "a party of germs, villainous people" who are worse than the "pagans" or the pre-Islamic Arabs (*jāhiliyīn*) who fought the Prophet. Even the earth reeled and shook in grief (line 59)—once again disruptions in the social order are mirrored in natural disasters. Lines 60–65 attempt to dramatize the great commotion that news of the takeover of the mosque had on the rest of the Muslim world.

Then, suddenly, there is a shift in al-Maᶜlah's commentary in line 66. From grief and shock the tone is transmuted into exasperation as he exclaims, "What is the use of talking to our unarmed generations? || It would be like shouting to deaf people." To whom is the question directed? As much to himself as it is to aṣ-Ṣūfī and the wider audience, but it becomes clearer as his poem proceeds that al-Maᶜlah is really addressing the youth of the country (and particularly his son), who are unmoved by moral exhortation. The shift in tone announces the theme broached in the original poem. The poet tells aṣ-Ṣūfī that he had apprehensions about the country's youth long before his friend did, apprehensions over the fact that they were embracing social change too quickly and abandoning their tribal traditions in the process, leaving society morally and politically weakened. Describing the present generation as "unarmed" implies that it is not interested in preserving the martial prowess that was the hallmark of tribal honor. Al-Maᶜlah, like aṣ-Ṣūfī, points to details of dress and fashion that he believes indicate that the young have turned their backs on tribal ways. When he sneers, "and that one, if he dons a *fūtah,* wears it long," he alludes to the fact that in tribal fashion the skirt should be worn at the knees. And when he derides Yemeni youth for wearing "their hair long [in] the style of the Christians," it is because tribesmen should ideally wear their hair cropped short. Instead, the youth are imitating heathens. His chagrin prompts the confession that "my heart bleeds over their loose morals." For both poets the change in dress is a symptom, not the cause, of a deeper spiritual decline, which is what truly produces their distress.

Of course, it is not coincidental that al-Maᶜlah laments the tragic takeover of the Grand Mosque at the same time as he castigates Yemeni youth. He invites listeners to entertain a parallel between the disaster occurring in Saudi Arabia and the social tensions mounting in Yemen—two quintessentially Arab states, both at one time fiercely tribal, both still religiously conservative, and both being catapulted from traditionalism to modernity—and it would be hard not to draw the inference that the poet believes a similar upheaval could also befall his country. We have in the Meccan incident an allegory of moral and political import, which the Yemeni people (and Muslims everywhere) are meant to heed as a warning.

How, then, to escape this dilemma of rapid social change that is imperiling morality and destroying the nation? The poet declares that the youth must be taught their proper identity. In four lines (85–88) al-Maᶜlah parallels aṣ-Ṣūfī's text-utterance almost exactly when he uses logical paradoxes to suggest that the youth have turned into something contrary to their nature. Thus, we are told that "the arrow of the bow is not equal to the mustard branch || nor dirt comparable to April wheat." But how to rescue them from this false transformation? First, he addresses his son in the poem in the voice of the stern, didactic father: "What is wrong with you? The real man is the one who says 'I'" (line 14). The last part of this line is a Yemeni saying. It is supposed to teach self-reliance, not dependence on connections to get ahead in life. In other words, concealed within the proverb is an admonition of personal autonomy and achievement, which are central to the values of tribalism. What is dramatized in the poem, then, is a miniature lesson in morality directed toward the youth of Yemen.

The instruction continues: "If the guest comes to you, say: 'Long life to the arrival'" (line 15). The greeting he quotes in Arabic, *ḥayyā bi-man jā-nī,* is a typical, diagnostic tribal greeting and therefore simultaneously accomplishes the act of hospitality and reinforces tribal tradition. Next, the son is given detailed instructions on how to behave toward the guest ("Make him feel at home; greet him and be thrilled by his arrival at your door. || Cherish him; do not take him to a neighbor's house. / Slaughter [animals for dinner] in his honor. . . . || Spend what you will from my house and storerooms. / Give presents. . . . The guest is always right. You must not deny him anything" [lines 16–18, 20]) and reminded that "he who honors his guests is never a loser" (line 19). The father is referring to the fact that honor accrues to the generous host and that maintaining honor in glorious deeds of hospitality is one of the core values of tribalism. After another injunction addressed to the son, he proceeds to explain where the boundaries of his tribe lie in line 22—a continuation of the tribal lesson directed toward the son, who must know the borders in order to defend them.

But the voice shifts slightly in lines 23–29 as the poet begins the customary greeting routine, for now he is addressing the great tribal personalities of Khawlān, which, one assumes, his son overhears so that he can acquaint himself with the roster of political leaders. The very elaborateness and passion with which the father performs the greeting is again meant to instruct the son by example, and in the speech act are embedded laudatory epithets that key for the son the central values of the society. "They are men of reliance on the day the roars of battle are heard. / Noble people, proud, enduring, and able to solve problems" (lines 25–26) means that the best of men, the paragons to be emulated, are loyal to the tribe, especially when it is under attack, dignified, hardened to adversity, and wise.

At the end of the poem, when al-Maʿlah instructs the messenger to ride through the territory of al-Ḥadā, his tribe, he uses these and similar epithets to describe the great Ḥadā personalities. "Go into the heart of al-Ḥadā, the place of nobility and source of tribal traditions" (line 90) is quite significant in the context of this poem, for precisely the survival of these traditions among the poet's people, the Ḥadā tribe, is at stake. The overriding concern in this passage, however, is with martial prowess: "The men of al-Farāṣī, who are from the frightening ʿAbīdah tribe, . . . Al-Bukhētī, whose army is famous: when it mobilizes, || the earth shakes. . . . He deals the enemy a hundred blows. . . . He is a deadly scourge. . . . If sounds of gunfire break out, al-Ḥadā is on the move" (lines 92–95, 97).

It is significant that the epithet "able to solve problems" extends to the conception of the poet, who is an analyzer and solver of pressing issues. In other words, by being a poet, and the very best one possible, al-Maʿlah is showing himself to be an ideal tribesman. Should there be any doubt on this issue, one need only refer to the last line (29) of the greeting routine: "And [greetings] to Sheikh Ṣāliḥ for the amazing poem which has *guided* [us]" (my emphasis). A poem is meant to be a moral map for its listeners; moreover, the whole idea of right guidance has powerful associations with prophecy and the Qurʾān.

Though not exactly beginning a separate section, line 30 opens a routine of greeting addressed specifically to aṣ-Ṣūfī and merits special comment. "I received a present which was like the most excellent date from Ḥalḥal." By this charming metaphor the poet crucially frames the poem as a gift. The specific form that the gift takes, a prized delicacy given to honor the guest, continues to drive home the lesson of generosity, but the general notion of gift exchange also nicely speaks to the notion of a poetic presentation demanding reciprocity. In fact, the poem not only matches aṣ-Ṣūfī's almost exactly in form but also intensifies it by the greater detail and number of lines devoted to the various sections. Al-Maʿlah continues to talk about poetic practice when he asserts that "by it our courageous friend has made a statement" (line 31), a key to the interpretation of this whole exchange, which I will turn to in a moment. Befitting his status as a close friend, aṣ-Ṣūfī receives an effusive greeting, one that extends for fifteen lines, and the way the speech act is performed once again highlights a central value of tribalism.

The remedy, then, according to the poet, for the ills that plague the contemporary moral order is to teach the young well. The instruction is to be carried out by implicit example as much as by explicit word. But aṣ-Ṣūfī stressed awareness of history as critical to reforming the moral conscience. And in this respect, too, al-Maʿlah follows his predecessor. In lines 76–83 he reminds his audience of Yemen's greatness: the wealthy, powerful kings of the spice trade, "who recorded for Yemen a history in inscription || full of glory, majesty, honor, and certainty"; the expulsion from the country of the Persian satrapy by Sēf bin dhī Yazin, perhaps Yemen's greatest culture hero; and Shem, the founder of the city of Ṣanʿā and a valiant fighter. As if to salute tribalism in Yemen, the poet concludes with a long, incantatory paean to the great names and places of the two regions from which the poets hail.

Significance of the Poetic Dialogue

It is clear that the two poems considered in this chapter confront the issue of social change in Yemen and the dilemmas it poses for a traditional society. How does one modernize yet not Westernize, reform the technological base yet not deform the traditions? Is not the very practice in which these two poets have engaged a poignant icon of what they are talking about? For example, the use of the tape recorder in their poetic production is a modern technological innovation, but instead of being destructive of tradition, it actually enhances it. This production implies that tribal traditionalism is possible *within* modernizing practices. Al-Maʿlah is a successful merchant, deeply embroiled in the conflicts created by the capitalist system, but nevertheless he can, or believes he can, reconcile this occupation with his poetic vocation. What makes this subtext especially moving is the fact that the tribal poetic system may itself be slowly disappearing. On another level of interpretation, therefore, the two poems are a plea for the preservation of their art form, but they may be fighting a rearguard action against a rapidly advancing foe.

We are left with the question of the significance of this poetic exchange within a wider political discourse centering on the nation-state. What is created is a particular voice that is traditional and tribal and in a certain sense in opposition to other tribal voices that can be heard in Yemen, such as al-Gharsī's. To borrow a phrase from Mikhail Bakhtin, we hear a polyphony of voices in the tribal discourse on the nation-state. This is as it should be, according to the tribal ideology of autonomous action. When I once discussed al-Gharsī's poetry with aṣ-Ṣūfī, he admitted, "Well, al-Gharsī does lean a little toward socialism in his verse. I do not share his political view"; but he said this with a smile and almost a shrug, as though the ideology of his friend's poetry was less important than the fact, the good fact, that he is heard. It would be contrary to what we have seen the nature of tribal political discourse to be were only one voice heard. The polyphony must lead somehow to a consensus. In other words, the leaders should be listening to the tapes and attempting to forge a consensus behind which the tribes and the rest of the country can unite.

But the main point here is the way in which tribal *communicative practices,* through the discourse they make available in a widely reticulated market system, significantly help shape the formation of the nation-state. We might expect such discourse to be disseminated via radio, television, or the newspaper, but in fact the medium is the tape recording, whose impact on societies like Yemen has yet to be adequately studied. In addition, what may seem surprising, because it goes against the Western conception of poetry and its uses, is the central importance of poetry to this communicative practice. Not sharing the positive outlook of educated urbanites toward the printed word and its forum in newspapers, the tribes (certain literate tribesmen notwithstanding) do not generally enter into that discursive practice. And as for the oral media, they, like the newspaper, are under the control of the central government and therefore cannot ensure the autonomy of the tribal voice. Furthermore, official political commentary among the Khawlānī tribes, though certainly not limited to poetry, is largely couched in it, so that the expression of political views in the *qaṣīdah* appears quite natural to them. The taped poem, then, is a significant communicative practice in which the tribal voice may be heard.

CONCLUSION

Poetry as Cultural Practice

According to literary critic Raymond Williams (1980, 47), "The true crisis in cultural theory, in our own time, is between [the] view of the work of art as object and the alternative view of art as a practice." He goes on to state:

> The relationship between the making of a work of art and its reception is always active, and subject to conventions, which in themselves are forms of (changing) social organization and relationship, and this is radically different from the production and consumption of an object. It is indeed an activity and a practice, and in its accessible forms, although it may in some arts have the character of a singular object, it is still only accessible through active perception and interpretation.

What Williams is saying of art, particularly literature, Kenneth Burke (1968a, 1973) had emphasized earlier in his notion of poetic process and, at approximately the same time, in the 1930s and 1940s, much the same idea was developed by Jan Mukařovský (1977a, 1977b) and Roman Jakobson (1960) of the Prague School into a richly conceived communicative approach. In the United States this direction in literary theory evolved into reader-response criticism (Culler 1975; Fish 1980; Rabinowitz 1987), in Germany into reception theory (Jauss 1982), which was also deeply influenced by phenomenological investigations of the text (Ingården [1931] 1973). Where Williams has taken a different turn—though it is a path that has been crossed by others[1]—

is in his project to "discover the nature of a practice and then its conditions" (Williams 1980, 47). In other words, in an important sense artworks, understood as a set of practices, are constrained by material reality and hence subject to historical change.

So far we have outlined two notions of practice that critically inform the discussion of poetry in this concluding chapter: the work of art as an activity or process of communication (production and reception), on the one hand, and that activity's dependence on, or constraint by, economic and social practices, on the other. There is a third notion of practice—one that Williams and Burke touch on but in my view only the Bakhtin circle elaborated in any complete and nearly convincing way—which we may call *constitutive* of social phenomena, particularly ideology. Artworks as practices are active agents, not just passive reagents, in history.

Practice as processes of producing and receiving an artwork, practices of an artwork as constitutive of ideology, and practices that are constrained by other social and particularly economic practices—these are the main ideas that will guide the following discussion. I will refer throughout to the ethnography of poetry just completed, but at times I will have to introduce new material to advance the argument, particularly in the final section, where I discuss the material constraints on, and historical changes of, the oral tribal poetic system. Elsewhere I will be forced to summarize previous material to clarify points for which no examples can be easily drawn from literary traditions more familiar to the reader. For example, I will illustrate what I mean by a system of poetic genres with copious references to the Yemeni material.

The three ideas of practice are not equally well developed in this chapter, a fact reflecting, perhaps, the state of the field of poetics. If we have come to know quite a bit about the literary work of art as a communicative process of production and reception, it has only been in the last two decades, when the work of the Bakhtin circle began to be translated and read in America and when anthropology began to be interested in the ways in which social, and particularly discursive, practices constitute cultural phenomena (Bourdieu [1972] 1977; Foucault [1970] 1973, 1972; Habermas 1984–87), that we have started to explore the second notion of practice in detail. Since the 1970s there has developed an interest in the emergence of poetic forms from economic forces, a problem to which Williams has devoted much attention but which the field of poetics as a whole has only begun to study.

Practices of Producing and Receiving the Poem

In the modern, Western, and elite artistic tradition, as Raymond Williams reminds us above, we tend to think of artistic practices as leading to a "finished" or "perfected" product, which is itself (and not the practices that make the product possible) the focus of aesthetic interest. Nonacademic viewers tend not to be interested in the act of creation that results in a particular canvas by Picasso or a dramatic performance by Olivier; only the result of that creative act is for public perception (though in the case of the actor the art is perhaps more spontaneous). There are exceptions to this generalization, of course, among them jazz and the theatrical happenings of the 1960s, in which the actual moment of creation, experienced as a process in time, is privileged. The equivalent of such an aesthetic experience would be to peer over Picasso's shoulder as he applies his brush strokes or to listen to a Furtwängler rehearsal of a Beethoven symphony—a proposition that strikes us as incongruous because our culture does not allow, usually, public receptions of the creative process *as* the work of art. Even when it does (as in the relatively rare cases of rehearsal recordings or the more frequent, but still uncommon, attendance of concert rehearsals), the focus is still on the final product, for most concertgoers feel frustrated when they hear only sections of a work and not the complete version chosen by the conductor for the recording studio.

In many non-Western, non-literate societies, however, process is given priority over product, or, as in the Yemeni tribal case, aesthetic appreciation is balanced in a continuum stretching from the reception of the creative process (as in the *bālah*) to reception of a perfected product (the *qaṣīdah*) to reception of works of art that are perceived simultaneously as practices of composition and as finished works of art (the *zāmil*). In the light of such a continuum, we begin to see how artificial, even misleading, it is to think of the work of art as an *object*. What we would call an object is really the end product of a creative process, a particular moment in a continuous practice, that has become privileged for reception in our tradition.

Conventional Practices: The Genre

Bakhtin and Medvedev ([1928] 1985, 129) remarked that "a work is only real in the form of a definite genre." What, then, is a poetic genre? To begin with, it should be clear that I have been thinking of genres as categories not of texts but of speech activities or practices in the sense understood by Vološinov ([1929] 1986) as well as Bakhtin and Medvedev and made more explicit in the ethnography of communication by the phrase "speech event" (Hymes 1974). But another defining feature of genre which we have not discussed—its *orientation*—comes out of the work on genre done by Bakhtin and Medvedev and is crucial to this study. According to them, a genre has two orientations: an "outer" one, which we might call the work's pragmatic orientation to the context of production and reception, and an "inner" one, which has more to do with a thematic content created by the unity of the work (Bakhtin and Medvedev [1928] 1985, 130–31).

As for the outer orientation, literary critics (with the exception of Kenneth Burke) are usually less prone to observe it in artworks, given the tyranny of immanent analysis in our theoretical tradition, even though it is always present in every work of art, no matter how autonomous and self-contained that work may appear to be. As VCR users are now beginning to realize, a cinematic epic produced for a large screen loses much of its power when transferred to television. As a result, we now have "made-for-television" movies as well as movies produced for theater showings. The feature that separates the genres is precisely their orientation to distinct contexts of reception. Another example is the symphony and the string quartet. Though we can hardly think of more autonomous works of art in the Western tradition, the symphony is definitely oriented to a large concert hall because of the sheer size of the orchestra and the volume of sound it produces, and the large hall accommodates a concertgoing public that has been growing since the nineteenth century. By contrast, the quartet is fitted for a more intimate space or "chamber." If the often cyclic and melodramatic plot of a Dostoyevsky or Dickens novel—in each chapter the story builds tensions that go unresolved, leaving the reader in suspense, until the next chapter—strikes us today as artificial, even crude, we should remember that these novels were often serialized, and a plot cycle or emotional arc corresponds roughly to one magazine installment. The point was to make the reader buy the next issue.

Perhaps more than is the case in the Western tradition, the genres in the oral tribal tradition of North Yemen are complexly and richly oriented to the contexts of production and reception. It is important to see artistic virtue in necessity here. The fact that an artwork "responds" to an external context should not be seen as a weakness or a shortcoming, as long as the response is incorporated into the overall aesthetic intention. Take, for example, the speech acts of greeting in the *bālah* oriented to various members of the audience, in particular to the groom on the occasion of his wedding: they are beautifully articulated in the meter, rhyme, formulas, and imagery conventional in this genre, and they form a unity expressive both of the ideal, tribal male self and of the coherence or integrity of the poem. Even more interesting is the challenge-and-retort routine of this genre, which contains a profound moral lesson about tribal social interaction and its rewards and hazards. At times it seems as though the competition over honor, as acted out through the hurling of taunts, threatens to break up the performance, but this conflict also intensifies the dramatic force of the poem. The orientation to social violence becomes aestheticized in the genre—art "contains" the dangers of strife—whereas the energy released by the confrontation between the poets invigorates the performance.

Bakhtin and Medvedev have less to say about the inner orientation, perhaps because it is such an old chestnut of traditional literary criticism, except to make it more or less synonymous with their notion of theme. But if they have apparently said little, they have intended much, for in their theory theme is not to be understood simply as what the work is about (Hamlet, for example, as a play about a Danish prince who tries to avenge the murder of his father) but rather as some more complicated meaning given by the unity of the piece. This notion in itself is not very different from the tactics of conventional literary criticism, except for their view of the work as an activity or a practice that is never encompassed by the text. The work is "the whole utterance as a definite historical act" (Bakhtin and Medvedev [1928]

1985, 132). Therefore, the unity—to the extent that it exists and however we wish to define it—is the unity of a speech event; it is not text-centered.

As important as these notions of inner and outer orientations are to our understanding of genre, they are perhaps still too vague to do us much good. The problem is not knowing *that* but rather *how* a poem can be oriented in one direction or another.

In my analysis of Yemeni tribal poetry I have made use of several constructs to explain how a poem is oriented to the specific contexts of its production and reception, among them speech acts, the theory of indexicals and icons, and the Bakhtinian notion of dialogue. Each genre can be seen to be composed of speech acts (religious invocation, prayers for Muḥammad and ʿAlī, greetings, a routine of challenge-and-retort or a message portion, and religious benediction). Furthermore, these speech acts are not just specific to the literary system (as are, e.g., conventional ways of beginning or ending a poem) but are clearly oriented toward everyday communication. It is, of course, possible to analyze Western literary works of art in terms of speech acts (Pratt 1977), but what is unique to the Yemeni tribal tradition, and I suspect to many other folkloric systems, is the closeness or directness with which poetic speech acts mirror nonpoetic ones. It may be necessary to distinguish on analytical grounds two kinds of speech acts in literature, according to how they are related to everyday communicative practices.

As I have already demonstrated in the ethnographic chapters, a theory of indexicals is crucial to an understanding of how such everyday speech acts work in context. For words to "do" anything in social action, more has to be referred to than the content of a wish or a state of affairs. They not only need to point to whatever the actors are presently engaged in verbally (promising, greeting, challenging) but also need to identify (perhaps even assign) the participants and indicate their roles in the communicative act ("*I,* the one who is speaking, am the one who is doing the promising; *you,* the one who is addressed, are the promisee"). J. L. Austin (1962) pointed out that speech acts need not be, and indeed infrequently are, of this overt or explicit I-say-hello-to-you sort and that every speech community has countless ingenious linguistic and nonlinguistic devices by which to signal this pragmatic information. The same is true, of course, of the Yemeni speech community, but it is interesting how often speech acts in poetry, particularly in the *bālah,* are explicit. I think the explanation has to do, on the one hand, with the cultural significance of the wedding and the central role that the *bālah* plays as a ritual within it—that is to say, words at this time and place are thought really to count for something—and, on the other hand, with the importance in Yemeni tribal culture of taking responsibility for one's words.

An outer orientation is also constituted through dialogue. Bakhtin (1981) insisted that any sentence not only reflects linguistic information—phonological, morphological, and syntactic—but also unavoidably betrays something about the speaker's ideological commitments to a specific social structure (whether class, tribe, or ethnic group). It is precisely this concept of the relationship of the utterance to the speaker's ideology that Bakhtin meant by the term *voice.* In turn, however, one speaker's ideology is always formed in political conflict or tension with the ideology of another speaker positioned in a different social group, so that voice also is properly understood only in relation to dialogue, or a colloquy of voices, rather than monologue. This sense of dialogue is perhaps most apparent in the middle portion of the *bālah,* when poets hold each other to account for their positions; but it is also critical to the *zāmil,* which is often delivered as a response or in such a way as to provoke a response or at least to answer one, and to the *qaṣīdah,* for many of the same reasons. Whether as individual poems or as speech acts within them, these utterances are dialogically linked to one another.

We now make the notion of an inner orientation in a poetic work of art analytically more precise, by referring to Jakobson's notion of parallelism.[2] It is important to realize that by parallelism Jakobson meant more than just the minute linguistic structures of a poetic text—meter, rhyme schemes, alliterations, and so forth. Entire blocks of lines, which he called strophes, can be parallel to other blocks of lines, forming what he called the architecture of the poem (Caton 1987a). The point is that some linguistic unit—whether limited to the sentence or going beyond it to embrace the speech act or even larger wholes—is made equivalent in the poem to a unit or units of the same type. Indeed, the architecture resembles a *hierarchy* of linguistic units (see Appendix B) ranging from phonological structures on the bottom to entire poems at the top.

Besides the diversity and hierarchical organization of linguistic structures, it is also important to bear in mind that for Jakobson parallelism—whether on the level of the particular device, such as rhyme or meter, or on the level of the architecture of the poem—must always have a poetic signification. On the micro level Jakobson ([1970] 1981) spoke of parallelism as having "subliminal" significations for the reader, which to a certain degree may influence his or her thought (an allusion to Jeremy Bentham's "linguistic fictions" as well as to the Sapir-Whorf hypothesis; see also Friedrich 1979a). Repeatedly in my analysis of Yemeni tribal poetry I have shown how parallel structures create significations that, though perhaps not consciously intended by the poets, were critical to the rhetoric of the debate. Indeed, because they were subliminal, they may have had an uncanny power over the receiver of the verse. As one begins to move from part to whole, from the device to the architecture, poetic signification still remains in play.[3] Recall that it is precisely the whole of the *bālah* performance that signifies the whole of the tribal male self. In fact, it is at this higher level of the work as a whole that the performance enters into a powerful relationship with social reality (Mukařovský 1977b), because the actor's complete set of existential experiences (piety, honoring the other in greetings, challenging the other in order to create one's honor, learning self-possession or control over passion, and so forth) becomes fully engaged, be he the poet or the auditor.

How, then, do we connect Jakobson's notion of parallelism and architecture with Bakhtin and Medvedev's inner orientation of the literary work of art? In brief, the architecture of the poem, understood in terms of parallelism, forms the unity of the poem, and this unity in turn creates a signification or theme.

Conventional Practices: The Genre System

I have been talking about genre as though it existed in isolation from other poetic or nonpoetic genres. This point is an oversimplification, for it should be clear that the genres of tribal poetry are not independent of each other. Breaking the genres down into various sorts of practices will help us understand their interrelationship.

COMPOSITION

Performance. One important factor of comparison has to do with the composition of verse in a public performance. The *bālah* is the most complex and absorbing of genres in this regard. A *bālah* poem should be composed instantly and without forethought, and the entire composition should be experienced as an act or a process rather than as the result of that process. Diametrically opposed to it is the *qaṣīdah,* which is not composed in performance at all. Recitations of *qaṣīdahs* are common, but the poet has as much time as he requires to create his product. The *zāmil* lies somewhere in between these two poles: even though the lines of verse should ideally be composed during the course of the performance, the drama of composition is greatly attenuated.

Collective versus Individual Composition. The *bālah* must be composed by several poets for it to be experienced as a game. The *qaṣīdah,* however, is to my knowledge never collectively composed. Moreover, the self-consciousness on the part of the *qaṣīdah* poet about taking personal responsibility for his words evinces an unmistakable individualism. Though the *zāmil* poem is also composed by one person, in this case individual composition is more a matter of empirical fact than one of cultural relevance. Sometimes the author is known; more often he is not. He usually is the mouthpiece of the group he represents rather than a spokesman for his own views.

Text-Utterance or Product. In the *bālah* the aesthetic focus is on the process of composition, not the particular details of the text-utterance. This is not to say that the process does not have its own aesthetic and dramatic structure, for it is a highly organized, and also potentially volatile, act. In the *zāmil* attention begins to shift from the aesthetic structure in the process of composition to the aesthetic structure in the *product* of composition (what I have called the text-utterance), a shift that is complete in the *qaṣīdah.* The audience is privy in the former to the step-by-step process in the composition of the poem, whereas in the latter it is entirely deprived of this insider's view.

Multiple Media versus Verbal Medium. Not only is the *bālah* quintessentially a performance composition; it also involves control over musical form (the chant, the antiphony of poet and chorus) and dance, factors it shares—albeit in a much reduced form— with *zāmil* composition. To some degree poets seem to be aware of song when they compose their verse (that is, they know that their lines can be sung to various traditional melodies), but the problem of precisely fitting word to song is one that the professional singer, not the poet, is supposed to solve. Performance in the *bālah* involves multimedia artistry (much as in opera), whereas in the *qaṣīdah* artistry is concentrated in the verbal product.

SPATIOTEMPORAL DISTANCE BETWEEN POET AND AUDIENCE

The spatiotemporal distance between poet and audience is greater in the *qaṣīdah* than in the *bālah*. In the latter the poet and his audience are located in the same room, so that the reception and production of the poem are immediate and coextensive in time and space. In the former the reception of the poem may be delayed for an indefinite time period after the composition is completed, and the poem may be delivered to an audience far removed in space. The *zāmil,* however, may be experienced as an artwork in either mode. That is, the poet may compose a *zāmil* poem in a performance that he and his audience are staging, or he may, at a different place and time, re-create it for the same or a different audience.

No less important here is the possibility of mechanical transmission of the *qaṣīdah* (and the *zāmil*), whether in writing or on tape. This possibility means that the poet may communicate with a more extensive audience in the towns and cities as well as other tribesmen and nontribesmen. In particular, the poet may end up trying to influence the discourse on the identity and form of the Yemeni nation by having his poem disseminated throughout the country by means of the market system, or conversely he may be co-opted by the state to disseminate to tribal populations the state's view of its own identity.

LOCATION WITHIN SOCIAL RITUALS

Genres also differ in the degree to which they can be said to be embedded within special social occasions such as weddings, religious festivals, and dispute negotiations. It is difficult, if not downright impossible, for tribesmen to perform the *bālah* out of context. I was repeatedly told that when the time came for a wedding to be celebrated, I would have ample opportunity to hear the performance, but not before then. The *qaṣīdah* resembles Western poetic genres in that the text is usually divorced from a specific social ritual.

REFERENCE TO HISTORICAL EVENTS

In the *bālah* references to significant historical events occurring in the world of the tribesmen are not expected. Even when such references are made (e.g. an allusion to a local war), they rarely occur as subjects of discussion or description (like Austin's constatives) but rather as verbal *acts* (like Austin's performatives) whose effects pertain to the historical issue (for example, directives or exhortations to battle). As we would expect, the case is different for the *qaṣīdah*. A *qaṣṣād*'s talent is based in part on his ability to discuss, analyze, and exhort all at the same time. A poet of the *zāmil* cannot provide much in the way of commentary because of the terseness of the genre, although we have seen how resonant its ellipses can be in skillful hands.

INTRATEXTUAL VERSUS INTERTEXTUAL DIALOGUE

This feature has to do with the extent to which the poet enters into a dialogue with other poets within the same poem (as in the *bālah*) or in different but linked poems (as in the *zāmil* and the *qaṣīdah*). The reason that the drama of the *bālah* is so intensely exciting is that a competition is created between poets, a competition that has both aesthetic appeal and social value. In the case of the other two genres the dialogue is between two or more linked poems.

One way to conceptualize the system of these genres is to place them along a continuum of cultural practices.[4]

Bālah	*Zāmil*	*Qaṣīdah*
Performative	↔	Nonperformative, text-product
Collective	↔	Individual
Multimedia	↔	Verbal
Intratextual dialogue	↔	Intertextual dialogue
Ritual	↔	Nonritual
Nonhistorical events	↔	Historical events

Why should a genre system be important? First, the structuralist principle for determining the value (or identity) of an element, be it a phoneme or a penny, also holds for a poem: only in opposition to other elements of the same poetic system does a given genre have a distinctive identity. Second, insofar as they have to be proficient in all three genres and shift gears from so-called spontaneous and dramatic verse back to a more lyrical, linguistically intricate poetry, from terse aphorism to rotund oratory, tribal masters of verse exhibit a range of talent rarely demanded of Western poets. Third, if the practices of one genre, say the *bālah*, are mastered, a poet has a foundation for composing verse in a more difficult genre, such as the *qaṣīdah.* Many a *qaṣīdah* starts out as a *zāmil,* which is then expanded. Fourth, cultural associations of one genre carry over into another with important consequences for the interpretation of social action. For example, the *bālah* has associated with it the cultural concept of a game; this cultural concept spills over into the use of *zāmil* poetry in war disputes, helping frame antagonisms expressed in poetic exchanges as symbolic or mock combat and thereby transforming conflict into play. Fifth, and most important, the genre system shows how poetic practices are essentially social practices. To be a *bālah,* a poem must be produced and received by a group in a ritual. The *qaṣīdah* may not appear to be social because it is composed by an individual in a nonritual setting, but this practice is combined with a discussion or analysis of actual politicohistorical events critical to the poet's community. The *zāmil,* in effect, contains the social practices of both the *bālah* and the *qaṣīdah.* Last, it is by keeping in mind the genre system that we can explain why some genres change or even drop out of sight and others remain unimpaired. This point, however, anticipates the final section, so I postpone its discussion until then.

The Emergence of Ideology in Poetic Practices

With this richly nuanced sense of practices for producing and receiving the poetic work, I will now delve into the problem that has preoccupied us in this book: how does culture as ideology emerge in such practices? Actually, this question should be broken down into two smaller ones: what do we mean by *emergence* of culture in social action? and, what do we mean by *ideology*? Only after answering both can we turn to the heart of the matter: *how* do poetic practices, as described in the first section of this chapter, constitute ideology?

Emergence of Culture

What is not often made clear in the anthropological literature is the difference between the reproduction of the cultural system and its emergence in communicative action. On the one hand, communicative action reproduces the cultural system of symbols and meanings crucial for social interaction. It cannot be the case that culture has to be created *de novo* each time or be negotiated or emerge in every new transaction. As a colleague put it, "That would be life as one continuous freshman year." On the other hand, neither can the cultural system be entirely given or presupposed. There are situations in which intersubjective understanding must be created in communicative action. Under which specific circumstances, then, does it make sense to talk about the emergence of culture?

I can delineate at least four types of social contexts in which an emergent notion of culture might be appropriate:

1. Contexts of socialization (and acculturation), in which cultural patterns must emerge in the adolescent's repertoire of behaviors; this was G. H. Mead's problem of analysis (see also Ochs 1988 for this problem with respect to language learning);
2. Contexts of socioeconomic change, in which the traditional system does not serve as an adequate model or precedent for social action and new patterns have to emerge in place of older ones, or blend with them, or coexist ambiguously with them;
3. Contexts in which misunderstandings, leading perhaps to serious conflict, arise in sociopolitical interaction and a new understanding or consensus has to be established; again, this problem was central to Mead and is also at the heart of Habermas's notion of communicative action;
4. Contexts of social reconstruction (for example, after natural disasters or warfare) or the formation of larger national and social entities.

The first context was at the forefront of my analysis of the *bālah;* the second and fourth were in that of the *qaṣīdah;* and the third dominated my analysis of the *zāmil.* Of course, all three poetic genres to some degree reproduce the cultural system of tribalism; but I have been most concerned with the emergence of cultural understandings in contexts where they cannot be simply given or presupposed.

Ideology as Semiotic Practice

Now let us try to define ideology. In one sense ideology approximates the anthropologist's notion of culture as a system of symbols and their meanings (Geertz 1973, Schneider 1976). However, in Marxist thought this system is seen as reflecting the conflict of class or, *ideology* (margin note)

Social Signs (margin note)

more generally, of social and economic relations. To Marx, as is well known, ideology is "mystifying" in the sense that the dominant class or group tries to impose its own notion—always a partial one—of reality on the rest of society, thereby achieving social preeminence and political predominance. Vološinov and Bakhtin, though certainly concerned with both of these notions of ideology, are more interested in the *practices* through which it is produced. As Vološinov argues in his book *Marxism and the Philosophy of Language*, "The reality of ideological phenomena is the objective reality of social signs" ([1929] 1986, 13). It was the Bakhtin circle, above all, that clarified the relationship between ideology and signifying practices, an approach that is obviously useful for our purposes.

Bakhtin and Medvedev ([1928] 1985) start with the observation, no longer radical after Vygotsky (1962, 1978), that ideas cannot exist unmediated by material signs: "The reality of the inner psyche is the same reality as that of the sign" (Vološinov [1929] 1986, 26). In a passage closely resembling the ideas of Peirce (1932), they claim that "understanding is a response to a sign with a sign. . . . And nowhere is there a break in the chain, nowhere does the chain plunge into inner being, nonmaterial in nature and unembodied in signs" (Vološinov [1929] 1986, 11). Vygotsky (1978) would say that thinking consists of semiotic practices that have become internalized.

These ideas of Bakhtin and Medvedev, Vološinov, and Peirce suggest that ideology is inseparable from communication, but there is still a practical problem of finding an empirical unit that constitutes ideological practice in any given society. Vološinov has solved this problem through his notion of the "behavioral speech genre" (Vološinov [1929] 1986, 20). He concludes that "*a typology of these forms is one of the urgent tasks of Marxism. . . .* Each period and each social group has had and has its own repertoire of speech forms for ideological communication in human behavior" ([1929] 1986, 20; emphasis in the original). Here we have an interesting anticipation in Marxist theory of the modern ethnography of communication (Gumperz and Hymes 1964; Hymes 1974; Bauman and Sherzer 1974), which purports to describe patterns of speaking in a cross-cultural perspective and to analyze the interrelations of these patterns and other forms of social life. However, the connection to Marxism is not explicitly made in the theoretical pronouncements of the ethnography of communication, nor is its primary focus the question of social conditions determining (or constraining) communicative genres, which in their turn constitute ideology.[5]

Ideology Emergent in Poetic Practice

If, as Bakhtin maintains, ideology is produced through speech genres, including artistic ones, the question then becomes: how does Yemeni tribal poetry do this? To answer that question, we need to recall the outer and inner orientations of genre, for it is through them, I contend, that ideology is constituted.

Let us begin with the outer orientation and return to the problem of the speech act and speech indexicals. As originally formulated by Austin (1962), speech acts are part of the social institutions they help to create. Yemeni poetry is shot through and through with such speech acts (the invocation of Aḷḷah; the greeting of guests; the issue of, or the response to, a challenge; the statement of a message), which orient the poets and their audiences to social contexts. Moreover, because the speech acts are of a sort found in ordinary or everyday discourse connected with fundamental ideological principles of society, Islamic and tribal, they end up constituting the same ideology in poetry as well. Through indexical devices—many of them contained in formulas used to construct the *bālah* poem or in everyday phrases tailored to fit the meter and rhyme of the *zāmil*—the producers and receivers of this poetry are constituted as exemplars of various ideological types. A poet in the *bālah* exclaims, "I mention Muḥammad [as many times as] the stars in the heavens revolve," and thereby constitutes himself as a type of pious Muslim. In another turn he might declare, "It pleases me to perform the *bālah* with such lions among men," and thereby constitutes the assembly he has addressed as honorable men.

One of these speech acts, the challenge-and-retort routine critical to the *bālah* performance, is explicitly dialogical in structure. A poetic line is always addressed *to* someone with the aim of eliciting a response. That is, in the middle section poets are expected to test each other through taunts, teasings, and other provocations. We have seen how the honor of actors is constituted in this dialogue, for honor can only be won in competition with another individual of equal status.

When we come to the *qaṣīdah,* the outer orientation begins to look somewhat different, for the context of producing this poem is not the same as the context of receiving it (as is the case in the *bālah*). But that is not all, for the *qaṣīdah* can be received by many different kinds of people in many different contexts; the context of reception becomes more highly generalized than is the case for any other genre. The indexes of the *qaṣīdah,* in turn, become more general in their reference. Insofar as the receivers are not part of the tribal community but belong to an urban, educated society, many of the poem's speech acts—with the exception of the religious ones—will have little relevance for its audience and thus drop out. The ideology of the *qaṣīdah* is now constituted primarily through a thematic speech act in which the poet analyzes, and gives his opinion on, some crucial issue. Ideology is constituted in the *bālah* in performative, and in the *qaṣīdah* in constitutive, speech acts.

At the same time as the ideology of a poem is constituted by its outer orientation, it is also created by its inner one. Parallelism (or architecture) is the main practice of this inner orientation, which belongs to the *bālah* no less than to the *qaṣīdah.* In the former case the architecture consists primarily of a parallel series of performative speech acts that constitute through their ensemble the ideal tribal self. In the case of the *qaṣīdah* the aesthetic focus is on the text-utterance (rather than the whole performance), and the architecture is made up of a parallel series of verse units or strophes (as well as smaller linguistic units such as alliteration and metaphor). I have said, following Jakobson, that these parallel structures create subliminal meanings that underscore key ideas in the theme. Because they are often covert, they are ideal weapons in an ideological struggle—hard to detect, yet profound in effect.

How is Poetic Practice Constrained by the Base?

Having dealt with one side of the relationship between society and poetry—the way in which poetry helps to constitute tribal ideology—it is now time to explore the effects that social and economic formations have on genres and the genre system, in order to complete this overview of poetry as practice. The preceding analysis leads, I believe, to the conclusion that a poem is a social practice and as such it cannot be crudely assigned to some abstracted superstructure or worldview.[6] This kind of layer-cake metaphor would only reintroduce the problem of how to connect literature and society, when my point has been, to quote Williams, that "literature is there from the beginning as a practice in the society" (1980, 44). As such, the poem would have to be seen as part of the base—that is, as part of social and political practices that, however, are not as primary as economic ones—that *constitutes* the ideology or worldview of a particular group.

The question then becomes: what economic and technological conditions make possible or constrain the poetic practices that constitute ideology and consciousness? Several routes might lead to an answer. One is to trace the historical transformation of audiences brought about by changing demographic patterns connected with economic change. Another is to consider the history of the technological means of artistic production leading up to a particular art form (Benjamin [1936] 1969). Yet the two are not unconnected, as Williams (1980) has so beautifully illustrated in his analysis of the rise of naturalism as a dramatic form in nineteenth-century English theater.

In Yemen two major changes—one technological, the other demographic—have had complex effects on poetic production and reception. I have already discussed the introduction of the portable tape recorder. As noted earlier, a great deal of poetry is recorded, then distributed to the dozens of stereo stores located in the capital as well as in large towns all over the country; tapes are bought largely by tribesmen but also by surprisingly large numbers of the religious elite, the urban middle class, servants, and other segments of society.

The fact, however, that the *qaṣīdah* is the only significant genre that has been recorded requires explanation. That explanation, I believe, is to be found in the nature of the genre system itself. I have said that the aesthetic focus of the *qaṣīdah* is on the final linguistic result or product of the act of composition; hence, a tape recording does not distort the aesthetic experience. On the contrary, one could argue that the recording enhances it by allowing the receiver to retrieve the text-utterance as many times as he or she likes and to intervene in the process of its reception by stopping the tape at any point, replaying it, or even slowing it down. The tape recording allows the listener to *appropriate* the text-utterance more completely than would have been imaginable in the days when its reception depended on a professional singer. As for production in this genre, it too is vastly facilitated by the tape recording, for now poets can hear one another's work cheaply and simply from all parts of the country.

Why is the *bālah* not suitable for tape recording? We have learned that it is the process of composition, not the final linguistic result, and participation in that process that are critical in the experience of this genre. A tape recording would seriously impoverish its aesthetic richness because it would make possible for the listener only the reception of, not direct participation in, its performance. The intervention of the tape recorder would transform the experience of this genre to the detriment of its aesthetic effect.

In short, not the whole but only a part of the poetic system is enhanced through the tape recording, because of the variable aesthetic practices of the genres. But the intervention of a new technology has had momentous consequences for the *qaṣīdah,* nonetheless. The audience that can be reached openly or surreptitiously is potentially vast. It is precisely in the dialogue of ideological constructions pertaining to the modern state, as we have seen, that the tape-recorded tribal *qaṣīdah* has its most significant impact. Through the tape recording the tribal *qaṣīdah* can become far more intrusive in that national dialogue.

But the technological intervention of the tape recording is by itself insufficient as an explanation for these changes in the poetic system. After all, the tape is bought by the stereo-store owners from a professional singer or poet (who is ideally not supposed to sell his talent, however) and then distributed for sale across the country. The dissemination of the tape recording thus depends largely on a capitalist market system. Unfortunately, little is known about this national market system—how deeply it penetrates into the remotest regions, how effective the black market is, whether it is a recent phenomenon produced by the boom economy of the 1970s, and who runs it—so I am unable to shed much light on this problem.

Besides a changing technology and the market system, another factor impinging on the poetic system is tribal migration. As the career of Muḥammad al-Gharsī demonstrates, many tribesmen have emigrated from the rural areas to the larger cities or abroad to the oil-producing countries of the Arabian Peninsula, where they stay for many years, amassing a small fortune in the construction industry and sending remittances to their families back home.

The effects of this migration on the poetic system have been complex and various. The young men who seek an education in the capital or accompany their fathers abroad either fail to learn or else forget how to compose the *bālah* and the *zāmil* because they do not have the opportunity to practice these performance genres. I know this partly from what the older men have told me and partly from having observed the reluctance of recent returnees to join their compatriots in the poetic performances. Most damaging of all, however, is the fact that the young men forget the speech acts of tribal social intercourse, such as greetings and the challenge-and-retort routine, which we have seen to be the mainstay of performance poetry. Children do not have access to formal instruction in this art but must acquire it through direct experience of rhythm, rhyme, alliteration, and speech acts to be found in ordinary conversation. If young men are deprived of this early experience, they lack the training to compose verse competently. The *qaṣīdah,* by contrast, can be learned on one's own through the tutelage of a more experienced poet and is not as deeply affected by the migration. It is not surprising, therefore, to find that the *qaṣīdah* thrives abroad.

As younger tribesmen start to attend school and become better educated, they cannot help but be influenced by the ambivalence that the literate culture harbors toward dialect and toward poetry composed in dialect. Doubts about the greatness of their own linguistic tradition are raised by the negative comments of their teachers, who are trying to educate them in the literary and scriptural heritage. It is to be expected that these young men will become alienated from their own spoken language and oral dialect poetry.

Their response to the tribal *qaṣīdah,* however, might be more ambivalent. The tribal *qaṣīdah* has been written for decades and is still thriving. Furthermore, it stands at the pivotal point between the tribal and the literate urban traditions, for it is presumed that the tribal *qaṣīdah* is a descendant of the ancient pre-Islamic ode whose forms served as the canons for classical Arabic poetry. Adopting a more "educated" or classical style, especially when addressing an urban audience, does not necessarily represent betrayal of the genre. In other words, even though the perceptions of the classical style may be different for a literate tribal audience and an illiterate one, neither is hostile to the intervention of writing and an educated register in the *qaṣīdah.*

What do all these effects on the poetic system amount to?[7] The performance genres will inevitably suffer from some neglect, perhaps even disappearing among large segments of the tribal population located in the urban areas or abroad. The tribal *qaṣīdah* may survive, though not necessarily in its traditional form. The older, essentially oral ode, with its lengthy routines, will continue to compete with a younger, essentially literate poem whose content stresses the topic and whose style varies from colloquial to standard language. Whether or not the more contemporary version wins out is perhaps less interesting than the fact that the tribal *qaṣīdah* will continue to be a vital ideological genre through which the tribes will be able to enter into national dialogue on the identity of the nation. Because the *qaṣīdah* bridges two central traditions—the tribal oral one and the urban literate one, which together draw the most powerful audiences in the country—it is accessible to virtually everyone.

The Yemeni state, unlike the guardians of Plato's "ideal" republic, will make sure that the tribal *qaṣīdah* survives as long as the state is unable to bring the tribes under its heel. In its attempts to co-opt various tribal poets for its own rhetorical purposes and then disseminate their poems in the marketplace, the state is trying to *persuade* a sizable and potentially hostile population to adopt its policies. On the other side of the rhetorical battle are to be heard traditionalists and tribalists like aṣ-Ṣūfī arguing with progressives like al-Gharsī over which ideology and platform will save the country from ruin. What one is hearing and will probably continue to hear is a dialogue of extraordinarily powerful and contentious voices whose arena is the *qaṣīdah.* Far from damaging it aesthetically, this conflict will render the genre more dynamic, vigorous, and fascinating.

I have been arguing that tribal poetry is constitutive of social reality in compelling ways precisely because of its integration with the forms of everyday and ritual life. Yet the previous chapter revealed that even the masters of the poetic word like aṣ-Ṣūfī and al-Maᶜlah are apprehensive about the future. For, ironically, this very anchoring of the poetic word in concrete social action is also its weakness when social intercourse changes, when ceremony becomes transformed, and particularly when the values associated with tribalism wane. It remains to be seen whether the traditional pattern will become unraveled under the impact of social changes or whether rural tribal Yemen will be tomorrow what it was yesterday. Emigration to the oil-producing countries has slowed down, and a new conservatism encouraged by an Islamic fundamentalist movement may indirectly work to preserve the poetic system pretty much as I encountered it in 1979–81. It is hard to say what the outcome will be. But I like to think that poetry is so close to the self-definition of Yemeni tribesmen that were the traditional poetic forms to disappear, new forms would be invented to give life to their indomitable spirit and their zest for play, argument, and humor.

APPENDIX A

Yemeni Tribal Arabic Phonology

The consonants of Yemeni tribal Arabic are displayed in Table A-1. Four of the consonants are velarized (or pharyngealized, depending on which phonological scheme is adopted; see Brame 1970) and are transcribed with a dot under the segment. (However, the segment /ḥ/ is not a velar but a pharyngeal; velarized /ḷ/ is marginal in the word *aḷḷāh* [God]). The hard velar /g/ corresponds to the *qāf* of Classical Arabic, which is pronounced as a uvular /q/. Thus, the standard Arabic verb *qāl* (he said) would be pronounced with an initial /g/ in North Yemeni tribal Arabic. This pronunciation is perhaps the most significant shibboleth of North Yemeni dialect (in the southern regions of the country around Taʿiz the /q/ pronunciation is preserved). Word-final consonants are unreleased after a long vowel and at the ends of phrases or sentences: [rutub̥, ḥayd̥, sēf̥].

One kind of phonemic merger is to be found in Ṣanʿānī/Khawlānī Arabic. In other dialects the words *ẓall* (be, become) and *ḍall* (go astray), one beginning with a continuant, the other with a stop, are distinguished, whereas in this dialect they merge into initial /ḍ/—that is, into the velarized dental fricative—even in the speech of highly educated persons.

Table A-1. *Consonants in Yemeni Tribal Arabic*

	Labial	*Dental*	*Palat.*	*Velar*	*Pharyn.*	*Glottal*
Stop	b	t(ṭ)/d		k/g		ʾ
Nasal	m	n				
Fricative	f	th/dh(ḍ)		kh/gh	ḥ/ʿ	h
Affricate			j			
Sibilant		s(ṣ)/z	sh			
Lateral		l(ḷ)				
Trill		r				
Glide	w		y			

The glottal stop is problematical. On the one hand, it seems to be phonemic because of minimal pairs such as /ʾahl/ (people) and /sahl/ (plain), or /saʾal/ (he asked) and /sāl/ (it flowed). Yet there is a strong tendency to delete the glottal stop in all positions, so that in rapid speech one often hears [sāl] (he asked), its meaning distinguished by the context. It is especially common to delete the glottal stop at the beginning of words: /lā/ as opposed to /ʾilā/ (to), or /ḥad/ as opposed to /ʾaḥad/ (someone); but deletion in word-medial position is not uncommon either: /mārib/ as opposed to /maʾrib/ (Mārib, large town in eastern Yemen), or /rēs/ for /raʾīs/ (president), where the glottal stop is deleted and the vowel shortened and diphthongized (see discussion of vowels below). In word-final position the glottal stop is almost never heard except to indicate emphasis. For example, "no" can be rendered as either /mā/ or /maʾ(a)/ depending on the context. Although the glottal stop tends to disappear, especially in rapid speech, speakers must be aware that it exists at some underlying level of representation because they often reinstate it when they have been misheard or when they wish to convey emphasis. In poetry a missing glottal stop will be reinstated to produce an additional syllable needed for the meter.

The glides /w/ and /y/ are also somewhat problematical when they occur in representations of long vowels: for example, /ī/ becomes /iy/ or /ū/ becomes /uw/. That is, long vowels become diphthongized. This process occurs sometimes in poetry, again for reasons having to do with meter (see Appendix B).

Table A-2 gives a summary of information on vowels in the dialect. Evidence of minimal pairs shows the phonemic status of the short and long vowels. Other long vowels such as /ē/ and /ō/, however, are surface manifestations of the diphthongs /ay/ and /aw/: for example, /bayt/ becomes /bēt/ (house), and /gawl/ becomes /gōl/ (saying). Not all central diphthongs undergo this process, especially when they occur in words thought to be of particularly ancient origin. Thus, the mountain Ḥaylān is almost always pronounced [ḥaylān], not [ḥēlān], but the region Khawlān is occasionally pronounced [khōlān]. The diphthong /ey/ can sometimes be heard, in /timshey/ (you walk [f. sg.]) as opposed to /timshī/ (you walk [m. sg.]).

Although phonetically words may appear with two initial consonants—[zghīr] instead of /ṣaghīr/ (small), [skǣ] instead of [ʾiskǣ] (get out of the way!)

Table A-2. *Yemeni Tribal Arabic Vowels*

	Front	*Central*	*Back*
High	i, ī		u, ū
Mid	ē		ō
Low		a, ā	
Diphthongs	ey (rare)	ay, aw	oy, ow (rare)

—phonemically such a cluster is not possible. Informants will insist that [zghīr], for example, is bisyllabic and will then enunciate it as [ṣaghīr] to prove the point.

Syllable Structures

According to my analysis, there are six basic syllable types:

1. Cv	*bi-* (with), *li-* (to)
2. Cv̄	*fī* (in), *mā* (no)
3. CvC	*gad* (already)
4. Cv̄C	*gāl* (he said)
5. CvCC	*tamm* (he completed)
6. Cv̄CC	*ḥājj* (pilgrim)

If a word begins in a glottal stop, it might lose its initial consonant if the preceding word ends in a consonant and the two words undergo elision—thus *gad ingalabat* (it was already overthrown) instead of **gad* ʾ*ingalabat.* This elision creates a new syllabification, *ga-din* instead of **gad-*ʾ*in.*

Sandhi Phenomena

Besides the disappearance of the glottal stop in the context of a preceding consonant, Yemeni tribal Arabic has a marked tendency to shorten vowels or diphthongize them at word junctures.

yā + ʾ*ahl* = *y-ahl* (O people)
fī + *al-bēt* = *f-il-bēt* or *fiy al-bēt* (in the house)
ruḥ-tū + *as-sūg* = *ruḥtu-s-sūg* or *ruḥ-tuw as-sūg* (you went to the market)

However, if the word following the vowel does not begin with a glottal stop, then these phenomena do not take place—for example, *fī maktab-ah* (in his office), not *fiy maktab-ah.*

Another junctural phenomenon peculiar to Yemeni tribal Arabic is the use of an epenthetic /a/ between a noun and the first-person plural possessive, as in *bēt* (house) + *-a-nā* (our). This rule is usually generalized to other persons as well, such as *-hā* (her) and *-kum* (your [pl.]).

Accent

The placement of stress, though variable, is not arbitrary. It depends on the structure of the syllable and its position in the word (see Caton 1984).

APPENDIX B

A Linguistic Theory of Meter

Why do we need a linguistic theory of meter to understand the *baḥr* of Yemeni tribal verse? After all, the great eighth-century Arab grammarian and aesthetician Ibn Aḥmad al-Khalīl devised an extremely sophisticated theory of pre-Islamic Arabic verse meter, deriving much of his data from Arabian Bedouin poetry. Therefore, given the plausible assumption that contemporary Yemeni tribal poetry is a residue of this more ancient system, would it not be simpler to apply his analysis to my data without worrying about the linguistic soundness of his conclusions? The Arabic philologist Count Carlo von Landberg (1901–13) had, for instance, discovered many of Ibn Aḥmad's metrical patterns (in addition to some new ones) in southern Arabian poetry; Albert Socin (1901) and Ettore Rossi (1938a, 1938b, 1939a) recapitulated these findings in poetry from central Arabia and North Yemen, respectively. I could easily follow the lead of these great Arabists and apply Ibn Aḥmad's system to the data, trying to account for the exceptions in as rule-governed a way as possible.

The problem is to develop a "natural" system of verse analysis given what we know about meter in other languages and poetries. Roman Jakobson, for example, has charged several noteworthy investigations of Slavic verse systems with

> one shortcoming: they remain largely within the framework of a single language and a single metrical system. Only the utilization of material from other languages for comparative purposes permits us to view metrical system as a special case and to appreciate fully the relationship between form and material. *Comparison is the indispensable foundation for the linguistic interpretation of any system of versification.*
> (Jakobson 1979, 122; my emphasis)

In other words, to gain insight into verse structure—by *insight* I mean something akin to what Chomsky has in mind, that is, an analysis that tells us something about the *universals* of verbal structure—we must compare the

Khawlānī verse system with other known systems in the world to see in what ways it does or does not conform to their structures. To put the point in more Chomskyan terms, if a certain distribution of linguistic items, such as the syllable weights (heavy versus light), can be analyzed according to a number of different patterns (all "descriptively adequate"), how do we know which pattern to choose on *explanatory* grounds?

Let me therefore try to build a universal theory of meter according to which my analysis of Yemeni verse will have to be evaluated.

The Syllable as the "Relevant" Linguistic Unit of Meter

John Lotz (1960, 137–38) has suggested that "the principle according to which we select the metrically relevant linguistic phenomena is the principle of metrical relevancy in analogy with the principle of relevancy in phonological and grammatical analysis." The verse systems of the world (cf. Wimsatt 1972) exhibit an extraordinary diversity. Some, like classical Greek and classical Arabic, depend on a regular repetition of syllabic weights, whereas in English iambic pentameter it is the prosodic feature of accent combined with a certain number of syllables that are relevant, and in French *vers alexandrin* the number of syllables per unit is the main organizing principle, with heavy stresses distributed regularly at certain positions of the line. I could give other examples, but the point would remain the same: whatever the particulars of the verse system, the basic relevant unit of meter is the *syllable*.

This assertion of the primacy of the syllable in versification systems begs the question of how to define the syllable as a linguistic unit. Herein lies one of the trickier and more neglected problems of linguistic analysis. As late as 1956 in his article "The Syllable in Linguistic Description" Einer Haugen jibed, "The syllable has become something of a stepchild in linguistic description. While sooner or later everyone finds it convenient to use, no one does much about defining it" (Haugen 1956, 213). Students of poetics find themselves in the awkward position of having to describe a key unit of verse meter that linguists have, unfortunately, ignored in their theoretical analyses until the early 1970s.

The Opposition of Metrical Syllables

In purely syllabic verse systems the number of syllables in a line becomes the foundation of the meter. Hence, to scan a line of syllabic poetry, one must be able to identify and count syllables. But in systems that add the prosodic feature of accent, tone, or quantity (weight), "the notion of the syllable alone will not suffice. A second concept has to be introduced: the organization of the syllabic material according to certain prosodic features, called long and short base for durational meter, and even and changing base for tonal meter" (Lotz 1972, 5). For example, though in colloquial English more than two stress levels are possible in the linguistic system, the verse meter only makes use of the opposition of stressed and unstressed syllables. In modern Mandarin Chinese, according to Frankel (1972), there are basically four phonemic tones, but the meter groups these into a binary opposition: the "level" (even) tone is contrasted with the other three, which are classified together as the "deflected" (changing) tone.

On the basis of these examples and the evidence of other prosodic systems around the world, Lotz (1972, 15) concludes that "dual opposition may prove to be a metrical universal or at least a universal tendency." That is, syllables (however they may be determined in a particular language) become members of a poetic-prosodic oppositional category relevant to the metrical analysis in a given verse tradition. If comparative metrics continues to bear out this finding, it will have important and interesting implications for linguistic theory, for it suggests that binary opposition plays as important a role in the poetic function as it does in the referential one (Jakobson and Halle 1956). Note that I am not saying that the poetic function feeds parasitically off of the referential one, thereby explaining the apparent homology in their more abstract structures. Rather, what I am suggesting is that on some deeper level the various subsystems of language corresponding to different communicative functions are cut according to the same abstract patterns.

The Hierarchical Arrangement of Units in Poetry

The hierarchical organization of language is well known to linguists who have studied the referential function. The principle is a simple one: similar units are contained within larger units, which in turn combine to form still more inclusive units, and so forth; the analogy is often made to a Chinese puzzle box or a branching tree. Thus, distinctive phonetic features combine in a "bundle" to comprise the morphophonemic segment; the latter is a constituent of lexemes, which concatenate in noun and verb phrases, which in turn form sentences. There is no reason to stop at the sentence, as linguists have conventionally done, for one could analyze still larger chunks of discourse in terms of the same organizing principle.

Several linguists have suggested that hierarchy is also crucial to understanding the structure of verse. In his article "Studies in Comparative Slavic Metrics" (1952) Jakobson used the concept of hierarchy to describe a particular verse tradition: "There are three degrees of segmentation which are directly imposed by the metrical pattern of Common Slavic recitative poetry, and which are constantly termed METRICAL. They are: (1) the foot, (2) the colon, and (3) the line. These metrical constituents can be arranged in a *hierarchy*" (Jakobson 1952, 55, my italics). De Groot (1957), one of the great phoneticians of this century, who was deeply interested in the aesthetics of natural language, noted the wide application of hierarchy across semiotic systems: "Hierarchy is segmentation, Grouping. The Groups in music are: notes, measures, phrases. In language they are: syllables, frame-morphemes (Trubetzkoy's 'Rahmeneinheiten'), words, phrases. In verse: syllables, periods or 'feet,' members of lines, lines, stanzas" (De Groot 1957, 392). What is important to our understanding of hierarchy is that the lowest structural units are identified in relation to the next higher ones. Thus, it is impossible to identify the phonemic sounds of a language without knowing which sounds discriminate lexemes and which do not. Similarly, one cannot identify the hemistichs except in terms of the line, nor the feet except in terms of the hemistich, nor the metrical syllables except in terms of the foot.

The Abstractness of Verse Meter

One of the fundamental postulates of Saussurean linguistics is the abstractness of linguistic form (later reiterated by Chomsky). Saussure's breakthrough in the study of language was to argue that analytical units that linguists hope to isolate and identify are more abstract than the surface phonetic facts of speech. Saussure was solely concerned with the referential function and hence the more abstract semantic units correlated with it; but one might well ask whether the principle of abstractness can also be applied to the study of form created in the poetic function.

It is in the light of such a principle that we might regard Jakobson's important distinction between "verse design" and "verse instant" (Jakobson 1960, 364–65). The verse design is the stable metrical pattern that "underlies the structure of any single line" (ibid.). As an illustration, Jakobson refers us to the Serbian epic meter (Jakobson [1933] 1966), in which the line contains ten syllables followed by a syntactic break. A word boundary is compulsory before the fifth and tenth syllables.

1 2 3 4 ## 5 6 7 8 9 ## 10

The compulsory presence of the verse feature is not audible, yet the verse design of the meter requires positing a caesura in the abstract. (See Jakobson 1963 for a discussion of this analysis.) One of the oldest debates in the analysis of the ancient Greek hexameter concerns the caesura that occurs in the third foot of the line. Some scholars maintain that the line is too long not to have a pause after a certain breath group, whereas others deny any justification for positing one when there is no phonetic evidence. Sturtevant (1924, 337) represents the extreme latter view when he states, "We may take it for granted that an obligatory feature of versification must in some way be audible."

This debate over the abstractness of verse pattern is relevant to a problem in the analysis of Yemeni tribal meter. The syllable structure #C$\bar{v}$C## appears, on the surface at least, to be monosyllabic, without a final vowel. Following Sturtevant's phonetic position, one would have to conclude that this structure is always monosyllabic regardless of its position in the verse design. But as we shall see, this interpretation of the surface facts leads to a different and more serious problem; namely, the pattern becomes in places highly irregular in spite of the protestations of informants to the contrary. Do we simply override the informants' intuitions? Or do we reinterpret the surface facts in such a way as to account for a perceived regularity by a more abstract metrical pattern? As in the case of grammatical facts, if informants' intuitions point us in a certain direction, we ought to revamp the analysis to account for them.

Variation: The Concept of Position

> One has to distinguish between "variation" and "irregularity" in meter: In syllabic-prosodic meters the numerical regulation refers not only to the syllabics as such but to the base classes as well; that is, in certain positions only one base class is allowed. Positions must, therefore, be introduced as a second numerical principle, in addition to the number of syllables, the sole characteristic of pure-syllabic meter. Positions which have to be filled out by a definite base class are called fixed. No syllabic-prosodic systems exist in which all positions are fixed. Free positions may be filled by either of the two base classes (anceps). Or there may be more complex substitutions.
>
> (Lotz 1972, 15)

This passage suggests that a metrical pattern admits of two kinds of positions: in one the occurrence of a base is fixed; the other position is free and allows one or the other base form to occur in that position. Every meter *must* permit variation in some positions of the pattern.

Meters of Tribal Verse

The phonological sketch in Appendix A reveals three linguistic features as possible candidates for a rhythmic contour of verse: accent, intonation, and syllabic quantity. The question is: which of these phenomena are the building blocks of meter in Yemeni tribal poetry? In oral poetic traditions the meter, if there is one, is not known through a *conscious* set of rules (Kiparsky 1972, 174). Nor is it obvious from a phonetic examination of a verse line.

A more abstract analysis of the surface line reveals syllabic quantity to be the constructional unit of meter. But to be convinced of this fact, we must first categorize the syllable structures of Yemeni tribal Arabic according to their metrical values of heavy and light. Appendix A reveals six syllable types in the dialect:

1. Cv	3. CvC	5. CvCC
2. Cv̄	4. Cv̄C	6. Cv̄CC (very rare)

Given that the theory is correct and the meter works through a binary opposition of heavy and light, a reasonable question to ask is: which syllables are felt to be light and which heavy? But the question cannot be answered without looking simultaneously at the next higher structural unit—the foot, if there is one, or the hemistich—and determining some kind of regular patterning on this level of organization according to which syllabic analysis we choose. For example, let us assume that the syllable structure Cv is light (⏑) and that every other syllable structure is heavy (–). Then the scansion of a *phonemicized* line such as the following will turn out to be:

– – ⏑ – – – ⏑ – – – – – ⏑ – ⏑ – – –
ḥayyā bi-man jā min gubal khawlān ʿārif || wa muḥtarim sinnat
⏑ –
bakīl

A pattern begins to emerge if we designate the foot as – – ⏑ –:

– – ⏑ – | – – ⏑ – | – – – – | ⏑ – ⏑ – | – – ⏑ –

According to this analysis, there are two irregular feet, – – – – and ⏑ – ⏑ –. My informants insisted, however, that the meter of the line is perfectly regular. There are two options: either attempt somehow to explain these anomalies, according to the linguistic theory of meter, or reject the analysis and start over again.

In regard, first of all, to the apparent irregularity in the foot | – – – – |, note that the second syllable is *-lān##* (type 4 above). If Jakobson is correct and the metrical design is more abstract than the given verse instance, we might ask ourselves whether in fact the scansion is as it appears on the surface of the line or whether it may be analyzed as something slightly different. In other words, is *-lān##* actually a monosyllable or is its underlying structure *bi*-syllabic (i.e. *-lā -n(v)##*) with the vowel of the second syllable suppressed or understood? A justification for the latter analysis needs to be given, but I will postpone it. Let us for now assume that this analysis is the correct one, for it renders the end of the first hemistich perfectly regular.

– – ⏑ – | –
khaw-lā-n(v) ʿā-rif

This analysis hinges on the hypothesis that structures of the type #Cv̄C## are fundamentally bisyllabic, a hypothesis that will have to be revised somewhat to account for other kinds of data to be presented momentarily.

There remains the anomaly of the fourth foot, ⏑–⏑–, beginning the second hemistich. Another part of the linguistic theory of meter says that some positions in the foot will be variable and others fixed. If we hypothesize that the first position in the foot is variable (i.e. the foot may appear either as ⏑–⏑– or as ––⏑–), the anomaly disappears, and we get in fact a perfectly regular hemistich.

To summarize the analysis thus far, I contend that meter in Yemeni tribal poetry is based on a binary opposition of light syllables (Cv) and heavy syllables (every other type). In other words, these are the "equivalent" units that are distributed in parallel fashion in the line, forming a foot. If we assume that the syllable type #Cv̄C# is fundamentally bisyllabic, thus making the verse design more abstract, and that the first position of the foot is variable rather than fixed, we obtain a scansion of the line that is regular, thus confirming informants' intuitions about the meter. The first assumption raises the question of whether the underlying structure of word-final heavy syllables of the types ##CvCC## and ##Cv̄CC## might be analyzed as bisyllabic as well. This question is important because roughly 10–20 percent of the lines turn out to be metrically irregular if they cannot be so analyzed. I have already said that the bisyllabic hypothesis may need some qualification in the light of data yet to be presented. But for now, can we justify positing an underlying syllable structure #Cv̄C-C(v)##?

An interesting parallel case comes from Latvian folksongs as analyzed by Valdis Zeps (1963). Zeps argues that the verse design is based on four syllables, with a word boundary obligatory after the fourth syllable and absent after the third. The surface phonetic facts are not necessarily consistent with this verse design, for sometimes there are only three syllables instead of four. One can account for this apparent anomaly, however, by positing a missing syllable in the morphophonemics of the language that "can be reinstated during recitation and singing" (Zeps 1963, 126). Similarly, we have seen that Jakobson in his analysis of the Serbian folk epic (1963) argued for an obligatory caesura in the verse line even though it may be phonetically absent, insisting only that the feature in question be potentially audible in speech. In what contexts does the underlying vowel we have posited appear?

The great South Arabian Arabist Count Carlo Landberg (1901–13,

2 [1–2]: 99–101) came up with a solution to the problem of scansion when he noticed that poetic meter became perfectly regular when the poem was chanted instead of delivered in spoken recitation. He always asked informants for the chanted version of the poem, so as to hear the metrical pattern. In examining his texts one finds that it is particularly the #Cv̄C## structures that appear with a final vowel (thus rendering the structure bisyllabic). Landberg concluded that the meter was "faulty" in spoken recitation, but in fact that judgment assumes that verse design is not abstract and therefore the same as verse instant, an assumption the linguistic theory of meter calls into question. Nevertheless, it is to Landberg's credit that he discovered the contexts in which the underlying vowel becomes "potentially audible." I came across the same contexts in North Yemeni tribal verse.

The justification, then, for bisyllabic analysis is that verse designs in other traditions also have underlying elements that must be posited if metrical intuitions are to be explained and that these elements eventually do turn up in certain contexts. In other words, the arguments are based on comparison with other traditions and on a linguistic theory of meter. But is the bisyllabic analysis correct as it now stands? Or does it require modification in the light of other data?

I argue that the hypothesis needs to be qualified: the segmentation of the syllable #Cv̄C## as one or two syllables is *optional* for the poet, and the choice depends on the position of the structure in the underlying metrical pattern. Verses such as the following are said to be regular by Yemeni tribal informants but would have an irregular scansion if #Cv̄C## were automatically bisyllabic:

> ⏑ – [⏑] ⏑ – | – – [⏑] ⏑ – | – – [⏑] – |– – ⏑ –
>
> ṣalāḥ ʿalē-k aḷḷāh wa sallam ṭūl yā mukhtār-ahā
>
> God's prayer and blessing be upon you, O Chosen One

The words *ṣalāḥ* and *aḷḷāh* have the structure in question, but if they are interpreted as being fundamentally bisyllabic, the line becomes irregular, contradicting informants' intuitions. (The line comes from a poem by one of Khawlān's greatest poets, who is particularly admired for his technical accuracy.) But if we assume that the syllable is monosyllabic, then the irregularities vanish. Given this data, then, I would conclude that the bisyllabic interpretation of the #Cv̄C## structure must be optional.

Assuming that this analysis is correct, let us return to the remaining problem of segmenting heavy syllables of the types #CvCC## and #Cv̄CC##. The first type is segmented automatically into CvC-C when another word follows. The reason for this segmentation is that three consonants may not occur together (see Appendix A): hence, if the following word begins in a consonant, an epenthetic /a/ is automatically inserted before the word boundary to create a bisyllabic structure, CvC-Ca## (e.g. *kull* [all, every] + *bēt* [house] = *kulla bēt*); and if the following word begins in a vowel, the last consonant of the syllable elides with it. As for the superlong syllable #Cv̄CC##, it is very rare and occurs usually in monosyllabic words (e.g. *tāmm* [complete]). I have never come across this structure in my collection of poetry and therefore cannot test a hypothesis regarding its segmentation.

Let me recapitulate the analysis and arguments up to this point. The syllable types are categorized as light (Cv) and heavy (Cv̄ and CvC). The scansion of type Cv̄C is problematical, and we must assume an optional rule of bisyllabic segmentation into one heavy (Cv̄) and one light (Cv) or else an interpretation of one heavy syllable Cv̄C, depending on the position of the structure in the verse design. Neither of the superheavy types, CvCC and Cv̄CC, is problematical, for reasons already noted. This analysis makes sense of informant assertions of metrical regularity. In accounting for this regularity, I have posited a certain patterning of the light and heavy syllables in a foot ––⏑– where the first position is variable (i.e. light or heavy) and all others are fixed. I do not doubt that there are details of scansion and metrical analysis that have been overlooked or may even turn out to be wrong on the basis of future data. Any empirical analysis is subject to revision, and mine is no exception. What I do assert, however, is that the justifications I have put forward for this analysis in terms of a general linguistic theory of meter ought to hold despite changes in the details.

Thus far I have analyzed the foundations of poetic meter but not what Lotz has called its "superstructures," that is, the structures that occur on higher levels of the architecture of the poem. It is to this problem that I turn next, for it is here that the issue of parallelism and its productivity in verse systems becomes important.

Metrical Parallelisms

Consider again the metrical example discussed in detail above, whose abstract design looks something like this:

––⏑–––⏑–––⏑––

Let me now perform an admittedly pedantic and rather laborious exercise for the sake of making what I hope is a meaningful point. The question is: what is the patterning of syllables? There are obviously many different ways in which to group the syllables so as to create a sense of form, some of them better than others. What are the reasons for preferring some to others? Here are some possible patterns:

1. Assume that the rhythm is based on a syllable count. The algorithm is

as follows: (a) there are 13 syllables to a hemistich; (b) every *other* odd syllable, starting with the first one (i.e. first, fifth, and ninth) is *variably* light or heavy, except for the last one, which is heavy; (c) every *other* odd syllable starting with the third one (i.e. third, seventh, and eleventh) is *fixed* as light; and (d) every even syllable is *fixed* as long. Although, as Chomsky might say, this algorithm is "descriptively" adequate in that it accounts for the data, does it explain what we know about verse systems generally? Syllable-count meters are not rare. For instance, in the French *vers alexandrin* and Japanese *haiku* counting syllables within the rhythmic unit is critical. But note that this solution is not "natural" in the sense that it requires one to do more than simply count the number of syllables in a unit like the hemistich; it actually requires one to *match up* particular numbered positions with particular metrical values of light and heavy—a far more complicated task. In the particular way that it counts syllables this pattern does not resemble any other known verse system. Therefore, the solution is not probable or believable.

2. The previous algorithm does away entirely with the concept of the foot, maintaining that there is no hierarchical level of organization between the syllable and the hemistich. But the linguistic theory of meter stresses the hierarchical structure of language in the poetic function and hence leads us to posit the foot as a likely constituent. The question now becomes: which of the following analyses is preferred and why?

a. – – | ⏑ – | – – | ⏑ – | – – | ⏑ – | –
b. – – ⏑ | – – – | ⏑ – – | – ⏑ – | –
c. – – ⏑ – | – – ⏑ – | – – ⏑ – | –
d. – – ⏑ – – | – ⏑ – – – | ⏑ – –

Other combinations are, of course, possible. But those listed above are enough for the discussion of the problem at hand, which is to determine some criteria for preferring one sectioning of a line to another. I think most listeners would intuitively prefer 2a and 2c. Close inspection reveals that those two solutions require us to posit fewer kinds of feet. To put it differently, the patterning is strong in 2a and 2c and weak in all the other scansions. But which of the two is preferable, 2a or 2c? Again, I believe intuition would lead listeners to choose 2c over 2a. From the analysis we see that 2c involves even fewer kinds of feet (one as opposed to two) and that its rule of patterning for the feet is simpler (repetition as opposed to alternation).

The principles, then, that I have invoked to identify 2c as the preferred solution are economy and simplicity which are precisely the ones put forward by Seymour Chatman (1965, 116) in his theory of meter: "Let us assume that scansion and that metrical analysis to be the best which most simply, economically and consistently account for all the facts, that describe with least complexity a mechanism by which language may create secondary rhythms." Unless one can perform psychological experiments on informants to determine the psychological reception of verse meter (even if such experiments of rhythmic perception did already exist—to my knowledge they do not—it is hard for me to imagine administering one of them to a Yemeni tribesman!), there seems no alternative but to invoke these explanatory principles of economy, simplicity, and consistency to account for the regularity or patterning of verse. In other words, they must be added to the linguistic theory of verse systems.

Thus far I have concluded that the foot is a necessary constituent of the analysis in order to account for patterning of light and heavy syllables in any fashion that reflects listeners' intuitions. The precise content of the foot must be decided on the basis of simplicity, economy, and consistency. I will now end the metrical analysis by examining the different kinds of feet that are possible, the different patternings resulting from the combination of these feet in the hemistich, and the extent to which this verse system may be productive (i.e. may produce new patterns).

The Pitter-Patter of Different Feet

Here is a line from a tribal poem:

–[◡] – –[◡] – – ◡ – – –[◡] – – ◡ – – ◡ – –
w-ēn marrē-t yā bū ḥulēgah || yōm tuṣbaḥ tinādī bi-ṣōt-ak
Where did you go, O Abū Ḥulēgah, || the day you began to shout?

What exactly is the metrical pattern? The simplest and most economical pattern seems intuitively to be as follows:

–◡–|–◡–|–◡–|–||

Analysis has thus revealed a second type of foot: –◡–. In this line, as in the previous line I examined, a larger pattern is created by repeating the foot a certain number of times (determined by the length of the musical chant).

Now consider this line:

– ◡ – – – ◡ – – – ◡ – – – ◡ – – – ◡ – –
sādat-ī ʾantum nujūm al-ʾarḍa dāyim || min saʿādat-kum nazal-nā
– ◡ – –
l-it-tahāyim
My lords, you are the everlasting stars of the world; || by your grace we descend to the Tihāmah

What is the pattern in each hemistich? The metrical feet we have available to us thus far in the analysis allow one solution:

–◡–|––◡–|––◡–|–

But this solution is hardly simple, consistent, or elegant. If we posit a third type of foot, –⏑––, we get a different sectioning of the line:

–⏑––|–⏑––|–⏑––

We now have three distinct kinds of feet: ––⏑–, –⏑–, and –⏑––. Each serves as the basis of a distinct metrical pattern by means of a simple repetition; the number of repetitions is determined by the length of the musical chant. Three additional patterns exist in the verse system on the basis of the alternation of two (and only two) distinct feet:

––⏑–|–⏑–|––⏑– . . .
–⏑––|–⏑–|–⏑–– . . . *or* –⏑–|––⏑–|–⏑–|– . . .
–⏑–|–⏑––|–⏑– . . .

Note that the second sequence is analyzable into two different patterns, making it structurally ambiguous. This ambiguity is not necessarily a fault of the analysis. That is, all structures—be they phonological, syntactic, or poetic—may be expected to be analyzable in more than one way. Note also that the above feet and the rule of alternation allow a seventh pattern and its reverse, but neither actually occurs in my corpus of texts:

––⏑–|–⏑––|––⏑– . . .
–⏑––|––⏑–|–⏑–– . . .

If we assume, however, that this system is productive, with rules of repetition and alternation of metrical feet that create parallelisms of the kind we have been examining, then there is reason to believe that either the absence of these patterns is an accident of my collection or else no one has yet created them but eventually someone will. I wish now that I had composed lines of verse on these patterns and tested them on my informants to see whether they would have accepted them; unfortunately, I did not complete this analysis of meter until after my departure from Yemen, and therefore the opportunity to test them never presented itself.

APPENDIX C

Transcription of the Sample *Bālah* Poem

Note: Phrases in italics are formulas. All others are nonformulaic.

1. wa yā lēlah bālah:

– – ⏑ –|– ⏑ –| – – ⏑ –| –⏑ –

Poet 1 ʾalā *w-abdaʿ bi-dhī lāmiʿ al-bārig wa dhī lāḥ b-ih*

– – ⏑ –|– ⏑ –| – – ⏑ – | – ⏑ –

ʾalā *yā man daʿ aḷḷāh karīm al-kaffa mā khayyab-ah*

2. wa yā lēlah bālah:

⏑ – ⏑ –| –[⏑]–| – – ⏑ –| – ⏑ –

Poet 1 ʾalā *w-an aḥmad aḷḷāh mā nōd aṣ-ṣabā habhabah*

⏑ – ⏑ –|– ⏑ – | – – ⏑ –|–⏑ –

ʾalā *wa manzal aṭ-ṭashsh[a] min jōw as-samā sākibah*

3. wa yā lēlah bālah:

⏑ – ⏑ –|– ⏑ –| – –[⏑] –| – ⏑ –

Poet 2 ʾalā *w-anadʿiy aḷḷāh dhiy al-mabdūʿ w-al-khitm[a] b-ih*

⏑ – ⏑ –|–[⏑] – | – –[⏑]–|– ⏑ –

ʾalā *w-an aḥmad aḷḷāh milyōnāt bā naḥsib-ah*

4. wa yā lēlah bālah:

– – ⏑ –| –[⏑] –|– – ⏑ –| – ⏑ –

Poet 1 ʾalā *ninjā min an-nār dhī hī nār-ah al-muzwabah*

– – ⏑ –|– ⏑ –|– – ⏑ –| – ⏑ –

ʾalā *yōm al-muḥāsib yiḥāsib kulla mā garrab-ah*

5. wa yā lēlah bālah:

– – ⏑ – | –[⏑] –| – – ⏑ – | – ⏑ –

Poet 1 ʾalā *dhī mihdiy an-nōb dhī tijnī ʿasal tishṭab-ah*

– – ⏑ – | –[⏑] –| – – [⏑] – | – ⏑ –

ʾalā *y-aḷḷāh ṭalabnā-k dhī f-il-bidʿ[a] w-al-migribah*

6. wa yā lēlah bālah:

– – ∪–|– ∪–| – – ∪ –|–∪–
Poet 1 ʾalā *ḥāfiḍ marākib ʿalā mōjāt-ah an-nājibah*
– – ∪–|– ∪–|– – ∪–|–∪–
ʾalā *w-adhkur muḥammad ṣalāt aḷḷāh ʿalā ṭayyibah*

7. wa yā lēlah bālah:

– – ∪–|– ∪–|– –∪–| –∪–
Poet 2 ʾalā *w-adhkur muḥammad ka-mā gad dhikrat-ah wājibah*
– – ∪ –|– ∪–|– –∪–| –∪–
ʾalā *yishfaʿ la-nā min jahannam ḥarra-ha l-lāhibah*

8. wa yā lēlah bālah:

– – ∪– |–[∪]–|– – ∪ –|–∪–
Poet 1 ʾalā *y-aḷḷāh ṭalabnā-k daḥḥan-nā min al-miḥnibah*
∪– ∪–| –[∪] –|– – ∪–| –∪–
ʾalā *w-agul masa l-khēr w-ānā min rijāl miḥribah*

9. wa yā lēlah bālah:

∪– ∪ –| –[∪] –|∪ – ∪ –| –∪–
Poet 2 ʾalā *masā-ka b-il-khēr w-ant[a] min gaḥūm manyibah*
– – ∪–|– ∪ –|– – ∪ –|–∪–
ʾalā *y-ahl an-niṣāl al-ḥaḍārim ḥidduw aṭ-ṭayyibah*

10. wa yā lēlah bālah:

– – ∪ –|–∪ –|– – ∪–|–∪–
Poet 3 ʾalā *ḥayyā-kum al-kulla w-ijʿal lā tarō nāyibah*
– – ∪ –|–[∪]–|– – – ?– | – ∪ –
ʾalā *yā marḥab ālāf lā yiḥṣā lā ḥad maḥsibah*

11. wa yā lēlah bālah:

– – ∪–|–[∪]–|– –∪–|– ∪–
Poet 3 ʾalā *w-akhdum li-ṣaffēn dhī hum ḥāmilīn uswabah*
– – ∪ –|– ∪–|– – ∪ –|–∪–
ʾalā *dhī yintadō f-il-muḥājī kulla ḥad martabah*

12. wa yā lēlah bālah:

– –[∪] –| –[∪] –| – – ∪–| –∪–
Poet 2 ʾalā *ḥayyā-k w-abgā-k mā shaddū ʿalā mirjibah*
– – ∪ –|–[∪]–|– – ∪ – | – ∪ –
ʾalā *yā kurmat aḍ-ḍēf ḥattā fī sanīn mijdibah*

13. wa yā lēlah bālah:

– – ∪ –| –[∪]–|– – ∪–|– ∪ –
Poet 4 ʾalā *yā lēlat al-khēr lā ṣāḥib ligī ṣāḥib-ah*
– – ∪ –| –[∪]–| – – ∪ –| –∪–
ʾalā *yā marḥab aḍ-ḍēf dhī mabʿad wa dhī magribah*

14. wa yā lēlah bālah:

– – ∪ –| – ∪ –|– – ∪ –| – ∪ –

Poet 1 ʾalā *w-akhdum ḥarīw as-saʿādah ʿaṭra min ṭayyibah*

– –[∪]–| – ∪ –| – – ∪ –|– ∪ –

ʾalā *w-aḍ-ḍēf ʾajnab* min al-ḥabḥab maʿā ʿunwabah

15. wa yā lēlah bālah:

– – ∪ –|–[∪]–| – – ∪ – | –∪–

Poet 2 ʾalā *w-abgā-kum aḷḷāh yā dhī taʿraf aṣ-ṣāyibah*

– – ∪ –| – ∪ –|– – ∪ –| –∪–

ʾalā *dhī tintamō f-il-muḥājī lā badat nāyibah*

16. wa yā lēlah bālah:

– – ∪ –| – ∪ –| – –[∪] –|– ∪ –

Poet 1 ʾalā *yā marḥabā* b-il-ḥukaymah gōl dhī yaʿjab-ah

– – ∪ –| – ∪ –| – – ∪–| – ∪ –

ʾalā *mā ḥanna raʿd-ah wa saggā fī bilād mijdibah*

17. wa yā lēlah bālah:

– – ∪ –|–[∪]–| – – ∪ –| – ∪ –

Poet 2 ʾalā *w-abgā-kum aḷḷāh yā dhī dhābiḥīn mitribah*

– – ∪ –| –[∪] –| – – ∪ –| – ∪ –

ʾalā *y-ahl al-karam* ṭūl mā hādhā la-nā mijribah

18. wa yā lēlah bālah:

Poet 3 Unintelligible

19. wa yā lēlah bālah:

– –∪ –| –[∪]–| – – ∪ –| – ∪ –

Poet 1 ʾalā fī dhālik ad-dār lā b-ih shēkh wa lā nēgabah

– – ∪ –| – ∪ –| – – ∪ –| – ∪ –

ʾalā gaḥm al-khalā f-il-jabal w-ath-thaʿla f-il-maʿzabah

20. wa yā lēlah bālah:

– – ∪ –| –[∪]–| – – ∪–| – ∪ –

Poet 3 ʾalā *yā marḥab aḍ-ḍēf jamʿah dhī ghilī manṣab-ah*

– ∪ –| –[∪]–|– – ∪ –| – ∪ –

ʾalā *w-al-ḥarīw ʿād zāyid kulla-mā yiṭlub-ah*

21. wa yā lēlah bālah:

– –∪ –| –[∪] –|– – ∪ –| – ∪ –

Poet 1 ʾalā yā ṣāliḥ *aḥyā-k lā tibgā la-nā harwabah*

– – ∪ –| –[∪] –| ∪ – ∪ –| –∪–

ʾalā *hū ḥuṣna maʿmūr mā hiy al-gurā khāribah*

22. wa yā lēlah bālah:

Poet 3 Unintelligible

23. wa yā lēlah bālah:

– –⌣ –| –[⌣] –| – – ⌣ –| – ⌣ –

Poet 1 ʾalā yā ṣāliḥ *aḥyā-k lā shiṭṭū l-ak al-magṭabah*

– –[⌣] –| – ⌣ –| – –[⌣] –| – ⌣ –

ʾalā *w-alfēn ṣaḷḷāh ʿalā mukhtār f-iṭ-ṭayyibah*

APPENDIX D

Transcription of the Sample *Bālah* Development Section

The Host-Guest Teasing Routine

– ∪ –| – ∪– –|– ∪ –|– ∪– – – ∪–| – ∪– –|
Host: marḥabā mā ṭalabtū law tagūlū nisānī || bā yijī f-il-fitar ʾaw
– ∪–|– ∪ – –
bā yijī fī gharārah

– ∪ –| ∪? – –| – ∪ –| – ∪– – – ∪–| – ∪– –|
Host: hiyya laʿbat al-bāl kulla-hā shūf ʿajā-nī || mā ṭalabtū w-ajadtū
–[∪] –| – ∪ – –
l-ēsh hādha d-dabārah

–|– ∪ – –| – ∪–| – ∪ – – – ∪ –|
Guest: yā saʿd an aʿrif yā karīm al-yamānī [meter short] || ʾal-ʿarab
– ∪– –|– ∪ –|– ∪ – –
jāwiʿah mā ʿād tarīd as-samārah

– ∪ –| –[∪] – –| –[∪] –|? ∪ – – ∪ – – ∪| –[∪]
Guest: ḥājja ḥayyā-k b-id-diggāg w-ath-thawānī || wa law ʿād abū-k
– –|– ∪ –| – ∪ – –
yā nāṣir yigaddim ḍimārah [faulty first foot]

– ∪ –| – ∪– –| – ∪ –| ∪– ∪– –
Guest: gad muḥammad taʿayyib yiddiy arbaʿah ṣiyānī [last foot
– ∪ –| – ∪– –| – ∪–| – ∪ – –
long] || shāhiy aswad miniʿniʿ min bilād al-ʾimārah

– ∪ –| – ∪ – –| –∪– | – ∪– – – ∪ –|–
Guest: zil wa ʿudd az-zamal l-ak wājiʿah f-in-niyānī || ʾashti l-ākul
–? –|? – –| – ∪ –| – ∪ – –
ḥattā l-aslā-nī bi-ḥabbah sigārah [meter faulty]

– – ∪ –| – ∪ – –|– ∪ –| – ∪ – –
Host: ʾantū tabō niddiy al-ḥāṣil w-adhī f-ith-thabānī [meter

– – ⏑ –| – ⏑ – –| –[⏑] – –| – ⏑ – –
faulty] || w-inna-k tubā la-k galīl siḥtēn fī sūg an-naḍārah [meter faulty]

– ⏑ ⏑| – ⏑ – –| – ⏑ –| – ⏑ – – – ⏑ –| –
Guest: w-ann asal-ak bi-gurmat dhī malān al-banānī || w-anta lā mā
⏑ – –| – ⏑ –| – ⏑ – –
gani^c^t-ah bā yuga^c^ b-il-ḥijārah

– ⏑ –| – ? – –| – ⏑ –| – ⏑ – – –[⏑] –| –
Host: gad ṭaḥanna l-ḥabbah w-al-jamāl f-is-sawānī || ḍēf mā shī
⏑ – –| – ⏑ –| – ⏑ – –
ma^c^ā-nā w-anta sir l-ak shirārah

– ⏑ –| – ⏑ – –| – ⏑ –| – ⏑ – – –[⏑] –|
Guest: shī maḥabbah li-ḥawla r-rub^c^a w-illā fa-shānī || kēf huh
– ⏑ – –| – ⏑ –| – ⏑ – –
silf-akum ninsā ḥarīw as-sarārah

The Poets' Duel

– – ⏑ –| –[⏑] –| – – ⏑ –| – ⏑ –
10. shawwag-niy al-bāl w-al-ghumrān wa m-ānā kasal
– – ⏑ –| – ⏑ –| – – ⏑ –| – –
w-illā fa-lā tinfa^c^ al-bālah la-dhī waddil [last foot short]
– – ⏑ –| –[⏑] –| – –[⏑] –| – ⏑ –
11. yā ḥallat al-bāl f-id-dīwān man jā yishill
– – ⏑ –| – ⏑ –| – –[⏑] –| – ⏑ –
shawwag-niy al-bāl ma^c^ al-ghumrān kam min baṭal
– – ⏑ –| –[⏑] –| – –?| – ⏑ –
16. yā ḥallat al-bāl w-ash^c^ār kam min jahal [third foot short]
– – ⏑ –| – ⏑ –| – – ⏑ –| – ⏑ –
dhī mā yiḥaggig ḥarūf-ah ^c^ind-anā lā yiḥill
– – ⏑ –| –[⏑] –| – –[⏑] –| – ⏑ –
17. w-antah yiḥayyī-k y-al-baddā^c^ m-ānā kasal
– – ⏑ –| – ⏑ –| – – ⏑ –| – ⏑ –
w-in shī ma^c^-ak ḥarfa hāt-ah w-al-^c^awēlah tishill
– – ⏑ –| – ⏑ –| – – ⏑ –| – ⏑ –
20. lā tingidū shī samiyy in guṣra w-inn-ah ṭuwal
⏑ –⏑ –| – ⏑ –| – – ⏑ –| – ⏑ –
wa tāliy ash-shi^c^ra ḥagg-ah shūf gad-uh f-is-sifal
– – ⏑ –| –[⏑] –| – – ⏑ –| – ⏑ –
21. w-antah yiḥayyī-k y-al-baddā^c^ ashūf-ak dhaḥil
– – ⏑ –| –[⏑] –| – – ⏑ –| – ⏑ –
w-ānā min aghmār dhī ta^c^dī wa dhī gad tishill
– –[⏑] –| – ⏑ –| – – ? –| – ⏑ –
23. w-at-tēs mugrin ᵓalā w-antah hag-na r-rakhal [third foot short]

– – ⏑ –| –[⏑]–| – – ⏑ –| – ⏑ –

mā nil^cab al-bāl ṭūl al-lēl wa shūf lā tidhill

– – ⏑ –| – ⏑ –|– – ⏑ –|– ⏑ –

26. min kuthr al-ash^cār adhī fōg-ak wa lā tihtadal

– – ⏑ –| – ⏑ –| – –[⏑]–| – ⏑ –

yā raḥmat-ah yā samiy-yī shūf lā tistagill

– – ⏑ –| –[⏑]– | – – ⏑ – | – ⏑ –

27. w-antah yiḥayyī-k yimlī ḥadd-anā w-al-maḥall

– – ⏑ –| –[⏑] –| – – ⏑ –| – ⏑ –

yā fakhriy aḥyā-k w-antah yā ḥimār adh-dhubal

– –[⏑]–|– ⏑ –|– – ⏑ –| – ⏑ –

28. yā bāl lā tit^cabī rub^c-ī bi-ḍarb al-mathal

– – ⏑ –|– ⏑ –|– – ⏑ –|– ⏑ –

kull-in yifaṣṣil yigaṭṭi^c gaṭ^ca mā ^cad yiḥill

APPENDIX E

Transcription of al-Gharsī's Poem

b-ism-ī wa b-ism al-jēsh[a] w-isma ʾal-bilād al-ʾāhilah || ʾabṭāl-ana
l-muttaḥdiyīn hawl al-manāyā w-al-ḥatūf
b-ism il-mawāgiʿ f-il-jibāl ash-shumakh al-mutgābilah || ʾagūl[a]
ʿāsh al-gāyid al-mughwār[a] maʿdūm al-waṣūf
ʿāsh az-zaʿīm al-ḥurra man gād al-yaman w-al-gāfilah || w-al-jēsh[a]
w-ibna sh-shaʿb[a] takrīm-an la-hu gāmū wagūf
tisʿah malāyīn yishhad aḷḷāh in takūn mitgālilah || w-illā fa-gad
taʿdād-ahā ʾaḥdī ʿashar yimkin-hā tanūf
wa kull-ahum ṭūʿ al-ʾawāmir w-al-guwā mitkāmilah || ʾalūf[a]
taḥdhū ḥadhwa-kum yā sīdī talawwa ʾal-ʾalūf
ʾa mā tarā tilk al-ḥashar w-al-ʿārimah w-al-ḥāfilah || mustanḍirīn
amr-ak la-tatḥarrak ʿalā m-antah tashūf
wa kulla ʾāmāl al-ʾulūf al-ḥāḍirah w-al-ghāfilah || ghāyah munā-hā
w-al-mirād al-jidda l-ingādh ar-riyūf
f-ar-rīf[a] miḥtāj al-ʾayād al-mukhliṣah w-al-ʿāmilah || mithl
al-ʿawāṣim gaddirū fī-ha l-muwāgif w-aḍ-ḍarūf
lā tasmaʿū mughriḍ fa-tabgā kulla ʿazlah ʿāzilah || w-al-ḥagga ʾinnā
ʾumm-anā lis-nā min al-maghraḍ ḥasūf
b-il-ʾamsa ʾayyadnā wa waḥḥadna l-gulūb al-māyilah || w-al-jihla
wallā w-anjalā ḍulm al-liyālī w-al-kasūf
wallā zamān al-fugra ḥaṭṭamna l-jasūr al-ḥāyilah || bēn
at-tagaddum w-al-binā biʾs al-maʿīshah f-il-kahūf
lākin ʾarēnā sagfa masjid-nā wa fī-h al-wāṭilah || hādha l-ladhī
khalla l-yaman yaḥmal silāḥah w-as-siyūf
yā rāyid at-taṭwīr[a] gad kull al-malāyīn āmilah || ʾinn-ak sa-tajlub
l-il-bilād al-khēr[a] w-al-ʾarā shafūf
ʾaḷḷāh[a] wallā-k al-yaman jaʿal yadē-k aṭ-ṭāyilah || lākin talaṭṭaf yā
ḥabīb ash-shaʿb[a] kun fī-nā raʾūf
ʾunḍur ʾilā ʾayat liwā maḥrūm[a] naḍrah shāmilah || hab l-ah min
at-taʿlīm[a] ḥaḍḍ-ah lumma tafrīg aṣ-ṣafūf

narjū-k[a] tadrak f-il-bilād al-ḥābilah w-an-nābilah || w-ibnō binā min ṣaḥḥa lā tibnō ʿala l-jadr ar-ragūf
f-al-joww[a] ghēr al-joww[a] w-al-bāriḥ bi-ʿaks al-gābilah || w-al-baḥr al-aḥmar min habūb al-ʿāṣifah ʾamwāj-ah tazūf [hemistich too long]
khiyūṭ[a] mansūjah wa barm al-khēṭ[a] ʿind al-ghāzilah || w-aṣ-ṣūf[a] yishti khaṣṣ[a] gabl al-ghazla w-illa ṣ-ṣūf[a] ṣūf
min ad-diyār al-khārijiyyah l-ad-diyār ad-dākhilah || nakhshā ʿalā dha-sh-shaʿb[a] min baʿḍ al-jihah hadm as-safūf
ʾafḥaṣ la-ḥattā tāʿraf aṣḥāb al-galūb al-ghāyilah || w-aʿraf natāʾij-hā wa ʿālij-hā bi-mā hī l-ah ʾalūf
wāḥid l-ah al-maʿrūf[a] yimshī b-ih wa wāḥid ʿāmilah || w-idha l-bashar mitjānisah f-ijnās-ihā ʿaddat ṣanūf
w-antum gad-ak khābir la-hādha l-ʾamra khibrah kāmilah || fa-lā tajāmil ḥad wa mōla l-ḥagg[a] mā min ḥad yakhōf
wa hā ʾanā b-ism al-yaman ʾaṭlub maṭālib ʿādilah || w-arjū ṣarīḥ amr-ak bi-lā dōrān[a] fī-hā ʾaw lafūf
ʾal-ʾawwalah shagg aṭ-ṭurug w-iṣlāḥ[a] mā hiy ʿāṭilah || fiy al-bilād an-nāʾiyah min faḍl-ak ukhruj waṭūf
w-ath-thāniyah tubnā madāris-nā bi-ṣūrat ʿājilah || min ajla taʿlīm al-binīn al-ʿilma lā ṣagf al-kafūf
w-ath-thālithah batrōl[a] nitmassak bi-guwwat hāʾilah || nidfaʿ balad-nā l-il-ʾimām baʿd at-takhalluf w-al-khalūf
baʿd ar-rawāsib w-ar-rawākid w-al-ʿugūl al-jāhilah || dhī min ʿamīg al-jahla manzūʿah wa maghrūfah gharūf
wa rābiʿ-an bāb az-zirāʿah ʿājilah lā ʾājilah || ḥarām[a] yibgā shaʿb-anā tharwat-ah ṣāyim ʿaṭūf [meter faulty]
hādhih fiṣāl arbaʿ nafāʿit-hā la-nā mitbādilah || bēn al-ḥakūmah w-al-mawāṭin l-ak wa-lī fī-hā ṣarūf
w-al-ʿafwu ʾin gad zayyad al-baddāʿ[a] shī fī zāmil-ah || f-ash-shiʿra fī-h ashʿār[a] min naḍm al-gawāfī w-al-ḥarūf

APPENDIX F

Transcription of aṣ-Ṣūfī's Poem

gāl al-fatā bū muḥammad kulla shī yukmal || wa kulla makhlūg[a] min dār al-ḥayāh fānī
yā ṭēr[a] siffāḥ[a] faḍḍ al-jō wa tawakkal || balligh bi-maḍrūf yiḥwī naḍma gayfānī
min ʿayn[a] khawlān[a] dhī mā tigbil ar-rowfal || wa lā shayāṭīn[a] min ʾinsin wa lā jānī
yā ṭēr[a] lā tihbiṭ illā fī dhamār ajmal || min kulla baldah sagā-h aḷḷāh[a] b-il-ʾamzānī
lā gad waṣalt al-madīnah lāzim in tisʾal || ʿan ibna mugbil muḥammad khērat insānī
ʿizz al-maʿālī shadīd al-bās[a] mā yibkhil || mars al-karam w-ash-shahāmah ṭūl al-azmānī
shibl al-ḥadā kulla mā shāf al-gharīb agbal || yigūl[a] yā marḥabā b-ik fōg al-aʿyānī
yaʿjab ʿala ḍ-ḍēf [a] min maṭlaʿ wa min manzal || mawā l-il-aghrāḍ[a] min gāṣī wa min dānī
shāʿir wa tājir wa lā f-in-nās[a] yitmaththal || kadhdhāb[a] man gāl[a] mithl-ah l-il-ʿulā bānī
maʿlah maʿallī taʿallā fī zamān awwal || min ṣubbat awlād mazīd[a] nasla thuʿbānī
jēsh al-ḥadā dhī yihizz al-ʾarḍ[a] lā zaḥfal || w-ar-rūs[a] tihtiz min-ah w-illā wa-l-amrīkānī
lā gāl[a] ʿilm-ak fa-gūl l-ah jīta l-ak mursal || bi-khaṭṭ[a] min ʿinda shāʿir jēsh[a] khawlānī
ṣadīg-akum dhī ʿalā mabdā-h[a] ma-tḥawwal || ʿala ṣ-ṣadāgah li-hāfiḍ sirra w-aʿlānī
salām[a] l-ak mā lamaʿ barg-ah wa mā sabbal || min rūs[a] l-agnāf [a] w-amsa r-raʿda ḥannānī
w-asga l-bilād al-jadībah b-il-maṭar w-ahmal || w-aḥyā thamar-hā wa ṭābat zahra l-aghṣānī

bi-ghshā-ka yā ʿārif ahl al-ʿagda w-ahl al-ḥall || wa ʿārif ahl al-ʾisāʾah w-ahl al-aḥsānī
b-il-miska w-al-mustakā w-an-nadda w-aṣ-ṣandal || wa ʿaṭra ʿambar wa mā wardī wa rīḥānī
makhṣūṣ[a] l-ak yā walad mugbil wa mustaʿjil || min ṣāliḥ aṣ-ṣūfiy ahdā b-ih la-kum ʿānī
mā shammar al-markab al-hindī wa mā naggal || ṣanāʿat al-hinda w-amlā kulla dukkānī
wa ʿadda mā kulla muʾmin bāt[a] yatnaffal || wa ṭāʿa rabb-ah bi-ʾakhlāṣ w-al-itgānī [hemistich short?]
yā mursilī kallim al-maʿlah wa lā takhjal || kallām[a] muṣaddig ṣadīg-ah khēr[a] ʾikhwānī
gul l-ah yigūl ibna gāsim bin ʿalī gad mall || ḥayāh[a] fī-hā ʿazīz an-nās[a] yihtānī
w-al-galba mā ʿād ʿalā hādha l-ḥayāh ʿaggal || w-idhā w-anā yōm[a] taḥṣīl al-ʿulā wānī
matāʿib al-wagta khallat galbiy atkassal || min ayna l-ī galba fī hādha l-ʿamar thānī
ʾan aʿtagid ʾinna mā b-ish galba yitbaddal || wa l-ibna muslim yugaʿ kāfir wa naṣrānī
wa lā muṣallī wa ṣāyim yidkhil al-maḥfal || dhī yidkhil-ah kulla mitkhanfas wa sakrānī
wa lā ʿasal min buṭūn an-naḥla yirjaʿ khall || dhī tishraʿ an-nōb[a] shihd-ah rās[a] ʿallānī
mā shī yugaʿ burtagāl ṣifar min al-ḥanḍal || wa lā balas janna yibdī fī rūmānī [meter short]
ka-lā wa lā dōm[a] yishbah ṣāfiy al-ḥalḥal || min bāsigāt an-nakhāyil ḥagg[a] najrānī
w-ad-durra w-al-lūla ṭūl al-wagta mā yakhtall || wa lā yawāgīt[a] titghayyar wa mirjānī
wa hākidha n-nās[a] titmayyiz wa tinfāḍil || mā hum sawa n-nās[a] dhī fī jumʿ al-awṭānī
yā ʾummat ad-dīn[a] lā ḥad minna-kum yijhal || gad sār[a] farʿōn[a] min bugʿā wa hāmānī
wa sār[a] nimrūd[a] hū dhī kān[a] yitgātil || wa sār[a] min-hā banī ʾaḷḷāh sulēmānī
wa sār[a] min-ha l-ḥabīb al-muṣṭafā l-afḍal || dhī ʾanzal aḷḷāh[a] fī-h ayyāt[a] gurʾānī
w-al-ḥaydarah dhī bi-sēf-ah l-il-ʿadā ḥandal || raḥal gafā mā gad aʿdam rūs al-igrānī
f-ēsh aklaf-ak yā yaman-na l-ḥurr[a] tatbahdhal || wa fī-ka kam-min ṣubī l-il-khaṣma ṭaʿʿānī

mā kunt aḍunn al-jibāl ash-shāmikhah tiftal || w-arbāb-ahā dhī ḥumū-h insāl[a] gaḥṭānī
dhī ḥaṭṭamū kulla ghāzī wagta mā yuṣal || bi-shēsh[a] khānah wa hirtiyyah wa sulṭānī
wa shalluw amwāl[a] jēsh ar-rōm[a] w-al-hitral || wa jēsh al-aḥbāsh[a] hum w-awlād[a] ʿuthmānī
yā shaʿb-anā kulla shājiʿ min ligā-nā dhall || hū jēsh-anā dhī ghazā fāris wa rūmānī
w-al-yōm[a] mā fād-ana l-ʾālī wa la l-jarmal || wa la l-madāfiʿ wa rashshāshāt[a] mēdānī
y-ibn al-yaman gaṣd-ak ar-rāḥāt[a] w-al-magyal || bi-bazrat al-gāt[a] dhī min kulla bustānī
mā taʿlam inn ad-duwal lā shaʿb-anā tarḥal || shūʿī wa baʿthī wa gadhdhāfī wa ṭulyānī
wa ḥizba nāṣir dakhal f-ish-shaʿba tawaghghal [meter short?] || wa ḥizba sūrī wa baghdādī wa lubnānī
wa ḥizba gharbī min al-giblah bi-yatsallal || wa ḥizba shargī yigūd-ah ḥayd[a] shamsānī
wa man waṣal lē-h[a] lā shahad wa lā hallal || hādhā majūsī wa hādhā ʿābid awthānī
mā ḥad fi l-aḥzāb[a] hādhih kull-ahum bismal || b-ism-illāh la-hū ʾal-mukawwin kulla mā kānī [meter long]
yā shaʿb-ana nhuḍ tayaggaḍ gabla mā tankal || fa-lā biyaghrū-ka maglūbīn al-adyānī
yikfī-k mashāṭ[a] tālāt ash-shiʿar y-aḥbal [meter short] || w-al-khanfasah ʾalfa ḥummā tāk al-adgānī
w-al-banṭalūnāt[a] hādh aḥlā wa hādh ashkal || khaḍrā wa ḥamrā tarā-h ashkāla w-alwānī
mā kāna shī mithla-mā hādha l-khēra yuʿgal [hemistich short?] || fī shaʿb-anā dhī min ahl ash-shirka muṣṭānī
y-ibna l-yaman law taghallag bāb-ak al-mugfal || mā yidkhal ash-shaʿba lā shirk[a] wa lā zānī [faulty hemistich]
yā maʿlah inṣaḥ rijāl ash-shaʿba tatgabyal || min gabla mā yidkhalū layyāta w-aghwānī
yā ḥayd[a] bēnān[a] gul l-in-nās[a] kēf tifʿal || wa gāyid ash-shaʿba yiḍrab kulla mikhtānī
raʾīs-ana l-bār[a] dhī yitgaddim al-maḥmal || wa yantagim kulla mujrim baʿda burhānī
subḥān[a] dhī yaghfir az-zillāt lā ḥad zall || man tāb[a] w-akhlaṣ fa-ʿand aḷḷāh[a] ghufrānī
yā rabba ṣāliḥ yinādī l-ak wa yatwassal || b-ism-ak wa ʿilm-ak wa ḥulm-ak yā kurīmānī

mā nadᶜiy ill anta fī māḍī wa mustagbil || yā man ᶜalē-k at-tawakkul w-at-tawākānī
w-asāl-ak al-ᶜafwu lā dhambī ᶜaleyy athgal || yā murtajā yā ṣamad ya ᶜāliy ash-shānī
ᶜafw-ak wa ṣafḥ-ak wa ghufrān-ak la-nā yishal || bēn aydē-ka yōm[a] nibᶜath fī-h[a] ᶜaryānī [meter faulty]
yōm al-mawāzīn[a] titrajjaḥ wa tatᶜaddal || yā ḥayya gayyūm[a] rajjaḥ fī-ha sīrān-ī
yōm al-ᶜugūl az-zakīnah kull-ahā tadhhal || wa yijtamiᶜ fī-h[a] mālik hū wa raḍwānī
w-azkā ṣalāt-i ᶜala l-mukhtāra tatsajjal || ṣalāt wa taslīm[a] min galb-ī wa lissān-ī
yā gōm[a] ṣallū ᶜalā man rabb-anā faḍḍal || muḥammad-an dhī sakan jannāt[a] ᶜadnānī

APPENDIX G

Transcription of al-Maʿlah's Poem

ʾakhū ʿalī gāl gad ʾal-wagta yiddāwal || w-aṭmāʿ bugʿah wa bugʿah mā la-hā mānī
mā bāgiy ill anta y-aḷḷāh yā wizā man dhall || yā dhī rafaʿt as-samā min ghēr[a] ʿamdānī
tibsiṭ wa tirfaʿ wa titnaḍḍar wa titʾammal || wa ḥukm-ak al-ḥagga w-antah farda rubbānī
subḥāna dhī kawwan ajwāf al-ghumar w-aṭ-ṭall || hū dhī khalag-nī wa ṣawwar-nī wa sawwā-nī
wa kawwan al-barga fī baṭn as-samā w-ahmal || min as-sama l-māʾa yirwī kulla ʿaṭshānī
w-aḥyā b-ih al-ʾarḍa min mēd b-il-ḥayāh taḥfal || w-al-khalga tirtāḥ[a] min ʿurb-an wa ʿijmānī
w-ash-shamsa fī burja-hā l-il-khalga tatjawwal || tahīsh li-ʾarzāg-ahā man kaffa milyānī
kāfī jamīʿ al-khalāyig jalla w-itkaffal || bi-kulla shī ʾinkhalag min dūn[a] nisyānī
bi-ḥamd-ah ar-raʿda shabbaḥ w-ath-thara stamthal || w-al-kōn[a] nādā bi-ḥamd-ah kull al-akwānī
wa kulla makhlūg[a] yitḥammad wa yitbahhal || li-mālik al-mulk[a] dhī hū ʿadla minnānī
w-an aḥmad-ah ʿadda-mā zād al-ʿashī sakhbal || ḥamd-ī wa shukr-ī li-rabb-ī ṭūl[a] m-aḥyā-nī
fī kulla ḥāl aḥmad-ah min wājib-ī w-aʿmal || fī ṭāʿat-ah kulla majhūd-ī wa ʾimkān-ī
min baʿda dha l-ḥīn[a] lā ḥillu ṣ-ṣubā ʾizhal || galb-ī min aḍ-ḍēg[a] yā maḍnūn-iy aḍnā-nī
yā mā l-abū-ka l-fatā man gāl anā y-aḥbal || mā hū shi man gāl abī lā kunta lugmānī
lā b-il-mathal ghirra f-antah baʿd-iy atmarjal || lā jāt-ak aḍ-ḍēf[a] gul ḥayyā bi-man jā-nī

raḥḥab wa sahhal wa ḥayy-ah w-irtawaʿ madkhal || wa gaddir-ah lā tasūg-ah bēt[a] jīrānī
w-idhbaḥ w-anā bū-ka lā tiglig wa lā tifshal || w-aṣruf la-mā shiʾta min bēt-ī wa makhzān-ī
w-ihdī ka-mā-nā li-ḍēf-ak yā fatā w-ikmil || gad anta fāhim bi-ʿādāt-ī li-ḍēfānī
y-ibnī tarā l-in-nashāmah kulla shī yubdhal || w-aḍ-ḍēfa man sharraf-ah mā hū bi-khasrānī
ʿawāgib aḍ-ḍēf[a] niʿmah mā la-ha mafṣal || w-aḍ-ḍēf[a] l-ah ḥagga lāzim lā tugaʿ dānī
min baʿda dha l-ḥīn[a] yā marḥab wa yā mashal || marḥab malā wādiy as-silʿah wa hirrānī
w-arḍ al-ḥadā min ṭaraf kōmān[a] lā mowkal || wa min gazan lā manāhal ḥadda bēḥānī
tarḥīb[a] gōsī wa ṣayyādī wa bin ḥarmal || dhī takrim aḍ-ḍēf[a] man ḥiyal wa tabʿānī
bi-ṣ-ṣūfiy al-jīd[a] dhī galb-ah ʿaley-ya dall || ṣāliḥ walad gāsim akbar shakhṣa w-āfā-nī
min gōm[a] khawlān[a] lā gad shaddat al-mahjal || gōm ad-darak yōm[a] ʿajjāt az-zaḥīmānī
w-ahl al-karam w-al-kubārah w-al-ʿanā w-al-ḥall || ʿawlat bin aṣ-ṣūfiy ashraf nās[a] fityānī
tashhad la-hum b-il-kubārah nāḥiyat hanshal || wa gōm[a] suhmī wa shaddādī wa suḥmānī
w-al-lōz[a] w-ahl al-bukērī kulla garn ashdal || wa min banī jabra w-aṣḥāb ar-ruwoyshānī
li-sh-shēkh[a] ṣāliḥ bi-gēfān il-ʿajab dhī dall || ʿāsh al-fatā bū muḥammad garn al-agrānī
jit-nī hadiyyah ka-ʾinni shayda min ḥalḥal || ʾaw-k-inna-hā shayda ʿallānī wa bēʿānī
bi-ha ṣ-ṣadīg al-kabīr ash-shājiʿ atgawwal || m-adrī ʿalē-sh-ah bi-faʿl al-khēra jāzā-nī
bin gāsim ash-shahma dhī ḍarab wa dhī sabbal || wa dhī gharaf min ʿamīg al-baḥra w-asgā-nī
jabbāha b-alfēn[a] maḍrab ʿaṭra yitshakkal || wardī wa naddī wa ḥāfūrī wa rīmānī
maʿ at-taḥiyyāti tablugh ʿadd-amā sayyal || barg as-sarāyā wa l-ah rāʿid wa hittānī
salām[a] l-ish-shēkh[a] w-al-ʿuggāl yitwaṣṣal || wa l-ir-riʿāyā yaṣal milyōn[a] faddānī
wa lakka fī lakka fī lakkēn[a] yitgābal || w-ithnēna milyōn[a] majmūlah bi-ḥisbānī

wa b-il-fata sh-shēkh[a] yā mursal[a] lā tifshal || law b-ih min al-farga sittīn alfa ṣannānī
l-ibnā muḥammad tasallim lā takūn tarsal || farʿ an-nigādhī la-hā rāʿī wa rihhānī
w-aṣnā-h[a] w-ibn akhwat-ah man shalla min-hum shall || min al-hadiyyah jabāh shēbah wa mirdānī
w-al-akhwa ṣāliḥ huwa n-nāmūs[a] w-al-haykal || karīm al-ikhlāg[a] dhī b-il-ʿarfa nādā-nī
wa kulla wāḥid min ahl al-ʿēn ana tnāwal || jabāha ʿishrīn[a] maḍrab ʿaṭra fannānī
dhī takrim aḍ-ḍēf[a] b-il-kōbish wa b-il-ḥiyyal || lā jāt-ah aḍ-ḍēf[a] yishbaʿ kulla jīʿānī
ʾama ṣ-ṣadīg al-ʿazīz al-farʿa dhī bāsil || bi-tilk al-abyāt[a] hū nashm-ī wa nishwān-ī
ʾan ashhad inn-ah bi-ṣōt al-ʿizza yitkallal || w-anā muʾayyid bi-tawgīʿ-ī wa ʿurfān-ī
l-il-akh ṣāliḥ wa bā-sarriḥ fiy al-jadwal [meter short] || dhī jā bi-gōl-ah wa lā rayt-ah wa lā rā-nī
yā wannat-ī mā yuwan ʾash-shājiʿ al-madhtall || wannēta min galba mitʾassif wa ghulbānī
min bāṭil al-wagta dhī khalā-niy atgafal || w-algā-niy agfēt[a] l-iṭ-ṭalaʿ m-al-gurfā-nī [meter short]
yigūl adhī bāt[a] ṭūl al-lēla yitgalgal || k-inn-ah ʿalā nār[a] damʿ-ah yinzil aḥfānī
min ḥādithah fī ḥaram makkah b-ih atsalsal || ḥizb al-jarāthīm[a] shallah nās wa ghiddānī
w-al-galba yaṭwī ka-ṭayy al-ghazla w-al-maghzal || w-an-nār[a] gad ḥarragat laḥm-ī wa ʿuḍmān-ī
ʿanāṣir al-baghyi b-il-ʾislām[a] tatmahzal || wa tuntahi-k rāyat al-ʾislām[a] bidhwānī
bāgī bigāya l-khidaʿ wa kulla jaḥsh ahbal || dhī ḥārabat ʾan-nabī ʾuthm-an wa ʿadwānī
w-al-yōm[a] dākhil ḥaram makkah bi-tatmashgal || binādig al-ḥarb[a] min hōzar wa hāwānī
thārū ʿalā man bi-makkah w-alṣuw al-mashʿal || lā mā bi-malik fī-hā w-al-ʿawānī [meter short]
wa haddadū-hā bi-ḥarb al-mīm[a] w-ash-shanjal || mā hākadh astaʿmalat ʿabād al-awthānī
fī giblat al-ʿurba lā ḥabbāsh wa lā nakhwal || wa lā li-khaybar wa lā gōm ibna jihlānī
lā mā samaʿt al-ʾidhāʿah fī rubā jarwal || tangal ʿulūm il-ʾisāyah damʿ-i ʾahjā-nī

kādat min al-ʿilma nafs al-hīm[a] titfilfil || wa bi-l-ʾasan zād-anī hamm-ī wa waddā-nī
w-al-arḍa ṣajjat wa rajjat w-ath-tharā ʾahbal || wa kulla dōlah bakat ʿuṭf-an wa ḥarmānī
baghdād[a] nādat ʿadan w-ash-shām wa ṣaffi t-tall || wa sūriyah khadhdharat libyā wa durmānī
wa maṣra nādat wa bērūt ablaghat nowfal || w-arḍ al-yaman ballaghat landan wa-ʾīrānī
w-an-najda ṣāḥat wa nāḥat l-id-duwal taʿjal || w-arḍ al-khalīj andharat tūnis wa baḥrānī
w-ash-shārigah raddadat kuwēt[a] yitzahhal || w-al-hinda wālat w-ar-rūs[a] w-al-yabbānī [meter short]
mustankirah kulla ma l-ḥizb ar-radī suwwal || fī giblat al-muslimīn afʿāl[a] sufhānī
wa kam wa yā kam min asbāb al-ʿawā nizʿal || kam yā mashākil wa kam yā nās[a] ghūbānī
mā fād-ana l-harja ʿind ajyāl-inā ʿazzal || ka-ʾinna-nā gad naṣayyiḥ bēn[a] dōrānī
shabāb-anā ʿan ṭarīg ajyāl-anā mayyal || bi-shakla yilgī kabīr al-galba ḍabḥānī
wa kam miʾāsī naʿānī w-ash-shabāb akhbal || magrūn[a] b-it-tiyya mitmarrid wa kharbānī
hādhā mukhanfas wa hādhā l-aḥtazam sarbal || w-ahl at-talāwīt[a] shallat silfa shamʿānī
wa kam naṣaḥnā ʿasā w-an-nās[a] titʿaddal || ʿan ghayya-hā yashhad aḷḷāh galb-iy admā-nī
nandhir wa naʿdhir wa nanṣaḥ kulla man tayyal || ʿabd al-bilāghāt[a] min ṣaddag wa-ʾaymānī
wa lā ḥadā minna-hum ḥarram wa lā ḥallal || ʾillā ʿalē-hā wa ṣall aḷḷāh farīḍānī
mā rāy-akum b-il-ʾimānah fī banī shaʿfal || lā sirt agūl l-ah yijawwib yōm[a] nilgā-nī
galad-niy aḷḷāh[a] yishtō ḍarba b-iṣ-ṣummal || wa ḥabs-ahum fī manāzil gaṣra ghamdānī
wa shaʿb-anā y-ibna gāsim jīl[a] yitḥakwal || min gabla m-aʿyā-ka yā ṣāliḥ gad aʿyā-nī
w-al-wagta maʿyūb[a] jaḥbal jamb[a] min jaḥdal || ʿādāt[a] lazzāt[a] tubbaʿ w-ibn[a] kanʿānī
dhī sajjalat l-il-yaman tarīkh[a] mustaʾṣal || ghazz-an wa majd-an wa tashrīf-an wa ʾaygānī
kam sēf[a] bin dhī yazan gātal wa kam nāḍal || wa ṭahhar ad-dīna fī maṣrā wa sūdānī

wa sām[a] bin nūḥ[a] kam shangal wa kam ʿangal || w-aʿlā la-dīn
ʿadālah fōg al-adyānī
w-iḥnā naṣaḥna l-mukhanfas yitrik ash-shanbal || w-al-khunfasah
dhī darab-hā taḥt al-ādhānī
w-ihṇā ʿalā thār-ahum y-ibn al-yaman naʿmal || nimshī maʿ al-ḥagga
fī darb al-ʿulā sānī
yā ʿizza ʿan wājibāt al-ḥagga lā tiksal || ʾarjū-ka lā yagtalib ṭabʿ-ak wa
tikhtānī
lā tāmin ad-dahra w-ad-dunya l-gharūrat taʿgal || gad sār[a] kisrā
wa gayṣar w-ibna marwānī
yigūl[a] bin mugbil ams al-galba yitdhallal || yadrus mawāḍīʿ[a]
min-ha l-galba khijlānī
mā yistawī sinnat al-gādim wa la l-maʿṭal || wa la dh-dhahab bā
yidānī l-il-ḥumēgānī
rumḥ al-ganā mā yisāwī ʿūdiy al-khardal || w-illa l-jadhār tasāwiy
al-burr an-nīsānī [meter faulty]
w-al-lōz[a] mā yistawī siʿr-ah maʿ al-fijjal || wa lā balas rōm[a] yihdī
fī-h[a] murgānī
w-illā samaʿt inna habba l-luʾla gad dhaḥḥal || wa lā min al-ʿāj[a]
yihdī rās[a] sēfānī
gūm yā rasūl ibna mugbil shidda mihr aḥjal || min ʿāṣimat ʿansa
w-ajzaʿ khalfa sufyānī
fuḍḍ al-ḥadā sāḥat ahl al-ʿizza w-al-manhal || gōm ad-darak l-aʿtanā
ʿarwā wa thōbānī
w-ibn al-maghaddī wa kōmān al-ʿana s-suffal || w-al-gaʿshamī
w-al-jarādī w-āl[a] ḥayyānī
w-āl al-farāṣī ʿabīdah gōm-ahā tidhhal || wa gōm[a] l-aʿmās[a] fī-h
aghmār[a] jadʿānī
w-al-baykhatah jēsh-aha l-mashhūr[a] lā jaḥfal || yihizza bugʿah wa
l-ah ruwwād[a] fityānī
mithla l-bukhētī muḥammad bin ʿalī l-ashtall || yifʿal li-khaṣmah
miyāt ḥufrah wa madḥānī
wa ʿāda bin gōs[a] f-il-haddāt[a] mōt azwal || ʿarīg al-amjād[a] sulṭān
ibna sulṭānī
ʿizz al-ḥadā ṣulb[a] nājī farʿa lā jaljal || tihtā b-ih aʿla l-jibāl
ash-shumm al-azbānī
lā shabba ṣōt al-ḥarāyig f-al-ḥadā tarḥal || baʿd-ah kam algīta
thōbānī wa ḍubyānī
tahjam ʿala l-khaṣm[a] b-irmāḥ al-gana s-summal || tashhad la-hā
f-il-yaman ṣaʿdah wa hamdānī
w-ānis wa sāgīn[a] min ʿabdān[a] lā nowfal || w-arḥab ʿayāl āl[a]
yaḥyā khalfa sinwānī

yā mursilī min zirājah w-aṭlaʿ an-nagwal || khalf al-ḥarūrah wa yās[a] ḥadd[a] gahlānī
ṭarīg-ak al-ʿēn[a] dhī birrāg-ahā khayyal || w-asga l-ḥadā min raḥīg al-misk[a] w-arwānī
min sāriy al-barga sharbah k-inn-ahā zawgal || lākinn-ahā ʾaththarat fī galb-iy ashjānī
w-asʾal ʿalā man bi-shiʿr-ah fi-l-ḥadā ṭawwal || bin gāsim al-jīda ṣāliḥ dhī taḥarrā-nī
min shigga khawlāni jēsh al-ʿizza lā saḥbal || lā gad nawa l-ʿazma yilgī-hā sulēbānī
min ʿizzat al-khōf[a] khallā shaʿb-anā gabyal || min baʿda mā shalla guwwāt-ah w-al-adwānī
wa kharraj-ah ʿarḍa min shaʿb al-yaman w-ankal || tilk al-guwa l-gādimah min arḍa ḥilwānī
salām[a] ma r-raʿda fī baṭn as-samā zaʿjal || wa sayyal-ah ʾasgā rubaʿ ghōshah wa haylānī
li-jēsh[a] khawlān[a] ṭāyil ʿadd-amā rattal || wa sabbaḥ aḷḷāh[a] ʿuthmān ibna ʿaffānī
salām[a] min lisna shāʿir laysa yitnazzal || ʿan wājib al-ḥagga yibshir man gad ahdā-nī
yitgabbal ar-radda mahmā fī ʿināh azbal || w-agḍī-h[a] w-arḍī-h[a] tagdīr-an la-m aʿṭā-nī
wa lā yijūz ibna gāsim minn-anā yamṭal || bil yistaʿad ʾal-gaḍā madbūl[a] majjānī
man gaddam al-jumla tagdīr-ah ʿalay-yā jall || wa ʿāda l-ah ḥagga zāyid fōg al-imtānī
w-al-khitma ṣallō ʿalā man rabb-anā faḍḍal || ʿalā muḥammad wa ʾāl-ah ṭūl al-izmānī

Notes

Chapter 1

1. The *'akhdām* are usually considered by tribesmen to be of African origin and are not descended, as are the *khaddām,* from the ancient tribes of Arabia. In chapter 2 I will relate the origin myth of the *khaddām.*

2. Although there is no ethnography of warfare per se, one can garner snippets from Evans-Pritchard (1940, 1949), Gellner (1969), Jamous (1981), and Peters (1967).

3. Perhaps the most perspicacious observer of the Arabian Bedouin when they still engaged in wide-scale raiding and warfare in the nineteenth century was the Swiss traveler John Lewis Burckhardt, who remarked:

> The Arab tribes are in a state of almost perpetual war against each other; it seldom happens that a tribe enjoys a moment of general peace with all its neighbours, yet the war between two tribes is scarcely ever of long duration; peace is easily made, but again broken upon the slightest pretence. The Arab warfare is that of partisans; general battles are rarely fought: to surprise the enemy by a sudden attack, and to plunder a camp, are chief objects of both parties. This is the reason why their wars are bloodless; the enemy is generally attacked by superior numbers, and he gives way without fighting, in the hopes of retaliating on the weak encampment of the other party.
>
> (1831, 133)

Described in this fashion, raiding was a game of honor with clear-cut rules its players had to observe to avoid losing face. "The Aenezes never attack by night; this they regard as *boag* . . . or treachery," Burckhardt explains, "for, during the confusion of a nocturnal assault, the women's apartments might be entered, and violence offered" (1831, 141). And he adds as one of the rules of this game, "An Arab never kills an unresisting foe unless he has to avenge the blood of some relation" (1831, 142). One of the ironies of this society is that "enemies" cooperate in observing the rules of raiding to an extent hardly shown by groups in corporate activities like pasturage and transhumance. Played out as a chivalrous contest, raiding and warfare had their code of honor, which opponents had to obey if they were to remain men of honor, and this value was internalized to such a degree that armed aggression minimized bloodshed. One was not out to kill the enemy in some willful, but blind, pursuit of self-interest but only to *shame* him and thereby enhance one's reputation for bravery and cleverness. Had the enemy been eliminated, the contest would have been over and no more honor gained.

4. With either the spoken or the chanted mode I had constantly to bear in mind the possibility that my interlocutor was in some way editing the text in a well-meaning attempt to make it more accessible. I did not discourage these spontaneous intralingual translations, but I always asked the reciter whether he could give me another version of the same poem using terms from his own dialect (especially if he happened not to come from the area in which I was doing research).

5. On several of my trips to the capital I sought out the help of Professor Muḥammad ʿAbduh Ghanem, one of Yemen's greatest classical poets, who is also an expert on the metrics of colloquial poetry, having written an excellent treatise on *ḥumēnī* verse. He analyzed a sample of the poems in my collection according to the same canons he had determined for his data. This basic framework gave me a start on the problem, and what remained was for me to alter the analysis somewhat to take into account a number of exceptions I encountered in my corpus of texts. Further changes were made once I had worked out a comparative theory of meter (see Appendix B).

Chapter 2

1. In the context of contemporary tribal society *marūwah* does not have the same range of meaning as it does in modern literary circles or even pre-Islamic Arabia. Generosity and chivalry are only secondary in importance to the notion of self-control or discipline. In this sense both women and men can be said to possess *marūwah.*

2. In the beginning of my fieldwork among the tribes of Khawlān, I spoke of poetry in terms of the thematic categories I had learned in my reading of *ḥumēnī* poetry and the critical literary works on that tradition, written in some cases by its greatest practitioners, but I eventually discovered that they have little relevance and as terms practically no currency among the tribes (they are seldom recognized and hardly ever used). First, there is the problem of delimiting categories according to subject matter. Practically the only clear-

cut division that exists is between love poetry (*ghazl*), political verse (*siyāsī*), which includes what the townsmen distinguish as social criticism (*shiʿr ijtimāʿī*), and religious poetry (*dīnī*). Nature poetry as a separate category is not recognized—an important difference between the two traditions, since this category of verse ranks high in the town canon. Furthermore, in the tribal tradition there is a lot more mixing of thematic categories in the same poem; a love poem invariably contains social or even political material, and a religious poem may end in virulent criticism of the country's youth, of materialism (which had become rampant in the boom economy of the 1970s), or of the "satanic" threat represented by the "atheist" regime of Marxist South Yemen. In brief, categorization by thematic content, though possible in a rough way, is not how the tribesmen primarily conceive of their poetry. Second, and more interesting, is the fact that the tribal poets generally hold *ghazl* or love poetry in much lower esteem than political and religious verse, and if any theme can be said to reign supreme, it is politics. Those poets I interviewed who admitted to having composed *ghazl* tended to denigrate it in comparison with their output on political subjects. This preference stands the town's valuation of subject matter on its head.

3. Both these facts, the occasionality of the poem and its composition on that occasion, lead to an explanation, perhaps not by itself complete, of the unevenness and peculiar lack of depth of the oral tradition. It is a sine qua non of folkloric research to incorporate, if at all possible, poems and stories that are part of the historical tradition. In Arabian folklore one would include the ancient Banī Hilāl cycle of tales, the pre-Islamic *qaṣīdah* (Berque 1978; Connelly 1986; Slyomovics 1988), and poems of the Ḥimyār in Yemen. It is generally assumed that if a tradition is an oral one, then the same poem or series of poems will be re-created over many centuries with only subtle changes apparent in formulaic usage and various kinds of textual embellishments. When I first arrived in Khawlān, I was excited by the expectation of discovering some ancient poetic saga or cycle; but in spite of my persistent efforts to elicit a recitation of such works, I never once came across a tribesman who had learned them or thought them important enough to teach me. This came as even more of a surprise as I realized how extremely important the ideology of history is to Yemeni tribesmen, a history which surely would be commemorated in the *words* of the ancestors, who are believed to have been master poets. But midway in my fieldwork it dawned on me that I had not been thinking about this tradition in the right terms. I had been assuming that it is the text per se that is important to remember, the verbal object we associate with printed poetry, when in fact it is either the *process of composition* that is to be remembered, as in the case of the *bālah*, or *the finished product of that process as it relates to a historically remembered situation*.

4. The most dramatic example of this kind I found for the urban literati

is gleaned from Yemeni scholar and poet Aḥmad ash-Shāmī's interesting essay "Yemeni Literature in Ḥajjah Prisons" (1975). In 1948 an unsuccessful coup d'état against Imam Aḥmad was carried out by a group of educated elite (*ʿulamā*) whose leader was the Imam's most trusted minister, ʿAbdullah al-Wazīr, a legendary figure in Yemen. Al-Wazīr and his companions were taken prisoner, as commemorated in the following famous poem from Khawlān composed some time in the same year:

> Khawlān captured (Mount) Nugm with its black army || and left brave men cringing.
> It carried off al-Wazīr to al-Ḥajjah in chains, || and al-Gardaʿī is now killed.

Al-Gardaʿī is also a folk legend, a great tribal sheikh who had been incarcerated by Imam Aḥmad's father, escaped from prison, and then returned to assassinate him, only to be killed himself in turn. Eventually al-Wazīr was beheaded along with many of his closest coconspirators, but ash-Shāmī and some others were spared. In verse they begged clemency for those condemned to die. "Truly the Imam was well-disposed toward poetry and the magic of words," ash-Shāmī remarks, "and had never failed to respond to them, for all that he was ruthless and tyrannical" (1975, 52). It is uncanny how closely this anecdote parallels the premise of the Thousand and One Nights, where an all-powerful and implacable ruler agrees to stay the execution of the narrator as long as her stories continue to catch his imagination.

5. Here is W. H. Auden on the question of poetry and politics:

> The characteristic style of 'Modern' poetry is an intimate voice, the speech of one person addressing one person, not a large audience; whenever a modern poet raises his voice he sounds phony. . . . Poets are, by the nature of their interests and the nature of artistic fabrication, singularly ill-equipped to understand politics. . . . Their natural interest is in singular individuals and personal relations, while politics and economics are concerned with large numbers of people, hence with the human average (the poet is bored to death by the idea of the Common Man) and with impersonal, to a great extent involuntary, relations. (Auden [1962] 1985, 47)

This declaration, surprisingly, comes from a poet who wrote much good poetry on deeply felt moral and political themes relevant to a whole generation (cf. his poem "Spain"). Indeed, although political poetry, even of a hortatory slant, has had a long and distinguished history in American literature (Walt Whitman, Ezra Pound, T. S. Eliot, Langston Hughes, e.e. cummings, Kenneth Rexroth, Robert Duncan, and Denise Levertov, to mention only a few), the predominant aesthetic of the white academic establishment (which is the "home" of most practicing poets today) still proclaims that poetry and politics do not mix. The unease many mainstream American poets feel about "politicizing" their poetry must also have to do with a more general cultural bias of the West against *utility* in art. Again Auden: "Whenever [our century] attempts to combine the gratuitous with the utile, to fabricate something which shall be both functional and beautiful, it fails utterly" (Auden [1962] 1985, 39). Leaving his peculiar prejudices aside, let us note, first of all, that the distinction between the "gratuitous" arts and the "utile" ones (how about *futile* and *utile?*), though perhaps not always so harshly drawn, is commonly found, often implicitly, in the writings on art of many modern critics and poets. Second, after having drawn the distinction, Auden puts forth the corollary that "gratuitous" art, when well done, has aesthetic merit, whereas "utile" art, regardless of the skill and imagination with which it is produced, can never measure up. Though I think many people would take exception to Auden's view that modern architecture has not produced significant buildings that are both functional and aesthetically beautiful, few would raise an eyebrow over his judgment that "a poet, painter or musician has to accept the divorce in his art between the gratuitous and the utile as a fact for, if he rebels, he is liable to fall into error" (Auden [1962] 1985, 39).

Ever since the late eighteenth century, capitalism and industrialism have produced a separation of experience into distinct categories (work versus leisure, science versus religion versus art) with the result that art has been, and continues even more today to be, divorced from other realms of reality. Along with this compartmentalization there has arisen, at least from the time of Théophile Gautier and then gaining strength with the Symbolist poets, a cultural aesthetic of *l'art pour l'art,* which has dominated Western European thinking and the practice of art ever since, in spite of sporadic writings by political poets who represented a "subversive" and at times even "secret" opposition to it, and in spite of particular poems that sounded a strong political protest. Not all poets in our tradition are narrowly centered in Western preconceptions, but the exceptions are few.

Chapter 3

1. Composing a *qaṣīdah* is to some extent a matter of expanding a *zāmil.* In response to a friend's inquiry, a poet once said that he was working on a *zāmil* and then proceeded to recite it, only to have his friend somewhat pedantically correct him because the poem in question was too long for a conventional *zāmil* (it covered more than six lines). His friend maintained that it

ought properly to be considered a *qaṣīdah.* The poet concurred in this opinion, explaining that it had begun as a *zāmil* but he found that he had more to say than he could fit into the shorter verse form.

2. The last two are said during the festival following the conclusion of Ramadan.

3. The *razfah* is similar in verse form to the *zāmil* but is performed to its own distinctive dance step and music.

Chapter 4

1. The *rōshān* is like the *bālah,* though it is performed outdoors and is far less elaborate.

2. In the example the melody has a two-part structure, the second part closing the cadence of the first. A short passage of three notes begins the chant. The two-part structure is a common feature of performance melodies and resembles the structure of the verse line, the second hemistich being identical in form to the first but completing the thought begun by it. Parallelism is at work in the musical structure as well as the verse line, where a paradigmatic and syntagmatic tension is maintained between the call and its response (or echo).

3. There was a time in my fieldwork when I suspected the verse structure to be dependent on musical structure, and so I took pains to transcribe the melodies exactly as I heard them (a far more difficult task than I had anticipated) and mark the delivery of the verse on them to see if there were some musical-poetic structure that synthesized the two. I found the verse structure to be independent of music.

4. Other metrical patterns for the *bālah* may exist, but I doubt it. The performance would otherwise become too difficult, I suspect, for the average person. It would become an elite game rather than one that ideally anyone could play, and the purpose of the *bālah* is to engage in the act or process of composition as many in the assembly as possible.

5. Like internal rhyme, alliteration is relatively uncommon in *bālah* poetry. It is, however, a prominent feature of other genres. The alliteration is of the simplest variety, for example, the repetition of word-initial consonants instead of the more complex root-consonant patterns alliterated in other genres. One of the more pronounced examples of alliteration is evidenced in this turn:

> w-abdaʿ b-ik adʿī-k yā min yadd-ak al-gādirah || yā mālik al-mulka
> yā dhī minn-ak al-maghfirah

> I begin with You, O from Your all-powerful hand, || O master of
> creation, O You from whose hand (we obtain) forgiveness.

In the first hemistich there is a noticeable alliteration of the consonants *b, d,* and ʿ as well as *y* and *k.* In the second hemistich there is an even more noticeable alliteration of word-initial *m* and word-final *k.* But on the whole this kind of texturing of the line by subtle sound repetitions is uncommon, at least in the *bālah,* and I cannot help wondering to what extent it may even be accidental, for we shall see that the heavy use of formulas does not permit much leeway in this respect. In other words, whatever alliteration appears may be the unconscious by-product of the formulas linked together to form a metrically regular line.

6. I believe that Milman Parry's definition is still the best: a formula is "a group of words which is regularly employed under the same metrical conditions to express a given essential idea" (1930, 80). Simple repetition is a necessary, though not a sufficient, criterion, for it is obvious that in many literary works single words, expressions, and sometimes even entire sentences are repeated—the refrain "Quoth the Raven, 'Nevermore'" would thereby falsely qualify as a formula in Poe's "Raven"—even though they are not part of a composition created in a performance. As Albert Lord wisely reminds us in his classic *Singer of Tales* (1960, 33), "Only in performance can the formula exist and have clear definition."

7. The word *ʾabṭāl* is the plural of *baṭal,* which means a person who is grasping something. The word *al-kirāsī* is the plural of *kursī,* which in this context refers to the rifle butt; it is qualified by the noun *ʿūj* (bend, curve) to describe the concave shape of the handle that rests against the marksman's shoulder.

8. Formula 1b is only one type that can follow formula 1a in the line; other possibilities are *ḥāmiliyīn aṣ-ṣamīl* (wielders of the club) and *shalliyīn uswabah* (sg. *ʾasīb*) (wielders of the scabbard and dagger). Thus, we could generate even more verses than those shown for 1a and 1b. If such formula types had many branches in their schema, Parry would speak of them having great "depth," by which he meant that they could be used to construct large numbers of poetic lines.

9. This analysis should be compared with work that has been done on productivity or generativity of formulaic usage. For a discussion, see Foley 1988.

10. *m-al* is the contracted form of *mā ʾal* (that which the . . .). The *mā* particle introduces an intensifier phrase for the speech act of greeting. The word *mittammarah* is a feminine Form V active participle: *mitatammar / mi-ttammar / mittammar* (deletion of the prefix vowel).

11. I prefer to use the term *turn* instead of *line* for the next higher structural unit in the *bālah* because, though it superficially resembles a line of *zāmil* or *qaṣīdah* poetry, its function is tied to a performance, specifically to a "turn" a poet takes at building a poem. Inside the turn, too, one finds an antiphony

between poet and chorus as well as an interweaving of refrain and verse. It thus has a musical structure all its own, which is entirely lacking in lines of poetry from other genres and needs to be analytically distinguished from them.

12. Alternatively:

> – – ᴗ –|– ᴗ –| – –[ᴗ]–| – ᴗ –
> f-il bidʿa ṣallū ʿal al-mukhtār sīd ar-rusal
> f-il bidʿa ṣallī ʿal al-mukhtār *bū fāṭimah*
> f-il bidʿa ṣallī ʿal al-mukhtār *Ṭāha l-faḍīl*
>
> In the beginning, pray to the Chosen One, the Lord of the Prophets
> In the beginning, pray to the Chosen One, *father of Fāṭimah*
> In the beginning, pray to the Chosen One, *the Outstanding One*

Having invoked the Prophet and his epithets, the poet can in the second hemistich beseech him to intercede with God on the Day of Judgment and persuade Him not to condemn man to Hell.

13. The *darūs* (sg. *dars*) are selections of the Qurʾān read over the sick.

14. Note in Appendix C the more "classical" verb form *yigrōn* as opposed to *yigrō* (read). The use of the variant form is another instance of where knowledge of Qurʾānic Arabic is drawn on for reasons of meter. See also pp. 104–5.

15. ʿAlī was the fourth caliph of Islam, though the Shīʿā contend that he was wrongfully overlooked to be the Prophet's immediate successor as head of the Muslim community. His martyr's death—he was stabbed in the midst of his prayers—also sanctifies him in the eyes of this sect of Islam.

16. This formula does not conform exactly to the meter. I cannot explain this exception, unless I and my informant did not hear the tape correctly or the poet made a mistake. If the latter, however, the audience did not catch it.

17. I recall an incident that illustrates this perception. Having somehow gotten into a discussion of comparative religious practices with a couple of Yemeni men, some nuns working for Catholic Relief Services were demonstrating their own mode of prayer, emphasizing that the act is a relatively simple one. They noted that the usual folding together of the hands was not obligatory, for the worshiper may adopt his or her own personal posture and style of utterance as long as the pietistic attitude was there. To the Yemenis, who are of course accustomed to set movements of head and hands as well as prostration, which the young men obligingly demonstrated to their inquisitive friends, such prayer seemed lackadaisical, if not actually an insult to God. How could it have any meaning, let alone effect, if it could be performed in any which way? Did Christians think too that one could write a letter or sing a song in any which way?

18. A parallel is obvious between verbal rituals and poetry, though it must be stressed that orthodox Muslims strongly deny it. Muḥammad vehemently disassociated the Qurʾān from poetry because it was believed that verse smacked too much of soothsaying and magic. Yet the fact that poetry is supposed to issue from emotions but be *controlled* in expression—that it is, especially in the case of the *bālah,* an *act,* moreover an act highly conscious of *form*—makes poetry very similar to the Muslim conception of ritual and would, I suppose, produce at least subliminal associations with it. It is therefore not in any way incongruous to find religious acts being performed in poetry, or for that matter poetry being performed in religious acts.

Chapter 5

1. Here are examples of hemistichs devoted to this routine.

– – ∪ –| – ∪ –| – – ∪ –| – ∪ –
w-aḷḷāh yighanni l-muḍayyif *gad ḍabaḥ jazwarah* ||

– ∪ –|– ∪ –
w-aḷḷāh yighanni l-muḍayyif gad *ḍābiḥī ʾath-tharāb* ||

– ∪ –| – ∪ –
w-aḷḷāh yighanni l-muḍayyif gad *mikrimīn ad-dafūr* ||

– ∪ –|– ∪ –
w-aḷḷāh yighanni l-muḍayyif gad *rabb-anā yijbar-ah* ||

And may God enrich the host, *he has butchered already droves of animals*
And may God enrich the host, *butchering the sheep*
And may God enrich the host, *generous ones to the arrivals*
And may God enrich the host, *may our Lord reward him*

I cannot omit the following highly original line, which I doubt was formulaic because I had never heard it before:

– – ∪ –| –[∪]–| – –[∪] –| – ∪ –
w-al-mā min al-bīr ʿabdaḷḷāh gad maghghar-ah

And the water in the well, ʿAbduḷḷah has turned it red

In other words, the host has butchered so many sheep in hospitality that he has turned the well water red with their blood.

2. The word *nisānī* comes from *nisnī* (we irrigate [from the well]) and the root S-N-Y. The lengthened medial *ā* is for reasons of rhyme.

3. The lexeme *ʿajā-nī* was explained to me to be a shortened form of *ʿajab-nī,* from the verb *ʿajab* (it pleased).

4. The literal translation is "O Saʿd, I know, O generous Yemeni."

5. These hemistichs were not uttered in an uninterrupted sequence as I

have presented them; rather, poets interjected turns from other speech acts (such as greeting guests). Furthermore, I have not included all the turns from this one performance that are part of the same routine, only a representative sample.

Chapter 6

1. One reason for the relative shortness of the *zāmil* formula is to be found in the rhyme scheme of the poem. As we shall see, the line is always divided by a caesura clearly marked by a rhyme, and often lines will contain more than two internal rhymes.

2. There are two ways, in fact, of making the short formulas fit a range of different metrical schemas. One way is to keep the wording but shift slightly the position of the formula in the line, so that syllabic length corresponds to the requirements of metrical length. Another way is to keep the position of the formula in the line but alter its syllabic structure or subtly change its wording. Both methods are employed in the *zāmil,* whereas I rarely encountered them in *bālah* poetry. In the latter genre the poet keeps the wording and position constant throughout.

3. *Ṣanī*ᶜ*ah* can also mean one who is skilled in crafts. That definition would ascribe to this poem a deeper political meaning, which it likely has because it was composed during the 1979 war between North Yemen and South Yemen.

4. Note the use of the second-person feminine singular attached pronoun *sh* to refer anaphorically to a city that is (covertly) feminine in gender.

5. Let us consider the *zāmil* dialogue in one of its more routine or institutional settings—the tribal wedding ceremony. I recorded the following three poems while attending a celebration in Bēt ash-Shanbalī (see Map 2), known also by the epithet *maḥall ash-shu*ᶜ*arā* (the place of poets). The first poem was uttered by the host party during the groom's *zaffah* (wedding procession through the town):

∪ – ∪ –| – –[∪]–| – – ∪ –| – – – ∪ –| –
muḍayyif-ak yā ḍēf gad raḥḥab wa sahhal || ḥayyā b-il-asḥāb
– ∪ –
al-gidām
– – ∪ –| – – ∪ –| – – ∪ –| – – –[∪]–| – –
ḥayyā bi-kum ma l-markab al-hindī taḥammal || w-al-mōt yitgassam
∪ –
gisām

Your host, O guest, has welcomed and entertained you; || greetings to the venerable companions.

Greetings to you [as precious as] what the boat from India brings, ||
[greetings as many times as] death's portion is distributed.

In the first line the host is greeting the guest and reminding him that he has been honored, that is, that the host has fulfilled his obligations to the guest by providing him with food and entertainment (the verb *sahhal*), by which he means the luncheon and the festivities of the *zaffah* and *gāt* chew. The second line is a restatement of the greeting, but this time with intensifier phrases honoring the guest. Note the formulaic expression of this intensification of feeling. The boat from India once carried precious cargo of gold, silks, and spices, and the poet is establishing a metaphorical equivalence between its sumptuous riches and the greetings he heaps on the guest. The second intensifier phrase is an original way of conveying the number of greetings bestowed on the addressee. Since death eventually claims every person, that number is great indeed.

As expected, the response to this *zāmil* came from the guests sometime in the course of the procession. Observe that they have preserved the original rhyme scheme and rhyming sounds, the meter, and the relative length of the hemistichs in the line (three feet in the first, two feet in the second):

⏑ –(⏑) –|– – ⏑ –| – –? –|– – – ⏑ –| – –(⏑)–
salām yitrattil ʿalā hādha l-gāyil || yibgī miyāt sabʿīn ʿām
– –(⏑) –| – – ⏑ –| – – ⏑ –|– ⏑ – ⏑ –| – – ⏑ –
taslīm yitfarraz ʿalā jāhil wa ʿāgil || wa man ḥaḍar hādha l-magām

Greetings chanted for this speaker; || may he live one hundred
years.
Greetings singling out each child and adult || and whoever is
attending this place.

Not as vivid as the original, the response nonetheless has interesting grammatical alliterations in the two lines (the two Form V verbs *yitrattil* and *yitfarriz* as well as the active participles *gāyil, jāhil,* and *ʿāgil*). Note also that some of the endings on these forms are internal rhymes, which add to the aesthetic appeal.

To top the guests, the host party replied with another *zāmil* in their honor, this one in answer to the second poem of the series:

– – ⏑ –| – –(⏑) –| – – ⏑ –| – – – ⏑ –| – – ⏑ –
yā dhī badaʿt al-gōl ḥayyā mā tanazzal || maznah fiy ignāf al-ʿamān
– – ⏑ –| – –(⏑) –| – – ⏑ –| – – – ⏑ –| – –
marḥab jamīʿ aḍ-ḍēf mā yirʿad wa sayyal || mā raḥbah al-jabrī
⏑ –
wa yām

O you who composed the saying: greetings as great as the rain that
falls || from the black cloud,

Welcome to all the guests, [a welcome] as powerful as the lightning
and as turbulent as the flood, || as generous as the Jabri and Yām.

The aesthetic structure is exactly as in the earlier poems of the series. The only difference is the highly formulaic nature of the language. "O you who composed the saying" is like the beginning of other *zāmil*s in my corpus of texts. The intensifier phrases all use stock formulas based on the ideas *rain falling from the sky, lightning flash,* and *the wadi in flood.* The only nonformulaic part of the poem is in the punch line, an unusual allusion to two tribes of Yemen of great and ancient nobility who were famous for their generosity. By metaphorical analogy the greeting is intensified, and the allusion to a central value of *gabyilah* in turn connects the present event with a heroic tradition.

6. The morpheme *bā* is the future-tense particle.

7. The lexeme *lā* is translated as "if" and is equivalent to the classical Arabic *law.*

Chapter 7

1. "Now persuasions are effected not only by argumentative speaking, but also by ethical [speaking]; for we are persuaded when we think the speaker to be a man of a certain character—that is, when he seems to be good, or well-disposed or both"; "The character [ethos] of the speaker is a cause of persuasion when the speech is uttered as to make him worthy of belief; for as a rule we trust men of probity more, and more quickly, about things in general, while on points outside the realm of exact knowledge, where opinion is divided, we trust them absolutely" (Aristotle 1932, 45, 8).

2. "This trust, however, should be created by the speech itself, and not left to depend on an antecedent impression that the speaker is this or that kind of man" (Aristotle 1932, 8).

3. Fernandez distinguishes two kinds of metaphor: persuasive or "colocative" metaphors and performative or "organizing" ones. He also distinguishes two aspects of metaphor: that it works by analogy, linking domains in unexpected and creative ways, and that it has much to do with feelings (1986, 7). Throughout his study of these two aspects, Fernandez stresses the "enactive" role of metaphor (i.e. that metaphor must be understood in an act of communication and not simply as a matter of symbolic representation or self-expression) and the fact that it can induce persons to act out the metaphor in ritual (i.e. it can become an icon or model for action).

4. It is perhaps wiser to eschew Fernandez's own metaphor of movement for describing the action of pronouns in quality space, a metaphor that might lead to the thought that personae do not themselves act but are acted on, that

they are moved by the rhetorical hands of other personae like pawns in a chess game.

5. *ʿagr* (pl. *ʿagāyir*) is any sacrificial animal, but in the context of a dispute mediation is usually a cow.

6. *maklaf* (pl. *makālif*) is a tribal term for "wife" or "woman."

7. *lā* is the preposition *ilā* and drops the initial glottal stop. Other examples are *yām* (days) for *ayām; mām* for *imām;* and *bū* for *abū* (father).

8. *ṣāyib* is understood in opposition to *ʿāwij.*

9. *ḥad* (someone) comes from *aḥad;* the initial glottal stop is dropped, as explained in note 7.

10. *ʿārif* (pl. *ʿurafā*) is a technical term meaning a person who has knowledge of tribal law and experience in dispute mediations.

11. *sārif* is not an easy term to translate. It has a general meaning of wrongdoer, but I am not very satisfied with my translation. I was not able to elicit greater clarification from my informants.

12. *khāṭir-kum,* like *barāy-akum,* is a formula used in saying farewell. The latter is particularly tribal in usage and is heard in other Yemeni speech communities as well.

13. *fajjat* (the *t* of the feminine ending appears before a vowel) is the space between the mountain walls of a wadi. It is in fact wider than a gap or pass but narrower than a valley.

14. *mashbūḥah* is the passive participle of *shabaḥ,* which colloquially means "hold or grasp firmly."

15. *taʿaywaj* is a peculiar form but has the same meaning as *taʿawwaj* (deviate from).

16. From *radam* (push).

17. In Islam it is believed that God revealed His truth in four sacred books: the Torah, the Book of Psalms, the New Testament, and the Qurʾān.

18. A *ḥākim* is a *sayyid* judge.

19. Note what seems to be a case ending in *kull-an,* which is used here for the meter. Examples can also be found in *bālah* poetry, such as in the formula *yōm[a] bard-an wa ḥarr* (the day of cold and heat), when *-an* is needed to preserve the meter; otherwise it is dropped.

20. Some readers have found the fact that I left Yemen before learning the outcome of the dispute to be a shortcoming of the case study. But disputes are rarely settled permanently. In many instances they are simply put aside for an indefinite period of time and then resurrected in connection with another altercation. Thus, even if, after I left, the ʾAʿrūsh were awarded ownership of the meadow, the Banī Shadād may eventually have tried to reassert control over it, and in time the conflict may have begun all over again. Nor is it fair to conclude, just because I cannot know the outcome of the case, that I

have not demonstrated my claim that poetry is being used by actors to try to persuade each other. As in many other cases, actors believe what they *want* to believe. Thus, the mediators finally got the Banī Shadād to come to the negotiating table, and they believe their poetry to have been instrumental in persuading them to do so, even though they cannot know this to be true in any empirical sense. And the ʾAʿrūsh believe that the mediators accepted their legal claims to the land in large part because their poetry is superior to that of their opponents, though they know that having written deeds to the land makes their position secure. Similarly, the Banī Shadād may in fact be trying to coerce their opponents into giving up the land; nevertheless, they are persuading themselves and others in their poetry that they are fighting to restore their honor. The mediators are in turn trying to persuade them of the reality of their "darker" motives, which pollutes the ideal of the tribesman. By the power of their poetry they believe they can persuade the addressee to make himself over into the ideal they hold up to him.

Chapter 8

1. For example, the formula *ṣallū ʿala l-mukhtār* (pray for the Chosen One) is linked with a small number of attributive phrases like *shafīʿ-anā min jahannam* (our intercessor [keeping us out of] Hell) or *dhī bayyan ad-dīn l-ak* (who announced the true religion) or *dhī faḍl-ah* (whose grace is [widespread, well known, etc.]). Caliph ʿAlī is usually referred to by his standard epithet, *al-ḥaydarah,* along with some mention of his role in the early days of Islam in fighting the infidels or an allusion to his martyrdom and that of his two sons at Karbala. These formulas are familiar from the *bālah.*

2. y-aḷḷāha yā man l-ak jabāh al-khalga takhḍaʿ b-is-sajūd || yā
 bāsiṭ ad-dunyā wa yā mursī li-sabʿ abjār-ihā
 b-isma-k wa ʿilm-ak w-al-galam w-an-nūr w-as-sajdah wa
 hūd || w-al-ʿarsha w-al-kursī wa b-ish-shams il-munīrah
 anwār-ihā
 ʿajjil bi-ghufrān-ak wa luṭf-ak yōm-anā taḥt al-laḥūd || yā ḥayya
 yā gayyūm[a] ʿafw-ak fī ḍalām aghdār-ihā
 ʿafw-ak la-nā yōm al-giyāmah yōm[a] mā mālik yagūd ||
 ʾal-mijrimīn ahl al-khiyānah lā jahannam nār-ihā
 ʾal-ḥamda l-ak mā yilmaʿ al-bārig wa mā ḥann ar-raʿūd ||
 w-ihmil bi-raḥmah nāfiʿah w-isga l-waṭan b-amṭār-ihā
 w-isgā basātīn al-yaman w-ikhḍir wa ʾifṭir kulla ʿūd ||
 w-al-ʾarḍa taḥyā w-izharat fī-hā jamīʿ ashjār-ihā
 ṣallū ʿalā ṭāhā shafīʿ al-khalga fī yōm al-waʿūd || ʾal-muṣṭafā dhī
 shāʿ[a] faḍl-ah fī ʿamūm agṭār-ihā

w-al-ḥaydarah dhī gātal al-kuffār[a] w-al-ᶜālim shahūd || w-aḥya
l-farāyiḍ w-ash-sharīᶜah w-aᶜtalā migdār-ihā
man tābiᶜ al-mukhtār[a] yiskun wasṭa jannāt al-khalūd ||
ṣallā ᶜalē-k aḷḷāh wa sallam ṭūl[a] yā mukhtār-ihā

3. gāl-aha l-muᶜtanī || hāt[a] yā milgan-ī || lā taᶜadhdhar
bi-nī || kuff al-aᶜdhārā
k-inn-ak arkant-anī || thumma ḍayyagt-anī || f-iz-zamān
ad-danī || b-it-taḥayyārā
gāla jīt-ak sarīᶜ || mā mathīl-ī yiḍīᶜ || ʾiltagif l-in-nazīᶜ || jāba
baḥḥārā

4. yā ṭārish-ī b-arsil-ak dha-l-ḥīn[a] taḥarrak || lā ḥaytha b-akhaṣṣa
l-ak b-il-khiṭwah itᶜannā-k.
dha-l-ḥīn[a] bā-ʾaᶜzam-ak bi-taksiy al-kādilak || ᶜazzim li-tōk
at-taᶜiz w-al-ᶜāṣimah mā wā-k.
sallim ḥarūf-ī darak mōla l-ᶜanā wādirak || l-il-gāᶜid
itkhabbar-ah gul l-ah bigā-k ibgā-k.

5. yā maᶜannā shidda l-ak mihr-an jawādī || lajjim-ah w-asawwiy
al-mahāmīz al-jiyādī
sābig-an k-ar-rīḥ[a] fī baᶜḍ al-nijādī || mā yahimm al-baᶜda
w-agfār al-fiyāfī
min maḥall ash-shambalī hijrah wa shīᶜah || gāhirīn al-khaṣm[a]
b-ir-ramiy al-waḍīᶜah
ᶜanda khalg aḷḷāh murātib-him rafīᶜah || ʾahla bāl-an wa faᶜāl-an
w-iᶜtarāfī
dhubba yā ᶜāzim min al-ḥaydēn[a] ghādī || w-al-ḥadā ḥadd
al-bukhētī w-az-ziyādī
wa ᶜanūs ibn asᶜad igṭaᶜ kulla wādī || w-al-masā maṭraḥ dhamār
bi-lā khalāfī
yōm[a] thānī yā rasūlī shidda bukrah || gāᶜ sayyah[a] w-aṭ-ṭurug
yamnah wa yasrah
wādiy al-ḥār altawī ᶜaṣrah bi-ᶜaṣrah || w-al-ghadā gaflān[a]
ṣayᶜād ash-sharāfī

6. yā marḥabā marḥab yaᶜizz || ahl al-ʾawālī w-al-jihaz || w-ahl
al-jarāmil w-al-kanīd
marḥab malān al-ᶜāṣimah || wa kulla markhā jāhimah || wa
yurwiy al-ḥad ar-raᶜīd
marḥab tarāḥīb al-maṭar || yimlī garā-hā w-al-ḥaḍar || yā gōm
taṭᶜan f-il-warīd
yā ᶜāmma ṣāliḥ marḥab-an || mā hazzat anwār aṣ-ṣubā || wa
hazhaz al-fōj al-barīd

7. balligh taḥayyāt-i min ṣāliḥ bi-ʾajmal ʿaṭūr || maḥlūl[a] b-il-warda w-al-ʿambar ʿala z-zaʿfarānī
rishshah li-wādī ʿabīdah mikrimīn ad-dafūr || ʾahl an-nafūs al-karīmah w-al-galūb al-ḥinānī
khuṣṣ al-mashāyikh bi-mā wardī wa ʿūdah baḥūr || wa khuṣṣ al-afrād[a] b-il-kādhī kharaj min ʿomānī
salām[a] min ṣāliḥ aṣ-ṣūfī maʿashshar jabūr || jabāh la-kum yā rijāl al-majidd[a] fī kulla ʾānī
salām[a] yimlī ḥaṣūn al-ʿizza dōr as-sarūr || marsa sh-shajāʿah ḥumāt ad-dīn[a] kam min fulānī
ʾahl al-karam w-ash-shahāmah gāṭifīn az-zahūr || min wādiy al-ʿizza dhī yishrib min ash-shadhrawānī
wādī ʿabīdah dhīy ahl-ah ʿābirīn al-jasūr || lā rāʿidah ḥanna mā l-il-arḍa min-ah kinānī

8. ballaghū min-nī ḥusēn ibn al-jamālī || bōraʿī rāʿī ḥusēnāt al-gafālī
yā ʿuḍūd al-jamb al-ayman w-ash-shamālī || l-ak salām-an wāzin akhshām al-kafāfī
w-ibziyā-nā dhī la-hum f-il-jūd ʿādah || mā baziy illā wa min khāl-ah ridād-ah
fī sawā w-illā ghawā w-illā jawādah || mā bazī-n illa n-namārah w-az-zirādī
khuṣṣ-ahum b-in-nidda w-al-ʿūd al-mashidhdhim || hum dhiyāb ad-damma l-al-ḥarbī taʿaḍḍam
mā yahābūn al-ligā fī kulla magdam || b-il-jarāmil dhī maʿāṣim-hā ṭafāfī
wa jamīʿ aṣḥāb-inā man kān gharrām || shambalī w-ashmal khubēgān ahl al-arwām
b-it-taḥīyah w-as-salām at-tāmma lammām || man sakan naḥw aṣ-ṣarīm wa f-il-jarāfī

9. yā rabb-an astaghfar-ak ʿaley-ya sitr-ak || anā taʿawwadhta b-ik min shī wa fī-h ishrā-k
dhikr an-nabī kulla mā fōj aṣ-ṣaba tḥarrak || wa hazz al-ashjār[a] w-aghṣān al-ʿanab w-ar-rāk

10. y-aḷḷāh taḥassan khitām-ī yā ghanī yā shakūr || ʿafw-ak wa ṣafḥ-ak wa ghufrān-ak wa luṭf-ak ʾamān-ī
w-al-khitma ṣallū ʿal al-mukhtār badr al-badūr || ʿalē-ha ṣallū jamīʿ al-khalga ʾinsan wa jānī
ṭāh al-ḥabīb al-munawwir siʿda man l-ah yazūr || dhī bayyan aḷḷāh[a] faḍl-ah fi-l-khuṭab w-al-idhānī

11. w-aṣ-ṣalāt taghshā-k[a] yā khitm ar-risāyil || mā ḥada l-ḥādī wa mā habb al-hilāyil
kulla mā nāḥū ʿalē-k ahl al-wisāyil || b-it-taraḥḥum w-it-taḥannun w-it-taḥāfī
yā bashīr-an yā nadhīr-an yā munīr-an || yā shafīʿ al-khalga min nār as-saʿīrā
man samaʿ ṣallī ʿalā ṭāhā kathīr-an || ʿadda mā yitlō fiy al-ʾawrāg ar-rahāfī

12. The first formula in the line, *w-al-khitma ṣallō ʿala* (and in conclusion, pray for), is familiar from the conclusion of the *bālah,* except that here it is used with a slight twist, for the vocative *yā ḥaḍūr* (O assembly) separates the verb from its preposition *ʿalā* (for). The reason for its intrusion in the formula is obvious: the vocative phrase provides the poet with an internal rhyme (*ḥaḍūr / badūr*), which the line requires, while at the same time completing the scansion of the metrical foot. The traditional epithet for the Prophet *badra l-badūr* (moon of moons) is used in the line for the same reasons of rhyme and meter. The third formula, at the beginning of the last hemistich, *shafīʿ min nār* (intercessor from the fire), is adapted from the formula so often used in the *bālah, shafīʿ-anā min jahannam ḥarr-ihā* (our intercessor [keeping us out of] Hell, its heat). The formula *nār al-waʿīd* (fire on the judgment day) is an original one. Again, there are good poetic reasons for having created it: *al-waʿīd* gives the meaning "the appointed time," which the religious tradition construes as the day of final judgment, and at the same time it carries the necessary end-of-line rhyme, *-īd.* The word *nār* (fire) is often used, as in the Qurʾān, to refer to Hell, thus reinforcing the meaning of the original formula. But the line is not quite finished, for one more adaptation is still needed—the deletion of the affixed possessive pronoun *-nā* (our) for reasons of metrical scansion. This deletion does alter, though not drastically, the meaning of the original formula.

This example illustrates the main problem of the poet's compositional use of formula. Recall that in the *bālah* he had to make the formula conform to the requirements of the performance. Rapid composition fostered the use of relatively fixed formulaic phrases (or formulaic systems). Skill was required in order to choose the right formula to initiate a particular routine (invoking God, praising Him, remembering and praying for the Prophet), and match it with other prefabricated formulas that would complete the line. But the use of formula in the *qaṣīdah* must meet other requirements of text-internal form. Hence, as we have seen in the examples, the poet must develop a kind of skill different from rapid composition—an ability to adapt formula to such formal considerations as diverse meter, internal rhyme, and alliteration.

13. yā ṣāḥ[a] ṣabr-ak ʾidhā m-ashtaddat al-ʾazmah || fa-lā fa-lā yā zaman sharʿ al-ḥalā maḥsūd.

14. The second example of onomatopoeia is also from al-Gharsī:

badāt[a] b-ism-āk w-ant idrāj ʿalay-y[a] luṭf-ak || yā mawla l-alṭāf dhī
mā khāfiyah tikhfā-k
mālik al-ʾamlāk mā l-ak nidda fī mulk-ak || mā lī sawā ʾagṣad-ah yā
mālik al-ʾamlāk
yā rabba man jā-k mitlawwī ʿalā ḥabl-ak || ʿabd-ak tarajjā-k tifʿal
l-il-ʿabād idrā-k
yā khēr fakkāk ʿand-ak l-il-mishākil fakk || ʾal-ḥall min-ak wa lā
ghēr-ak la-hā fakkāk

I began with Your names, bestow on me Your benevolence || O
Most Benevolent One, to whom nothing is secret.
Master of Creation, You have no equal in Your wealth || I mean
only Him, O Master of Creation.
O God, he who comes dangling on Your rope || Your slave begs You
to bring men to their senses.
O Best Solver, You have the solution to all problems || The solution
comes from You, and no one but You.

There are several interesting and unusual sound patterns in this poem. The beginning *badāt[a] b-ism-āk[a]* contains both an alliteration of *b* and an echo of the consonant-vowel pattern CāCa (the native listener likely is subliminally attuned to such patterns because of the morphology of Arabic). The *m-l-k* pattern is repeated throughout the second line; these repetitions are formed not only morphologically, in derivations of root and consonant-vowel patterns, but also syntactically, as in *mā l-ak* (you have no). But most arresting is the alliteration of the *k* phoneme because it appears not only in the rhyme but also several times in the same line. The effect is almost overwhelming and is consistent with the underlying meaning, for the poet is invoking the Divine Spirit addressed as *-k* (you).

15. gāl ibna nāṣir gad ikhtall ash-shaʿūr || w-aḷḷāh wa gad ḍayyaʿ
ash-shiʿr ash-shaʿīr.

16. ʾahwēn[a] yā gōm[a] yā jasr al-ʿabūr || ʾathār[a] m-antū mathīl
az-zamharīr
lā rāḥ[a] ḍāmī wa gad fī-h aḍ-ḍarūr || fa-yaḥsab-ah baḥra lāwī
mistadīr
ḥattā ʾidhā jāh[a] baʿd an-naḍūr [last foot short] || fa-lam yajid
shī ʾamām-ah f-il-gafīr
kaʾinna ḥad gal la-kum l-il-khalfa dūr || w-al-bōrajī ṣāḥ[a]
fī-kum w-an-nafīr
wa durtuw al-kulla yā gōm ad-dabūr || ʾaḷḷāh[a] yigbaḥ ʿad
yimīn aḍ-ḍamīr

17. takhallalat-na l-gaḍāyā w-aṣbaḥ ash-shōr[a] ʿāṭil || w-al-yōm
al-aḥwāl[a] min baʿḍ al-gaḍāyā ʿaṭīlah
yā sēl[a] sīl min rās al-jabal w-as-sawāyil [meter short] || y-ahl
al-ḥagūl aḍ-ḍawāmī jā-kum aḷḷāh bi-sabīl-ah
bidʿ-ah barākīn[a] tanfajir wa ʿugb-ah zalāzil || w-akhsha
l-kawārith tugaʿ min ḥāshidah lā bakīlah
wa bā taʿumm al-maṣāyib kāfat ash-shaʿb ṭāyil || bi-kulla
shaṭrē-h lā mā hī tabanshar ʿajīlah

18. ṣārat ʿalē-k al-gharārah w-anta yā shaʿb-anā ghāfil || wa rāʿiy
al-bill[a] ḍayyaʿ-ahā wa ṣārat hāmilah
narjū-k[a] tadrak f-il-bilād al-ḥābilah w-an-nābilah || w-ibnō
binā min ṣaḥḥa lā tibnō ʿala l-jadr ar-ragūf
min ad-diyār al-khārijiyyah la d-diyār ad-dākhilah ||
nakhshā ʿala sh-shaʿb[a] min baʿḍ al-jihah hadm as-safūf

19. ḥāshid tanādī yā bakīl al-jūd[a] niksir l-il-giyūd || y-ahl
al-janāḥēn al-yaman lā yimtaḥī ʾathār-ihā.

Chapter 9

1. With regard to tribal confederacies and political hierarchies, one ought to consult the excellent work of Beck (1986), Tapper (1979), Garthwaite (1983), and others; for the relations of the so-called Islamic saints and the tribes, see the classic statements of Gellner (1969, 1981).

2. True, there was, and continues to be, a spectacle in the act of delivering the text-utterance, as exhibited, for example, in the *dōshān*'s sung performances or in the poet's own spoken recitation before an audience that repeats the line rhyme; but in fact the *dōshān*'s tapes are widely sold in the market, receiving critical acclaim, and there is nothing to prevent an audience from resoundingly repeating the end rhymes and clapping to themselves as they listen to the recording (which indeed happens). The case is clearly otherwise for the *bālah.* To tape its performance would be to capture the hearing of its text-utterance only, which is absurd, for it is the entire bodily enactment and competition of poetry that is crucial to this genre. To listen to a single *bālah* poem over and over again would be contrary to the whole point of a performance in which poets, chorus, and audience get together to create "spontaneously" and chant the poem collectively. The *zāmil,* whose text-utterance is passed down through the generations, could also be recorded without great damage to its aesthetic integrity, but it usually is not. I suspect that its brevity makes it easier to remember than the text-utterance of the *qaṣīdah;* it is not considered as grand as either of its sister genres and therefore is not deemed

worthy of preservation; most important of all, the *zāmil* is still largely confined in its use to local affairs rather than to the affairs of the nation-state (the example of the civil war poems notwithstanding), hence its statement may be thought not important enough to preserve on tape (we shall see, by contrast, that the *qaṣīdah* is quintessentially concerned with the affairs of the nation-state).

3. It would not be surprising to find that the newer mode of poetic production in turn influences the creation of a new kind of tribal *qaṣīdah*. Perhaps the last *qaṣīdah* we studied in the previous chapter, which was bare of the more traditional beginnings and endings and therefore strikingly different in content at least from the more traditional poem, is an exemplar of this new type of tribal "taped" *qaṣīdah*. But the reasons for the difference are complex and still relatively obscure to me, involving a host of factors—among them al-Gharsī's increasing knowledge of the taste of the urban milieu, which transcends the purely tribal audience, and the fact that the tribesmen who live in the large towns and cities are beginning to change their communicative and social patterns of interaction, so that the changing *qaṣīdah* form is in a sense harmonious with these newer routines. (The elaborateness of greeting routines fades in everyday urban situations in comparison with the tribal milieu; the image of a messenger going on a journey to deliver a poem may no longer seem apt when the reproduction of poetry is so closely tied to the tape recorder and the market place; and the religious routine may become associated with a certain, let us say, conservative political outlook unsuitable to a "progressive" or "liberal" voice.) Equally important is the knowledge the educated or more literate poets acquire of the literary tradition, which boasts its own *qaṣīdah*, said to have historical roots in the ancient tribal genre. But again these ideas are only speculative and require an in-depth study of the lives of the urban tribal poets and a comparative study of the *qaṣīdah* produced by them and the social modes of poetic production in the nontribal regions as well as their possible effects on the *qaṣīdah* form.

4. This might be biblical and Qurʾānic Haman. I owe this suggestion to Orin Gensler.

Conclusion

1. For Marxist criticism in general, see Benjamin ([1936] 1969), Lukács ([1920] 1971), Adorno ([1970] 1984), Goldman (1975), Eagleton (1976), and Jameson (1971, 1981).

2. Given that Bakhtin and Medvedev explicitly attacked the Formalists, Jakobson among them, for their narrowly conceived, text-centered poetics, my suggestion might seem doomed from the start. However, I am not so sure that by the time Jakobson developed his notion of parallelism and poetics in the 1960s—about four decades after the Bakhtinian critique of Formalism—

he had not moved fairly close to their position. For one thing, he, like the Prague School in general, tended to view the poem as a speech event comprised of many different functions. For another, an extension of his notion of parallelism, which is developed in this chapter, allows us to incorporate speech practices, not just semantic structures of language, into the unity of the poem.

3. Or so Jakobson claimed. His critics, however, were right in asserting that signification seemed to approach the vanishing point as Jakobson took the bird's eye view of the poem. Perhaps one can respond to these critics by asserting that he did not always have a signification (theme) in mind; rather, what was signified was the structural laws of relationship for the poetic function (Caton 1987a, 245–46). Regardless of whether we find this interpretation convincing, we need not abandon the hope of finding signification of the thematic sort in the architecture of the poem.

4. There are several problems with this kind of representation, however. The image of a continuum suggests that what differentiates one genre from another is the *degree* to which it possesses certain features. For example, most *bālah* poems do not contain references to historical events, but a few do, whereas the reverse is true of the *qaṣīdah* poems; the *zāmil* tends to be composed on ritual occasions and relatively infrequently for private use, whereas the *qaṣīdah* is almost never composed for a ritual occasion. Yet this description in terms of proportions is not sufficient, for categorical differences of plus and minus do exist, such as the fact that the *bālah* is always composed in a performance, the *qaṣīdah* never. These categorical differences are slight, however. Another problem with the continuum representation is that it falsely suggests that the *bālah* and the *qaṣīdah* are far apart from each other in the system. But we have learned that the text of the *bālah* is called a "*qaṣīdah*" (i.e. the text is referred to by tribesmen as "the *qaṣīdah* of the *bālah*") and from this metapragmatic statement alone we can infer that in the audience's estimation the two genres share a crucial connection. In addition, my analysis revealed marked similarities in their respective contents. Nor is it the case that the *zāmil* is unconnected with either of these two genres. As we have seen, it resembles the *bālah* in its performance, albeit in a much less elaborate form, and we also know that some *qaṣīdah*s are natural outgrowths of one or more *zāmil* poems. One genre—the *zāmil*—is like a musical movement within a larger symphonic genre; another—the *qaṣīdah*—is like a transposition into a different musical mode. To understand these connections, it might be better to represent the system of genres as a triangle:

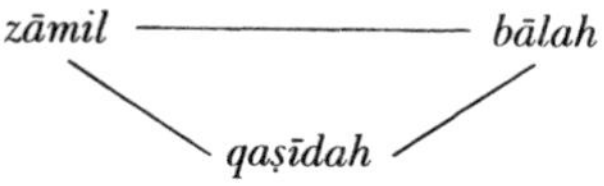

where each genre is seen to be interconnected with the others.

There is no need to choose between these two ways of representing the system. One emphasizes the distinctiveness of the genres according to one set of criteria, the other their similarity according to a different set of criteria; both points of view are valid.

5. According to Marxist theory, the ideological sign is "refracted" through the differential social interests of the community, which resembles Bakhtin's concept of dialogue. In some places of the text Vološinov speaks of this refraction as the "social *multiaccentuality* of the ideological sign" ([1929] 1986, 23). What is exciting and crucial about this idea is that it connects the sign with social conflict or struggle, as an arena for, not a refuge from, such conflict. In other words, discourse itself is the locus of—or more exactly, the focus of—contending social forces. Given this refraction of the ideological sign, it stands to reason that speaking in the Bakhtinian world is always dialogical, not in the narrow sense of a two-way conversation but in the sense of any utterance being an expression of the speaker's own necessarily partial perspective on the world and at the same time being directed at the antecedent or prospective utterance of his or her listener(s).

6. There has been a tendency in orthodox Marxism to abstract the concepts *base* and *superstructure* from real, concrete activity and then to reify them in ways that are counterproductive to our understanding of them, especially as regards the analysis of art. If we read carefully the famous passage on language, consciousness, and practical activity in part 1 of Marx and Engels's *German Ideology*, we realize, first of all, that these three phenomena are conceived of as indissolubly linked in a structural whole in any human activity. Williams gives the clearest analysis of this problem of reification:

> In the transition from Marx to Marxism, and then in the development of expository and didactic formulations, the words used in the original arguments were projected, first, as if they were precise concepts, and second, as if they were descriptive terms for observable "areas" of social life. The main sense of the words in the original arguments had been relational, but the popularity of the terms tended to indicate either (a) relatively enclosed categories or (b) relatively enclosed areas of activity. These were then correlated either temporally (first material production, then consciousness, then politics and culture) or in effect, forcing the metaphor, spatially (visible and distinguishable "levels" or "layers"—politics and culture, then forms of consciousness, and so on down to "the base"). The serious practical problems of method, which the original words had indicated, were then usually in effect bypassed by methods derived from a confidence, rooted in the popularity of the terms, in the relative enclosure of categories or areas expressed as "the base," "the superstructure." (Williams 1977, 77–78)

As Williams goes on to remark in the same essay, the result of separating these categories from each other and from specific practical activities is to end up reifying the base and the superstructure as empirical "objects" or "separate spheres of life" or "states" as opposed to empirical activities or processes, thus leaving out of account their essentially dynamic, interrelated, and even contradictory nature.

Second, far more problematical—one might, as Williams does, assert it to be the *most* problematical element of Marxist cultural theory—is the question of *determination* of the superstructure by the base. In its crudest forms Marxism asserts that the base directly determines the superstructure. Then there are the more dialectical versions, of which Bakhtin and Medvedev ([1928] 1985) is an example. Another attempted way out of the problem has been to assert that cause is rarely, if ever, ascertainable; only "constraints" or "limits" on the otherwise purposive acts of goal-oriented actors are. Finally, some formulations shy away from constraint altogether, begging the question of whether a Marxism without at least some such concept can be a Marxism at all.

7. Insofar as I hope in this book to contribute to the understanding of poetry as practice, I have developed in full the first two notions of practice outlined at the beginning of this chapter, but not the third. In defense of this insufficiency, I must point out that literary theory has hardly begun to catch up with the problem of how poetic forms change over time. Perhaps it is in this direction that research should now be headed.

Bibliography

Abu-Lughod, Lila

1984 *Honor, modesty, and poetry in a Bedouin society: Ideology and experience among Awlad ʿAli of Egypt.* Ph.D. diss., Harvard University.

1985 Honor and the sentiment of loss in a Bedouin society. *American Ethnologist* 12:245–61.

1986 *Veiled sentiments: Honor and poetry in a Bedouin society.* Berkeley and Los Angeles: University of California Press.

Adorno, Theodor

[1970] 1984 *Aesthetic theory.* Translated by C. Lenhardt. Edited by Gretel Adorno and Rolf Tiedemann. London and New York: Routledge and Kegan Paul.

Adra, Najwa

1982 *Qabyalah: The tribal concept in the central highlands of the Yemen Arab Republic.* Ph.D. diss., Temple University.

al-Ānasī, ʿAbd ur-Raḥmān bin Yaḥyā

N.d. *Tarjīʿ al-aṭyār bi-marqaṣ il-ashʿār* (The song of the birds at the poetry dance). Beirut: Dār ul-ʿAwdah. Ṣanʿā: Dār al-Kalāmah.

al-Baradūnī, ʿAbdaḷḷāh

1977 *Riḥlah f-ish-shiʿr al-yamānī* (A journey through Yemen's poetry). Damascus: Dār al-ʿilmi l-iṭ-ṭabāʿati w-in-nashr.

1981? Funūn al-adab ish-shaʿbī f-il-yaman (Folklore in Yemen). N.p.

al-Khafanjī.

N.d. *Ṣalaqāt al-ʿadas wa lays al-galas f-il-muḍaḥḥikat w-ad-dalas.* Typescript from the Ministry of Public Works, Ṣanʿā, Y.A.R.

Allen, W. Sidney

1973 *Accent and rhythm, prosodic features of Latin and Greek: A study in theory and reconstruction.* Cambridge: Cambridge University Press.

al-Muqāliḥ, ʿAbd al-ʿAzīz

1978 *Shiʿr al-ʿāmmīyati f-il-yaman* (Colloquial poetry in Yemen). Beirut: Dār al-ʿAwdah.

Alpers, Svetlana

1983 *The art of describing: Dutch art in the seventeenth century.* Chicago: University of Chicago Press.

1988 *Rembrandt's enterprise.* Chicago: University of Chicago Press.

Aristotle

1932 *The Rhetoric.* Translated by Lane Cooper. Englewood Cliffs, N.J.: Prentice-Hall.

1970. *The Poetics.* Translated by Preston H. Epps. Chapel Hill: University of North Carolina Press.

ash-Shāmī, Aḥmad Muḥammad

1965 *Qiṣṣat al-adabi f-il-yaman* (The story of literature in Yemen). Ṣanʿā?: al-maktab at-tijārī l-iṭ-ṭabāʿati w-at-tawzīʿi w-an-nashr (Commercial office for printing, distribution, and publication).

1974 *Min al-adab il-yamānī* (On Yemeni literature). Beirut: Dār ash-Shurūq.

1975 Yemeni literature in Hajjah prisons 1367/1948–1374/1955. *Arabian Studies* 2:43–59.

Auden, W. H.

[1962] 1985 The poet and the city. Reprinted in *Poetry and politics: An anthology of essays,* ed. Richard Jones, 36–51. New York: Morrow.

Austin, John L.

1962 *How to do things with words.* New York: Oxford University Press.

Bakhtin, Mikhail

1981 *The dialogic imagination: Four essays.* Edited by Michael Holquist. Translated by Caryl Emerson and Michael Holquist. Austin: University of Texas Press.

1984 *Problems of Dostoeyevsky's poetics.* Translated by Caryl Emerson. Minneapolis: University of Minnesota Press.

1986 *Speech genre and other essays.* Edited by Caryl Emerson and Michael Holquist. Translated by Vern McGee. Austin: University of Texas Press.

Bakhtin, Mikhail, and Pavel Medvedev

[1928] 1985 *The formal method in literary scholarship.* Translated by Albert J. Wehrle. Cambridge, Mass.: Harvard University Press.

Basso, Ellen

1981 *A musical view of the universe.* Philadelphia: University of Pennsylvania Press.

Basso, Keith

1979 *Portraits of 'the whiteman.'* Cambridge: Cambridge University Press.

Bateson, Gregory

1972a A theory of play and fantasy. In *Steps to an ecology of mind: Essays,* by Gregory Bateson, 177–93. New York: Ballantine Books.

1972b Style, grace, and information in primitive art. In *Steps to an ecology of mind: Essays,* by Gregory Bateson, 128–52. New York: Ballantine Books.

Bauman, Richard

1978 *Verbal art as performance,* with supplementary essays by Barbara A. Babcock. Rowley, Mass.: Newbury House Publishers.

Bauman, Richard, and Joel Sherzer, eds.

1974 *Explorations in the ethnography of speaking.* New York: Cambridge University Press.

Baxandall, Michael
1972 *Painting and experience in fifteenth-century Italy.* Oxford: Oxford University Press.
Beck, Lois
1986 *The Qashqa'i of Iran.* New Haven: Yale University Press.
Beeman, William O.
1986 *Language, status, and power in Iran.* Bloomington: Indiana University Press.
Ben-Amos, Dan
1972 Toward a definition of folklore in context. In *Toward new perspectives in folklore,* ed. Americo Paredes and Richard Bauman, 3–15. Austin: University of Texas Press.
Benjamin, Walter
[1936] 1969 The work of art in the age of mechanical reproduction. Reprinted in *Illumination: Essays and reflections,* by Walter Benjamin, ed. Hannah Arendt, 217–51. New York: Schocken Books.
Bennett, Tony
1979 *Marxism and formalism.* London and New York: Methuen.
Benveniste, Emile
1971 The nature of pronouns. In *Problems in general linguistics. Essays,* by Emile Benveniste, trans. Mary Elizabeth Meek, 217–22. Coral Gables, Fla.: University of Miami Press.
Berque, Jacques
1978 *Cultural expression in Arab society today.* Austin: University of Texas Press.
Blanc, Haim
1970 The Arab dialect of the Negev Bedouins. *Proceedings of the Israeli Academy of Sciences and Humanities* 4 (7): 112–39.
Blau, J.
1972–73 On the problem of the synthetic character of classical Arabic as against Judaeo-Arabic (Middle Arabic). *Jewish Quarterly Review* 63:29–38.
Bloch, Maurice, ed.
1975 *Political language and oratory in traditional society.* New York: Academic Press.
Bly, Robert
[1970] 1985 Leaping into political poetry. Reprinted in *Poetry and politics: An anthology of essays,* ed. Richard Jones, 129–37. New York: Morrow.
Bourdieu, Pierre
1966 The sentiment of honour in Kabyle society. In *Honour and shame: The values of Mediterranean society,* ed. Jean G. Peristiany, 191–242. Chicago: University of Chicago Press.
[1972] 1977 *Outline of a theory of practice.* Translated by Richard Nice. Cambridge: Cambridge University Press.
1984 *Distinction: A social critique of the judgment of taste.* Translated by Richard Nice. Cambridge, Mass.: Harvard University Press.

Bowra, C. M.
1966 *Heroic poetry.* London: Macmillan.
Brame, Michael
1970 *Arabic phonology: Implications for phonological theory and historical implications.* Ph.D. Diss., Massachusetts Institute of Technology.
Bühler, Karl
1934 *Sprachtheorie.* Jena: Fischer.
Burckhardt, John Lewis
1831 *Notes on the Bedouins and Wahabys.* London: Colburn and Bentley.
Burke, Kenneth
1965 *Permanence and change.* New York: Bobbs-Merril.
1968a *Counter-statement.* Berkeley and Los Angeles: University of California Press.
1968b Dramatism. *International Encyclopedia of the Social Sciences,* 7:445–52. New York: Macmillan.
1969a *A grammar of motives.* Berkeley and Los Angeles: University of California Press.
1969b *A rhetoric of motives.* Berkeley and Los Angeles: University of California Press.
1973 *Philosophy of literary form.* Berkeley and Los Angeles: University of California Press.
1984 *Attitudes toward history.* Berkeley and Los Angeles: University of California Press.
Cantineau, Jean
1936 Etudes sur quelques parlers de nomades arabes d'Orient (premier article). *Annales de l'Institut d'Etudes Orientales* 2:1–118.
1937 Etudes sur quelques parlers de nomades arabes d'Orient (second article). *Annales de l'Institut d'Etudes Orientales* 3:119–237.
Caton, Steven C.
1984 *Tribal poetry as political rhetoric from Khawlān aṭ-Ṭiyāl, Yemen Arab Republic.* Ph.D. dissertation. University of Chicago.
1985 The poetic construction of self. *Anthropological Quarterly* 58 (4): 141–51.
1986 Salām Taḥīya: Greetings from the highlands of Yemen. *American Ethnologist* 13 (2): 290–308.
1987a Contributions of Roman Jakobson. *Annual Review of Anthropology* 16:223–60.
1987b Power, persuasion, and language: A critique of the segmentary model in the Middle East. *IJMES* 19:77–101.
Chatman, Seymour
1965 *A theory of meter.* The Hague: Mouton.
Chelhod, Joseph
1973 Les cérémonies du mariage au Yémen. *Objets et mondes: la revue du Musée de l'homme* 13 (1): 3–34.
Chomsky, Noam
1965 *Aspects of the theory of syntax.* Cambridge, Mass.: MIT Press.
1966 *Cartesian linguistics.* New York: Harper and Row.

Clifford, James
1988 *The predicament of culture.* Cambridge, Mass.: Harvard University Press.
Cole, Donald P.
1975 *Nomads of the nomads: The Āl Murrah Bedouin of the Empty Quarter.* Chicago: Aldine.
Connelly, Bridgit
1986 *Arab folk epic.* Berkeley and Los Angeles: University of California Press.
Corriente, F.
1971–72 On the functional yield of some syntactic devices in Arabic and Semitic morphology. *Jewish Quarterly Review* 62 : 20–50.
1973 Again on the functional yield of some syntactic devices in Arabic and Semitic morphology. *Jewish Quarterly Review* 64 : 154–63.
Culler, Jonathan
1975 *Structuralist poetics.* Ithaca: Cornell University Press.
De Groot, A. W.
1957 Phonetics in its relation to aesthetics. In *Manual of phonetics,* ed. Louise Kaiser, 385–400. Amsterdam: North Holland.
Diem, Werner
1973 *Skizzen Jemenitischer Dialekte.* Orient-Institut der Deutschen Morgenländischen Gesellschaft, Band 13. Beirut.
Dorsky, Susan
1986 *Women of ʿAmran: A Middle Eastern ethnographic study.* Salt Lake City: University of Utah Press.
Doughty, Charles M.
1921 *Travels in Arabia Deserta.* London: Cape.
Dresch, Paul K.
1984 The position of sheykhs among the northern tribes of Yemen. *Man,* n.s., 19 (1): 13–49.
1986 The significance of the course events take in segmentary systems. *American Ethnologist* 13 (2): 309–24.
1989 *Tribes, government, and history in Yemen.* Oxford: Clarendon Press.
Dumont, Louis
1972 *Homo hierarchicus.* London: Paladin.
Dundes, Alan
1980 *Interpreting folklore.* Bloomington: Indiana University Press.
Dundes, Alan, Jerry W. Leach, and Bora Özkök
1972 The strategy of Turkish boys' verbal dueling rhymes. In *Directions in sociolinguistics,* ed. John J. Gumperz and Dell Hymes, 130–60. New York: Holt, Rinehart and Winston.
Eagleton, Terry
1976 *Criticism and ideology: A study in Marxist literary theory.* London: Humanities Press.
Eickelman, Dale F.
1981 *The Middle East: An anthropological approach.* Englewood Cliffs, N.J.: Prentice-Hall.

Eliot, T. S.
1975 Tradition and the individual talent. In *Selected prose of T. S. Eliot,* ed. Frank Kermode, 37–44. New York: Harcourt Brace Jovanovich.

Erlich, Victor
1965 *Russian formalism: History, doctrine.* 2d ed., rev. The Hague: Mouton.

Evans-Pritchard, E. E.
1940 *The Nuer.* Oxford: Oxford University Press.
1949 *The Sanusi of Cyrenaica.* Oxford: Clarendon Press.

Feld, Steven
1982 *Sound and sentiment.* Philadelphia: University of Pennsylvania Press.

Fernandez, James W.
1986 *Persuasions and performances: The play of tropes in culture.* Bloomington: Indiana University Press.

Finnegan, Ruth
1977 *Oral poetry.* Cambridge: Cambridge University Press.

Fish, Stanley
1980 *Is there a text in this class?* Cambridge, Mass.: Harvard University Press.

Foley, John Miles
1988 *The theory of oral composition.* Bloomington: Indiana University Press.

Foucault, Michel
[1970] 1973 *The order of things.* New York: Random House.
1972 *The archaeology of knowledge and the discourse on language.* Translated by A. M. Sheridan Smith. New York: Pantheon.

Fox, James J.
1977 Roman Jakobson and the comparative study of parallelism. In *Roman Jakobson: Echoes of his scholarship,* ed. Daniel Armstrong and C. H. Van Schooneveld, 59–90. Lisse: Peter de Ridder Press.

Frankel, Hans H.
1972 Classical Chinese. In *Versification: Major language types,* ed. William K. Wimsatt, 22–37. New York: Modern Language Association.

Friedrich, Paul
1979a Poetic language and the imagination: A radical reformulation of the Sapir-Whorf hypothesis. In *Language, context, and the imagination: Essays,* selected and introduced by Anwar S. Dil, 441–512. Stanford, Calif.: Stanford University Press.
1979b The symbol and its relative non-arbitrariness. In *Language, context, and the imagination: Essays,* selected and introduced by Anwar S. Dil, 1–61. Stanford, Calif.: Stanford University Press.
1986 *The language parallax.* Austin: University of Texas Press.

Frost, Robert
1969 *The poetry of Robert Frost.* Edited by Edward Connery Lathem. New York: Holt, Rinehart and Winston.

Gadamer, Hans-Georg
[1960] 1986 *Truth and method.* New York: Crossroads.

Garthwaite, G. R.
1983 *Khans and shahs.* Cambridge: Cambridge University Press.

Geertz, Clifford
1973 *The interpretation of cultures*. New York: Basic Books.
[1976] 1983 Art as a cultural system. Reprinted in *Local knowledge: Essays*, by Clifford Geertz, 94–120. New York: Basic Books.
1988 *Works and lives: The anthropologist as author*. Stanford, Calif.: Stanford University Press.
Gellner, E.
1969 *Saints of the Atlas*. Chicago: University of Chicago Press.
1981 *Muslim society*. Cambridge: Cambridge University Press.
Gerholm, T.
1977 *Market, mosque, and mafraj*. Stockholm: University of Stockholm.
Ghanem, Muḥammad ʿAbduh
N.d. Shiʿr al-ghināʾ aṣ-ṣanʿānī (Sung poetry of Ṣanʿā). Center for Yemeni Studies and Research, Ṣanʿā. Beirut: Dār ul-Kitāb il-ʿarabī.
Goffman, Erving
1974 *Frame analysis: An essay on the organization of experience*. New York: Harper and Row.
1981 *Forms of talk*. Philadelphia: University of Pennsylvania Press.
Goldman, Lucien
1975 *Towards a sociology of the novel*. Translated by Alan Sheridan. London and New York: Tavistock.
Gombrich, E. H.
1961 *Art and illusion*. Princeton: Princeton University Press.
Gossen, Gary H.
1974 *Chamulas in the world of the sun*. Prospect Heights, Ill.: Waveland.
Gumperz, John, and Dell Hymes, eds.
1964 *The ethnography of communication*. Washington, D.C.: American Anthropological Association.
Habermas, Jürgen
1984–87 *The theory of communicative action*. Vols. 1 and 2. Translated by Thomas McCarthy. Boston: Beacon.
Halle, Morris, and Samuel J. Keyser
1966 The iambic pentameter. In *The structure of verse: Modern essays on prosody*, ed. Harvey Gross, 179–93. New York: Ecco Press.
1971 Illustration and defense of a theory of iambic pentameter. *College English* 33:154–76.
Haugen, Einar
1956 The syllable in linguistic description. In *For Roman Jakobson*, ed. M. Halle, H. Lunt, and H. MacLean, 213–21. The Hague: Mouton.
Hauser, Arnold
1982 *The sociology of art*. Translated by Kenneth J. Northcott. Chicago: University of Chicago Press.
Heath, Shirley B.
1983 *Ways with words*. Cambridge: Cambridge University Press.
Hooper, Joan B.
1972 The syllable in phonological theory. *Language* 48 (3): 525–40.

Hopkins, Gerard Manley
1953 *A Hopkins reader.* Edited by John Pick. London: Oxford University Press.
Hrushovski, Benjamin
1980 The meaning of sound patterns in poetry. *Poetics Today* 2 (1a): 39–56.
Huizinga, Johan
1950 *Homo ludens: A study of the play element in culture.* New York: Roy.
Hyman, Larry M.
1975 *Phonology: Theory and analysis.* New York: Holt, Rinehart and Winston.
Hymes, Dell
1964 Introduction: Toward ethnographies of communication. In *The ethnography of communication,* ed. John J. Gumperz and Dell Hymes, 1–34. Washington, D.C.: American Anthropological Association.
1974 *Foundations in sociolinguistics.* Philadelphia: University of Pennsylvania Press.
1981 *"In vain I tried to tell you": Essays in Native American poetics.* Philadelphia: University of Pennsylvania Press.
1987 Anthologies and narrators. In *Recovering the word: Essays on Native American literature,* ed. Brian Swann and Arnold Krupat, 41–84. Berkeley and Los Angeles: University of California Press.
Ingarden, Roman
[1931] 1973 *The literary work of art.* Translated by George G. Grabowicz. Evanston, Ill.: Northwestern University Press.
Jakobson, Roman
[1933] 1966 Über den Versbau der serbokroatischen Volksepen. Reprinted in *Selected Writings of Roman Jakobson,* 4:51–60. The Hague: Mouton.
[1933–34] 1973 Qu'est-ce que la poésie? In *Questions de poétique,* ed. Roman Jakobson, 113–26. Reprint. Paris: Editions du Seuil.
[1935] 1981 The dominant. Reprinted in *Selected writings of Roman Jakobson,* 3:751–56. The Hague: Mouton.
1952 Studies in comparative Slavic metrics. *Oxford Slavonic Papers* 3:21–66.
1956 The metaphoric and metonymic poles. In *Fundamentals of language,* by Roman Jakobson and Morris Halle. The Hague: Mouton.
[1957] 1971 Shifters, verbal categories, and the Russian verb. Reprinted in *Selected writings of Roman Jakobson,* 2:130–47. The Hague: Mouton.
1960 Linguistics and poetics. In *Style in language,* ed. Thomas A. Sebeok, 350–77. Cambridge, Mass.: MIT Press.
[1962] 1971 Efforts toward a means-ends model of language in interwar Continental linguistics. Reprinted in *Selected writings of Roman Jakobson,* 2:522–26. The Hague: Mouton.
1963 On the so-called vowel alliteration in Germanic verse. *Zeitschrift für*

Phonetik, Sprachwissenschaft und Kommunikationsforschung 16: 84–92.

[1966] 1981 Grammatical parallelism and its Russian facet. Reprinted in *Selected writings of Roman Jakobson,* 3: 98–135. The Hague: Mouton.

[1968] 1981 Poetry of grammar and grammar of poetry. Reprinted in *Selected writings of Roman Jakobson,* 3: 87–97. The Hague: Mouton.

1969 O cheshskom stikhe preimushchestvenno v sopostavlenii s russkim. Introduction by Thomas G. Winner. Providence, R.I.: Brown University Press.

[1970] 1981 Subliminal verbal patterning in poetry. Reprinted in *Selected writings of Roman Jakobson,* 3: 136–47. The Hague: Mouton.

1979 Afterword of 1926. In *Selected writings of Roman Jakobson,* 5: 122–30. The Hague: Mouton.

1981 Retrospect. In *Selected writings of Roman Jakobson,* 3: 765–89. The Hague: Mouton.

Jakobson, Roman, and Claude Lévi-Strauss

[1962] 1981 "Les chats" de Charles Baudelaire. Reprinted in *Selected writings of Roman Jakobson,* 3: 447–64. The Hague: Mouton.

Jakobson, Roman, and Morris Halle

1956 *Fundamentals of language.* The Hague: Mouton.

Jakobson, Roman, and John Lotz

1941 *Axiomatik eines Verssystems am mordwinischen Volkslied.* Stockholm: Ungarisches Institut.

Jakobson, Roman, and J. Tynjanov

[1928] 1981 Problems in the study of language and literature. Reprinted in *Selected writings of Roman Jakobson,* 3: 3–6. The Hague: Mouton.

Jameson, Fredric

1971 *Marxism and form.* Princeton: Princeton University Press.

1981 *The political unconscious.* Ithaca: Cornell University Press.

Jamous, Raymond

1981 *Honneur et baraka.* Cambridge: Cambridge University Press.

Jauss, Hans Robert

1982 *Toward an aesthetic of reception.* Translated by Timothy Bahti. Minneapolis: University of Minnesota Press.

Jespersen, Otto

[1935] 1979 Notes on meter. Reprinted in *Structure of verse,* ed. Harvey Gross, 105–28. New York: Ecco Press.

Katakura, Motuko

1977 *Bedouin village.* Tokyo: University of Tokyo Press.

Keeler, Ward

1987 *Javanese shadow plays, Javanese selves.* Princeton: Princeton University Press.

Keenan, Elinor

1975 A sliding scale of obligatoriness: The polystructure of Malagasy oratory. In *Political language and oratory in a traditional society,* ed. Maurice Bloch, 93–112. London: Academic Press.

Keil, Charles
1979 *Tiv song.* Chicago: University of Chicago Press.
Kiparsky, Paul
1968 Metrics and morphophonemics in the Kalevala. In *Studies presented to Professor Roman Jakobson by his students,* ed. Charles Gribble, 137–48. Cambridge, Mass.: Slavica.
1972 Metrics and morphophonemics in the Rigveda. In *Contributions to generative phonology,* ed. Michael Brame, 171–200. Austin: University of Texas Press.
1973 The role of linguistics in a theory of poetry. *Daedalus* 102:231–44.
Lancaster, William
1981 *The Rwala Bedouin today.* Cambridge: Cambridge University Press.
Landberg, Carlo, count
1901–13 *Etudes sur les dialectes de l'Arabie méridionale.* 3 vols. Leiden: E. J. Brill.
1920–42 *Glossaire datînois.* 3 vols. Leiden: E. J. Brill.
Lévi-Strauss, Claude
1963 The structural study of myth. In *Structural anthropology: Essays,* by Claude Lévi-Strauss, 202–28. New York: Anchor Books.
Lord, Albert
1960 *The singer of tales.* Cambridge, Mass.: Harvard University Press.
Lotz, John
1960 Metric typology. In *Style in language,* ed. Thomas A. Sebeok, 135–48. Cambridge, Mass.: MIT Press.
1972 The elements of versification. In *Versification: Major language types,* ed. W. K. Wimsatt, 1–21. New York: New York University Press.
Lukács, Georg
[1920] 1971 *The theory of the novel.* Translated by Anna Bostock. Cambridge, Mass.: MIT Press.
Malinowski, Bronislaw
1923 The problem of meaning in primitive languages. Supplement to *The meaning of meaning,* by C. K. Ogden and I. A. Richards, 296–336. New York: Harcourt, Brace and World.
Marcus, G., and M. Fischer
1986 *Anthropology as cultural critique.* Chicago: University of Chicago Press.
Marx, Karl, and Friedrich Engels
[1846] 1970 *The German ideology.* Translated by C. J. Arthur. London: Lawrence and Wishart.
Mauss, Marcel
[1920] 1967 *The gift.* Translated by Rodney Needham. New York: Norton.
McCarthy, John J.
1979 On stress and syllabification. *Linguistic Inquiry* 10 (2): 443–65.
Mead, George H.
1934 *Mind, self, and society.* Chicago: University of Chicago Press.
1964 *Selected writings of George Herbert Mead.* Edited by Andrew J. Reck. Chicago: University of Chicago Press.

Meeker, Michael E.
1976 Meaning and society in the Near East: Examples from the Black Sea Turks and the Levantine Arabs. *IJMES* 7:243–70, 383–422.
1979 *Literature and violence in North Arabia.* Cambridge: Cambridge University Press.
Middleton, John, and David Tait
1958 *Tribes without rulers.* London: Routledge and Kegan Paul.
Mitchell, T. F.
1960 Prominence and syllabification in Arabic. *BSOAS* 23:369–89.
Mitchell, W. J. T.
1986 *Iconology: Image, text, ideology.* Chicago: University of Chicago Press.
Mitchell, W. J. T., ed.
1982 *The politics of interpretation.* Chicago: University of Chicago Press.
Montagne, Robert
1935 Contes poétiques bédouins. *Bulletin d'Etudes Orientales* 5:33–121.
Mukařovský, Jan
1964 The esthetics of language. In *A Prague school reader on esthetics, literary structure, and style,* ed. Paul L. Garvin, 31–69. Washington, D.C.: Georgetown University Press.
1977a Art as a semiotic fact. In *Structure, sign, and function: Selected essays,* by Jan Mukařovský, ed. and trans. John Burbank and Peter Steiner, 82–88. New Haven: Yale University Press.
1977b Two studies of poetic designation. In *The word and verbal art: Selected essays,* by Jan Mukařovský, ed. and trans. John Burbank and Peter Steiner, 65–80. New Haven: Yale University Press.
1979 *Aesthetic function, norm, and value as social facts.* Translated by Mark Z. Suino. Ann Arbor: University of Michigan Press.
Munn, Nancy
1973 *Walbiri iconography.* Ithaca: Cornell University Press.
Musil, Alois
1907–08 *Arabia Petrea.* Vienna: A. Holder.
1927 *Arabia Deserta.* American Geographical Society of New York, Oriental Explorations and Studies, no. 2. New York: Crane.
1928 *The manners and customs of the Rwala Bedouins.* American Geographical Society, Oriental Explorations and Studies, no. 6. New York: Crane.
Myntti, Cynthia
1978 *Women in rural Yemen.* Ṣanᶜā, Y. A. R.: United States Agency for International Development.
Niebuhr, Carsten
[1792] 1972 *Travels through Arabia and other countries in the East.* 2 vols. Translated by Robert Heron. Beirut: Librairie du Liban.
Ochs, Elinor
1988 *Culture and language development: Language acquisition and language socialization in a Samoan village.* Cambridge: Cambridge University Press.

Ong, Walter J.
1982 *Orality and literacy.* New York: Free Press.
Parry, Milman
1930 Studies in the epic technique of oral verse-making, 1: Homer and Homeric style. *Harvard Studies in Classical Philology* 41:73–147.
1932 Studies in the epic technique of oral verse-making, 2: The Homeric language of an oral poetry. *Harvard Studies in Classical Philology* 43:1–50.
Peacock, James L.
1968 *Rites of modernization.* Chicago: University of Chicago Press.
Peirce, Charles S.
1932 *Collected works.* Vol. 2. Cambridge, Mass.: Harvard University Press.
Peters, Emrys
1960 The proliferation of segments in the lineage system of the Bedouin of Cyrenaica. *Journal of the Royal Anthropological Institute* 90: 29–53.
1967 Some structural aspects of the feud among the camel-herding Bedouin of Cyrenaica. *Africa* 37:261–82.
1968 The tied and the free. In *Contributions to Mediterranean sociology,* ed. J.-G. Peristiany, 167–88. Paris: Mouton.
Philby, Harry St. John
1955 *Saudi Arabia.* New York: Praeger.
Pike, Kenneth
1971 *Phonemics: A technique for reducing languages to writing.* Ann Arbor: University of Michigan.
1981 *Tagmemics, discourse, and verbal art.* Ann Arbor: University of Michigan Press.
1982 *Linguistic concepts: An introduction to tagmemics.* Lincoln: University of Nebraska Press.
Pratt, Mary Louise
1977 *Toward a speech act theory of literary discourse.* Bloomington: Indiana University Press.
Pulgram, Ernst
1970 *Syllable, word, nexus, cursus.* The Hague: Mouton.
Rabinowitz, Peter
1987 *Before reading.* Ithaca: Cornell University Press.
Richards, I. A.
1936 *The philosophy of rhetoric.* Oxford: Oxford University Press.
Riffaterre, Michael
1966 Describing poetic structures: Two approaches to Baudelaire's *Les chats.* In *Structuralism,* ed. Jacques Ehrman, 188–229. New York: Anchor.
Rosaldo, Michelle Z.
1973 I have nothing to hide: The language of Ilongot oratory. *LSoc* 2:193–223.
1980 *Knowledge and passion: Ilongot notions of self and social life.* Cambridge: Cambridge University Press.

Rossi, Ettore
1938a Appunti di dialettologia del Yemen. *Rivista degli Studi Orientali* (Roma) 17:230–65.
1938b Nuove osservazioni sui dialetti del Yemen. *Rivista degli Studi Orientali* (Roma) 17:460–72.
1939a *L'arabo parlato a San(â).* Roma: Istituto per l'Oriente.
1939b Vocaboli sud-arabici nelle odierne parlate arabe del Yemen. *Rivista degli Studi Orientali* 18:299–314.
Said, Edward
1978 *Orientalism.* New York: Vintage.
Samatar, Said
1982 *Oral poetry and Somali nationalism.* Cambridge: Cambridge University Press.
Sapir, Edward
1921a *Language.* New York: Harcourt, Brace and World.
1921b The musical foundation of verse. *JEGP* 20:213–28.
Sapir, J. David
1977 The anatomy of metaphor. In *The social use of metaphor: Essays on the anthropology of rhetoric,* ed. J. David Sapir and J. Christopher Crocker, 3–32. Philadelphia: University of Pennsylvania Press.
Saussure, Ferdinand de
[1916] 1959 *Course in general linguistics.* Translated by Wade Baskin. New York: McGraw Hill.
Schneider, David
1976 Notes toward a theory of culture. In *Meaning in anthropology,* ed. Keith H. Basso and Henry A. Selby, 197–220. Albuquerque: University of New Mexico Press.
Searle, John R.
1969 *Speech acts.* Cambridge: Cambridge University Press.
Sebeok, Thomas A.
1960 *Style in language.* Cambridge, Mass.: MIT Press.
Serjeant, Robert B.
1951 *South Arabian poetry, 1: Prose and poetry from Hadramawt.* London: Taylor's Foreign Press.
1957 *The Sayyids of Hadramawt.* School of Oriental and African Studies. London: University of London.
1977 South Arabia. In *Commoners, climbers and notables,* ed. C. A. O. van Nieuwenhuijze, 226–42. Leiden: E. J. Brill.
Sharif ad-Dīn, Muḥammad
N.d. *Mubayyatāt wa muwashshaḥāt.* Beirut: Dār al-ʿAwdah; Ṣanʿā: Dār al-Kalamah.
Sherzer, Joel
1983 *Kuna ways of speaking.* Austin: University of Texas Press.
1987 A discourse-centered approach to language and culture. *American Anthropologist* 89 (2): 295–309.
Silverstein, Michael
1976 Shifters, linguistic categories, and cultural description. In *Meaning*

in anthropology, ed. Keith H. Basso and Henry A. Selby, 11–55. Albuquerque: University of New Mexico Press.
1981 Meta-forces of power in traditional oratory. Paper presented to the Anthropology Department, Yale University, December.

Simmel, Georg
1955 *Conflict.* Translated by Kurt Wolff. *The web of group affiliations.* Translated by Reinhard Bendix and Kurt Wolff. Glencoe, Ill.: Free Press.

Slyomovics, Susan
1988 *The merchant of art.* Berkeley and Los Angeles: University of California Press.

Smith, Barbara Hernstein
1968 *Poetic closure.* Chicago: University of Chicago Press.
1977 Surfacing from the deep. *PTL* 2:151–82.
1978 *On the margins of discourse.* Chicago: University of Chicago Press.

Socin, Albert
1900–1901 *Diwan aus Centralarabien.* Leipzig: B. G. Teubner.

Sowayan, Saad A.
1985 *Nabati poetry: The oral poetry of Arabia.* Berkeley and Los Angeles: University of California Press.

Stankiewicz, Edward
1974 Structural poetics and linguistics. In *Current trends in linguistics,* vol. 12, ed. Thomas Sebeok, 629–59. The Hague: Mouton.
1977 Poetics and verbal art. In *Perfusion of signs,* ed. Thomas A. Sebeok, 54–76. Bloomington: Indiana University Press.

Steffen, H., et al.
1978 *Yemen Arab Republic: Final report on the Airphoto Interpretation Project of the Swiss Technical Cooperative Service.* Berne, Zurich.

Steiner, George
1975 *After Babel.* Oxford: Oxford University Press.

Steiner, Peter
1984 *Russian formalism.* Ithaca: Cornell University Press.

Steiner, Wendy
1982 *The colors of rhetoric.* Chicago: University of Chicago Press.

Stevenson, Thomas B.
1985 *Social change in a Yemeni highlands town.* Salt Lake City: University of Utah Press.

Stookey, Robert W.
1978 *Yemen: The politics of the Yemen Arab Republic.* Boulder, Colo.: Westview Press.

Sturtevant, E. H.
1924 Doctrine of the caesura: A philological ghost. *American Journal of Philology* 45:329–50.

Swagman, Charles
1988 *Development and change in highland Yemen.* Salt Lake City: University of Utah Press.

Tapper, Richard
1979 *Pasture and politics.* London: Atheneum.
Tedlock, Dennis
1977 Toward an oral poetics. *New Literary History* 8 (3): 507–19.
1983 *The spoken word and the work of interpretation.* Philadelphia: University of Pennsylvania Press.
Thompson, Robert T.
1974 *African art in motion.* Berkeley and Los Angeles: University of California Press.
Van Der Meulen, D., and H. Von Wissman
1964 *Hadramawt: Some of its mysteries unveiled.* Leiden: E. J. Brill.
Van Gennep, Arnold
[1908] 1960 *The rites of passage.* Translated by Monika B. Vizedom and Gabriella L. Caffee. Chicago: University of Chicago Press.
Varisco, Daniel M.
1982 *The adaptive dynamics of water allocation in al-Ahjar, Yemen Arab Republic.* Ph.D. diss., University of Pennsylvania.
Vennemann, Theo
1972 On the theory of syllabic phonology. *Linguistische Berichte* 18 : 1–18.
Vološinov, V. N.
[1929] 1986 *Marxism and the philosophy of language.* Translated by Ladislav Matejka and I. R. Titunik. Cambridge, Mass.: Harvard University Press.
Vygotsky, Lev S.
1962 *Thought and language.* Translated by E. Hanfman and G. Vakar. Cambridge, Mass.: MIT Press.
1978 *Mind in society.* Cambridge, Mass.: Harvard University Press.
Weil, G.
1913 ʿArūḍ. *Encyclopedia of Islam,* 1 : 463–71.
1960 ʿArūḍ. *Encyclopedia of Islam,* 1 : 667–77.
Wellek, René
1955 *A history of modern criticism: 1750–1950.* Vol. 1. New Haven: Yale University Press.
Wenner, Manfred W.
1967 *Modern Yemen 1918–1966.* Baltimore: Johns Hopkins University Press.
White, Hayden
1973 *Metahistory: The historical imagination in nineteenth-century Europe.* Baltimore: Johns Hopkins University Press.
1987 *The content of the form: Narrative discourse and historical representation.* Baltimore: Johns Hopkins University Press.
Williams, J. E. C.
1971 The court poet in medieval Ireland. *Proceedings of the British Academy* 57 : 85–135.
Williams, Raymond
1958 *Culture and society: 1780–1950.* New York: Columbia University Press.

1977 *Marxism and literature.* Oxford: Oxford University Press.
1980 *Problems in materialism and culture.* London: Verso.
1982 *The sociology of culture.* New York: Schocken Books.

Wimsatt, William K., ed.
1972 *Versification: Major language types.* New York: New York University Press.

Winner, Thomas G.
1973 The aesthetics and poetics of the Prague linguistic circle. *Poetics* 8:77–96.

Zeps, Valdis J.
1963 The meter of the so-called trochaic Latvian folksongs. *IJSLP* 7: 123–28.

Zwettler, Michael
1978 *The oral tradition of classical Arabic poetry.* Columbus: Ohio State University Press.

Index

Abu-Lughod, L., 20, 110–11
ʿAdnān, 34
Adra, Najwa, 25, 67
Ahl al-khums (people of the fifth), 34
Aḥmad, Imam, 65
ʾ*Akhdām*, 7, 305n1
ʿAlī, 188, 312n15
ʿAlī, U., 74
Allegory, 204
Alliteration: in *bālah* poetry, 310n5; as cultural concept of form, 43; in *qaṣīdah* poetry, 322n14; and underlining ideas, 177; in verbal games, 58; in *zāmil* poetry, 140–41, 174
Allusion, 19; in children's games, 57–58; in *qaṣīdah* by al-Gharsī, 212; Qur'ānic, 204; in *zāmil* poems, 146, 152, 168
Alpers, S., 51
Arabic, 18; accent in Yemeni, 273; oral, 23, 25, 271; supposed purity of oral, 35. *See also* Consonants; Literacy; Vowels
Aristotle, 31, 124, 156–58
Art: and society, 179; for art's sake (*l'art pour l'art*), 308n5
ʾAʿrūsh tribe, 29, 161–78. *See also* Dispute; al-Ghādir, N.; Shadād tribe
Auden, W. H., 308n5
Audience: and genre system, 258; reaction of, 44; reaction of, in *bālah* performance, 82; reaction of, in *zāmil* performance, 128
Austin, J., 99, 254, 263
Autonomy, 31–32
ʿ*Awāj* (deviation), 172

al-Baddā, A., 190
*Baddā*ʿ (poet), 56, 147
Baḥr (meter), 43, 45
Bakhtin, M., 252, 253, 255, 262; circle of, 250, 262, 327n6. *See also* Medvedev, P.; Vološinov, V.
Bālah, 28; beginning of, 99; bridegroom in relation to, 126; conclusion of, 107–8; dance movements in, 81–83; in contrast with epic poetry, 98; as game of violence, 79; and ideological production, 22; meter in, 85–86; musical tunes of, 83; performers of, 80; as poetic competition, 29; refrain in, 83; rhyme in, 86; speech act in, 99; as symbolic violence, 121–22; as term in poetic metalanguage, 45; terms used in analysis of, 80; turn-taking in, 84–85; women's composition of, 23. *See also* Alliteration: in *bālah* poetry; Formula; *Sharaf*
Banī Hilāl, 98, 307n3
al-Baradūnī, A., 39
Base: and superstructure, 264, 326n6. *See also* Poem
al-basīṭ, 85
Basso, E., 20
Basso, K., 21

Foreign aid, 221–22
Foreign workers, 223
Formula, 61; and *bālah,* 107, 118; and construction of self, 94–96; of everyday speech versus poetry, 103–4; in greeting, 60–61, 103, 104–5; versus nonformulaic lines, 96; productivity of, 311 n9; and *qaṣīdah,* 197; system and productivity of, 88–90; system in *bālah,* 86–93; and *zāmil,* 134–35
Foucault, M., 250
Frankel, H., 276
Friedrich, P., 50, 80
Frost, R., 3–4

Gabīlī (tribesman), 26, 36–37
Gabyilah (tribalism), 25, 80, 233, 247, 316 n5
Gadamer, H., 123
al-Gāḍī, Ḥ., 161–65
Gaḍīyah (issue), 39–40
Gāfiyah (rhyme), 43; in poem of al-Maᶜlah, 241; in poem of aṣ-Ṣūfī, 228. See also *Bālah; Zāmil*
al-Gardaᶜī, A., 131–32, 308 n4
Garthwaite, G., 323 n1
al-Gaᶜshamī, 64
Gāt, 8, 39
Geertz, C., 19, 20, 26, 50, 261
Gellner, E., 305 n2, 323 n1
Genre: inner versus outer orientation of, 252, 255–56, 263–64; as speech event, 252; structural relationships of, 76
Genre system, 256–59, 325 n4; and social rituals, 258; and text-utterance, 257
al-Ghādir, N., 11, 75, 142, 150–51, 152–53, 229
Ghanem, M., 39, 306 n5
al-Gharsī, M., 54, 180–215, 266, 268; biography of, 205–8; masterpiece of, 209–11
Ghazl (love poetry), 53
Ghinā (singing), 56
Glorious deed, 27, 28, 112. *See also* Meeker, M.
Goffman, E., 80, 115
Gossen, G., 20
Greeting, 60; and *ᶜīd al-kabīr,* 71; *ḥāl,* 67. See also *Bālah; Qaṣīdah; Zāmil*
Gumperz, J., 262

Habermas, J., 250, 261
al-Ḥadā (tribe), 223–45
Ḥāfiḍ (memorizer), 130
Haiku, 283
Hājis (poetic genius): compared to *shāᶜir,* 182; invoking of, in *qaṣīdah,* 190–91; and other human faculties, 37–38, 116
Hajr (atonement), 73–74
Ḥalgah (circle, in a performance), 81
Halle, M., 276
al-Ḥamdī, I., 208–9
Ḥaram Mosque, 241–43
Ḥarf (hemistich), 43
Ḥaṣaᶜah (*zāmil*), 45
Ḥasan, al-ᶜAmrī, 153
Ḥāshid confederation, 204–5, 223
Haugen, E., 275
Heath, S., 21
Hierarchy, 255, 276
History, 35
al-Hizām, M., 9. *See also* Fieldwork
Honor code, 25. See also *Sharaf*
Hospitality, 28, 114. See also *Karāmah*
Huizinga, J., 79
Ḥumēnī poetry, 39, 306 n2
Hymes, D., 20, 21, 252, 262

Ibn Sinbul, 53
Iconic index, 94
Iconicity, 82–83, 102, 129, 159, 178, 233
Ideology, 26, 110, 255; emergent in poetry, 261–64; as semiotic practice, 260
Illocutionary force, 61
Indexicality, 101, 105, 125, 147, 254
Individual, 181–85
Ingarden, R., 249
Intensification, 80

Jakobson, R., 249; and Bakhtin circle, 324 n2; and comparative metrics,

Breinigsville, PA USA
22 August 2010
244041BV00001B/88/A

9 780520 082618